MONEY IN INTERNATIONAL EXCHANGE

Money in International Exchange

THE CONVERTIBLE CURRENCY SYSTEM

Ronald I. McKinnon

New York   Oxford
OXFORD UNIVERSITY PRESS
1979

Copyright © 1979 by Oxford University Press, Inc.

Library of Congress Cataloging in Publication Data

McKinnon, Ronald I
  Money in international exchange.

  Includes index.
  1. International finance.   2.   Monetary unions.
3.   Foreign exchange problem.   I.   Title.
HG3881.M2737   332.4'5   78-673
ISBN 0-19-502408-7
ISBN 0-19-502409-5 pbk.

ALGEN—111274—TSI

First printing March 1979
Second printing September 1979

TO MARGARET

sary to allow traders to hedge themselves at reasonable cost against currency fluctuations. Public policies that either support or obstruct the world's money machine are critically evaluated. Hence, focus is on the monetization of international trade *per se*, and not on the macroeconomic implications for domestic income and employment within individual countries.

To illustrate, consider how the socialist economies of Eastern Europe, or less developed countries, monetize their foreign trade. Neither group provides domestic monies that are internationally convertible. Similarly, what explicit and implicit conventions must the Western industrial economies observe for their currencies to be used freely for international purposes? How has the key-currency role of the United States dollar evolved in the transition from fixed to floating exchange rates? Is the striking development of offshore Eurocurrency markets an aberration due to loopholes in financial regulations, or is it essential for banks and trading companies to hedge against exchange risk? Why have exchange-rate fluctuations themselves been so unexpectedly large since floating became general in 1973? The interested reader will find answers to questions such as these.

The book encompasses two audiences. The first is university students who have lacked a textbook that focuses on the microeconomic and monetary aspects of international exchange itself; existing texts have treated international finance mainly as an extension of domestic macroeconomic theory to an open economy. The second is professionals in universities, banks, and research institutes who will, I hope, find herein much that is new and hitherto unexplored.

R. I. McKinnon

Stanford, California
June 1978

Preface

Fixed parities for exchange rates among the currencies of Western industrial countries were central to the Bretton Woods Agreement of 1945, which was the legal basis for the successful international monetary system prevailing after World War II. By 1973, the system had disintegrated into a regime of floating exchange rates that, superficially, seems chaotic. Yet, in most economies, international trade continues to grow more rapidly than Gross National Product despite the fact that no purely international money exists and none is in prospect.

This book describes how the use of national currencies, only some of which have the important international property of being convertible, allows most of world trade to be effectively monetized rather than bartered. For a large proportion of foreign trade, but by no means all, firms and individuals throughout the world experience no difficulty in making "money" payments to buy foreign goods—even if they can no longer predict exchange rates between the national currencies for which they are liable. But the underlying monetary order, and observed conventions of exchange, cannot be taken for granted.

The main text analyzes common financial practices of merchants and manufacturers, commercial banks, and central banks. Interesting new data indicate how particular national monies are selected as currencies of invoice for exports, how the conventions of extending trade credit from buyer to seller have changed from the gold standard era, and what banking institutions are neces-

Contents

MONEY IN INTERNATIONAL EXCHANGE

There cannot be intrinsically a more insignificant thing in the economy of society, than money; except in the character of a contrivance for sparing time and labour. It is a machine for doing quickly and commodiously, what would be done, though less quickly and commodiously, without: and like many other kinds of machinery, it only exerts a distinct and independent influence of its own when it gets out of order.

J. S. Mill (1848)

But money has one feature that these other machines do not share. Because it is so pervasive, when it gets out of order it throws a monkey wrench into the operation of all the other machines. The Great Contraction is the most dramatic example but not the only one.

. . . The first and most important lesson that history teaches about what monetary policy can do—and it is a lesson of the most profound importance— is that monetary policy can prevent money itself from being a major source of economic disturbance.

Milton Friedman (1968)

1

In Search of International Money: The Convertible Currency System

With the fall of gold as a means of payment and as a unit of account (but not yet as a store of value) in international commerce, and with the failure of any international bureaucracy to provide a generally acceptable fiat money, the world monetary system is not easy to understand. At least conceptually, the pre-1914 gold standard was simple: the domestic and international means of payment were the same. But in the modern world, a curious mélange of national currencies determines the efficiency of multilateral trade in goods and services on an enormous and increasingly global scale. Transfers of capital from one country to another hinge on financial markets whose efficiency is also dependent on the international qualities of national money(ies). Understanding how individuals, firms, banks, and governments so utilize national currencies in foreign trade is necessary to avoid unwise policies that would provoke instability and conflict.

Insofar as its national currency is externally "convertible"—a term continually metamorphosing and for which a precise working definition is provided below—each country contributes to the availability of international money. A convertible currency can be held and used by foreigners, even those from countries whose own currencies are inconvertible. In this important respect, therefore, the provision of a convertible currency is an international "public good"; reciprocal access to convertible foreign currencies can, in turn, benefit domestic nationals.

Unlike most public goods, however, providing an attractive convertible currency to the rest of the world need not be costly for the donor country except, perhaps, in the case of centrally planned "command" economies. This is demonstrated in Chapter 3. In general, neither communist states in Eastern Europe or Asia, nor most less developed countries in Asia, Africa, and Latin America, have convertible currencies with international qualities, although they themselves benefit from the presence of international money. Here our conceptual search for international money is confined to the 40 or so countries, including the major Western industrial economies, providing currencies that the International Monetary Fund (IMF) currently deems convertible—what I shall call the *convertible currency system.*[1]

For organizational convenience, the nature of the demand for international money is differentiated quite sharply according to the viewpoint and utility of the principal economic agents in the foreign exchanges:

1) nonbank firms and individuals;

2) commercial banks; and

3) national governments, normally represented by their central banks.

Under carefully specified conditions, firms and households need hold only domestic money for international transactions; whereas the peculiar role of commercial banks requires a broad portfolio of foreign monies, while central banks typically hold a much narrower portfolio of foreign exchange. But this remains to be demonstrated in the course of outlining the necessary "rules of the game" for clearing international payments and setting foreign exchange rates within the convertible currency system.

Convertibility and Commercial Trading: Official Restraints on Asset Choice

The ways in which governments limit the choice of foreign exchange assets by private firms and banks—whether they be foreign or domestic residents— can be conveniently derived from a working definition of a convertible currency, as still commonly accepted under Article VIII (of the articles of agreement) of the International Monetary Fund:

No member shall, without the approval of the Fund, impose restrictions on the making of payments and transfers for *current* international transactions . . .

1. As listed in *28th Annual Report: Exchange Restrictions* (Washington, D.C.: International Monetary Fund, 1977), pp. 516–20.

Each member shall buy balances of its currency held by another member if the latter, in requesting the purchase, represents:

i) that the balances to be bought have been recently acquired as the result of current transactions.

ii) that their conversion is needed for making payments for current transactions . . .

The buying member shall have the option to pay either in the currency of the member making the request or in gold. (Or, in practice, in an internationally acceptable currency such as United States dollars.)[2]

While dollar-area countries such as Canada and the United States have maintained convertibility since 1945, it wasn't until the late 1958 that major European trading countries achieved free convertibility with the rest of the world.

On December 29, 1958, fourteen Western European countries—Austria, Belgium, Denmark, Finland, France, Germany, Ireland, Italy, Luxembourg, the Netherlands, Norway, Portugal, Sweden, and the United Kingdom—made their currencies externally convertible for current transactions; that is, nonresidents would now be freely permitted to exchange their earnings of these currencies from current transactions into any other currency at rates within the official margins.[3]

Only Germany went further to grant nonresident convertibility on capital account. Japan did not formally achieve convertibility, by fully accepting the obligations of Article VIII, until April 1, 1964. By December 31, 1975, 44 out of the 128 members of the International Monetary Fund had formally accepted convertibility under Article VIII—but this includes all the wealthier, nonsocialist trading countries and covers the bulk of world trade.[4] Most of these countries still retain substantial restrictions on capital account, which are much tighter for residents in comparison to those on nonresidents—a distinction investigated in more depth in a later chapter on Eurocurrency markets.

This current-capital account distinction is not sharp and has one very important qualification. While the formal definition of convertibility extends only to current transactions, commercial credits normally granted by exporters or received by importers are considered current for the purposes of satisfying Article VIII. Sweden is quite typical in this respect: merchants engaging in foreign

2. Italics and parentheses added by author. *The International Monetary Fund, 1945–1965*, Vol. III, *Documents* (Washington, D.C.: International Monetary Fund, 1966), p. 196.
3. Ibid., Vol. II, *Analysis*, p. 277.
4. Formal acceptance is not tantamount to actually achieving convertibility in practice. Many of the 44—such as Argentina and Bolivia—have still, *de facto*, inconvertible currencies with many restrictions on foreign payments for current transactions.

trade are quite free to give or receive credit as long as it conforms to normal commercial practice.

> The Riksbank permits exporters, however, to cover their normal suppliers' credits through foreign borrowing. Suppliers' credit granted by Swedish shipyards may be refinanced abroad even if it serves to finance sales of ships to Swedish shipowners. Swedish importers can be also granted permission to take up credit abroad to finance contemplated imports. Borrowing by way of suppliers' credit is not controlled, and other borrowing to finance imports is approved where the borrowing itself and the repayment terms are in conformity with commercial practice in the trade concerned.

In contrast, the freedom of domestic residents of Sweden to buy or sell foreign exchange on capital account, other than commercial credits, is much more restricted:

> The purchase of listed, as well as unlisted, foreign securities by residents from nonresidents, requires authorization. As a rule, such authorization is not granted.

> Residents who wish to receive loans or credits other than normal suppliers' credit from nonresidents must receive authorization to do so; each case is considered on its merits. Long-term borrowing abroad is under certain conditions permitted (for periods of at least ten years) to facilitate the financing of industrial investment in Sweden; otherwise borrowing to finance economic activity in Sweden is not, in principle, authorized.[5]

Convertibility can be defined independently of the exchange rates with foreign currencies that a government may be obligated to maintain. Let us distill, therefore, a concise working definition that corresponds to common usage. A currency is *convertible* if:

> Domestic nationals wishing to buy foreign goods and services, not specifically restricted, can freely sell domestic for foreign currency in a unified market at a single but possibly variable exchange rate covering all current transactions inclusive of normal trade credit; whereas foreigners (nonresidents) with balances in domestic currency arising from current transactions can sell them at the same foreign exchange rate or purchase domestic goods freely at prevailing domestic-currency prices.

For semantic accuracy, note that my definition of convertibility is somewhat weaker than the way in which the term has been used historically. Earlier definitions attached an official obligation to maintain a par value in the rate of exchange between domestic currency and foreign money. In particular, the domestic currency balances of nonresidents were to be redeemed at a known parity. In the nineteenth century a currency was deemed convertible only if nonresidents could obtain gold at a fixed price with their balances of that

5. *25th Annual Report: Exchange Restrictions* (Washington, D.C.: International Monetary Fund, 1974), p. 406.

currency.[6] Under the Bretton Woods System, specifically Article IV that was honored by most countries until August 1971, governments were obliged to provide the requisite foreign currency demanded by nonresidents at a rate of exchange not to differ more than one percent from parity.

Under our common usage definition, however, an official parity obligation is no longer necessary for a currency to be considered convertible. Indeed, even when the Canadian dollar floated without an official parity from 1950 to 1962, it was commonly considered to be a convertible currency as were the currencies of the industrial economies after general floating began in 1973. The breakdown of fixed exchange-rate obligations, so dramatically portrayed in Figure 1.1, has not impaired the effective convertibility of the currencies depicted.

Nonbank individuals and firms resident in those countries whose currencies are convertible in our current-account sense may be able to engage in capital inflows or outflows only to the extent they vary the leads and lags in giving or accepting normal commercial credits in international exchanges. But commercial credits are a large and sometimes dominant component of gross capital flows through the foreign exchanges that can be manipulated to influence net capital flows, as we analyze in more depth in Chapter 7. However, directly acquiring foreign exchange assets including money, or incurring debt to foreigners, is much less convenient for nonbank firms and individuals if not related to commercial transactions. Only residents of financially open countries such as the United States, Canada, or Germany are virtually unrestricted by any domestic regulation on what foreign currency positions they may take. However, in these countries, governments have occasionally imposed, and then removed, relatively mild restraints on capital transactions in what were imagined to be extraordinary circumstances.

Nevertheless, not too much should be made of these capital-account restraints.[7] As long as a country maintains convertibility, most domestic merchants, manufacturers, and even households can treat their balances in domestic currency *as if* they were international money; for all current transactions they represent almost instant command over (liquidity in) foreign goods at known prices. Even those engaged directly in the import or export business find domestic currency quite convenient for making international payments. Unless the domestic currency becomes terribly unstable in its command over real goods and services, *domestic* nonbank firms and individuals would normally have little use for checking accounts or currency hoards held abroad in foreign monies.

6. Hence, during the American Civil War, the American paper greenback was called "inconvertible" because it did not trade with gold at par. However, since the greenback could be freely sold to or purchased from foreigners, it was "convertible" in the modern sense of the word.
7. From the viewpoint of any single trading country. As we shall see, the international monetary system, in the aggregate, requires at least some major countries to maintain open capital markets.

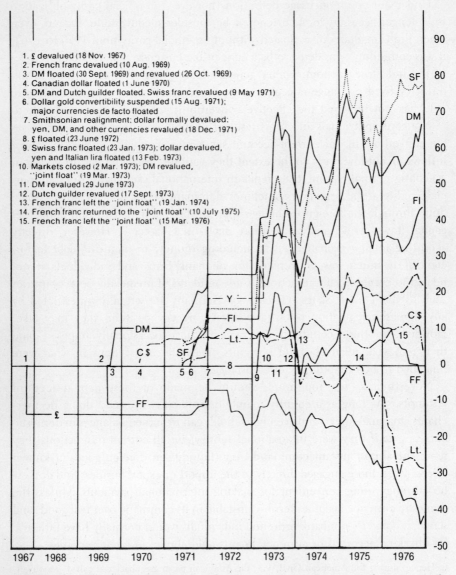

1. £ devalued (18 Nov. 1967)
2. French franc devalued (10 Aug. 1969)
3. DM floated (30 Sept. 1969) and revalued (26 Oct. 1969)
4. Canadian dollar floated (1 June 1970)
5. DM and Dutch guilder floated. Swiss franc revalued (9 May 1971)
6. Dollar gold convertibility suspended (15 Aug. 1971);
   major currencies de facto floated
7. Smithsonian realignment; dollar formally devalued;
   yen, DM, and other currencies revalued (18 Dec. 1971)
8. £ floated (23 June 1972)
9. Swiss franc floated (23 Jan. 1973); dollar devalued,
   yen and Italian lira floated (13 Feb. 1973)
10. Markets closed (2 Mar. 1973); DM revalued,
    "joint float" (19 Mar. 1973)
11. DM revalued (29 June 1973)
12. Dutch guilder revalued (17 Sept. 1973)
13. French franc left the "joint float" (19 Jan. 1974)
14. French franc returned to the "joint float" (10 July 1975)
15. French franc left the "joint float" (15 Mar. 1976)

FIGURE 1.1   Foreign exchange rates of major currencies: Percentage deviations with
respect to dollar parities of October 1967 (end of month figures)

SOURCE: OECD *Observer*, (November/December 1976), p. 101.

The Interbank Market
for Convertible Currencies

What is the role of the commercial and central banks in the international exchange of convertible currencies? Banks have long been dominant intermediaries in the foreign exchanges. Indeed, the market for foreign exchange as commonly conceived is essentially a telephone and telex network across leading commercial banks in major trading countries. Regulatory agencies such as central banks recognize the convenience of this commercial practice and place fewer restraints on duly authorized commercial banks dealing in foreign exchange in comparison to nonbank firms and individuals. Again, take Swedish regulations of authorized commercial banks, as of December 1972, to be representative of convertible currency countries:

> Authorized banks may buy from and sell to other authorized banks any foreign currency on a spot basis against another foreign currency or Swedish kronor. Also, they may purchase, spot, from foreign banks and other nonresidents foreign currencies against any foreign currency or Swedish kronor credited to a regular account. They may sell, spot, to foreign banks and other nonresidents foreign currencies against any other foreign currency or Swedish kronor debited to a regular account. *Regular accounts* may be held by residents of all countries. . . . regular accounts do not normally bear interest. The Riksbank is empowered to impose a negative interest charge on any excess credit balances in regular accounts held by foreign banks or banking firms; at the end of 1973 this authority was not being invoked.[8]

The banking system as a whole is a financial intermediary where for practical purposes *all* spot and forward foreign exchange transactions are cleared. That is, commercial exporters and importers don't barter foreign exchange spot or forward directly with each other. Unlike domestic trade, hand-to-hand currency is not used significantly except for some tourist transactions. One can adopt Paul Einzig's five different banking planes on which this crucial clearing role operates:[9]

1) Between commercial banks and customers;

2) Between commercial banks in the same country;

3) Between commercial banks in different geographical centers;

4) Between commercial banks and central banks; and

5) Between central banks outside the "open" market made by the commercial banks.

8. IMF, op. cit. p. 404.
9. Paul Einzig, A *Textbook on Foreign Exchange* (New York: Macmillan, 1966), p. 15.

Foreign exchange transactions take place on each of these five planes. The market's efficiency in facilitating international trade in goods and services depends in part on the similarity of quotations for any given foreign currency, and on the narrowness of the bid-ask spread at the retail level: the quotations for buying and selling foreign exchange that banks provide to their nonbank customers. This similarity of quotation and narrowness of spread at the retail level depends heavily on the efficiency of the wholesale interbank market—in which central banks may or may not participate directly.

This key intermediary role of the interbank market as a wholesaler of foreign exchange is worth spelling out in more detail. Domestic merchants and manufacturers engaged in either the export or import trade—shipping, textiles, computers, and so on—have a continuous need to buy or sell spot foreign exchange as bills become due or are paid by their customers. It would be inconvenient for them to keep large noninterest-bearing working balances in foreign currencies to cover uncertain future import needs, or for exporters to worry continually about finding other merchants or manufacturers on the import side who wish to acquire the various types of foreign exchange arising from their export proceeds. This is the natural role of banks.

How then do the commercial banks select their asset positions in foreign currencies in performing this vital clearing role in the spot market for foreign exchange? If a Swedish importer of silicon chips makes immediate payment to the American manufacturer, the process is normally quadrangular; the importer, the exporter, a foreign commercial bank, and the domestic commercial bank are involved. The importer can simply write a check against his domestic account for the foreign-currency amount to be credited the exporter in his bank. The Swedish bank then performs the conversion by obtaining the required foreign exchange—at a price known within narrow limits by the importer—and debits the importer's account for the domestic currency equivalent, say 10,000 kronor.

Would the Swedish bank buy exactly 10,000 kronor of foreign exchange— say dollars—in the interbank market to make the conversion? It is unlikely to do so in any immediate sense.

First, wholesale trade among the commercial banks is done on a very large scale—often with the assistance of foreign exchange brokers. Once the expense of making a contract is incurred, there is a cost saving in operating on large scale—say in million krona round lots at the wholesale level in comparison to a few thousand kronor in odd amounts at the retail level.

Secondly, bid-ask spreads and quotations in the interbank market change frequently. An aggressive foreign exchange department in a large commercial bank continually looks for the best buy or sell offer. Although these dealers sit by their telephones and computerized quotation boards and thus may be some-what paunchy, they have been likened to prize fighters circling each other. They must continually look for chinks in their opponents' armor—say, an unduly low offer price to sell foreign exchange by a foreign counterpart. They may then be jabbed in return by having their own extant offer to buy foreign exchange suddenly taken up in an amount greater than anticipated, just prior to having the exchange rate move. Hence dealers would lose too much flexibil-ity if required to match their bank's retail commitments exactly.

If one is left in any doubt regarding the excitement and the intensive com-petitive pressure that prevails in the wholesale interbank market, the technical note to this chapter shows that typical bid-ask spreads are very narrow relative to the potential exchange rate movement prevailing in any one trading day.[10] The two are related, however. For example, on September 29, 1972, the bid-ask spread to buy spot Deutsche marks (in terms of dollars) was only .016 percent of the spot rate, in a period where governments were intervening to maintain the value of the exchange rate within a narrow band under the Smithsonian agreement. Whereas on October 1, 1974, when official exchange-rate obliga-tions had been forcibly suspended, and when spot rates not infrequently moved as much as one or two percent in a day or 20 to 25 percent within a few months, the bid-ask spread widened to 0.106 percent of the spot rate—almost a sevenfold increase!

In short, the bid-ask spread reflects the costs (brokerage) and risk (potential of taking capital losses) of operating in the interbank market. Yet due to competi-tive pressure among commercial banks willing to perform the vital clearing role, the bid-ask spread remains very narrow as a percentage of the spot ex-change rate. Of course a widening of the bid-ask spread in the wholesale interbank market will be reflected back in increased retail bid-ask spreads (or other service charges) of each bank to its customers—who quite understandably prefer to specialize in trading macadamia nuts or manufacturing jellybeans rather than directly buying and selling foreign exchange. If the bid-ask spread becomes substantial and the price of foreign exchange more uncertain, the international "moneyness" of domestic currency is reduced.

Although each authorized commercial bank operates continually in the for-eign exchange market on behalf of its nonbank retail customers viewed collec-tively, we have inferred that each order to buy or sell foreign exchange by a retail customer is not matched by an exactly similar transaction in the whole-sale market. Hence, the banks themselves act as *dealers* rather than pure

10. The technical note to this chapter provides a sample set of foreign exchange quotations (both spot and forward) facing name banks—those who can contract freely without credit checks. More on the taking of names appears in Chapter 9.

brokers. The net foreign exchange due to be paid on behalf of a commercial bank's retail customers (in return for domestic currency) may be a bit greater or somewhat less than net purchases of foreign exchange (customarily due within two trading days) in the wholesale interbank market. Therefore authorized commercial banks find it convenient to hold working balances in foreign exchange with correspondent banks in other countries. For example, a Swedish commercial bank may hold working demand deposits in dollars with Chase Manhattan in New York as a means of covering any intended or unintended shortfalls in dollar payments that it must make on behalf of its retail customers. Similarly, Chase Manhattan may well hold deposits in kronor with Swedish commercial banks in the regular accounts just indicated. Hence, commercial banks have a very definite demand for working and precautionary balances in a variety of international currencies.

With the gradual return to convertibility and free exchange among major industrial economies after World War II, the holding of working balances by commercial banks steadily gained in importance. Robert Heller calculated that holdings of foreign exchange by commercial banks in the industrial countries rose from about 4.4 to 11.7 percent of imports from 1951 to 1966 as shown in Table 1.1.[11] After 1966, the IMF data become more difficult to interpret because growth in working balances of foreign exchange (say, largely demand deposits with correspondent banks) become swamped by a huge rise in interbank *Eurocurrency* deposits. As explained Chapter 9, these Eurocurrency deposits are more akin to forward rather than spot positions in foreign exchange—but are an essential part of the overall market for making and clearing foreign payments nevertheless.

On the other hand, nonbank *domestic* residents—commercial firms and individuals—are likely to hold directly only minor amounts of foreign currencies (checking accounts), for making payments even when permitted to do so legally. Rather, their domestic bank can hold foreign correspondent balances at lower cost because of economies in dealing with many customers at retail, and because of its ease of access to the wholesale interbank market. In effect, these foreign correspondent balances are international reserves against checking accounts in domestic currency that may be drawn down to buy foreign goods.

Therefore the private demand by nonbank domestic residents for international money(ies)—in the narrow sense of working balances of making payments—is best considered primarily an intermediated demand that operates through that country's commercial banks rather than being directly comparable

11. Foreign trade had risen so sharply that official reserve holdings, as a proportion of imports, actually declined.

TABLE 1.1   Foreign Exchange Holdings by Central and Commercial Banks

	Central banks' reserves/imports	Commercial banks' foreign exchange/imports
1951	0.616	0.044
1952	0.633	0.046
1953	0.687	0.053
1954	0.679	0.053
1955	0.615	0.050
1956	0.575	0.056
1957	0.528	0.057
1958	0.574	0.066
1959	0.541	0.077
1960	0.510	0.078
1961	0.506	0.089
1962	0.479	0.092
1963	0.464	0.091
1964	0.430	0.096
1965	0.402	0.103
1966	0.373	0.117

SOURCE: From H.R. Heller, "The Transactions Demand for an International Means of Payment," *Journal of Political Economy* (January/February 1968), p. 143.

to the demand for money in domestic trade and commerce. Indeed, the domestic currency itself (providing it is convertible) is likely to be viewed as international money by those private parties not directly responsible for currency conversion. And in the model of exchange-rate determination presented below, I assume that households and nonbank firms hold only domestic money.

The Monetary Conditions
for Long-Run Exchange Stability*

Consider a floating exchange rate where the commercial banks intermediate the flow demands and supplies of foreign exchange by merchants and manufacturers. There is no direct intervention in the foreign exchange market by central banks. If we experience a sustained period (over a year) of a stable exchange rate that is expected to be maintained, then domestic and foreign prices of internationally tradable goods will become more or less perfectly aligned through commodity arbitrage. What are the conditions for such a

---

*Nontechnical readers may prefer to skip this section on the first reading. The main argument can be picked up in Chapter 2 without loss of continuity.

determinant and stable exchange rate to be established between the convertible domestic currency, say, guilders, and the foreign currency, say, dollars?

Since the advent in 1973 of generalized floating among major convertible currencies, rates of exchange have moved quite sharply. Movements of one half of one percent in a day have not been uncommon (Table 1.2). Over six-month intervals some rates have moved as much as ten to twenty percent— only to be reversed later as in the case of the Deutsche mark and the U.S. dollar (Figure 1.1). During these short periods in which such sharp rate changes occur, the empirical evidence (Chapter 6) suggests that commodity arbitrage is insufficient to align national price levels. Hence the important question of exchange instability in this short run, where national price levels become detached and exchange rates move sharply, is deferred to Chapters 7 and 8.

Here I concentrate on the long run, where domestic prices of tradable goods are aligned with international prices. Perform the conceptual experiment of setting a given exchange rate (guilders per dollar) for the period of a year or more. All agents in the foreign exchange market have stationary expectations: the current exchange rate is their best guess of that rate which will prevail in the future. Interpret exchange rates recorded on the vertical axis of Figure 1.2 in this long-run *ex ante* sense. A spot rate R_s is "called out" and then held for a period of a year over which transactions involving exports and imports can take place freely so that domestic prices are aligned with their foreign counterparts.

A second characteristic of the hypothetical long-run exchange equilbrium, described by Figure 1.2, is the absence of net capital flows to or from the country in question. While current-account convertibility holds, capital-account restrictions are such that domestic nationals can neither acquire finan-

TABLE 1.2   Changes in Selected Currency Rates Against the U.S. Dollar (Average daily percentages)

Country	1973				1974				1975
	First quarter	Second quarter	Third quarter	Fourth quarter	First quarter	Second quarter	Third quarter	Fourth quarter	First quarter
Canada	0.14	0.06	0.07	0.15	0.11	0.11	0.12	0.08	0.12
France	0.54	0.45	0.86	0.56	0.76	0.41	0.27	0.29	0.45
Germany, Fed. Rep. of	0.47	0.52	0.82	0.47	0.64	0.64	0.32	0.47	0.48
Italy	0.26	0.46	0.40	0.24	0.47	0.31	0.17	0.20	0.33
Japan	0.53	0.10	0.09	0.09	0.49	0.28	0.29	0.07	0.28
United Kingdom	0.29	0.21	0.29	0.21	0.64	0.29	0.17	0.21	0.27

NOTE: Average percentage change from previous day in spot exchange rate against U.S. dollar (New York noon quotation).

SOURCE: International Monetary Fund *Annual Report, 1975*, p. 26.

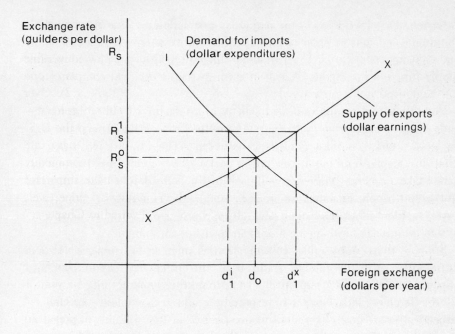

FIGURE 1.2   The market for foreign exchange in the long run

cial claims on foreigners net over the course of a year, nor can foreigners acquire net claims on them. Hence, the flow demand per year for foreign exchange, measured on the horizontal axis of Figure 1.2, is strictly a derived demand for commodity imports I from abroad; and the flow of supply of foreign exchange per year is derived from domestic exports X. In short, importing firms pay domestic cash for the foreign exchange to buy imports, and exporters convert fully the proceeds from overseas sales into domestic money.

Most basic textbooks in international economics present the demand for imports and supply of exports in a setting of *partial equilibrium*.[12] They derive the downward sloping demand for imports—the curve II in Figure 1.2—by summing the net demands, computed individually, for all imported commodities. It is partial equilibrium because the general purchasing power of the domestic currency is given irrespective of the state of the foreign exchanges. An increase in R_s raises the *relative* (guilder) prices of imported wheat, apples, sewing machines, and so on such that the demand for them diminishes in comparison to other (unspecified) domestic commodities, whose guilder prices

12. See, for example, the exposition of Herbert Grubel in *International Economics* (Homewood, Illinois: Irwin, 1977), pp. 216–23.

are given. One then looks at the particular characteristics of a wide variety of commodity markets in order to predict the quantitative effects of a change in the exchange rate. (In such a partial-equilibrium setting, an upward sloping supply function for exports—based on summing up individual components— can be derived in the same way.)

But this partial-equilibrium approach is unsatisfactory if either the foreign trade sector is large or an exchange rate somehow reflects the general purchasing powers of two monies. (This latter concern is taken up in more empirical detail in Chapter 6 on purchasing power parity.) To remedy these deficiencies, here I take a *general-equilibrium* approach to the derivation of import-demand and export-supply functions in order to obtain the conventional slopes portrayed in Figure 1.2. This more general approach requires explicit consideration of the market for domestic money in terms of commodities.

Suppose the country under consideration is small in two respects. (1) It is sufficiently open to foreign trade that the prices of exportables and importables—P_x^g and P_i^g respectively—dominate the domestic price level; and (2) the foreign (dollar) prices of exportables and importables— $\bar{P}_x^d$ and $\bar{P}_i^d$ respectively—are given exogenously, irrespective of the amounts imported or exported by the country in question. In the long run under consideration (but only then), the domestic guilder prices of exportables and importables will be aligned with their foreign dollar prices at the existing spot exchange rate, R_s:

$$P_x^g = R_s \, \bar{P}_x^d \qquad \text{(exportables)} \qquad (1.1)$$

and

$$P_i^g = R_s \, \bar{P}_i^d \qquad \text{(importables)}. \qquad (1.2)$$

To keep matters as simple as possible, but without any real loss of generality, assume the country in question has fixed stocks of land, labor, and capital that it does not augment during the period under consideration. It is a stationary state where unchanging resources are fully employed producing tradables— some of which are domestically consumed. Because the *relative* prices of tradable goods are fixed on world markets, domestic output of the exportable good—Y_x—and the importable—Y_i—are both predetermined over the year. "Real" national output, Y , then is just the weighted sum of Y_i and Y_x , where the weights correspond to their relative prices:

$$Y = \bar{P}_x^d \, Y_x + \bar{P}_i^d \, Y_i. \qquad (1.3)$$

In equation (1.3), the externally fixed dollar prices are the weights defining "real" income or national output. Hence "money" income—or the guilder value of national income—is:

$$P^g \cdot Y = P^g_x Y_x + P^g_i Y_i = R_s Y \tag{1.4}$$

from equations (1.1), (1.2), and (1.3). The reader will note that units for the domestic price level, P^g, have been chosen such that

$$P^g = R_s. \tag{1.5}$$

The index defining the domestic price level is simply equal to the guilder price of dollars—the exchange rate.

Preserving the stark simplicity of the algebraic model that has no bonds or international capital flows, suppose that the domestic stock of guilders M is the only financial asset available for Dutchmen to hold. M is the stock of checking deposits and currency held by the nonbank public—although other monetary aggregates may, on occasion, be more germane analytically. Households and firms have a determinant target stock for their *real* cash balances as denoted by M/P_g or M/R_s. This stock demand is stable because Dutchmen have stationary expectations regarding the purchasing power of guilders: tomorrow's commodity prices in guilders are expected to be the same as today's. People strive for portfolio balance by aligning their real guilder holdings to their unchanging real income, Y.

If financial disequilibrium should accidentally occur, people adjust their real cash balances downwards or upwards by allowing their flow of current consumption, C, to rise above or below Y for some short period of time. In particular, the flow demand for importables, C_i, depends directly on real cash balances and on current income:

$$C_i = C_i \left(\frac{M}{R_s}; Y \right)$$
$$\quad + \quad + \quad$$
(demand for importables). (1.6)

Hence, if R_s decreases, leading to higher real cash balances, people consume more importables.

By definition, real imports I are simply the difference between production and consumption:

$$I = C_i - Y_i. \tag{1.7}$$

Hence, the derived demand for imports is also directly dependent on cash balances and the exchange rate:

$$I = I \left(\frac{M}{R_s}; Y \right)$$
$$\quad + \quad + \quad$$
(demand for imports). (1.8)

Thus the downward sloping demand function for foreign exchange (dollars)

portrayed in Figure 1.2 is simply equation (1.8) multiplied by $\bar{P}_i^d$, the fixed
dollar price of imports.

But why should the export-supply function in Figure 1.2 slope upwards?
Note that the consumption demand for exportables also depends directly on
real cash balances and current income:

$$C_x = C_x\left(\frac{M}{R_s}; Y\right) \qquad \text{(demand for exportables).} \qquad (1.9)$$
$$+ \;\; + \phantom{\frac{M}{R_s}\right)}$$

The flow of actual exports, X, is the difference between production and
consumption:

$$X = Y_x - C_x. \qquad (1.10)$$

Hence, in general equilibrium, the derived export supply is *inversely* related to
real cash balances:

$$X = X\left(\frac{M}{R_s}; Y\right) \qquad \text{(export supply).} \qquad (1.11)$$
$$- \;\; + \phantom{\frac{M}{R_s}\right)}$$

As R_s increases, leading to domestic price inflation in guilders, the real value
of domestic cash balances declines. Dutchmen then cut back their consumption of exportables which releases more goods for export at the given dollar
price. This generates the standard upward sloping export supply function for
foreign exchange—albeit one that might only be operative in the long run.
(Short-run problems associated with downward sloping supply functions are
considered in Chapter 7.)

But this upward slope is essential in ensuring that the foreign exchange
market (and domestic money market) is stable. By some random shock, suppose
R_s rises to R_s^l as portrayed in Figure 1.2. Then the resulting excess supply of
dollars will drive R_s back to R_s^o. Hence a determinant exchange rate exists if the
import-demand and export-supply functions are stable, which is so if the supply
of nominal guilders M is given, and the demand for real money, M/P_g, is
stable.

Consider the domestic dual of this equilibrium in the foreign exchanges.
Define aggregate domestic consumption in "real" terms (using fixed dollar
weights) to be:

$$C = \bar{P}_i^d C_i + \bar{P}_x^d C_x. \qquad (1.12)$$

With investment zero in our stationary state, the aggregate demand for all
goods and services depends positively on real cash balances:

$$C = C\left(\frac{M}{P_g}; Y\right).$$
$$+\quad+$$

(1.13)

From the classical assumption of full employment, real domestic output is fixed at Y. Equilibrium in the domestic market between commodities and money requires that current consumption just exactly match production:

$$Y = C\left(\frac{M}{P_g}; Y\right)$$
$$+\quad+$$

(domestic equilibrium).   (1.14)

Otherwise, if Y differed from C in long-run "equilibrium," firms and households would be chronically adjusting their cash balance (guilder) positions; this contradicts the assumption that the long-run target demand for money is stable.

How then does domestic monetary policy influence the equilibrium position of the economy? Assuming that the demand for real money is stable, suppose a once and for all increase in M by the authorities. Individuals find themselves with excess real balances at the old price level P_g. As individuals, they try to raise C above Y. Hence, this bidding for tradable commodities raises P_g and depreciates the domestic currency in the foreign exchange market—raising R_s equivalently to P_g. When real balances are reduced to their original level, the desired flow of consumption again equals income where

$$Y = \bar{P}_i^d C_i + \bar{P}_x^d C_x.$$

(1.15)

Substituting equations (1.7) and (1.10) into equation (1.15) reveals that the dollar value of imports now equals the dollar value of exports:

$$\bar{P}_i^d I = \bar{P}_x^d X$$

(foreign exchange equilibrium). (1.16)

Equilibrium in the domestic money-commodities market implies equilibrium in the market for foreign exchange! The value of R_s equal to R_s^0 in Figure 1.2 just balances the *flow of* foreign exchange earned by exporters with the flow demanded by importers. But R_s^0 is also that value of P_g where, on net balance, domestic residents want neither to accumulate or decumulate their *stock* of real guilders. If M *is* given, a stable exchange rate does exist in long-run equilibrium even though the government does not intervene directly in the foreign exchange market to maintain an official parity.

"If M is given"—that is a big if. The domestic authorities can lose control over M for many reasons. Wayward fiscal policy leading to large government deficits that have to be financed by issuing domestic currency, or ineffective control by the central bank over its commercial banks, are two common possibilities. And if M is not under the firm control of the domestic central bank, then neither will a floating foreign exchange rate be determinant.

However, the story has a happy side. A government that is capable of controlling the stock of domestic money has an excellent prospect of stabilizing its exchange rate over the long term—unless the outside world is in chaos. Such exchange stability, together with maintained convertibility on current account transactions, imposes on the national economy the same prices for tradable goods and services as those that exist in the world economy at large.[13] Only with this equalization of purchasing power is the convertible domestic currency as good as international money. And the freedom of individuals and enterprises to use international money to trade at world prices implicitly underlies the famous classical and neoclassical theorems—from Adam Smith[14] to David Ricardo[15] to Paul Samuelson[16]—that demonstrate the welfare gains from international trade.

13. After taking transport costs and fiscal distortions such as import tariffs into account.
14. Adam Smith, *The Wealth of Nations*, 1776, Vol. I, ed., E. Cannan (London, 1961), pp. 418–36.
15. David Ricardo, *Principles of Political Economy and Taxation* (London: J. Murray, 1821), Chapter 7.
16. Paul Samuelson, "The Gains from International Trade Once Again," *Economic Journal*, Vol. 72 (1962), pp. 820–29.

A TECHNICAL NOTE TO CHAPTER 1:
Foreign Exchange Quotations

The following pages provide quotations on interbank bid-ask spreads, kindly provided on an informal basis by the foreign exchange division of a large American bank. The quotations do not necessarily represent the exchange rates at which trade actually took place among banks—in fact, the stated spreads may underestimate the spreads in actual trading. Moreover, customers of the banks involved might face wider bid-ask spreads—although direct data on this seems unavailable. There is reason to believe, however, that these last two factors are fairly constant, and do not distort the significant changes in interbank quotations that have occurred from the 1960s or from a fixed-rate year like 1972, to floating rates in 1973–74.

Rather than a formal statistical analysis of changes in bid-ask spreads, I shall simply present "raw" data on the dollar prices of major foreign currencies available to a foreign exchange trader for four representative points in time: September 29, 1972; June 18, 1973; January 31, 1974; and October 1, 1974. Further information going back to the 1960s is hard to get on a strictly comparable basis. However, fragmentary information for some countries from the 1960s can be informally compared to the data presented in the tables for 1972, 1973, and 1974.

In each of the four tables, bid-ask spreads in distant futures are greater than for spot quotations or near futures. As we pass from 1972 to 1974, bid-ask spreads widen substantially at every maturity—particularly for those currencies that had been pegged under the old Smithsonian system. However, measured as a percent of the spot exchange rate itself, the bid-ask spread in *distant* futures has widened much more with the advent of floating rates. For German marks for example, the bid-ask spread in 1972 for six-month futures was two basis points (.006 percent), whereas by January 1974 this spread had risen fourteen basis points (.04 percent). Back in December of 1971 (not shown in tables), the spread was only about 5/8 of a basis point.

Looking at the percentage forward premia and discounts (from the figures in parentheses), major turning points in spot exchange rates—as portrayed in Figure 1.1—were not predicted accurately at all. The high premium on the Japanese yen in September 1972 is about the only accurate indication of changes in exchange rates to come in 1973. On the other hand, on June 18, 1973, almost all forward quotations showed (incorrectly) premia against the dollar just two or three months before the dollar rose sharply.

TABLE 1.3 Interbank Foreign Exchange Quotations: September 29, 1972 (Dollars per unit of foreign currency)

	Spot U.S. terms		1 Month		3 Months		6 Months		12 Months	
	Bid	Offer	Bid	Offer	Bid	Offer	Bid	Offer	Bid	Offer
Sterling Floating	2.4205	2.4210	2.4148 (2.83D)	2.4159	2.4040 (2.73D)	2.4050	2.3879 (2.69D)	2.3892	2.3625 (2.40D)	—
Canadian dollar Floating	1.0165	1.0167	1.0165 (0.12P)	1.0170	1.0167 (0.12P)	1.0172	1.0168 (0.07P)	1.0172	1.0158 (0.06D)	1.0166
Belgian franc C = .022314	0.022625	0.022635	0.022658 (1.75P)	0.022679	0.022735 (1.94P)	0.022765	0.022835 (1.86P)	0.22865	0.022970 (1.48P)	—
French franc C = .1955	0.1995	0.1995	0.1995 (0.30P)	0.1997	0.1998 (0.65P)	0.1999	0.2001 (0.58P)	0.2002	0.2004 (0.48P)	—
German mark C = .3103	0.3122	0.3122	0.3131 (3.56P)	0.3132	0.3149 (3.56P)	0.3151	0.3174 (3.36P)	0.3176	0.3215 (2.99P)	0.3218
Dutch guilder C = .3082	0.3088	0.3089	0.3098 (3.79P)	0.3100	0.3118 (3.79P)	0.3119	0.3139 (3.29P)	0.3142	0.3170 (2.65P)	0.3174
Italian lire C = .001720	0.001718	0.001719	0.001715 (2.44D)	0.001717	0.001709 (2.09D)	0.001712	0.001701 (1.98D)	0.001704	0.001685 (1.92D)	0.001788
Swiss franc C = .2604	0.2630	0.2631	0.2638 (3.88P)	0.2640	0.2655 (3.80P)	0.2656	0.2676 (3.54P)	0.2648	0.2712 (3.12P)	0.2714
Japanese yen C = .003247	0.003321	0.003322	0.003378 (5.78P)	0.003344	0.003381 (7.33P)	0.003393	0.003473 (9.15P)	0.003491	—	—

NOTE: Figures in parentheses are percent per annum discount or premium over spot offer rate.

*C indicates central rate under the short-lived Smithsonian System.

TABLE 1.4 Interbank Foreign Exchange Quotations: June 18, 1973 (Dollars per unit of foreign currency)

	Spot U.S. terms		1 Month		3 Months		6 Months		12 Months	
	Bid	Offer	Bid	Offer	Bid	Offer	Bid	Offer	Bid	Offer
Sterling	2.5840	2.5845	2.5818 (0.84D)	2.5827	2.5745 (1.39D)	2.5755	2.5643 (1.49D)	2.5653	2.5432 (1.55D)	2.5445
Canadian dollar	1.0001	1.0004	1.0017 (2.22P)	1.0022	1.0038 (1.56P)	1.0043	1.0054 (1.12P)	1.0060	1.0056 (0.59P)	1.0063
Belgian franc	0.026705	0.026725	0.026805 (5.84P)	0.026855	0.026935 (3.89P)	0.026985	0.027080 (3.18P)	0.027150	0.027440 (3.09P)	—
French franc	0.2360 0.2370	0.2362	0.2362 (1.65P)	0.2365	0.2365 (1.04P)	0.2368	0.2370 (1.06P)	0.2374	0.2380 (0.75P)	0.2385
German mark	0.3909	0.3912	0.3911 (1.38P)	0.3916	0.3928 (2.25P)	0.3934	0.3955 (2.56P)	0.3962	0.4011 (2.74P)	0.4019
Dutch guilder	0.3686	0.3690	0.3696 (4.23P)	0.3703	0.3718 (3.79P)	0.3725	0.3739 (3.09P)	0.3747	0.3786 (2.93P)	0.3795
Italian lire	0.00165	0.00155	0.001654 (5.07P)	0.001663	0.001662 (3.63P)	0.001670	0.001667 (2.78P)	0.001678	0.001675 (2.11P)	—
Swiss franc	0.3289	0.3292	0.3303 (5.83P)	0.3308	0.3329 (5.10P)	0.3334	0.3358 (4.34P)	0.3363	0.3412 (3.95P)	—
Japanese yen	0.003779	0.003778	0.003792 (5.71P)	0.003800	0.003849 (8.46P)	0.003862	0.003919 (8.20P)	0.003937	—	—

NOTE: Figures in parentheses are percent per annum discount or premium over spot offer rate.

TABLE 1.5 Interbank Foreign Exchange Quotations: January 31, 1974 (Dollars per unit of foreign currency)

	Spot U.S. terms		1 Month		3 Months		6 Months		12 Months	
	Bid	Offer	Bid	Offer	Bid	Offer	Bid	Offer	Bid	Offer
Sterling	2.2690	2.2710	2.2390 (15.22D)	2.2422	2.2070 (10.57D)	2.2110	2.1710 (8.45D)	2.1750	2.1115 (6.85D)	2.1150
Canadian dollar	1.0113	1.0116	1.0113 (0.24P)	1.0118	1.0110 (0.04D)	1.0115	1.0105 (0.1D)	1.0110	1.0095 (0.09D)	1.0100
Belgian franc	0.023545	0.023575	0.023485 (0.8D)	0.023560	0.023380 (2.5D)	0.023425	0.023275 (1.8D)	0.023360	—	—
French franc	0.1963	0.1966	0.1946 (7.9D)	0.1953	0.1922 (7.5D)	0.1929	0.1904 (5.6D)	0.1911	0.1867 (3.8D)	—
German mark	0.3590	0.3600	0.3583 (1.3D)	0.3596	0.3575 (1.1D)	0.3590	0.3570 (0.8D)	0.3584	0.3568 (0.5D)	0.3584
Dutch guilder	0.3452	0.3457	0.3442 (2.8D)	0.3449	0.3423 (2.9D)	0.3432	0.3403 (2.6D)	0.3412	0.3382 (1.7D)	0.3392
Italian lire	0.001511	0.001514	0.001502 (4.0D)	0.001509	0.001490 (4.5D)	0.001497	0.001475 (4.0D)	0.001484	—	—
Swiss franc	0.3045	0.3050	0.3040 (0.4D)	0.3049	0.3034 (0.9D)	0.3043	0.3034 (0.3D)	0.3045	0.3034 (0.2D)	0.3040
Japanese yen	0.003347	0.003348	0.003306 (11.8D)	0.003315	0.003223 (13.5D)	0.003235	0.003172 (9.6D)	0.003188	—	—

NOTE: Figures in parentheses are percent per annum discount or premium over spot offer rate.

TABLE 1.6 Interbank Foreign Exchange Quotations: October 1, 1974 (Dollars per unit of foreign currency)

	Spot U.S. terms		1 Month		3 Months		6 Months		12 Months	
	Bid	Offer	Bid	Offer	Bid	Offer	Bid	Offer	Bid	Offer
Sterling	2.3360	2.3368	2.3320 (1.85D)	2.3332	2.2194 (2.76D)	2.3207	2.2983 (3.18D)	2.2996	1.1590 (3.25D)	1.1605
Canadian dollar	1.0151	1.0154	1.0152 (0.65P)	1.0159	1.0162 (0.55P)	1.0168	1.0165 (0.33P)	1.0171	1.0169 (0.25P)	1.0176
French franc	0.2113	0.2114	0.2103 (5.10D)	0.2105	0.2085 (4.92D)	0.2088	0.2053 (5.39D)	0.2057	0.2003 (4.82D)	0.2010
German mark	0.3774	0.3778	0.3779 (2.22P)	0.3785	0.3796 (2.65P)	0.3803	0.3808 (2.01P)	0.3816	0.3838 (1.88P)	0.3846
Dutch guilder	0.37045	0.37075	0.37085 (1.94P)	0.37135	0.37245 (2.37P)	0.37295	0.37365 (1.83P)	0.37415	0.37355 (0.97P)	0.37410
Italian lire	0.001514	0.001515	0.001506 (4.75D)	0.001509	0.001486 (6.86D)	0.001489	0.001450 (7.92D)	0.001455	0.001389 (6.93D)	—
Swiss franc	0.3395	0.3398	0.34015 (2.83P)	0.3406	0.3410 (1.47P)	0.3416	0.3423 (1.50P)	0.3439	0.3448 (1.46P)	—
Japanese yen	0.003352	0.003355	0.003350 (0.45P)	0.003357	0.003337 (1.18D)	0.003346	0.003335 (0.66D)	0.003344	0.003324 (0.35D)	—

2

Intervention by Central Banks in a World of *N* Currencies

The interbank market for foreign exchange could, in principle, operate without any direct intervention by central banks acting as executors of national governmental policies.

After all, the primary legal mandate of each national central bank is first, to secure the interregional clearing of domestic payments—as among, say, various Federal Reserve districts in the United States; and second, it is to control the stock of *domestic* money that, indirectly, might be sufficient in the long run to stabilize the exchange rate. A central bank may also be considered "the government's banker" and the regulator of domestic credit markets.

In contrast, international legal obligations are less firm. Under the Bretton Woods agreement of 1945, quite specific obligations to maintain official parities by *direct* short-run intervention to buy and sell foreign exchange were abrogated on occasion. Even before the general breakup of this parity system, Canada floated its exchange rate from 1950 to 1962. But official parities or not, governments tend to intervene continually in the foreign exchanges. By looking at reserve turnover, John Williamson[1] has calculated that official buying and selling of foreign exchange has not declined significantly since the Smithsonian par values were suspended in February 1973. Although individual experiences vary, some countries intensified their turnover of official exchange reserves after floating began.

1. John Williamson, "Exchange-Rate Flexibility and Reserve Use," *The Scandinavian Journal of Economics*, Vol. 78, No. 2 (1976), pp. 327–39. See also Esther Suss, "A Note on Reserve Use Under Alternative Exchange-Rate Regimes," IMF *Staff Papers* (July 1976), pp. 387–94.

Before asking the really big—and as yet insufficiently defined—question of whether any official intervention in the foreign exchanges is warranted (the fixed versus flexible exchange-rate controversy), two prior questions are worth considering:

1)   If the government of a convertible-currency country does have exchange-rate objectives, how might these be consistently achieved through direct intervention?

2)   What then are the implications of official direct intervention for the interbank clearing mechanism?

The direct techniques employed by the central bank to establish an official parity—or simply maintain the open-market price of foreign currency(ies) within narrow limits under floating rates—also determine the division of labor between the commercial banks and the central bank in clearing international payments. A narrow band within which foreign exchange rates are confined—say, the Bank of England endeavors to keep the pound sterling between US$1.68 and US$1.72—is an example of a rule-of-thumb commonly employed.

If an excess supply of sterling in the interbank market (among authorized commercial banks) drives the price down to $1.68, the Bank of England steps in and buys sterling for United States dollars. Similarly, only when sufficient excess demand drives the price to $1.72 need the Bank of England enter to sell sterling and buy dollars. Ordinarily, the great bulk of interbank transactions occur between $1.68 and $1.72 (as long as these official limits are themselves credible to the private market) so that only the commercial banks are active. Even when sterling falls to its support point of $1.68, the Bank of England sells dollars only to the commercial banks at wholesale, who in turn intermediate or retail the dollars to their nonbank customers.

Overall, therefore, the Bank of England need not be in the market continuously, and when it does enter at a support point, it can do so in a few large transactions. In principle, one man on a foreign exchange desk working at less than full capacity (but with the national reserves of dollars and unlimited sterling credit behind him) can preserve official parities, while the great bulk of the administrative work in clearing international payments devolves on the commercial banks.

N Currencies and N-1 Exchange Rates

Is this not altogether too simple? What about all convertible currencies other than dollars? Shouldn't the Bank of England intervene in Belgian francs, French francs, Deutsche marks, Dutch guilders, Australian dollars, Austrian schillings, kronor and so on, in order to fulfill either hypothetical parity obligations or other foreign exchange objectives? In fact, if there are N convertible currencies in the world, there exist $N-1$ exchange rates between sterling and other currencies towards some of which the Bank of England may have a parity objective, or at least a market view. Indeed, one of the proposals considered at the Nairobi Conference on International Monetary Reform in September 1973 was to have symmetrical multiple intervention by each central bank in all convertible currencies.

Administratively, if nothing else, continual intervention by one central bank in many currencies would seem complicated. Each country's official reserves would have to be held in South African rand, Canadian dollars, Italian lire, Greek drachma, and so on, including about forty currencies. Moreover, continual shifts might occur between those convertible currencies that seem worth supporting and those that the central bank certainly would not want to be caught holding. Mexican pesos in the early 1960s were strong, for example, whereas the peso of the late 1970s might seem less attractive.

Should the Bank of England be directly responsible for the sterling price of French francs, the sterling price of Spanish pesetas, the sterling price of Deutsche marks, and so forth? If so, what should be the *reciprocal* obligations of the Bank of France, the Bank of Spain, and the Bundesbank? Fairly complex rules could be devised that delineate when the Bank of France, for example, should be in the interbank market for sterling so as not to conflict with the Bank of England buying and selling francs. Indeed, even the close-knit European Monetary Union's experience with reciprocal rules governing multiple intervention has not been altogether satisfactory. Here it suffices to say that harmonious multiple currency intervention is incredibly complex if carried beyond a small number of countries closely bound together by common economic and political objectives. At this superficial level, therefore, it is perhaps not surprising that official intervention by any one central bank historically has never encompassed all or even most convertible currencies in the world. Usually only *one* foreign currency is used for official intervention; and in the postwar period, that one currency has been mainly the United States dollar.

More than mere convenience in reducing the bureaucracy necessary to run the foreign exchange departments of central banks is involved. The strong verdict of history, where official intervention is confined to the same single foreign currency, reflects the inherent logic of harmonizing exchange-rate objectives of at least $N-1$ of the N central banks in the simplest manner—no little virtue in a world of great complexity. For ease of exposition, suppose that the common *intervention currency* is the United States dollar. (In an earlier era, gold or sterling might have sufficed, and in the future perhaps it will be some fiat international money.) How then does an official exchange rate—

established by buying or selling U.S. dollars—influence the rate of exchange of
the domestic currency with the other $N-2$ national currencies on the one
hand, while minimizing potential conflict with the exchange rate goals of the
other $N-2$ central banks on the other?

Consider first the case when $N=2$—a world consisting only of Canada and
the United States. Our general principle is that there are only $N-1$ independent exchange rates to be determined in a world of N convertible national
currencies. In this two-country case, that leaves just one.

When the Bank of Canada buys and sells U.S. dollars with Canadian dollars
so as to maintain the Canadian dollar between US$0.99 and US$1.01, there can
be no rate outside these limits for the U.S. Federal Reserve to set without
provoking conflict. Indeed, in the postwar history of the two countries, over
several phases of formally pegged and then floating (no par) exchange rates, the
Bank of Canada intervened continually while the Federal Reserve passively
stayed out. In a two-country world, therefore, either one alone can have an
independent exchange-rate policy, or the single rate is agreed on jointly and then
maintained by purchases and sales closely coordinated by the two central banks.

Official Parities and Triangular Arbitrage

The *triangular* case of three countries, $N=3$, is interesting because it further
accentuates the need for an orderly rule to decentralize official foreign exchange interventions, and because it introduces an additional role for the
commercial banks in the multilateral clearing of international payments. In a
world consisting of, say, Canada, Germany, and the United States, there are
only two independent exchange rates to be determined, although there now
exist three rates quoted in the interbank market. For example, if the Bank of
Canada fixed the Canadian dollar between US$0.99 and US$1.01, and the
Bundesbank fixed the Deutsche mark between US$0.495 and US$0.505, then
the value of Deutsche marks in Canadian dollars would be contained within
Can$0.49 and Can$0.51. No official transactions would be needed between
Canadian dollars and Deutsche marks to maintain this parity range if all three
currencies remained convertible in the open market.

To see why only two official parities are necessary, suppose the Canadian
dollar rises to its maximum parity rate of US$1.01, whereas the Deutsche mark
falls to its minimum of US$0.495. Then algebraically:

$$(A) \quad \frac{\text{U.S. dollars}}{\text{Deutsche marks}} \times \frac{\text{Canadian dollars}}{\text{U.S.dollars}} = \frac{\text{Canadian dollars}}{\text{Deutsche marks}}$$

$$= \quad 0.495 \quad \times \quad \frac{1}{1.01} \quad = \quad 0.490099 \cong 0.49$$

That is, each Deutsche mark is valued at Can$0.49 to be consistent with the *two* official parities.

But what is the mechanism that maintains the rate of Can$0.49 per Deutsche mark in the absence of direct official intervention in the market for Canadian dollars and Deutsche marks? The answer is *triangular currency arbitrage* by the commercial banks. Suppose for some fleeting moment the two official parities were maintained as described above, but an importunate commercial dealer bid Can$0.492 per Deutsche mark in the Canadian-German interbank market. Then pressure would develop from other commercial banks to buy marks with U.S. dollars at the fixed official rate of US$0.495, sell the marks for Canadian dollars at Can$0.492, and then repurchase the U.S. dollars with Canadian at the official rate of US$1.01. If a commercial bank could actually move as much as US$100.00 along this triangular route without altering the quoted rates, the profits of doing so would be:

(B)   Step (1) $\dfrac{US\$100.00}{US\$0.495/DM}$ = DM 202.0202 purchased

Step (2)   DM 202.0202 × Can$0.492/DM = Can$99.393939 purchased.

Step (3)   Can$99.393939 × US$$1.01/Can$ = US$100.3878788 purchased.

Profits exclusive of brokerage fees:

US$100.3879 − $100.00 = US$0.3879 or .3879%

Although steps (1), (2), and (3) are actually necessary in order to make the arbitrage profit, the expected percentage yield can be seen directly from the degree of disalignment in the three rates. Specifically, take the percentage difference between the rate quoted directly in the Canadian dollar/Deutsche mark market *and* that implied by calculation (A) from the other two exchange markets:

(C) $\dfrac{Can\$0.492 - Can\$0.490099}{Can\$0.490099}$ = Can$0.003879 or .3879%.

The percentage profit of .3879 in (C) is the same as in (B). Given that the other two rates are officially supported, Deutsche marks will continue to be sold for Canadian dollars until their quoted rate falls to Can$0.490099, and the potential profit shown in (C) disappears.

The conceptual lesson to be learned from this simple arithmetic goes beyond how to make profits from triangular arbitrage—a ferociously competitive business in which high-speed computers ensure that nobody is going to get rich as long as official interventions are rational. If disalignments rise as described above, they are eliminated almost immediately. Rather, the arithmetic shows how supporting the U.S. dollar price of Canadian dollars by the Bank of Canada, and the U.S. dollar price of Deutsche marks by the Bundesbank, together are sufficient to determine the whole constellation of foreign exchange rates with the aid of private triangular arbitrage.

Yet more strongly, perhaps, there is no room for either central bank to supplant private arbitrage by setting an independent rate in the Canadian dollar/Deutsche mark market. Returning to our particular arithmetical example: if it were the Bundesbank (instead of a hapless private dealer) who offered to buy Deutsche marks at the disaligned rate of Can$0.492, an unlimited flood of offers to sell DM—purchased from the Bundesbank's own coffers with U.S. dollars—would be forthcoming. Other foreign exchange transactions would be disrupted as all private banks arbitraged at the Bundesbank's expense until either the three exchange rates were brought into mutual alignment, or the Deutsche mark became inconvertible so that it could not be purchased freely. In short, if the Bank of Canada is maintaining one parity by active intervention, only one independent choice is left either to the Bundesbank or to the Federal Reserve within a system of convertible currencies.

This important principle of decentralization of official foreign exchange policies is easily generalized to N convertible currency countries, where the total number of exchange rates (all currency pairs) is $N(N-1)\frac{1}{2}$. If $N-1$ central banks intervene to establish the parity value of their currencies in terms of the currency of the Nth, then these $N-1$ interventions together with triangular private arbitrage serve to determine all the remaining cross rates.[2] Because, by this reckoning, the number of exchange rates increases roughly proportionately to the *square* of the number of currencies, limiting official interventions to $N-1$ is a substantial organizational convenience. Effective decentralization occurs because each of the $N-1$ central banks has one, and only one, parity or other objective for its foreign exchange policy.

By implication, the role of the Nth country is to passively abstain from *direct* intervention in the foreign exchanges, in order to avoid conflict or inconsistency in the setting of rates. Of course, there is nothing to prevent authorities in the Nth country from consulting with the others in order to support—or to persuade them to modify—their exchange-rate targets. Indeed, this was sometimes done by the U.S. Federal Reserve during the Bretton Woods parity regime. (For the most part, however, the U.S. allowed individual trading partners to set exchange rates as they pleased.) But, if the principle of a single common intervention currency is dropped, mutual consultation would have to take place among all of the forty-odd countries, and not merely

2. Transacting in only three currencies is sufficient to determine all cross rates from these official parities provided that the intervention currency—say, the U.S. dollar—is common to all. The cross rate between any pair of currencies can be derived from knowing the parity rate of each with the common currency of intervention, without reference to other $N-3$ parities in the system. Hence arbitrage over more than three currencies is unnecessary to align N exchange rates.

between each one and the United States—an imposing strain on international goodwill!

Does this argument on the need to decentralize and limit official intervention make an implicit case for a floating exchange-rate regime with no official parity obligations? Unfortunately, the same potential problems of conflict and inconsistency exist in a no-par system because governments persist in having exchange-rate objectives. In the Canadian float from 1950 to 1962, the Bank of Canada was continually leaning against the market by buying and selling U.S. dollars in order to dampen (quite successfully) short-run movements in the exchange rate. In the massive general floating that began in February 1973, Williamson has noted that direct official intervention is almost as intense (mainly in U.S. dollars) as under the old parity regime.[3] Moreover, governments may intervene indirectly by manipulating domestic rates of interest and providing special forward contracts to induce their own commercial banks to buy or sell foreign currencies. The pros and cons of those interventions are considered later on; here it suffices to note that a consistent parity system serves to formalize certain rules of the intervention game—a version of which is still *implicitly* required in the no-par system observed so far.

The selection of a common currency for official intervention carries with it a further asymmetry. Exchange-rate margins will typically be twice as wide among the other $N-1$ currencies (as governed by private triangular arbitrage) than between each of the $N-1$ and the Nth currency itself. This doubling of margins is common among all $N-1$ currencies, and reflects a kind of exchange-rate pyramiding due to the fact that official foreign exchange objectives are established through an intermediary currency.

The old Bretton Woods system provides a good example of this pyramiding effect. Central banks outside of the United States were obligated to maintain their currencies within one percent of their official dollar parity, resulting in a maximum band of variation of two percent vis-à-vis dollars. The illustrative quotations of the Canadian dollar varying between U.S.$0.99 and US$1.01, and the DM varying between US$0.495 and US$0.505, exemplify the old legal requirements of the International Monetary Fund (IMF). Then from our calculations, triangular arbitrage will limit the Deutsche mark between Can$0.49 and Can$0.51—a four percent margin of variation just *twice* as wide as the official band of either currency with the U.S. dollar.[4]

3. Op. cit. p. 329.
4. More as a curiosity than anything profound, further pyramiding could take place if, say, the Dutch guilder was pegged to the Deutsche mark within a two percent band but not directly pegged to the U.S. dollar—the German and Canadian parity obligations in U.S. dollars remaining unchanged. Then the maximum range of variation between guilders and Canadian dollars would widen to six percent. Recourse to more intervention currencies would permit an even wider spectrum of possible variations in cross rates.

The Choice of the Nth Currency

We now address a more controversial question: Is the asymmetrical selection of an *Nth* currency an arbitrary choice for accounting convenience—finding a numeraire for our system of $N(N-1)\frac{1}{2}$ exchange rates—or must it necessarily devolve on a particular convertible currency with peculiar international characteristics?

One convertible currency is virtually as good as another in facilitating private triangular arbitrage at *a point in time*. Arbitrageurs—mainly commercial banks—simply buy and sell foreign exchange to make cross rates among $N-1$ currencies consistent with the $N-1$ bilateral exchange rates of each with an *Nth* currency. The *Nth* reference currency can be arbitrarily chosen for this purpose without having the properties of a special international money. Triangular round trips for arbitrage purposes, as illustrated by equations (1), (2), and (3), require virtually insignificant holdings of open positions in foreign currencies, and would seem independent of the presence or absence of a dominant international money. With the large intertemporal change in relative international currency values during 1973–78, the constellation of exchange rates at any point in time was never seriously disaligned in its multilateral consistency—a testimony to the robustness of triangular arbitrage.

However, the consistency and stability of a decentralized system of official interventions *through time* does depend in an essential way on (1) the economic size of the passive *Nth* country and (2) on the acceptability of its money as an international store of value. For this important dual role, *one* country with an attractive convertible currency is likely to dominate—although not necessarily indefinitely.

Consider country size and the meaning of a passive foreign exchange policy. As described above, only $N-1$ independent interventions are possible, so in a purely technical sense the *Nth* country must stay out unless some agreement is reached so it may substitute for one of the other $N-1$. But is this cloak of passivity as easily worn by Belgium (1977 GNP about US$81 billion) as by the United States (1977 GNP about US$1,890 billion), which is about twenty-three times as large in economic size?

To strip the monetary veil, note that the setting of an exchange rate is normally viewed as an instrument to influence the balance of international payments. Indeed, raising the price of the intervention currency, thereby depreciating the domestic currency against all others, is seen as increasing the net combined surplus on current and capital accounts.[5] Hence $N-1$ exchange-rate

5. In Chapter 1, it was demonstrated how raising R_s—the guilder price of dollars—would improve the domestic (Dutch) trade balance temporarily provided that the domestic money supply was under control. The argument can be extended to include the capital account as well.

policies correspond approximately to $N-1$ balance-of-payments targets. If the accounting is such that the sum of the world's payment surpluses equals the sum of all deficits,[6] the balance-of-payments position of the Nth is determined from the other $N-1$. Again, to avoid conflict and insure consistent decentralization of balance-of-payments policies, the natural counterpart of a passive foreign exchange policy is a passive balance-of-payments policy.

In order to provide the world with a quantitatively significant degree of freedom in setting $N-1$ balance-of-payments targets that are not in direct conflict, the Nth country must be of substantial economic size both in domestic GNP and in its foreign trade. In this respect, exports from the United States in 1977 were about twelve percent of world trade—slightly more than Germany's, while American GNP was a much larger proportion of world GNP than any other country's. Hence, an American balance of payments deficit— without becoming overwhelming to the United States itself—can reflect the collective desire of the other $N-1$ countries to run surpluses (deficits) in the course of determining their *speeds of adjustment* to full equilibrium. These temporary imbalances vis-à-vis the United States are an important safety valve or balance wheel for the system as a whole.

On the other hand, the equivalent payments deficits or surpluses that Belgium could run without provoking internal dissent would be trivially small for having this balancing impact—although the Belgian franc is an acceptable convertible currency for triangular arbitrage and for normal trading purposes. At the extreme, the Monégasque franc would be of no use whatsoever in this Nth currency role of facilitating foreign official interventions and allowing temporary payments imbalances by other nations.

The asymmetry in achieving decentralized balance of payment objectives carries over into the demand for "money" by central banks in the interbank market. As long as the U.S. dollar is the main intervention currency, other national central banks will acquire and hold dollars through time to facilitate their exchange-rate policies. Demand deposits are held in American commercial banks, or perhaps in a special account with the Federal Reserve Bank of New York, for writing checks to make international payments. Whereas longer term precautionary reserves are held either as direct claims on the United States, such as U.S. Treasury bills or certificates of deposit in American commercial banks, or as indirect dollar claims in the Eurocurrency markets.[7]

Other reserve assets held by national central banks can coexist with holdings

6. This is true if one uses an official-settlements definition of each country's balance of payments and excludes newly mined gold or the issue of direct monetary liabilities of some international agency.

7. To be described in more depth in Chapter 9.

in the *Nth* currency—such as gold or interest-bearing assets denominated in other currencies. Here it suffices to say that there will be a significant convenience demand by $N-1$ central banks to hold assets denominated in the *Nth* currency—reserves that may be deemed international money for official purposes. The dominant importance of U.S. dollars in world exchange reserves is shown in Tables 2.1 and 2.2, which are reproduced from IMF data. In 1977, over 60 percent of official reserves were either direct dollar claims on the United States, or Eurodollar deposits. And these are the more active reserves, where turnover is greater than in, say, gold holdings.

TABLE 2.1   Official Reserves, 1955–77 (Billions of SDRs at end of year)

	Gold	SDRs	Reserve positions in fund	Foreign exchange	Total
1955	35.0	—	1.9	18.1	55.0
1956	35.7	—	2.3	19.2	57.1
1957	36.9	—	2.3	18.4	57.7
1958	37.6	—	2.6	18.5	58.7
1959	37.6	—	3.3	17.5	58.3
1960	37.7	—	3.6	19.9	61.2
1961	38.6	—	4.2	20.5	63.3
1962	38.9	—	3.8	21.3	64.0
1963	39.8	—	3.9	24.1	67.9
1964	40.5	—	4.2	25.6	70.3
1965	41.5	—	5.4	25.4	72.3
1966	40.7	—	6.4	26.1	73.2
1967	39.4	—	5.7	29.3	74.4
1968	38.7	—	6.5	32.5	77.8
1969	38.9	—	6.7	33.0	78.7
1970	37.0	3.1	7.7	45.4	93.2
1971	35.9	5.9	6.4	75.1	123.2
1972	35.6	8.7	6.3	95.9	146.5
1973	35.6	8.8	6.2	102.0	152.6
1974	35.6	8.9	8.8	127.1	180.3
1975	35.5	8.8	12.6	137.8	194.7
1976	35.3	8.7	17.7	160.6	222.3
1977	35.5	8.1	18.1	199.3	261.8

SOURCE: International Monetary Fund *Annual Report, 1976*, p. 34. Data for 1976 and 1977 come from the International Financial Statistics.

NOTE: The SDR is the IMF's accounting unit and is worth about US$1.25. The price of gold is the official rather than the market price.

TABLE 2.2 Official Foreign Exchange Holdings by Type of Claim (Billions of SDRs at end of year)

	1970	1971	1972	1973	1974	1975	1976	1977
Official claims on United States	23.8	46.6	56.7	55.4	62.8	68.9	79.2	103.8
Official sterling claims on United Kingdom	5.7	7.3	8.1	6.5	8.3	6.4	3.2	3.3
Official Deutsche mark claims on Fed. Rep. of Germany	1.3	1.0	1.4	2.2	2.4	2.5	4.3	5.7
Official French franc claims on France	0.6	0.8	1.0	1.2	1.1	1.1	0.9	0.8
Other official claims on countries denominated in the debtor's own currency	0.9	1.0	0.9	1.6	1.5	2.7	3.8	4.6
Official foreign exchange claims arising from swap credits and related assistance	0.7	—	—	0.4	1.6	1.3	1.5	1.2
Identified official holdings of Eurocurrencies								
Eurodollars								
Industrial countries	5.1	3.4	5.6	7.3	6.5	7.0	7.9	14.7
Primary producing countries								
More developed countries	1.6	1.7	3.2	3.4	3.0	3.8	3.7	4.8
Less developed countries	3.8	5.4	9.2	10.3	22.8	27.7	34.0	38.5
Western Hemisphere	1.0	1.6	3.6	4.0	5.0	5.6	5.9	7.3
Middle East	0.6	1.1	1.9	2.3	12.0	16.7	19.1	20.6
Asia	1.1	1.1	2.0	2.7	3.0	3.5	5.9	7.8
Africa	1.1	1.6	1.7	1.3	2.8	2.0	3.1	2.9
Memorandum item: Major oil exporting countries	1.6	2.8	3.9	4.0	15.6	20.7	23.7	25.8
Total identified Eurodollars	10.5	10.4	18.0	21.1	32.3	38.5	45.6	58.0
Other Eurocurrencies	0.4	1.1	3.2	5.3	5.8	7.2	7.6	12.3
Total identified holdings of Eurocurrencies	10.9	11.6	21.2	26.4	38.0	45.7	53.1	70.3
Identified claims on IBRD and IDA	0.7	0.6	0.6	0.6	0.9	1.8	2.5	2.1
Residual	1.0	6.2	6.3	7.7	10.4	7.1	12.1	9.3
Total official holdings of foreign exchange	45.4	75.1	96.1	102.0	126.9	137.5	160.6	201.2

SOURCE: International Monetary Fund *Annual Report 1978*, p. 53.

NOTE: SDR is the IMF's accounting unit and is worth about US$1.25.

With other countries holding their reserves in the Nth currency, our second important criterion (other than sheer economic size) is that the Nth currency should maintain its real value through time measured by an international price index of goods and services, while allowing an attractive interest and liquidity yield to foreign official holders. Otherwise holding dollar balances would not be economically acceptable to most countries. Thus stabilizing the *dollar* price level of tradable goods is a key American obligation—in its role as the Nth country—to the smooth functioning of the convertible currency system. The disruptive consequences of inflation in the United States are analyzed in more detail in Chapter 11.

The United States Dollar as a Vehicle Currency for Commercial Banks

Just as central banks settle on a common *intervention* currency to minimize the cost of transacting, so do commercial banks choose a common *vehicle* currency within the interbank market for foreign exchange.

Consider first the spot market for making current payments. With N convertible currencies from active trading countries, commercial banks have $N(N-1)\frac{1}{2}$ potential cross rates of exchange that they must be prepared to quote to their retail nonbank customers—or lose the custom. If an Australian firm is considering importing Greek olives invoiced in drachma, it may well ask its local commercial bank to quote a price for drachma in terms of Australian dollars. Not making any such market itself, the Australian commercial bank then refers to the wholesale interbank market for an appropriate quotation.

There, an active wholesale market for Greek drachma in terms of Australian dollars is unlikely to exist either. The volume of trade between these two currencies is simply too small to warrant the establishment of an elaborate system of bid-offer quotations (see the Technical Note to Chapter 1) at which major name banks are willing to trade directly. That would involve the already harrassed (but highly paid) foreign exchange dealers in watching and operating in too many markets—$N(N-1)\frac{1}{2}$ to be exact. Instead, costs are minimized by having most rates for national currencies, traded in the interbank market, quoted against a single vehicle currency. If all convertible currencies are actively traded *only* against the U.S. dollar, the number of markets required is reduced to $N-1$—a substantial resource saving indeed!

And most direct interbank trading involves the U.S. dollar on a one-on-one situation with each other currency. Occasionally in spot trading, two large trading partners—say France and Germany—might generate sufficient activity to warrant the direct exchange of DM for francs. But this is the exception.

Typically the U.S. dollar is used as an intermediary. For example, exchanging Australian dollars for Greek drachma is consummated by first buying U.S. dollars with Australian dollars; and then the U.S. dollars are used to buy Greek drachma.

$$\frac{\text{Australian dollars}}{\text{U.S. dollars}} \cdot \frac{\text{U.S. dollars}}{\text{Greek drachma}} = \frac{\text{Australian dollars}}{\text{Greek drachma.}}$$

Therefore, when the Australian bank quotes a retail price for the Greek drachma to the Australian importer of olives, the quote includes the cost of the two enabling transactions at wholesale—each using the U.S. dollar.

While the occasional spot market may function independently of the dollar, *all* forward transacting in the interbank market utilizes the American dollar as an intermediary vehicle currency. Commercial banks make direct forward quotes (of the kind listed in the Technical Note to Chapter 1) only against the American dollar. The reason is clear enough. Forward trading involves the introduction of many markets, each corresponding to a maturity date in the future, no one of which has a terribly high volume of transactions. This lack of volume would become even more acute if direct forward markets were introduced between arbitrarily chosen pairs of convertible currencies, instead of funneling all trading through a common vehicle currency.

In summary, our analysis implies that the American dollar is a fairly universal kind of interbank money in the foreign exchanges, although nonbank enterprises and individuals (not engaged in trade with the United States) may comfortably invoice much trade in goods and services in other convertible currencies.[8]

Inconvertibility, Less Developed Countries, and Pegged Exchange Rates

Do we live in a world of generally floating exchange rates? The collapse in February 1973 of the short-lived Smithsonian agreement, which established official par values for major currencies against the American dollar, is widely regarded as the herald of a new era of unrestricted exchange-rate flexibility. But appearances and casual newspaper commentary are deceiving. Of the 122 currencies tabulated by the International Monetary Fund in Table 2.3, only 11 were floating independently as of June 30, 1975. They include the major Western industrial economies such as the United States, Japan, Britain, France, Italy, Canada, Switzerland, etc., and one or two oil-rich countries

8. The extent to which nonfinancial firms and individuals invoice their foreign trade in nondollar, but convertible, currencies is taken up explicitly in Chapter 4.

TABLE 2.3   Exchange Rate Practices of International Monetary Fund Members
(As of June 30, 1975)

	Number of currencies	Percentage share of trade of fund members
Currencies that float independently	11	46.4
Currencies pegged to a single currency, of which:	81	14.4
Pegged to U.S. dollar	54	12.4
Pegged to French franc	13	0.4
Pegged to pound sterling	10	1.6
Pegged to Spanish peseta	1	—
Pegged to South African rand	3	—
Currencies pegged to a composite of other currencies of which:	19	12.4
SDR	5	5.0
Other	14	7.4
Currencies pegged to others but that change the peg frequently in light of some formula	4	2.0
Currencies that are floating jointly	7	23.2
Total	122	98.4

SOURCE: International Monetary Fund *Annual Report, 1975.*

such as Saudi Arabia and Nigeria with ample supplies of foreign exchange for preserving free currency convertibility. These independent floaters account for about 46.4 percent of world trade.

Another small group of Western European countries, with a somewhat revolving membership, maintain common currency margins with each other and are said to be joint floaters: Belgium, Denmark, Germany, the Netherlands, Norway, and Sweden. These joint floaters account for another 23 percent of world trade.

Otherwise, the remaining 104 countries whose exchange practices were sufficiently systematic to permit classification in Table 2.3, all peg to a convertible foreign currency such as the U.S. dollar or the French franc; or they peg to a statistical index or a composite of currencies from the major industrial countries. But even in the latter case, a single intervention currency (usually the U.S. dollar) is the financial instrument for adjusting the international value of the domestic currency to the weighted index of other currencies. The great majority of these 104 are the poor less developed countries of Latin America, Africa, and Asia with *inconvertible* currencies.

While it is clear that countries with fully convertible currencies have the option of pegging or not pegging, those with exchange controls and restrictions on making foreign payments are virtually *compelled* to peg—either implicitly or explicitly—to a convertible foreign currency of a major trading partner.[9] Why should one associate pegged exchange rates, for most of the 104 countries, with currency inconvertibility and with economic underdevelopment?

Governments in less developed countries (LDCs) often lack the internal political power, and the accompanying fiscal and administrative capability, to allocate domestic resources directly by centralized fiat in the manner of the communist centrally planned economies. Nevertheless, these same governments are usually not enamoured with the idea of a decentralizing economic decision making through the unrestricted use of equilibrium prices and free markets. Rather, the government has a domestic plan and perhaps planning agency; its political office is seen as a mandate to control or influence as much economic activity as possible. However, the strongest instrument for internal economic control that can be freely manipulated by LDC governments is often the market for foreign exchange—where the clearing of international payments can be fairly easily brought under a single authority.[10] Since imports and exports usually pass through centralized ports and border-crossing stations, they are more easily monitored and taxed by a weak governmental authority than is commerce in the domestic hinterland.

While fiscal and financial devices that are used to manipulate the flow of trade through the foreign exchanges are legion, some of the more common practices are listed below. The government in the guise of the foreign exchange authority can:

1) Allocate import licenses and the associated economic rents to particular firms and individuals while excluding others.

2) License in favor of particular importable (exportable) commodities—wheat, machinery, etc.—so as to reduce (raise) their domestic-currency prices relative to potential imports that are disallowed.

3) Raise general revenue for the government by:

    i) Auctioning off licenses to import to the highest bidder (seldom used).

    ii) Raising the domestic-currency price of foreign exchange charged to importers above that paid to exporters (often used).

    iii) Formally levying tariffs or other taxes on potential importables (frequently used but not easily manipulated in the short run).

4) Introduce multiple exchange rates, such that different imports can enter at several different prices for foreign exchange; or export proceeds can be sold for domestic money at favored or less favored rates of exchange.

9. And several such as Australia and Venezuela continue to peg to the U.S. dollar.
10. A more complete rationale for the ways in which LDC governments intervene in the foreign exchanges is provided in R. McKinnon, *Money and Capital in Economic Development* (Washington, D.C.: Brookings Institution, 1973), Chapters 3 and 10.

Such an elaborate maze of controls, where markets are segmented and different individuals are meant to see very different prices for importables or exportables, requires *currency inconvertibility* as a necessary administrative adjunct. Clearly, if all domestic firms and individuals were free to spend the domestic currency for foreign goods—using commercial banks as unrestrained financial intermediaries—the government's control would be undermined. Therefore, the clearing of foreign payments usually devolves on the *central bank* in LDCs—or the commercial banks act as tightly regulated agents of the central bank in enforcing a complex system of exchange restrictions. The central bank initially collects all foreign exchange earnings from exporters, holds all reserves, and then sells the foreign exchange for domestic currency to duly licensed domestic importers in particular exchange-rate categories. Hence commercial banks are not free to create a unified market for foreign exchange, either spot or forward, as they might do with a floating convertible currency or one floating within given exchange margins.

Willy-nilly the central bank is cast into the role of announcing exchange rates for the various categories of transactions listed above, and then providing the necessary foreign exchange to those traders satisfying the rules and regulations. To make this potentially herculean administrative task manageable, the central bank uses a single international numeraire for specifying its structure of exchange rates, and then uses that same foreign convertible money as the transactions currency for actually providing foreign exchange to domestic claimants. Usually, the foreign currency is that of one major industrial country.

For example, the Central Bank of Indonesia can announce official exchange rates in rupiahs per dollar, and then sell dollars to favored Indonesian importers who can trade dollars, if necessary, in the foreign interbank market for other convertible currencies. The upshot is that the rupiah is effectively pegged to the U.S. dollar, and Indonesian reserves are held in dollars.

Notice the acute problems that would arise if the exchange controls were managed using several foreign convertible currencies. No longer would the government have a single numeraire for exchange rates. Moreover, if the government did announce rates of exchange between the rupiah and several foreign currencies simultaneously, the cross rates of exchange would become quickly obsolete in a world where the mark, dollar, yen and so forth are all floating vis-à-vis each other. Indonesian exporters and importers (duly licensed of course) would attempt triangular arbitrage at the expense of the foreign-exchange authority. Any time the dollar moved with respect to the mark or yen in the open markets for foreign exchange, the authorities would have to alter their official quotations in each of the foreign currencies they were prepared to buy and sell. Hence, virtually all countries with inconvertible currencies peg to one important foreign money with international properties—usually the U.S. dollar.

There is some opportunity cost to maintaining a peg-of-convenience to a single convertible foreign currency. The country with the inconvertible currency then has to accept the exchange fluctuations of its partner currency with other independently floating convertible currencies, or at least consciously make adjustment for such fluctuations.[11] However, these costs would seem low in comparison to holding and managing a portfolio of several foreign currencies for payments purposes, or having no peg (numeraire) at all when there is no unified market between the domestic currency and foreign monies.

The official pegging of the exchange rate is a convenient device for organizing the foreign payments mechanism in the short run. However, most countries with inconvertible currencies do not maintain a fixed exchange rate with their partner currency in the long run. In Chapter 1, we established that a stable exchange rate could only be maintained in the long run if the domestic money supply was sufficiently controlled so that chronic excess demand for foreign goods did not develop. This condition has generally been met neither in most LDCs nor in many developed countries, so that the pegged official price of foreign exchange is often adjusted upwards—frequently under great duress. These common crises, involving discrete movements in official pegs, are discussed in more depth in Chapter 7.

Fixed Versus Floating Exchange Rates

Clearly, unrestricted floating is only feasible when the currency in question is convertible. Only then can the commercial banks make a unified market in foreign exchange by intermediating the unrestricted demands and supplies of their nonbank customers. Not only is fairly complete freedom to make and receive payments on current account necessary, but some modicum of flexibility in the movement of short-term private capital is also required.[12]

But suppose sufficient freedom in making and receiving foreign payments is allowed so that the domestic currency is effectively convertible. Accepting the fact that we live in a world where several currencies are floating, when should the authorities in any *one* country opt to peg it to that of a trading partner? (Remember, only one independent intervention is feasible.)

11. Some of the statistical anomalies of passively accepting the exchange-rate fluctuations of the partner country are outlined by Stanley Black, "Exchange Policies for Less Developed Countries in a World of Floating Rates," D. Leipziger (ed.), *The International Monetary System* (Washington, D.C.: Agency for International Development, 1976), pp. 13–66.
12. This important point is demonstrated more rigorously in Chapters 5 and 7. For example, an active forward market in foreign exchange depends heavily on allowing free movement of short-term capital.

The first and fairly trivial observation is that the trading partner itself must have a fairly stable monetary system. In this respect, the United States has remained relatively stable while Britain in the 1970s has lost its position. Many countries no longer wish to peg to the pound sterling as they did several decades ago, and have switched their pegs to the U.S. dollar or float independently.[13] But even a potentially stable trading partner may experience vicissitudes in its monetary policy, and experience exchange-rate changes vis-à-vis third countries that are inappropriate for the country under consideration.

A further condition—particularly important for small countries—is that they be highly integrated with the country or area to which they are pegging: the old argument on optimum currency areas.[14] Then, if the partner country does succeed in establishing domestic price stability, the substantial trade between the two, at a fixed exchange rate, will impose price stability (in the long run) on the country in question through unhindered commodity arbitrage. Also, a stable exchange rate is important to exporters and importers for reducing risk; they would benefit more when the partner country dominated the foreign trade of the country in question.

At bottom, however, there is a more fundamental issue. What is the best way for a country to organize its monetary policy *and* preserve currency convertibility at the same time? In opting for a freely floating exchange rate, our country is also opting for monetary independence—and it had better be sure it has the will and financial capability of exercising that independence in an appropriate way. In Chapter 1, we established the long-run relationship between a stable domestic money supply, which was independently determined, and a stable exchange rate.

On the other hand, in opting for a rigidly fixed exchange rate over the long run and free convertibility, control over the domestic money supply must be subordinated to the foreign exchange mechanism and (implicitly) to the partner country. Otherwise the fixed exchange rate cannot long endure without inciting a speculative crisis.[15] A balance of payments deficit signals that there is an excess of domestic money (guilders) in circulation: domestic firms and individuals are trying to rid themselves of money to buy foreign goods or securities net. To preserve the fixed exchange rate, the central bank, in the guise of the foreign exchange authority, naturally eliminates this excess supply by selling exchange reserves (dollars) and purchasing guilders, which thereby withdraws

13. See Stanley Black, op. cit. p. 59. In 1973 alone, Cyprus, Malta, Malaysia, and Singapore all discontinued their peg to sterling.
14. This argument is developed in more detail in Chapter 8, and can also be found in R. McKinnon, "Optimum Currency Areas," *American Economic Review* (September 1963), pp. 717–25.
15. Of the kinds described in detail in Chapter 7.

them from circulation. And consistency requires that the guilders so removed stay out of domestic circulation.

Similarly, suppose the central bank does not create guilders fast enough, by domestic open market operations or discounting, to satisfy the existing demand for guilders at the given price level (exchange rate). Then a surplus will appear in the balance payments where individuals and firms are net sellers of goods and securities to foreigners for money (dollars). The official exchange stabilization fund purchases the excess dollars from domestic nationals in return for guilders—thereby relieving the shortage of domestic currency while preventing its appreciation in the exchange market. A domestic money-supply operation is always the dual of a purchase or sale of foreign exchange, and the fixed exchange rate requires that the domestic dual not be undone.

In contrast, an *inconsistent* domestic monetary *cum* foreign exchange policy would be where excess guilders (at the existing price level) are pumped into the economy by domestic techniques—say, an uncontrolled deficit in the government budget covered by printing guilders. Then, under a fixed exchange rate *and* free convertibility, this excess would quickly appear as a deficit in the balance of payments, leading to a loss of exchange reserves that may well be unsustainable. A crisis, a discrete devaluation or perhaps several devaluations, are then forced on the economy; or convertibility and free trade are undermined as the authority resorts to direct exchange controls to protect its reserve position. In either case, this inconsistent monetary policy detaches the domestic price level—and the *relative* prices of tradable goods—from those prevailing in world trade. Serious economic dislocation and losses in allocative efficiency result.

From 1954 to 1970, Mexico followed a consistent monetary *cum* exchange-rate policy in pegging the peso at 12.5 to the U.S. dollar *and* allowing incipient deficits in the balance of payments to contract the domestic monetary base in the short run, while permitting a secular increase in the supply of pesos from domestic sources to be more or less in line with the growing demand for them. Between 1954 and 1970, the Mexican price level in pesos was fairly stable and exchange controls and other restrictions were absent. From 1971 to 1976, however, the Mexican government embarked on a much higher rate of monetary expansion from domestic sources. This could not be fully offset by drawing down dollar reserves—supplemented with heavy borrowing in the New York money market— to repurchase the excess pesos being created domestically. The result was a collapse in the value of the peso to 24 to the dollar in the fall of 1976, a spectacular internal price inflation, and the temporary imposition of exchange controls.[16]

16. A more complete analysis of the Mexican experience can be found in G. Ortiz, "Capital Accumulation and Economic Growth: A Financial Perspective on Mexico," Ph.D. dissertation, Stanford University, 1977. Most of the exchange controls were subsequently removed.

The moral of our story is clear. The old argument on fixed *versus* floating exchange rates is misspecified when posed that way. Rather, ensuring *consistency* in monetary *cum* exchange-rate policy—with either a fixed or a floating exchange rate—is probably the more important policy decision in preserving free convertibility.

3

Currency Inconvertibility and the Foreign Trade of Centrally Planned Economies

Since World War II, three fairly distinct groups of countries have had inconvertible currencies in varying degrees. The centrally planned econmies (CPEs) of Asia and Eastern Europe deliberately use inconvertibility to support their domestic price structures and planning mechanisms. Most other less developed countries (LDCs) have done so more by accident than design (Chapter 2) because of fiscal problems and their difficulties in aligning exchange rates.[1] A third prototype group, Western European countries in the 1940s and early 1950s, lacked foreign exchange reserves due to a general shortage of capital that could be used in clearing multilateral payments. Their return to convertibility under the Marshall Plan is discussed in Chapter 11.

Despite the diverse nature of the countries involved, all experienced inefficiencies and anomalies in their foreign trade that wcrc (are) mitigated by their use of convertible currencies—international money provided by other nations. Here I focus on the socialist economies (CPEs) because they provide the most striking illustrations of the problems involved in organizing foreign trade without having domestic currencies that are internationally convertible.

Because inconvertibility can be a matter of degree rather than an either/or

1. Even as late as 1973, 86 out of the 128 members of the International Monetary Fund failed to satisfy their convertibility obligations under Article VIII. All 86 are normally classified as "less developed"—the poor countries of Asia, Latin America, Africa, and so on. Communist countries, with the exception of Yugoslavia, are not members and have no legal convertibility obligation.

concept, let us further refine its common usage definition to distinguish among several forms of inconvertibility governing current-account transactions:[2]

1) *Commodity inconvertibility* holds when domestic currency owned by nonresidents cannot be freely used to purchase domestic goods and services at prices prevailing in domestic trade. In particular, such balances arising from authorized current-account transactions cannot be freely spent on domestic goods for *export*. In general, only an authorized state trading agency may purchase domestic goods for export; and relative export prices may be quite different from domestic prices of the same goods.

2) *Foreign exchange inconvertibility for nonresidents* implies that the national monetary authority is not obligated to repurchase domestic-currency balances (arising from authorized current-account transactions) from foreigners at a known parity either with convertible foreign exchange or with the foreigners' own currency. Nor are foreigners allowed to sell their domestic balances in a unified open market for foreign exchange.

3) *Foreign exchange inconvertibility for residents* holds when domestic residents cannot freely utilize their own currency to buy foreign exchange in a unified market in order to *import* goods and services on current account. Either a strict licensing procedure exists, or the import trade is concentrated in the hands of a single state agency. Again, there need be no close relationship between the relative prices of imports in foreign currency and their relative prices in domestic currency.

These distinctions are important because normally all three kinds of inconvertibility hold for centrally planned economies, although foreign exchange inconvertibility for nonresidents could, in principle, be relaxed. LDCs normally prevent domestic currency held by residents from being freely converted into foreign exchange in order to ration imports of goods and services in the presence of a disaligned exchange rate. But these same LDCs are usually anxious to expand exports and typically don't practice commodity inconvertibility; they may also allow some degree of foreign exchange convertibility for nonresidents. In the 1940s and early 1950s, many Western European countries imposed foreign exchange inconvertibility on both residents and nonresidents towards the dollar area and other strong currencies, but they allowed free commodity convertibility for the most part.

Central Planning and Commodity Inconvertibility

In a communist country, the state owns the means of production and determines investment priorities in this or that sector of the economy. However, the absence of private property *per se* is not sufficient to warrant inconvertibility on

2. Chapter 1, p. 7.

the *current* account of the balance of payments. (Nor does the absence of private property prevent international lending and borrowing—it only forestalls trade in equities or the use of collateral that could constitute an equity claim.) It is not difficult to imagine a variety of state-owned enterprises, in commerce or in manufacturing, purchasing industrial materials abroad when the relevant foreign prices seemed attractive at the prevailing exchange rate. Similarly, these same enterprises could divide their output between domestic and foreign sales, either by direct exportation or because foreign buyers are free to acquire balances in domestic currency to bid for domestic goods. Currency convertibility would allow such decentralized decision making in foreign trade—the domestic currency would be internationally liquid—even though the participating enterprises were state owned and perhaps each was collectively managed by its workers. But such decentralization does require that domestic prices accurately reflect economic scarcity.

Instead, the current output of producer goods and industrial materials is centrally allocated by administrative fiat in communist countries, sometimes called command economies.[3] Prices serve only a residual role in accounting for cash flows when goods pass from one enterprise to another. Since prices are not used for allocative purposes domestically, it is inconceivable that foreigners be permitted what domestic enterprises cannot do, i.e., freely exercise monetary claims to purchase whatever domestic goods seem attractive at prevailing prices. Not only would nationally administered materials allocations be upset, but low price tags on some potentially exportable domestic goods may well conceal the fact that they are either very costly in real resources or are in actual shortage. Formal accounting prices need bear no systematic relationship to their value in use as seen by the planners. Hence, commodity inconvertibility is necessarily universal in centrally planned economies—otherwise central planning through materials allocations could not exist.

A natural concomitant of commodity inconvertibility, therefore, is the concentration of all export trade in a single agency that purchases domestic goods to be sold abroad at what might be a very different relative prices.[4] Centralized

3. Beyond the retail level, Yugoslavia was the first communist state to experiment in a sustained way with using market prices to decentralize economic decision making—but not so far as to allow free currency convertibility into foreign exchange. In recent years, Hungary also has liberalized domestic prices somewhat and now departs substantially from the model of a pure command economy.
4. "The complete lack of relationship between Soviet internal and foreign trade prices over most of the period 1929–1956 is demonstrated below. . .In 1937, for example, some goods were exported at less than 10 percent of their domestic prices, some at 300 percent above domestic prices, with the rest scattered between. This suggested that the USSR required not just two exchange rates, to equate internal and world prices, one for producer goods and one for consumer goods, but dozens." Franklyn Holzman, *Foreign Trade Under Central Planning* (Cambridge, Mass.: Harvard University Press, 1974), p. 13.

state trading agencies act as buffers between foreign and domestic relative prices—a need that is made more acute in the presence of taut or high pressure planning techniques where materials shortages are commonplace. Such agencies ignore any profits (or losses) to be made from buying domestic goods at one price in domestic currency and selling for another in foreign currency, which is converted at an official exchange rate. The higher the domestic-currency price of the foreign currency, the greater will be these accounting profits. Yet the export agency's decision making is mandated from the center so that the setting of the exchange rate (as well as the structure of domestic prices) is an unimportant element in its selection of goods to be exported—most unlike the situation in convertible-currency countries where the correct alignment of domestic and foreign prices through the exchange rate is a critical matter.

For these same reasons, foreign exchange inconvertibility also holds: individuals and firms cannot freely convert their domestic-currency balances into foreign exchange in order to import foreign goods. Not only do the domestic prices of goods seen by household differ substantially from those seen by enterprises, neither set accurately reflects their real costs in domestic resources. In a noncommunist less developed country, this latter discrepancy may arise primarily because the official price of foreign exchange is kept too low, making imports look unduly cheap. In a centrally planned economy on the other hand, the discrepancy is not so uniform: many domestic prices would be too low at the official exchange rate and incorrectly signal that imports are not wanted—and vice versa. In command economies, therefore, the import trade is also concentrated in a single comprehensive state agency (perhaps the same one responsible for exports) that sharply discounts the importance of domestic accounting prices in making its trading decisions.

What criteria might the agency bring to bear on what to import or to export? A standard procedure in mathematical planning models is to calculate shadow prices that do, more or less accurately, reflect domestic scarcity. Undoubtedly, a state trading agency would have to make similar very complex calculations to evaluate each traded commodity—if only implicitly. In general, however, very little formal theory can be brought to bear on how state trading decisions are actually made.

Multilateral Exchange With the West

In their growing trade with the West, CPEs heavily utilize Western convertible currencies as a means of payment and as a unit of account in order to facilitate trade on a multilateral basis. Unlike the immediate postwar years, some small countries in Eastern Europe such as Poland and Hungary now have as much as 50 percent of their foreign trade directed towards Western countries with convertible currencies.

Take first the case of a single hypothetical CPE, Transylvania, that has a domestic currency we will call "franks," which are inconvertible in both the commodity and foreign exchange senses. Initially, consider Transylvanian trade with countries having convertible currencies. No foreign exporter, say from Sweden, is willing to set prices or be paid in franks because they can't be freely used to buy either goods or foreign exchange. The Swedish exporter will demand payment either in Swedish kronor—normal commercial practice—or in some mutually agreeable third currency such as U.S. dollars. Hence, the Transylvanian state trading agency acquires and holds convertible currency(ies) for making payment. The system is asymmetrical because Transylvanian exports to Sweden will also be invoiced in kronor or in a third currency—rather than in franks as ordinary commercial practice (among convertible-currency countries) might suggest. Sven Grassman has calculated[5] that 87.8 percent of Swedish exports to Eastern Europe were invoiced in kronor and 12.2 percent in other convertible currencies; whereas 75.6 percent of all Swedish imports from Eastern Europe were invoiced in kronor while 24.3 percent were invoiced in other convertible currencies. World prices were the unit of account so that the moneyness of Eastern European currencies was not utilized at all in Swedish trade.

Most importantly, Transylvania can freely engage in multilateral trade with other countries having convertible currencies. If it has an export surplus with Sweden and a trade deficit with Austria, the excess kronor balances can be sold—using a Swedish or other Western commercial bank as an agent in the interbank market—to obtain Austrian schillings. If Austrian exporters do not have a strong commercial preference for invoicing in schillings, Transylvania may denominate all its trade in only one currency—say U.S. dollars.[6] The multilateral aspects of foreign trade would be quite efficient if exchange rates among convertible currencies were sufficiently stable. Then the state trading agency could easily assess the economic value, at the margin, of goods shipped to Sweden in comparison to the marginal value of those imported from Austria—relative to other potential trading partners quoting prices in convertible currencies. Moreover, Transylvania can easily run a trade deficit with the West by borrowing abroad in, say, the Eurocurrency market; or it could deposit the proceeds from a trade surplus in a conveniently liquid form with Western banks.

5. Sven Grassman, *Exchange Reserves and the Financial Structure of Foreign Trade* (Westmead, Eng.: Saxon House, 1973), pp. 32–33.
6. The selection of the currency of invoice is considered in Chapter 4.

However, commodity inconvertibility still leaves open the more basic question of whether Transylvanian foreign trade is efficient in terms of the domestic resource costs of her imports and exports. Transylvania still lacks a domestic money with international qualities to guide the efficient selection of a domestic bill of goods to enter foreign trade. This remains true for trade with other CPEs as well as with capitalist economies.

Bilateralism Within the Council
for Mutual Economic Assistance (CMEA)

Although CPEs utilize convertible currencies in their multilateral trade with the West, they have been reluctant to use such international money as a means of payment in intrabloc trade or in trade with many less developed countries. Political distaste for formally making payments in the convertible currencies of noncommunist countries, or unwillingness to invest in the necessary foreign exchange reserves, has led each pair of state-trading agencies to enter into long-term trade agreements that strive for bilateral balance. Multilateral trade within the communist bloc (CMEA) seems to be small and difficult to organize.

Michael Michaely did an exhaustive study of the degree of multilateral versus bilateral balancing for the worldwide trade of 65 diverse industrial and less developed countries in 1958. His statistical rank-ordering of dependence on multilateral trade showed that the five CPEs included were at the bottom: on an average, 9.6 percent of their trade was multilateral, whereas for the noncommunist countries the proportion was 29.2 percent.[7] This remarkable difference arose because the trade of the CPEs was then mainly intrabloc, which itself is dominantly bilateral.

In comparison, for the year 1938 Michaely calculated that proportion of multilateral trade in the total trade of these same five countries was 23.7 percent. Of course, bloc trading did not then exist because only the Soviet Union was communist. Hungary, Poland, Czechoslovakia, and Bulgaria were

---

7. Michael Michaely, "Multilateral Balancing in International Trade," *American Economic Review* (September 1962). His statistical index for multilateralism was

$$T_j = 100 \cdot \frac{\sum_{s=1}^{n} \left| \dfrac{X_{sj}}{X_j} - \dfrac{M_{sj}}{M_j} \right|}{2}$$

where X_{sj} stands for exports of country j to country s, and X_j stands for country j's total exports during the year, and n is the total number of countries being considered. A similar interpretation holds for the Ms on the import side. This measure of multilateralism becomes defective if there are large net capital transfers between trading partners.

freer to organize their trade multilaterally despite the substantial disorganization of the convertible-currency system in the 1930s.

For the 1960s, C. H. MacMillan found that only about 5 percent of Russian trade within the CMEA was multilateral (measured by Michaely's index); whereas about 25 percent of Russian trade with convertible currency countries was multilateral.[8]

To get a further picture of the pronounced bilateral character of intrabloc trade, Henryk Francruz used the same statistical technique as Michaely in order to measure multilateralism as proportion of trade *within* the communist bloc—in contrast to Michaely who was concerned with the total trade of each of his 65 countries.[9] For our five CPEs plus Rumania and East Germany he found that only 4.8 percent of intrabloc trade was multilateral in 1960–1963; this declined to 2.9 percent between 1964–1967. Extensions of Francruz's calculations, by the present author, to the 1968–1972 period indicate that multilateral trade remained at about four percent of total trade within the CMEA. Table 3.1 presents individual indices of the percent of multilateral trade in the total CMEA trade of each Eastern European country.

These numbers may overstate the degree of bilateralism within the bloc insofar as *indirect* multilateral trade may occur when, say, Poland receives goods that it doesn't want and exports them to third countries. Indeed, the Polish state trading agency may take delivery of the goods in an international port such as Rotterdam, where a special barter agent arranges for their disposal for payment in convertible currencies.[10] But the disposal of such surplus goods is costly, and the whole process is not equivalent to uninhibited multilateral trade based on international money as a means of payment.

On the other hand, the indices in Table 3.1 understate the degree of bilateralism among CPEs insofar as swing credits are given annually between pairs of trading countries to cover export deficits or surpluses. Generally, each pair of CMEA countries strives for bilateral balance over five-year planning horizons, but may not make it exactly on the annual basis referred to in Table 3.1.

This pronounced bilateral balance in trade between CMEA countries is a direct consequence of their payment procedures. Western convertible currencies serve as a unit of account in establishing relative prices for intra-CMEA trade as described below. However, their unwillingness to use these Western

8. "The Bilateral Character of Soviet and Eastern European Foreign Trade," *Journal of Common Market Studies*, No. 1 and 2 (1975), p. 11.

9. Henryk Francruz, "The International Bank for Economic Cooperation," IMF *Staff Papers* (November 1969).

10. "Back to Barter," *The Economist* (London: December 14–20, 1974), pp. 52–53.

TABLE 3.1   Indices of Intra-CMEA Trade Multilateralization (As a percent of total CMEA trade)

CMEA countries	1960	1961	1962	1963	1964	1965	1966	1967	1968	1969	1970	1971	1972
Bulgaria	1.9	3.6	6.1	1.2	3.4	3.5	1.5	2.6	2.6	2.5	2.5	2.9	5.9
Czechoslovakia	2.1	5.1	4.4	3.9	1.4	5.8	4.4	2.1	3.4	5.0	1.8	5.9	3.5
Germany, Eastern	5.5	9.4	8.7	7.7	3.2	5.1	6.9	5.9	4.5	4.1	6.2	5.1	4.0
Hungary	3.2	5.3	2.8	3.4	2.0	5.6	3.6	2.6	3.4	4.4	3.5	3.9	3.2
Poland	4.4	8.2	10.3	10.6	6.4	9.5	7.5	6.6	3.9	3.7	2.6	6.5	10.1
Rumania	3.1	8.9	5.1	9.8	2.9	3.9	3.7	4.9	3.2	7.1	6.0	7.5	7.1
U.S.S.R.	4.4	6.8	5.1	2.8	3.2	3.4	3.1	1.0	2.3	1.8	4.1	3.9	2.4
Mean (unweighted)	3.5	6.8	6.1	5.6	3.2	5.2	4.4	3.7	3.3	4.1	3.8	5.1	5.2

SOURCE: Indices for 1960–1967 are from Henryk Francruz, "The International Bank for Economic Cooperation," IMF *Staff Papers* (1969). The 1968–1972 indices are calculated from various issues of the *United Nations Monthly Trade Statistics*.

NOTE: CMEA refers to the Council for Mutual Economic Assistance, sometimes called Comecon.

NOTE: Statistical Index of Multilateral Trade:

$$100 \frac{\sum\limits_{s=1}^{n} \left| \dfrac{X_{js}}{X_{jc}} - \dfrac{M_{js}}{M_{jc}} \right|}{\sum\limits_{s=1}^{n} \left(\dfrac{X_{js}}{X_{jc}} + \dfrac{M_{js}}{M_{jc}} \right)}$$

where: X_{js} = exports of country j to country s
X_{jc} = total exports of country j to CMEA area
M_{js} = imports of country j from country s
M_{jc} = total imports of country j from CMEA
n = number of countries in the CMEA

monies as a means of payment has left the centrally planned economies without an effective system for clearing multilateral balances within the CMEA, despite their strenuous efforts to set up an independent multilateral clearing mechanism.

The Determination of Foreign Trade Prices in the CMEA

How are prices set in trade among communist countries? The maintenance of strict commodity inconvertibility ensures that each sovereign CPE has an essentially different internal price structure. Even if one set of internal prices— say the Russian—was chosen to apply to trade among all CMEA countries, the Soviets need not be particularly happy. Internal ruble prices of goods and services within the Soviet Union do not accurately reflect their economic scarcity in Russia, and the Russians may well be unwilling to trade with foreigners at such relative prices! Nevertheless writers within the CMEA have continually stressed the desirability—both ideologically and economically—of having an independent socialist pricing system for intrabloc trade.

> While it was clear that as marginal traders the USSR and nations of Eastern Europe had to trade with the West at world prices it was not clear what kind of pricing would prevail in intrabloc trade. Literature produced by the bloc consistently stressed the need for an "own" pricing system, one generated by intrabloc trade and scarcity relationships. Some Eastern European writers, and following them some Western writers, asserted that an "own" price system based on bloc or Soviet costs was, in fact, in use. While a theoretical possibility, this was not and could not be the case, however, because of the basic irrationality of the domestic prices and exchange rates of each bloc nation. The search for an "own" pricing system continues, however.[11]

In the trade of CPEs with Western countries, commodity prices have been generally established in world markets and denominated in Western convertible currencies as we have seen. Because of the nonoperative nature of their purely internal price systems, therefore, CPEs have been driven by practical necessity to transfer systematically most of these international price relationships to intrabloc trade. What then is the administrative machinery within the CMEA for facilitating this transfer, and what are the advantages and disadvantages of collectively imposing an agreed-upon set of prices—lifted from somewhere else—on trade between any pair of CPEs?

The CMEA consists of the six European socialist states listed in Table 3.1, Mongolia, about which information is scant, Cuba as of 1972, and North Vietnam as of 1978. It provides a multilateral secretariat for bringing socialist countries together to secure a common strategy on foreign trade prices. While

11. F. Holzman, op cit. p. 12.

much—perhaps most—adjustment in individual prices may eventually take place bilaterally, in 1958 the IX Session of the CMEA published a set of procedures—which had evolved in the previous ten years—for establishing a common set of prices in particular commodity categories upon which future trade was to be based:[12]

1) The selection of a basic world market and thus a world price: market quotations; catalogs; price lists; or possibly prices estimated from foreign trade statistics of noncommunist countries.

2) The adjustment of this world price for "value distorting influences"—possibly the purging of seasonal and cyclical influences by averaging backwards over several years.

3) Adjustment of world prices for transport costs to compensate for the CMEA's geographical location.

4) The alteration of a few prices beyond that called for in (1), (2), and (3) in order to stimulate production of certain commodities—perhaps to make the CMEA bloc more self-sufficient.

These procedures for establishing relative commodity prices remain formally part of the decision making process in the CMEA to the present day.

Another major institutional step was taken in 1963 with the formation of the International Bank for Economic Cooperation (IBEC). A new currency—the *transferable ruble* (sometimes called the trade ruble) was specifically introduced as an accounting unit for the CMEA prices established by the above procedures.[13] For example, suppose the dollar price of wheat, P_w, was agreed on by procedures (1) to (4). The price of wheat in transferable rubles would then be simply $P_w^S \cdot \frac{rubles}{dollars} = P_w^R$.[14]

Formally, any individual CMEA country that exports to another member builds up a credit balance in transferable rubles with IBEC; when it imports from that member or any other, its ruble account is debited. In a *pro forma*

12. This analysis of decision making in the CMEA closely follows that of Edward Hewett, *Foreign Trade Prices in the Council of Mutual Economic Assistance* (London: Cambridge University Press, 1975), pp. 31–35.

13. Hence it is distinct from the Russian ruble that is the unit of account for the very different prices prevailing within the Soviet Union.

14. As long as exchange rates among Western currencies were fixed, the choice of ruble/dollar exchange rate was essentially arbitrary and did not affect relative prices within the CMEA. A trickier exchange adjustment would arise if some goods are initially evaluated in DM according to procedures (1) to (4), and then the DM/dollar rate changes—whence comes the evident hostility of socialist planners to floating exchange rates among convertible currencies. Should the relative prices of dollar and DM commodities, on which the CMEA commission agrees *ex ante*, be altered with fluctuations in the dollar price of DM?

sense, therefore, IBEC provides a straightforward procedure for multilateral clearing.

A further financial step by IBEC to encourage the multilateral exchange of goods within the CMEA is to allow the multilateral extension of credit as well. "Countries with an end-of-the-year overall deficit can receive short-term loans rather easily at interest rates between two percent and five percent. Medium-term loans (up to three years) are available. . . ."[15] These loans are extended by IBEC itself and are an attempt to move away from exclusive reliance on short-term swing credits that have been extended bilaterally between each pair of CMEA countries. This extension of credit by IBEC to cover shorter term imbalances should make it easier for, say, a creditor member to shop around in the CMEA for goods on which to spend its credit balances. The potential selling country can, of course, be different from the CMEA member with whom the creditor earned the export surplus. Thus, the institutions of the CMEA and IBEC combined seem to provide a common mechanism for setting prices and clearing payments through which multilateral trade *could* take place.

Why doesn't it work? Ruble transferability in a technical legal sense hardly affects economic practice as Francruz's calculations suggested. In order to spend a credit balance—arising from bilateral trade—with a third CPE, commodity inconvertibility requires detailed negotiations with the state trading agency of the third country to determine which goods can actually be obtained. Hence, complex three-cornered negotiations are required before the country in question can determine whether or not it is worthwhile to run the initial bilateral surplus. The evident complexity of this multilateral bargaining helps explain the continued predominance of bilaterally balanced trade within Comecon—as documented earlier.

To further understand why bilateralism remains so rigid in practice, consider the difficulties of achieving—by implementing procedures (1) through (4)—a common socialist price system. Agreement among the government representatives from the six or seven CMEA countries requires detailed and lengthy negotiations over which foreign price quotations to use. Procedures for purging "random" or "monopolistic" elements from world market prices—point (2)—are also difficult to implement conceptually; and some simple average of world prices going back three to five years has been the smoothing technique used in the past. More difficult might be agreement on some conscious deviation from world prices—say, to raise the price of automobiles above world market-clearing levels—that necessarily improves the terms of trade of at least one CMEA country but causes a deterioration for others.

15. E. Hewett, op. cit. p. 15.

Hence, once a complex many-sided negotiation was brought off successfully, it was expected to last for several years.

> The 1966–70 agreements were negotiated first using 1959–62 prices and then using 1959–63 prices, as the 1963 prices became available. These prices still left the exporters of raw materials with unfavorable terms of trade. Finally, with the increases of the prices of raw materials on world markets in 1964, a 1960–64 price base was selected at the December 1964 Executive meeting, as the official new base for CMEA foreign trade prices during the 1966–70 period.[16]

However, with more substantial movement in relative prices in the world economy in the 1970s, pressure from those CMEA countries that were disadvantaged was brought to reopen the complex negotiations more frequently. A system involving annual adjustments in CMEA prices, based on five-year moving averages of world prices, now seems to have evolved:

> Until recently price adjustments within the framework of five-year periods were made very rarely, and then only concerning individual commodities, because price fluctuations on the world markets did not have deep economic roots.

> But the changes in world prices in the past two or three years bear, in the general opinion of the CMEA partners on the whole, a fundamental character. They reflect the profound structural changes in today's world economy.

> . . . the countries of the Socialist community intend in the course of the forthcoming five-year plan period (1976–1980) to make price adjustments annually, each time assuming as a basis the average world prices for the previous five years. Such practice will give price formation more flexibility in the conditions when a more or less long-term level of world prices have not yet been established. . . . [17]

Even with this last more rapid adjustment, however, CMEA prices have a high degree of obsolescence in world market terms. The result is the distinction between "hard" and "soft" commodities commonly made in intra-CMEA trade. Hard commodities are those that are essentially underpriced in world market terms and thus in short supply within the CMEA, whereas an incipient surplus of soft commodities exists in the CMEA—those that are relatively overpriced. Since this distinction is well recognized by trade negotiators, any single socialist country becomes more reluctant to run a surplus in its bilateral balance of trade with a given CMEA trading partner. True, such an export surplus would build up a credit balance in IBEC that could in theory be spent in any other socialist country. However, other potential trading partners at most would offer only soft commodities in exchange. Thus, any one country that

16. E. Hewett, op. cit. p. 40.
17. Quoted from a Soviet economist, B. Rachov, "Why Comecon Had to Raise Its Prices," *The Guardian* (May 31, 1975), p. 10.

runs a substantial surplus with any one trading partner—with no prospect of being cleared bilaterally in future years—will lose a lot of bargaining leverage.

If Poland is selling hard commodities, it will normally demand hard commodities in return from a CMEA trading partner. Otherwise, it could do better to sell its hard commodities at more favorable terms of trade in the world market. Similarly, if Rumania plans to import soft commodities, some other member of the CMEA would be chosen as the supplier *only if* that supplier would accept soft commodities in exchange. So there is a natural tendency to exchange hard for hard, and soft for soft, commodities in a bilaterally balanced fashion. Indeed, as long as a particular CPE can always sell hard commodities on the world market and buy soft ones, intra-CMEA trade is forced into a more rigidly bilateral mould. Hence the rapid liberalization of the foreign trade of communist countries with the West in the 1970s is quite consistent with increased bilateralism in trade between CMEA countries! Effectively, CMEA trade is cleared multilaterally through the world market, which limits the losses in economic efficiency arising from bilateralism within the CMEA itself.

Recognizing the rapid obsolesence of moving averages of world prices denominating intra-CMEA trade, there are other difficulties with transferring price information from outside the bloc. Homogeneous primary commodities such as oil, wheat, copper, and so forth usually have well-defined international prices—perhaps commonly quoted in a single international currency such as the U.S. dollar on a recognized international commodity exchange in, say, Rotterdam or Chicago. Thus there is little difficulty in ascertaining what world prices actually are, and averaging them through time. And observers agree that relative primary commodity prices used by the CMEA seem to be approximately correct using this criterion.

However, there are no commonly recognized international price quotations for types of machinery or manufactured consumer durables. Indeed, homogeneous commodity classification systems simply don't exist for such manufactures as they do for the various grades of wheat. Furthermore, exports of industrial goods tend to be invoiced in the home currency of the capitalist exporter, if that currency is convertible.[18] Hence, when exchange rates change in the short run, the "law of one price" is violated—even across capitalist countries with perfectly convertible currencies. Given that servicing and quality aspects of CMEA industrial goods may also vary markedly from their Western counterparts, what are the hapless negotiators within the CMEA to do in finding a mutually agreeable set of outside prices?

The answer seems to be that the formal multilateral pricing protocol of the

18. As illustrated in Chapter 4.

CMEA—as described by points (1) to (4)—breaks down for complex industrial goods. Machinery prices are established mainly on a bilateral basis between each pair of trading partners. To be sure, these bilateral negotiations use the prices of industrial goods denominated in Western convertible currencies as a point of reference. But the bargains struck for each pair of countries might involve quite different ruble prices. Since these separate bargains probably aggravate the distinction between hard and soft commodities within the CMEA as well as violating the notion of commonality in price setting, further impetus is given for keeping intra-CMEA trade on a strictly bilateral basis.

In summary, the unwillingness of CPEs to use international money (convertible currencies) as a means of payment forces intrabloc trade into a primarily bilateral pattern. However, this bilateral trade is not pure barter because international money still serves as a unit of account in establishing relative prices—in an imperfect but perhaps indispensable fashion.

Barter, Command Planning, and Economic Sovereignty

If the prices of commodities in international markets (denominated in convertible currencies) are difficult to transfer to intra-CMEA trade as we have seen, and if the internal systems of accounting prices within each CPE are not designed to reflect economic scarcity, why don't the CMEA negotiators simply give up their search for an *ex ante* set of prices? One can imagine state-trading agencies bargaining (albeit bilaterally) over a bill of goods—perhaps hundreds of commodities—to be exported by country A in return for several hundred commodities to be imported from country B over a five-year time horizon. Implicit prices, in the form of commodity exchange ratios, would be established at the time agreement is reached on actual quantities to be bartered in each commodity category. This moneyless exchange seems consistent with Marxian ideology that is hostile to the cash nexus; and it also seems consistent with the mode of internal commodity exchange within each centrally planned economy—where *ex ante* prices are generally not used as guidelines by individual socialist enterprises in determining what they will give and what they will receive.

The basic objection to such pure barter is not that it is administratively impossible *per se*; rather it is only infeasible if the economic sovereignty of each trading country is respected. *Ex ante* agreement on an acceptable set of prices and valuation procedures permits the centrally planned economies to enter into *voluntary* mutual exchange. Without the benefit of these *ex ante* prices—even if they are somewhat modified by negotiation—extensive trade between any two

CPEs would sacrifice national sovereignty to a supernational planning authority that allocates goods by fiat between the countries in question.

Why should pure barter between sovereign state trading agencies be so difficult to organize? Suppose there are 100 commodities. Without a price system, the negotiators would need to agree on effective exchange ratios between every two commodities amounting to $100 \times 99/2 = 4,950$ different exchange rates! It would surely be easier to agree on only 100 prices to begin with, and then calculate the effective exchange ratios from the preselected prices. Having a unit of account (standard of value) in terms of the 100 preselected prices permits the negotiators to look at individual items *one at a time* for inclusion as an import or export. Exports or imports of raw materials, consumer goods, and capital goods can each be bargained separately. One can then add up the value of all such individual items in order to strike a bilateral balance of trade. It is unnecessary to pair each individual import with one or more export goods—a pairing that might have to take earlier pairs into account,[19] although the distinction between hard and soft commodities previously mentioned somewhat undermines this one-at-a-time procedure.

The upshot is that two sovereign (independent) state trading agencies are unlikely to be able to strike any comprehensive bargain under pure barter that is mutually satisfactory. With thousands of commodities involved in the world of modern technology, the administrative complexities would be overwhelming; and the negotiators would be unlikely to understand whether international trade so organized increased or reduced the economic welfare of the countries involved. Thus, severe truncation in the scope of foreign trade is the likely result, where a few relatively simple and obvious exchanges—e.g., coal for tropical foodstuffs—take place on an individually paired basis. Most of the gains from a rational international division of labor among socialist economies would be lost.

One way out is to yield national sovereignty to a supernational planning agency that allocates resources internationally much in the way that the individual national agencies plan resource allocation within each CPE. Indeed, the optimum international allocation of all economic resources within the CMEA could be viewed as a solution to a giant programming problem that simultaneously determines production, consumption, and the flow of goods and services across national boundaries. The preferences of the international planning authority for producing this or that commodity would be imposed in addition to the agency's allocation of consumer goods to particular countries. Shadow prices accurately reflecting scarcity within the CMEA (given the planners'

19. I am indebted to my colleague Robert Wilson of Stanford University for clarifying the above argument.

preferences) would be mutually determined in the grand solution; but these *ex post* prices would be redundant as allocative devices—as well as being different from historical accounting prices in each country.

The other way out—consistent with national economic sovereignty for individual CMEA countries—is to treat world market prices denominated in convertible currencies *as if* they were the solution to our general programming problem and did reflect modern technology so as to approximate scarcity relationships within the CMEA itself. *Ex ante*, world prices serve as neutral or disinterested outside arbiters of value relationships within the CMEA that negotiators can take as a starting point. This limited use of international money then allows substantial voluntary trade (albeit bilateral) between centrally planned economies on a *quid pro quo* basis.

Quixotically, if the convertible currency system were to collapse, perhaps as a result of worldwide communist revolution, centrally planned economies could be driven toward economic autarky vis-à-vis each other—or, alternatively, be forced to yield national sovereignty in economic planning.

A Gold Ruble?

Reforms in the foreign trade practices of the socialist economies can be considered on two distinct levels:

1) Assuming continued national central planning by materials allocation rather than prices, can trade among CMEA countries be liberalized multilaterally and put on a more economically efficient basis?

2) In the course of more sweeping reforms associated with the relaxation of centralized command planning in some of the smaller socialist economies, what does the elimination of commodity and foreign exchange inconvertibility portend for domestic monetary control and the problem of exchange-rate stability?

Consider first the relatively simple problem posed under (1). Can a multilateral clearing mechanism within the CMEA be arranged that does not depend *directly* on the use of Western currencies as a means of payment—and thus is more politically acceptable? Suppose that the transferable ruble—the depository claim on the International Bank for Economic Cooperation (IBEC)—was made convertible into international money at a known parity, and was thus transmuted into the gold ruble.[20] CMEA countries with credit balances in gold

20. For a discussion of the gold ruble, see Oscar Altman, "Russian Gold and the Ruble," IMF *Staff Papers* (April 1960), p. 434. The term "gold ruble" as used here is simply a short-hand expression for allowing transferable rubles to be exchanged for convertible currencies. The gold ruble need have no specific gold content; although Marx himself, and the Russians even now, had a preoccupation with gold as establishing the real value of money.

rubles would have the option of either spending them in other CPEs or in buying convertible currencies. The log jam in multilateral trade would be broken. An individual CPE could run a bilateral surplus with a CMEA neighbor without negotiating simultaneously on how to dispose of the gold rubles so acquired. As the surplus accumulated, the CPE in question could shop leisurely for goods with other state trading agencies in the CMEA; if insufficient CMEA goods were available, the remaining credit balance could be converted into international money to buy Western goods.

A further step is to eliminate foreign exchange inconvertibility for nonresidents of the CMEA. Foreigners would then be eligible and perhaps willing to hold gold rubles, and hence no longer insist on payment exclusively denominated in Western convertible currencies. Commodity inconvertibility and foreign exchange inconvertibility for *residents* of each CMEA country would be retained, however, as necessary adjuncts of national central planning.

Without using convertible currencies directly, this gold ruble system has the political advantage of keeping all payments within CMEA confined to transferable gold rubles even as multilateral trade among CPEs is encouraged. The Western convertible-currency system becomes the ultimate clearing mechanism for surpluses in gold rubles, and the arbiter of their economic value. Indeed, this is what would encourage individual CMEA countries to run bilateral surpluses, or to accept bilateral deficits, in gold rubles.

How should the parity rate for the gold ruble be determined in a world where Western currencies are floating vis-à-vis each other? Because of continued commodity inconvertibility, the real value in terms of goods and services of the gold ruble could not be established within the CMEA itself. Rather, the gold ruble could be given international standing only if it were pegged to a major currency (such as the DM or the U.S. dollar) whose purchasing power over real goods and services *is* well established. But the proper choice of any one Western currency is difficult when their relative values continually change. Hence, the CMEA authorities might choose some representative basket or index of Western convertible currencies as the numeraire—although a single intervention currency should be selected.[21] Uninhibited floating of the gold ruble would be ruled out precisely because its rate of exchange with any Western currency would be indeterminant if commodity inconvertibility was retained.

In order to make the parity obligation of the gold ruble credible, the IBEC would hold some Western convertible currencies as reserves against ruble de-

21. In the mode of central bank interventions commonly used in less developed countries with inconvertible currencies, as described in Chapter 2.

posits outstanding. Deposit claims on the CMEA, which are potentially convertible into foreign exchange, are indirect foreign exchange claims on individual CMEA members with debit balances in IBEC. So the resulting foreign exchange reserves of CMEA members would have to be arranged accordingly. However, communally held exchange reserves could well economize on the reserves of convertible currencies now held individually by CMEA members.[22]

Hence, no net foreign exchange cost need accompany the introduction of the gold ruble system. Indeed, IBEC itself could simply borrow in the Eurocurrency market to secure working balances of convertible currencies (as individual CMEA members have been doing in recent years). The net cost to IBEC would be the difference between its borrowing rate of interest and the deposit rate(s) earned on its reserves.

What then is the basic political objection to the gold ruble or something like it? While international money is used as a unit of account in bilateral bargaining between CPEs, there is substantial political pressure to insulate such trade from the West. Prices of a few goods may be raised above or reduced below their international level through negotiation. Indeed, in the early postwar period, the Russians may have used their superior political position to extract tribute from the others by simply turning the terms of trade in their own favor. At the present time, poorer bloc members may claim favored price treatment. Free multilateral clearing through a gold ruble system would develop great pressure to impose *current* world prices on intrabloc trade, thereby reducing the scope for significant deviations in the bilateral terms of trade. A disadvantaged trading partner would find it easier to turn to the convertible-currency world. More fundamentally, perhaps, long-term bilateral trade agreements, which are a concomitant of eschewing international money as a means of payment, are a convenient vehicle for tying economies together politically and economically.

Full Liberalization and the Monetary Conditions for Exchange-Rate Stability

While useful, the gold ruble system represents only a partial step toward complete currency convertibility. Evolving full currency convertibility in any one socialist economy—where individual enterprises could buy or sell freely abroad—necessarily is associated with the decentralization of pricing and output decisions. But the pros and cons of such a sweeping reform that jettisons command planning by centralized materials allocations is well beyond my

22. Much in the way that credit and debit balances in the old European Payments Union (EPU) economized on the need of Western European countries to hold reserves directly in U.S. dollars in the early 1950s prior to their return to full convertibility (Chapter 11).

purview. Instead, let us simply assume such a major liberalization does occur—an assumption not too far-fetched for Yugoslavia or Hungary. Then consider the narrower problem of establishing and maintaining a stable exchange rate—which individual enterprises can take as given in the course of importing and exporting on a decentralized basis.

It was established in Chapter 1 for a stationary state that a sufficient condition for exchange stability was for the central bank to maintain strict control over the quantity of money in circulation; and appropriate generalizations of this monetary rule to growing economies are discussed in Chapter 10. Are there any peculiar characteristics of the banking-monetary systems in socialist economies that might make this control problem unusually difficult?

In a strictly centrally planned economy such as that of the Soviet Union, the State Bank holds *all* the deposit claims of firms; and the Bank makes loans to firms (not households) in the form of short-term credits that determine the volume of such deposits in circulation. In this vein, the State Bank will extend any amount of credit to enterprises on demand if they are purchasing materials, supplies, or labor in conformity with the central plan. Similarly, the deposits of an enterprise can only be spent if the State Bank determines that these expenditures for materials conform to official planning directives. Therefore, the State Bank serves mainly as an auditing agency for the central planners rather than one charged with controlling the volume of deposit money in circulation.

Indeed, the domestic quantity of "money" in circulation at any one point in time may be indeterminant in an economic sense because many enterprises have excess cash balances for which they have no mandate to spend, whereas the State Bank must provide unlimited lines of credit to yet other enterprises on the instruction of the planning authority. Thus the effective quantity of money is difficult to measure and wanders around in an indeterminant fashion. This indeterminacy need not be particularly disruptive however, because the aggregate demand and supply for goods and services in each commodity category is balanced through the central plan itself. All output from any one enterprise is directly allocated to yet other enterprises at arbitrarily fixed accounting prices. Conceptually, these strict administrative allocations of goods make unnecessary strict control over the quantity of money as a means of preventing either general inflation or general deflation.

Now, suppose our major reform occurs. Buy and sell decisions are decentralized to individual enterprises and domestic currency prices are set according to the principle of supply and demand. In addition, unrestricted importing and exporting take place at a unified exchange rate for foreign currency. Then the quantity of money in circulation becomes important both for limiting fluctuations in the exchange rate and for stabilizing the domestic price level. Hence the Soviet State Bank, or its successor, could no longer extend credits on demand to individual enterprises at very low rates of interest as it does now. Nor would the blocking of particular deposit balances held by domestic enterprises or foreigners be consistent with this full liberalization.

Rather the State Bank would have to evolve less direct—but nevertheless effective—techniques of monetary control. But how sophisticated need this control mechanism be to maintain full convertibility? For small open economies like Hungary and Yugoslavia, the answer depends heavily on whether a pegged or a freely floating exchange-rate system is selected.

In the case of a floating exchange rate, the whole panoply of monetary control devices used in advanced industrial economies becomes necessary. Discretionary open-market operations to actively alter the domestic money supply, and a discount rate of interest that effectively limits borrowing by enterprises, are two such techniques. If the lending and deposit functions of the State Bank were themselves decentralized to a subsidiary set of commercial banks, the Central Bank would then worry about the proper reserve to deposit ratio and the proportion of coin and currency vis-à-vis deposits in private portfolios. For a fledgling central bank to get the supply of money under its complete control—and then accurately estimate the aggregate domestic demand for it—would be extremely difficult in an economy where individuals and enterprises have little experience with free choice in money holding and capital markets are imperfect. Yet such strong monetary control would be necessary to stabilize the domestic price level on the one hand, and to stabilize a floating foreign exchange rate on the other.

There is an easier way out. If the international economy is tranquil such that commodity prices in the convertible foreign currency of a major trading partner are themselves reasonably stable, our liberalizing CPE could simply peg its exchange rate to that currency. With free convertibility on current account in both the commodity and foreign exchange senses, the price level in domestic currency would be established. Without knowing quite what it is or what it should be, the domestic authorities could then allow the domestic money supply to be *endogenously* determined through foreign exchange transactions designed to maintain the pegged exchange rate.

Minimal reserve requirements on commercial banks and some limit on their discounting privileges would then be sufficient for internal monetary control. Suppose an incipient surplus developed in the balance of payments; this would signal the authorities that there was an excess demand for domestic money over that being currently supplied. This excess demand would automatically be accommodated when the authorities purchased the convertible foreign currency and provided domestic base money in exchange in order to maintain the pegged exchange rate (prevent the domestic currency from appreciating). Provided the economy in question had the requisite reserves of foreign exchange, domestic money could be removed from the economy in a symmetrical fashion when a deficit in the balance of payments signaled that there were excess cash balances in domestic circulation. These would then be redeemed by the domestic authorities by selling foreign currency rather than relying on some more complex open-market operation in domestic bonds—when an open bond market may not yet exist.

Yugoslavia has had chronic inflationary problems during its struggle to liberalize. A policy of pegging the dinar to the more stable Deutsche mark (DM), and allowing the domestic supply of dinars to be endogenously determined, might commend itself at the present time on these narrow technical grounds of economic efficacy.[23]

After the successful German monetary reforms of 1948–49 and the partial return to external convertibility, the German economy was left without substantial open markets in primary securities. Thus the German authorities wisely pegged to the U.S. dollar as a means of stabilizing the internal German price level, and to stabilize private price expectations that had been shaken by the severe German inflation. Then as the German economy grew rapidly without inflation, the supply of base money in DM was increased by the simple expedient of the Bundesbank purchasing dollars in the foreign exchange market. This was reflected in German balance of payments surpluses throughout the 1950s and 1960s. Of course, a liberalizing CPE could adjust its money supply by expanding domestic credit so as to avoid running a chronic surplus in its balance of payments.

23. As suggested by my colleague Paul Evans. The mechanics of monetary manag ment under a fixed exchange rate are discussed in Chapter 10.

4

Hedging by Exporters and Importers

Return now to the problem of organizing foreign trade between countries with convertible currencies. Private exporters are free to sell goods and services to importers. They negotiate on price, on the extension of trade credit, on the currency of invoice for making payments, and on whether or not to buy foreign exchange forward to cover any obligations arising therefrom.[1] Under floating exchange rates that move sharply on a week-to-week or month-to-month basis, hedging against foreign exchange risk in these negotiations is essential to prevent international commodity trade from atrophying for want of private capital.

Before setting up a formal model of hedging, however, let us define precisely what is meant by foreign exchange risk for nonfinancial trading firms and manufacturing enterprises.[2]

Assume that the convertible national money (home currency) is the *preferred monetary habitat* of domestic importers and exporters. Resident firms view their domestic currency as the relatively riskless asset into which they want their profits translated, and strive to stabilize the liquidity (realizable) value of their asset portfolios in terms of the domestic money. Despite the recent currency upheavals and increasing openness of national economies, I claim that this

1. The analytical structure developed in this chapter is based largely on the empirical work of Sven Grassman of the Institute for International Economic Studies, Stockholm. See his *Exchange Reserves and the Financial Structure of Foreign Trade* (Westmead, Eng.: Saxon House, 1973).
2. Hedging against exchange risk by financial firms, such as banks, is taken up more explicitly in Chapters 8 and 9.

working hypothesis is well suited to portray the short-run behavior of most trading enterprises.

Take as a starting point that the firm has a well-defined manufacturing or trading interest in a particular commodity: say, a Canadian exporter of newsprint or a Swedish importer of pocket calculators. In the short time horizon under consideration, the firm is committed to producing or merchandising that commodity, having previously developed expertise in this particular line. Because the firm wants to concentrate on its merchandising or manufacturing specialty from whence its main profit flow comes, international financial affairs are organized in a purely dependent and defensive way: the taking of open positions in foreign currencies is associated *only* with that trade and is always kept to a minimum.[3]

The validity of this highly simplified approach, based on the minimization of foreign exchange exposure, rests on two kinds of arguments.

First, in capturing the essentials of hedging in the markets for foreign exchange, one cannot and should not try to model the whole of the firm's manufacturing and merchandising operation. Rather, in the short run, I simply assume ongoing implicit commitments to pay for wages in the domestic currency, for most supplies in the domestic currency, and that domestic creditors such as commercial banks are the dominant sources of capital unless otherwise specified. Hence, risk is minimized when the firm's net foreign exchange position is hedged back into the domestic currency in which the firm's principal obligations are denominated.

Second, while the owners of the firm may view profits as a means to future consumption, and that consumption could take the form of goods imported from abroad, it still behooves the firm to maximize the certainty of its earnings in terms of the domestic currency *only*. Then, knowing that the firm is following this simple and rather common rule-of-thumb, the rather diverse shareholders (and possibly other creditors) of the enterprise can adjust their portfolios of both domestic and foreign exchange assets to take their own particular patterns of future consumption into account. We have thus a *separation axiom:* the managers minimize the variance of cash flow solely in terms of the domestic currency, and, knowing this but not knowing the firm's exact week-to-week or month-to-month decisions, the shareholders decide on their own degree of portfolio diversification into foreign exchange assets.[4] It would be entirely im-

3. As long as an exchange rate is not obviously disaligned because of some unsupportable official intervention. Hence, speculation by merchants is not considered here, although this issue is taken up later in Chapter 7.
4. No attempt is made here to model the behavior of these shareholder-investors. In any event, they are likely hampered by foreign exchange regulations and the absence of a broad base of

practical if the shareholders were forced to follow the various open foreign exchange positions the firm could take, on the assumption the firm was *not* hedging, in order that they hedge their individual portfolios against what the firm is doing.[5]

This view of domestic money as a preferred habitat of the resident domestic firm is implicit in most formal theories of hedging and speculation, and I shall explicitly carry it forward here. Because of the domestic character of this assumption, the model of hedging based on it is not meant to apply to truly multinational corporations for which the home currency is not immediately obvious; then diversification for its own sake across assets in different national currencies might be sought. Nor would firms officially resident in small countries like Liberia, Panama, or Monaco likely use the domestic currency as the preferred habitat—given the absentee character of the owners.

Similarly, an upheaval in managing the home currency might lead to currency diversification by firms with impeccable credentials as domestic residents. To illustrate, a sharp loss of confidence in the domestic currency requiring (1) either the imposition of strict exchange controls and loss of convertibility,[6] or (2) a rapid depreciation in the foreign exchange value of the domestic currency for which high domestic nominal rates of interest cannot compensate,[7] is clearly inconsistent with domestic monetary claims being the preferred currency habitat of domestic nationals—including firms. One then has to change the model.

Another fundamental assumption is that our importer or exporter faces a capital constraint—perhaps defined by his own equity—that limits the size of his enterprise and the merchandising profits arising therefrom. Hence he hedges not so much because he is personally risk averse, but because his ability to raise capital hinges on the riskiness of his enterprise as *perceived by others*. For example, the amount any gimlet-eyed banker might lend him—and the favorableness of the interest-rate terms he might negotiate—depends on minimizing the probability of default. In the extreme, he might face, for a given expected yield and riskiness of his enterprise, absolute capital rationing. No

information on overseas investment opportunities. A pure model of overseas portfolio diversification, assuming the absence of exchange controls or informational uncertainty, is provided by Bruno Solnik, "An Equilibrium Model of the International Capital Market," *Journal of Economic Theory* (August 1974), pp. 500–24.

5. For the contrary approach that shareholders have full information on what foreign exchange exposure the firm might undertake, see D. P. Baron, "Flexible Exchange Rates, Forward Markets, and the Level of Trade," *American Economic Review* (June 1976), pp. 253–66.

6. As with, say, Peru at the present time.

7. As with the German currency in 1922–23.

bank would lend him funds beyond a certain level no matter how high the rate of interest for which he is willing to contract.[8]

Finally, to minimize our concern with the firm's technical production problems, simply assume that a fixed production and sale opportunity is carried over from the past: the firm is committed to selling X units of a single specialized export (or import) commodity in a given time interval in commerce with one other country. It then designs inventory and financial policies across the two currencies in order to yield an optimum mix of expected yield and risk for these X units.

Our model of a nonfinancial firm has thus been narrowed to one whose primary business is to make merchandising profits from exporting or importing, including associated manufacturing. The analytical simplifications imposed on our trader's financial behavior are summarized thus:

A.   The convertible domestic currency is the trader's preferred monetary habitat.

B.   He is limited to selecting asset portfolios connected only with the export-import trade.

C.   He is subject to a capital constraint that in large measure depends on the riskiness of his enterprise as seen by his banker.

D.   He faces a fixed production opportunity for either exporting or importing from one other country. Hedging against exchange risk involves only two currencies.

What then are the principal economic decision variables left open to our trading firm anxious to minimize currency risk?

1)   The selection of a currency of invoice—domestic or foreign.

2)   The terms of normal commercial trade credit:

   i) cash on delivery

   ii) on account credit

   iii) payment by a bill, drawn on the importer by the exporter, with a fixed term to maturity.

3)   The degree of forward covering of foreign-currency payments due in the future.

4)   The means by which deferred payments in a foreign currency should be covered forward including:

   i) either a specific forward contract negotiated with the bank for delivery in a specified number of days; or

8. For an interesting analysis of capital rationing in general, and this possibility in particular, see Dwight Jaffee, *Credit Rationing in the Commercial Loan Market* (New York: John Wiley and Sons, 1971).

ii) the spot purchase of an interest-bearing foreign exchange asset, with or without a definite maturity date.

Let us consider each in turn.

The Currency of Invoice: Tradables I and II

Until recently, economists had very little empirical information on how particular currencies are selected to invoice goods that flow in international trade—a selection that is critical in dividing currency risk between exporters and importers. Somewhat cavalierly, the U.S. dollar (and sterling in an earlier era) has been dubbed "international money" in the literature of international finance. From this the unwary might naturally infer that most trade, even among countries other than the United States, was actually invoiced in dollars (or sterling). Such is not the case. In Tables 4.1 and 4.2 on Sweden, and Table 4.3 on Denmark, Sven Grassman has shown how the dominant currency of invoice is normally the home currency of the exporter—a result that generalizes to most convertible-currency countries.[9] Sixty-six percent of Swedish exports were invoiced in kronor, and 59 percent of Swedish imports were invoiced in the currency of the selling country. This latter percentage was substantially higher than 59 percent for Swedish trade with other convertible-currency countries, and was close to zero for imports from centrally planned economies and less developed countries because they have inconvertible currencies.

Despite this striking empirical regularity evident in Tables 4.1 to 4.3, there remains a residual asymmetry. Direct trade with the center or Nth country is mainly invoiced in that country's currency. For example, 64.5 percent of Swedish exports to the United States (and Canada) were invoiced in U.S. dollars, and 94.3 percent of Swedish imports from the United States (and Canada) were also invoiced in U.S. dollars. Hence, one would suspect that Canadian foreign trade—most of which is with the United States—is very

9. Sven Grassman, "A Fundamental Symmetry in International Payments Patterns," *Journal of International Economics* (May 1973), pp. 105–06; and "Currency Distribution and Forward Cover in Foreign Trade: Sweden Revisited," *Journal of International Economics* (May 1976), pp. 215–22. Tables 4.1, 4.2, and 4.3 are Grassman's and reproduced here without alteration. One should remember that this currency symmetry is associated with *nonbank* firms and individuals. For trading among commercial and central banks in the interbank market, the U.S. dollar is more dominant (Chapter 2). Subsequently a number of other empirical studies have verified that exports from the industrial countries (with convertible currencies) are predominantly invoiced in the home currency. For a compendium, see Stephen Carse, John Williamson, and Geoffrey Wood, *The Financing Procedures of British Foreign Trade* (London: Cambridge University Press, forthcoming).

TABLE 4.1 Distribution of Sweden's Foreign Trade Payments by Invoice Currency

Currency	Exports (%)		Imports (%)	
	1973	1968	1973	1968
Swedish kronor	67.4	66.1	25.7	25.8
U.S. dollars	14.1	12.3	20.0	22.0
Deutsche marks	4.8	3.8	19.7	17.4
Pound sterling	4.6	11.2	10.3	17.3
Danish kronor	0.9	1.8	4.5	3.9
Norwegian kronor	1.0	0.7	3.6	2.2
Dutch guilders	0.05	—	2.8	—
Swiss francs	1.6	0.05	2.4	2.4
French francs	0.07	0.8	2.1	2.5
Italian lira	0.1	0.03	1.9	1.8
Other	4.3	2.5	7.0	4.7
Total	100	100	100	100
Total*	51.200	24.600	45.800	26.200

SOURCE: Sven Grassman (1976).
*Millions of Swedish kronor.

TABLE 4.2 Currency Denomination in Foreign Trade Payments, Sweden, 1968

Currency	Exports (%)	Imports (%)
Selling country's	66*	59
Purchasing country's	25	26*
Third country's	9	15
Total	100	100

SOURCE: Sven Grassman (1973).
* Swedish kronor.

TABLE 4.3 Currency Distribution Used in Foreign Trade Payments, Denmark, 1971

Currency	Exports (%)		Imports (%)	
Danish kroner	41	—	19	—
U.S. dollars	22	(7.9)	25	(8.4)
Pounds sterling	15	(19.3)	14	(13.5)
Deutsche marks	8	(12.4)	15	(18.5)
Swedish kronor	6	(16.2)	11	(16.5)
Swiss francs	2	(3.0)	4	(2.4)
Other	6	(41.2)	12	(40.7)
Total	100	(100)	100	(100)

SOURCE: Sven Grassman (1973), and the Danmarks Nationalbank Report and accounts for the year 1971, and OECD, overall trade by countries, October 1972.
NOTE: The share of Denmark's trade due to the countries whose currencies are shown in the table is given within brackets.

unrepresentative of world payments patterns in that exports or imports are seldom invoiced in Canadian dollars. Fieleke analyzed 123 firms in the Boston area that had financial or commercial dealings with Canadian residents in 1970. For only 23 of these firms were any payments made in Canadian dollars, but even here, American dollars were also used. When asked about currency risk and a possible need to hedge, the general tenor of the American firms' replies were "since payments are made in American dollars, we have no problems."[10]

Let us therefore put aside direct trade with the center country, and look analytically at trade between two more representative countries with convertible currencies.[11] What motivates exporters to invoice in their home currency? Under what circumstances might they prefer, or be induced, to invoice in a foreign currency?

International trade theorists make a convenient analytical dichotomy between tradable goods and nontradables—those that can be neither imported nor exported because of prohibitive transport costs. In the extreme, a person living in San Francisco cannot purchase from Hong Kong a haircut or gardening services, nontradables par excellence, within any feasible range of domestic American prices. While this tradable-nontradable dichotomy is convenient analytically,[12] in reality there is a continuous spectrum of goods with virtual perfect tradability at one extreme (precious metals and manufactures with a high economic value relative to weight) and nontradable labor services at the other.

Accepting this distinction between tradables and nontradables, let us further divide the tradables category into tradables I and tradables II.

Tradables I are those in which producing firms can control (set) the market prices for their own particular products. In the short run at least, producers of tradables I face a downward sloping demand curve from foreign and domestic buyers.[13] Usually tradables I are manufactured products with distinctive characteristics—if only a brand name. This heterogeneity allows different market prices to exist for similar (although not identical) products in the relevant market. The Volvo automobile is a convenient prototype tradable I, but Swedish furniture, glassware, and so on could also fit.

Automobile manufacturing may be deemed a competitive industry in the sense that firms are confined to making only normal profits; nevertheless prices

10. Norman Fieleke, "The Hedging of Commercial Transactions Between U.S. and Canadian Residents," *Canadian-United States Financial Relationships* (Boston: Federal Reserve Bank of Boston, 1971), pp. 171–78.
11. The American share of world exports is now down to about twelve percent as of 1977.
12. Particularly in considering the economic impact of exchange-rate changes. See for example, R. McKinnon, "Optimum Currency Areas," *American Economic Review* (September 1963).
13. As under monopoly, oligopoly, or monopolistic competition.

do not fluctuate according to daily or weekly supply and demand, although inventories do. Rather a certain constancy of price is a considerable administrative convenience in production and marketing, not the least of which is the information content of this constant price to potential buyers who consider a range of slightly differentiated automobiles before making a final purchase decision. In this sense, automobiles in particular and tradables I in general are what John Hicks calls "fixprice" goods.[14] Although each price is not inalterable in discrete steps, it is fairly rigid through continuous time.

Tradables II are more homogeneous commodities where one firm's output may be graded and precisely compared to that of others. Take wheat as a prototype tradable II, but most primary products drawn at random would fit. Daily and weekly fluctuations in the price of wheat are quickly arbitraged across the international boundaries of convertible-currency countries unless prevented by specific quota barriers or redundantly high tariffs. Tradables II are what John Hicks would call "flexprice" goods and are neither firm-specific nor country-specific, unlike most manufactured goods.[15]

Let us now consider the optimal invoicing strategy for a firm exporting tradables I. A Swedish producer of Volvos has money costs of production that are specified in kronor. Long-term wage contracts are drawn up fixing the krona costs per man-hour—although not necessarily the number of man-hours that need be purchased. Parts suppliers and subcontractors in Sweden typically bill the Volvo company in kronor (although foreign sources of supply may invoice in their home currency). Hence, the Volvo Corporation avoids risk by having its sales prices fixed in kronor, to both domestic and foreign buyers, over fairly long contractual periods.

The Volvo company's inventory policy towards automobiles held by the factory and by distributors complements this rigid pricing strategy. Inventory changes are used to clear discrepancies between current sales and production, and for this reason the existing stock is often out of equilibrium (the preferred level) given the rigid pricing structure. However, the company's control over price insulates its inventory from pure price risk. That is, most situations of excessive inventories can be met by reducing production and liquidating stocks at the given krona price. Only in extreme circumstances would it be forced into distress sales at sharply reduced prices. Hence the rigid krona price acts as an

---

14. J. R. Hicks, *The Crisis in Keynesian Economics* (New York: Basic Books, 1974), Chapter I.
15. It should be emphasized that this distinction between tradables I and II is not one between monopoly and competition. The common international market price of wheat could be raised by a determined cartel of wheat producers. Similarly, while Volvo faces a downward sloping demand curve for its product, excess economic rents can be competed away in the manner of the usual model of monopolistic competition.

implicit forward sale that hedges the krona value of domestic inventories—a feature that appeals to risk-averse Swedish bankers who provide inventory financing. Distributors of Volvo cars work closely as agents of the Volvo Corporation, and as such share this price umbrella over the *krona* value of their inventories. (Insofar as these agents are importers in other countries, they are subject to currency risk.) Swedish exporters of other tradables I (fixprice goods) also invoice in their home currency, whence the high proportion of krona invoices in Grassman's statistics on Swedish exports.

In considering tradables II (flexprice goods) that are often primary products, one can more sharply distinguish primary producers (farmers) from merchants. Because wheat is a standardized commodity, the identity of any particular farmer's wheat is not important. Distribution and storage devolve on merchant specialists who can exploit economies of scale in wheat merchandising: the ability to purchase or sell a specified quantity of wheat at a given geographical location at one point in time. Each merchant is usually a small part of the total world market and is himself a *price taker*. The prices at which he purchases and sells are determined within narrow limits by global supply and demand including the willingness of other merchants to add to their inventories. Unlike the Volvo distributor, the value of the merchant's wheat inventory cannot be protected by an administered wholesale or retail price and fluctuates in the open market.

With sufficiently homogeneous tradables II and high-volume international trade, a centralized commodity exchange may register worldwide supply and demand at a single geographic basing point—often in a country with a commonly used international currency. Britain has highly developed commodity exchanges in metals, homogeneous and storable tropical produce, and ship chartering (the Baltic exchange) to name but a few. Hence prices in these particular products are often quoted in sterling. Despite the relative decline in the international use of sterling, the long history and familiarity of these exchanges seems to ensure their continuance. However, American cities such as New York and Chicago have been rapidly acquiring more commodity exchanges of higher volume—with some overlap with London. For example, U.S. dollar prices of various grades of wheat are registered daily with the Chicago Board of Trade, from which transportation costs can be added or subtracted to establish spot prices in dollars anywhere in the world. In addition to these spot markets, futures markets up to eighteen months in maturity for any commodity with a high volume representative grade may exist if inventory holding is important.

In summary, commodities sufficiently homogeneous to be registered in a centralized international exchange will usually have sale prices quoted in sterling or dollars rather than in the domestic currency of the exporter. Such commoditiees are tradables II. But the market for *all* tradables II need not be formalized by an official trading exchange. Petroleum and gasoline products have long been traded throughout the world at fairly uniform spot prices (except in crisis situations) without such a geographically centralized exchange. Moreover, without a representative grade among the mélange of crude and refined products, generalized futures trading has never developed in the petroleum industry. Nevertheless, almost all quoted prices and payments for oil products that cross international boundaries are in U.S. dollars as of 1978— mostly under the auspices of the OPEC (Organization of Petroleum Exporting Countries) cartel.

Prior to December 1974, a rather charming anachronism had several states in the Persian Gulf demanding payment for their oil in sterling because they were historically part of the sterling area; nevertheless they quoted prices and set tax obligations in U.S. dollars because of the dollar's more stable international purchasing power. The sterling-dollar exchange rate on a particular day then had to be specified to effect the conversion because of this separation between the standard-of-value and means-of-payment function of international monies. However, the important point for our purposes is that governments and nonfinancial firms were quoting prices (or receiving payments) in dollars or sterling for petroleum products—tradables II—whatever the country of origin or destination.

What is the moral for our Swedish merchant exporter of wheat (tradables II)? Since he is a price taker, he does not have the market power to fix the krona price of his own sales in order to protect the value of his inventories or other costs. Moreover, there is a substantial administrative convenience in quoting export prices in dollars to his overseas customers, who can compare them with Chicago prices and may actually be purchasing for resale in terms of dollars. Thus he goes ahead and invoices wheat and other tradables II in dollars or sterling. Grassman's data in Table 4.1 show that about 70 percent of Swedish exports not invoiced in kronor were invoiced in dollars or sterling—with the former being more common in trade with third countries.

Having thus established that tradables I are likely to be invoiced in the home currency of the exporter, and that tradables II are invoiced mainly in U.S. dollars (or sterling), what then are the implications for hedging against currency risk and the extension of trade credit?[16]

16. I have stressed the distinction between tradables I and tradables II according to the characteristics of the goods involved—whether they are fix- or flexprice. An alternative approach is to explain differences in currencies of invoice according to the country in which trade is financed. For example, the prevalence of sterling invoicing in international trade in the late 19th and early 20th centuries in part stemmed from the fact that Britain was a financial center where trade bills from

Currency Risk and
the Structure of Trade Credit

The amount of net credit extended from exporter to importer, and *pari passu* from one country to another, depends on the exact timing of payment relative to shipment of goods.[17] Except for items that have a long lead time in production or are very specific to the needs of a particular buyer, it is normal commercial practice for the seller to give credit by allowing the buyer to defer payment, until well after he has received the goods, for the following reasons:

a)   The buyer wants time to examine the quantity and quality of the goods shipped.

b)   The buyer may be a wholesaler who himself does not receive payment until the goods are resold.

c)   In case of default, the seller (more than other creditors) may conveniently reclaim the goods as collateral.

The financial instruments by which trade credit is extended from exporters to importers are several, and have greatly changed since the heyday of the sterling bill. In dividing currency risk between exporter and importer, "the important line of demarcation between different forms of payment lies between transactions settled on open account and those in which payment obligations are settled in some other way." *Open account* is where the exporter simply keeps his own books on receivables from his customer, who are typically given a maximum term within which to pay but no fixed date on which payment is to be made. The customer must pay within the delivery month, within 30 days, 80 days, or something similar. "There is no formal instrument of credit, the observation of payments obligations being a matter of confidence."[18] Interest may or may not be charged on outstanding receivables; often a significant price discount is offered by the seller in the event of early payment. One can see from Table 4.4 that open-account credits were given in 55 percent of Swedish export transactions and in over 70 percent of import transactions.

---

anywhere in the world were discounted at low rates of interest. As we shall see later, the selection of a currency of invoice is not a pure technological matter reflecting the economic character of the goods being shipped. But in the modern world where opportunities among convertible currency countries for financing trade are more symmetrical, it is convenient at this point in our analysis to rest the distinction between tradables I and II on the character of the goods themselves. Then having so made this distinction, the implications for selecting a mode of finance can be derived— rather than the other way around.

17. Similar distinctions have been made by Bent Hansen in his pioneering analysis of the financial structure of Swedish trade. See Bent Hansen, *Foreign Trade Credits and Exchange Reserves* (Amsterdam: North Holland, 1961).

18. Sven Grassman, *Exchange Reserves and the Financial Structure of Foreign Trade*, op. cit., p. 27.

This prevalence of open account credits in Swedish trade can be linked to our previous distinction between tradables I and tradables II—where the former was more common. By invoicing his goods in kronor, the Swedish exporter absolves himself of currency risk. (Similarly, foreign exporters absolve themselves of currency risk by invoicing in their home currency). The foreign importer must now bear the foreign exchange risk of using his home currency to buy kronor. In return, I hypothesize that *open-account credits from the exporter allow the importer to exercise discretion in timing repayments as a quid pro quo for bearing currency risk*. More empirical evidence remains to be collected to verify this hypothesis.[19]

Thus open-account credits allow the importer more flexibility in hedging. For example, he can decide to pay in three months time and cover a portion of this payment with a forward purchase of kronor maturing exactly on the day that payment is made. Or the foreign importer may leave an open short position in kronor and simply repay as his inventory of imported goods is liquidated.

On the other hand, if the Swedish exporter is selling tradables II invoiced in U.S. dollars to some third country, he has much less incentive to give indeterminate open-account credit to his overseas customer. The exporter is now bearing currency risk when he receives dollar payments and converts back to kronor. The uncertainty surrounding this conversion is needlessly aggravated if

TABLE 4.4   Foreign Trade in 1968 by Forms of Payment

Form of payment	Exports		Imports	
	Kronor (millions)	%	Kronor (millions)	%
Open account	13,513	55.0	18,369	70.2
Whereof consignment	516	2.1	451	1.7
Advance (whole amount)	146	0.6	600	2.3
Cash against documents	5,214	21.2	2,741	10.5
Acceptance	1,194	4.9	1,635	6.3
Sight documentary credit	829	3.4	418	1.6
Time documentary credit	283	1.2	419	1.6
Contractual quotas	2,894	11.8	1,580	6.0
Whereof more than 50 per cent in advance	172	0.7	304	1.2
Free deliveries	507	2.1	401	1.5
Total	24,580	100	26,163	100

SOURCE: Sven Grassman, *Exchange Reserves and the Financial Structure of Foreign Trade*, op cit., p. 28.

19. The reader is referred to the forthcoming study by Carse, Williamson, and Wood, for an in-depth empirical analysis of British forms of payment.

the exact timing of this payment is unknown. Hence, the exporter is less likely to give credit in the first place, and if credit is extended it will be in the form of a precise bill or acceptance payable in, say, exactly 30 days in U.S. dollars.

An empirically testable implication of the above analysis suggests itself: *open-account trade credits should be relatively more common for exports invoiced in the home currency* that I have called tradables I. Grassman did not test this hypothesis for Swedish data, but testing should not be difficult with the data he has collected. More casually, the shift away from the use of fixed-term trade bills and acceptances towards open-account credits over the last 30 years of Swedish experience with foreign trade—as noted by both Hansen and Grassman—may parallel a shift away from sterling as an international currency towards invoicing in the home currency of the seller.[20]

Inventory Valuation Adjustment Versus Forward Covering

To what extent should deferred payments in a particular foreign currency be secured by forward financial cover, if a trader wants to hedge against currency risk as completely as possible? Analytically, the question can be addressed in a general and a narrow sense.

A more general accounting would look at all the company's outstanding debts and assets arising from many possible transactions denominated in the foreign currency—including those anticipated in the near future. A multinational corporation that has many dealings with its overseas affiliates would be a logicial candidate for the general approach. Offsetting total assets against liabilities depicts the company's net position in the foreign currency, and calls for a decision to cover some or all of this net position as it is reported (translated) back into the home currency at the end of every accounting period.

The problem with this general approach is deciding on a uniform accounting rule for undertaking this translation every three months or so. Should only current assets and liabilities be revalued as the spot exchange rate fluctuates, leaving noncurrent assets valued in terms of old exchange rates? Or, should only monetary claims and liabilities directly denominated in the foreign currency be adjusted as the exchange rate changes—leaving all nonmonetary assets abroad (inventories, buildings, and equipment) unadjusted? Until the U.S.

---

20. As a previous note suggested, the choice of a currency of invoice may be as much a financial phenomenon as one dependent on the technical characteristics of the goods in question. Still, in the Swedish case, a shift toward invoicing in the seller's currency of exports and imports could also reflect the rising importance of manufactured goods, and the declining shares of Britain and the United States, in world commodity trade.

Financial Standards Accounting Board in Statement 8 (January 1, 1976) declared that *all* American corporations should use the latter monetary-nonmonetary technique, American firms had been free to choose their own consistent procedures. FASB-8 is highly controversial. In distinguishing true economic foreign exchange risk from nominal accounting risk under FASB-8, one must undertake a complex taxonomy of different situations in which a multinational corporation might find itself—and for only some of these would the new rule be appropriate.[21]

Here I take a much narrower approach to trader hedging by focusing on only *one* international transaction, and that by a nonmultinational company that doesn't have other assets or liabilities denominated in foreign exchange.[22] My concern is to minimize economic risk in foreign trade *per se*, rather than to analyze the benign or perverse effects of particular accounting rules imposed on multinational firms with overseas affiliates. Finally, the distinction between tradables I and tradables II is highlighted within an appropriately designed hedging procedure, a distinction that would carry over into analyzing the translation problem under alternative formal accounting rules.

Consider first a prototype Dutch importer of tradables I—say, Swedish Volvos invoiced in kronor to be paid on open-account credit. Volvos arrive in discrete lots; on January 1, the importer receives his complete inventory of Volvos that he expects to sell in the next three or four months. To keep matters simple, suppose initially that he decides to repay in full in 90 days (on April 1) in order to take advantage of a favorable discount offered by the Swedish Volvo Corporation. How much kronor should he now purchase 90 days forward in order to minimize the variance in his income position from possible fluctuations on the krona/guilder exchange rate?[23]

The answer depends heavily on the extent to which he can adjust the *guilder price* of Volvos in response to exchange-rate changes. Suppose the krona unexpectedly appreciated against the guilder by 10 percent after the importer had incurred uncovered krona debts but before he sold any automobiles. The guilder value of his accounts payable has now risen by 10 percent. However, if the importer can raise the guilder selling price of his inventory by 10 percent—perhaps because the main competition is from other dealers in imported auto-

21. A nice summary of some of these issues can be found in Linda Snyder, "Have the Accountants Really Hurt the Multinationals?" *Fortune* (February 1977).
22. Norman Fieleke provides evidence that this kind of isolated transaction is empirically important: "The 1971 Flotation of the Mark and the Hedging of Commercial Transactions Between the United States and Germany," *Journal of International Business Studies* (Spring 1973), p. 54.
23. Or equivalently, purchase kronor at the existing spot rate to hold for 90 days against his future payment. The least-cost financial route for securing forward cover is explored in some depth in Chapter 5.

mobiles who face the same change in exchange rate, this inventory valuation adjustment exactly offsets the fact that his krona debts are 10 percent more expensive in guilders—his currency habitat. His loss on currency trading is just counterbalanced by the increased guilder prices of Volvos yet to be sold—a process that is exactly reversed if the guilder had appreciated in terms of kronor. Hence, without forward financial covering, the Dutch importer can insulate the value of his net cash flow in guilders from currency risk.

Indeed, had he covered his foreign monetary liabilities by buying kronor 90 days forward, with inventory price adjustments responding to exchange-rate changes as described above, the *ex ante* variance in his cash flow position would have *increased:* a depreciation of the guilder would lead to a windfall inventory profit and an appreciation would lead to a windfall inventory loss, neither of which is offset by gains or losses in his covered krona debts due in 90 days. In precisely circumstances like this, FASB-8 would work perversely! The Dutch importer would, under FASB-8, cover his monetary krona debts forward, while ignoring his nonmonetary inventory valuation adjustment.

However, the circumstances where the importer can rely wholly on inventory valuation adjustment to eliminate currency risk are very limited. If Volvos are sold for guilders before the exchange rate changes, then inventory valuation adjustment cannot be used for those particular automobiles. Hence the Dutch importer might do well to actually purchase kronor forward against his intended April 1 day of payment as automobiles are sold from his inventory. (Or equivalently, the flexibility of open-account credits might allow him to repay the Volvo Corporation in kronor directly as he sold his cars, without waiting until April 1.) In general, the importer's need for forward financial cover increases as his inventories are reduced before the 90 days elapse.

What might prevent the guilder price of Volvos in inventory in Holland from fully adjusting kronor to exchange-rate changes?

First, for a series of small upward and downward movements in the krona/guilder exchange rate, the Dutch importer cannot conveniently continually alter the sticker prices on the automobiles in his showroom. Indeed, Robert Dunn has shown that for minor fluctuations in the Canadian/American exchange rate from 1952 to 1962, Canadian importers left unchanged the prices in Canadian dollars of goods imported from the United States—and vice versa.[24] Insofar as these minor changes can significantly influence the *net* profit position of the importer, if they occur prior to making payment, he should increase his forward cover.

Second, for major discrete exchange-rate changes—say a 10 percent devalua-

---

24. Robert Dunn, "Flexible Exchange Rates and Oligopoly Pricing: A Study of Canadian Markets," *Journal of Political Economy* (January/February 1970), pp. 140–51.

tion of guilders relative to kronor and all other major currencies—the Dutch importer may be unable to raise the guilder price of Volvos by a full 10 percent. If his principal competition comes from domestic automobile manufacturers, their guilder costs and prices may rise by much less that 10 percent or even not at all. But other importers of automobiles may face the same exchange-rate change and are anxious to boost their guilder prices.[25] The net result is likely some partial upward price adjustment—say, six percent. Insofar as this commodity-price adjustment is incomplete, the risk-averse importer should partially cover forward.

The distinction between tradables I and tradables II bears on the correlation between commodity-price and exchange-rate changes. If the Dutch firm had been importing wheat (tradables II) invoiced in U.S. dollars, and if the guilder depreciated by 10 percent, international commodity arbitrage would be nearly perfect. The homogeneous nature of wheat would cause the value of the Dutch merchant's wheat inventories to be bid up by the full 10 percent. Hence for a given level of commodity inventories relative to deferred payment obligations, importers of tradables II would seek less forward cover than would importers of tradables I.

In conclusion, our risk-averse Dutch importer with outstanding krona debts should seek *more* forward financial cover when:

1) the more imperfect is the correlation between the guilder price of commodities he has in inventory and the value in international exchange of the guilder; and

2) the smaller are existing commodity inventories relative to the magnitude of deferred payments.

The precise quantitative determination of the optimal level of forward financial cover is both difficult to make and an important determinant of the stability of the importer's cash flow. A simple algebraic model of the optimum hedge is developed in the technical note to this chapter for the stochastic case where exchange-rate movements and inventory-price adjustments are jointly distributed random variables.

Financial Predominance, Tradables II, and the Optimum Double Hedge

Our analysis of hedging has concentrated on tradables I, which are invoiced in the seller's currency. Trade credit was granted from exporter to importer,

25. There is a further complicating currency asymmetry. If the krona appreciates by only 10 percent relative to guilders and to all other currencies, Dutch importers of automobiles from other countries will not feel impelled to raise their prices at all. Whether the krona appreciates or the guilder depreciates makes a significant difference once third-country effects are taken into account. The reader can work out this particular taxonomy for himself.

and—implicitly—domestic banks financed domestic traders in each participating country. The Swedish exporter of Volvos could draw on Swedish banks for krona credits, and the Dutch importer might draw on Dutch banks for guilder credits, provided that both parties remained hedged against exchange risk denominated in their home currency.

This *financial symmetry* implies that banks in each convertible-currency country have a comparative advantage in extending credit to, and receiving deposits from, domestic residents in the domestic currency. Given the existence of default risk and capital rationing, local banks are in the best position to judge the credit-worthiness of domestic importers or exporters who wish to borrow to finance international trade. Concomitantly on the supply side, the banks in any one country are not asymmetrically restricted in their ability to lend or to attract deposits in domestic currency. Usury laws and other restrictions on loan portfolios are, on balance, no more repressive in one country than another.[26] Notice that this model of financial symmetry does not rule out net capital flows from one country to another, it simply implies that domestic banks in each country are efficient intermediaries in their own currencies.

Financial predominance, on the other hand, implies that the capital market in the center country or *Nth* currency is not only more efficient in serving its own nationals, but also accepts deposits or makes loans to exporters or importers (resident in other countries) on more favorable terms than can their domestic banks or capital-market institutions. This greater efficiency at the center may be due to fewer official restrictions on financial institutions and international capital transfers, economies of scale in finance, the greater stability of the national currency, accumulated financial wisdom, or various combinations of the above.

The classic example of financial predominance is the pre-1914 London capital market. A very high proportion of international trade among countries other than Britain was financed by sterling bills drawn on importers by exporters, which were due in 90 days or 6 months. If these commercial bills were guaranteed against default by an acceptance house, exporters in turn could freely sell these sterling bills to a London bank (discount house) at the world's lowest open-market rates of interest. Because international traders from all nations financed trade credits in sterling through London, the minimization of currency risk led to trade between second and third countries being invoiced in sterling.

---

26. In contrast, domestic banks in less developed countries are often severely restrained in their ability to finance foreign trade. See R. McKinnon, *Money and Capital in Economic Development*, (Washington, D.C.: Brookings Institution, 1973), Chapter 7.

At the present time, however, neither London nor New York have capital markets that dominate international finance in the manner of the pre-1914 London market. Hence the model of financial symmetry seems empirically more appropriate in describing commerce in tradables I between any randomly chosen pair of convertible currency countries—neither of which is Britain nor the United States. This is consistent with Grassman's data on the common practice of invoicing in the home currency of the exporter. Moreover, most industrial economies encourage domestic banks to provide export finance, and sterling has declined as a world currency because of exchange controls and inflation. Restraints on short-term credits by American banks to third parties were only lifted in January 1974.

Nevertheless, the financial predominance model may still apply to commerce in tradables II, which is invoiced in dollars or sterling anyway. One might expect the capital market in the center country to have a comparative advantage in financing this trade—given the propensities of borrowers and lenders to avoid currency risk. Since tradables II are largely primary commodities with high price variability, commodity futures markets in the center country are likely to be an important adjunct to its capital market. Consider now the interesting dual problem of how to hedge against currency risk on the one hand, and against commodity-price risk on the other.

Let us take as our principal analytical focus the problem of hedging foreign trade between two convertible currency countries—neither of which is the United States—but which are exchanging tradables II invoiced in U.S. dollars. Again, take wheat as the prototype tradables II, and consider exports of Australian wheat to Japan under the assumption that Australian dollars and Japanese yen are the preferred monetary habitats of Australians and Japanese respectively. How will currency risk be allocated between the Australian exporter and Japanese importer, and how does this allocation influence the extension of trade credit?

Because the Australian exporter invoices and receives payments in U.S. dollars, he bears currency risk, as does the Japanese importer. Hence he has much less incentive to extend flexible on-account credit to the importer than did our Swedish exporter of Volvos to the Netherlands. Indeed, the more uncertain the timing of the Japanese importer's payments in U.S. dollars, the more needless currency risk the Australian exporter faces. Hence, insofar as trade credit is extended from exporters to importers, i.e., payment is deferred, we would expect the timing and terms to be very precise. Fixed term trade bills or acceptances—say 30 days—could well be the mode of finance.

The net trade credit extended might also be much less if a third currency is used. For example, one might expect a high proportion of commercial sales of

wheat to involve cash against documents where no trade credit is extended—
perhaps to be shipped in long-term contracts where cash payments approximately
balance the flow of wheat. Cash against documents may also be the mode for a
homogeneous and easily graded commodity such as wheat because the buyer
need not defer payment until the quality of goods shipped is ascertained.[27]

In order to draw a sharp analytical distinction, let us assume that the Australian exporter extends *no* net credit to the Japanese importer. Payment is made
by cash (U.S. dollars) against documents when the wheat is shipped. Does the
Australian exporter thereby absolve himself of risk? Insofar as he is a merchant
(rather than a farmer) who acquires wheat inventories over time for sale overseas, he must worry about hedging the value of those inventories against fluctuations in the world (U.S. dollar) price of wheat as well as guarding against
currency risk. In this respect, highly developed wheat futures markets in Chicago could be useful to him given the fact that wheat is invoiced in U.S.
dollars. He could sell wheat short in Chicago futures as his inventories build
up. When a contract is signed to deliver wheat at a fixed U.S. dollar price to
Japan a short period hence, he would eliminate his short position in Chicago
for that amount of wheat.[28] The cash proceeds from his inventories are then
fixed *ex ante* in terms of U.S. dollars.

One then better understands the complementary nexus among invoicing
tradables II in the currency of the center country, having highly developed spot
and futures markets in commodity exchanges in that country, and allowing
foreign nationals to have easy access to finance at the center. For example, if

27. Grassman's data on Swedish export credits provide some limited support for this hypothesis.
While exports are not classified according to whether they are tradables I or II, it seems as if
foodstuffs and timber products are closest to the definition of tradables II. In both these categories,
the average credit period extended by Swedish exporters is much shorter than for the rest of
Sweden's export bill (Grassman, op. cit. p. 63). For foodstuffs, the average credit period is 17 days,
and for timber products it is 24 days. The average for the export bill as a whole is 78 days. If
foodstuffs and timber products were further broken down into homogeneous primary materials and
manufactured goods, the former could well show even shorter credit periods.
28. The usefulness of the Chicago hedge to our hypothetical Australian exporter hinges on two
important technical considerations:

   1)   The extent to which the f.o.b. price of wheat in Australian ports varies rigidly in tandem
         with Chicago prices. The fact that both the U.S. and Australia export wheat to Japan
         probably means that prices are highly correlated.

   2)   Longer-term futures prices (in which the exporter hedges) are closely correlated with
         near-term forward prices.

In technical terms, both (1) and (2) establish the basis—the difference between the Chicago
futures price and the forward price (short-term) at which wheat can be sold to Japan. The Chicago
market is useful to the Australian wheat exporter as long as this basis is fairly constant.

our Australian wheat exporter wishes to borrow to finance his inventory acquisitions, he might readily negotiate a U.S. dollar loan (on attractive terms) from
an American (or other) bank on the strength of the fact that his position in
U.S. dollars is hedged against fluctuations in the world price of wheat. Thus he
can assuredly repay the U.S. dollar loan. Indeed, hedging is best viewed as a
means of relaxing the underlying capital constraint that traders and enterprises
generally face.

But what about currency risk *per se:* the problem of translating back into
the Australian dollar that is, by assumption, the monetary habitat of the
exporter? The wheat exporter used the complementary futures and financial
markets in the center country to hedge against fluctuations in the U.S. dollar
price of wheat, but he needs to pay his labor and storage costs in Australian
dollars, and possibly redeem his own equity capital in terms of Australian
dollars. He should sell U.S. dollars forward for Australian dollars for the full
value of his inventory of wheat (assuming the whole is to be sold to Japan)
less whatever U.S. dollar loans are outstanding. Presuming that he is making
a profit as a wheat merchant, this forward sale of U.S. dollars would just
cover his merchandising costs in Australia plus his own equity capital once
the wheat inventory is sold off. Insofar as he borrowed Australian dollars to
finance his wheat inventory (that is to some extent in violation of our financial predominance assumption), his optimal forward sale of U.S. dollars for
Australian dollars would increase in order to cover his domestic bank loan.

Hedging against changes in the exchange rate between U.S. and Australian
dollars is necessarily incomplete. As the merchant accumulates wheat and
hedges against *commodity price risk* in U.S. dollars, he has only an approximate idea of when he can sell the wheat for cash. Indeed, as a merchant
holding inventories, he provides an important convenience service to others
whose needs and timing of purchases may be uncertain. Hence, the merchant
does not know exactly the future dates at which he will want to convert U.S.
dollars into Australian dollars. Thus forward sales will only reduce but not
eliminate his currency risk.[29]

In summary, the exporter's dilemma in hedging can be neatly characterized
as requiring a double hedge: to avoid commodity price risk measured in U.S.
dollars, and to avoid currency risk in coming back to Australian dollars. How-

29. The risk avoidance problems of the Japanese importer of wheat invoiced in U.S. dollars are
sufficiently similar (although not identical) that they do not warrant separate analytical treatment.
Suffice it to say, that the importer may wish to hedge commodity price risk by going long in
Chicago wheat futures depending on his own commitment to sell wheat for yen. The Chicago
wheat futures market then becomes a truly international register of the future demand and supply
of wheat. He also hedges currency risk by buying U.S. dollars forward for yen—forward purchases
that are reduced insofar as he finances the imports of Australian wheat by a U.S. dollar bank loan.

ever, with the uncertain timing of overseas sales, and with the imperfect nature of the Chicago futures hedge, even this double hedge optimally applied will not eliminate risk altogether. Insofar as residual risk remains, bankers (financiers) will require that our exporter put up a substantial amount of his own equity to finance his inventories—whence the capital constraint on his operations. The financial aspects of this capital constraint, as related to forward covering, are discussed further in Chapter 5.

A TECHNICAL NOTE TO CHAPTER 4:
Optimum Forward Cover

This algebraic note supplements the text on hedging by inventory valuation adjustment versus hedging by forward covering.[30] Our Dutch firm, with a preferred currency habitat of guilders, imports on January 1 exactly 100 Swedish Volvos—each worth one Swedish krona. The full 100 kronor are to be paid in 90 days on April 1.

In order to encapsulate the algebraic analysis into one discrete time period of 90 days, assume further that the Dutch importer keeps the inventory (perhaps in transit) for 90 days, and then sells the whole consignment for the best price depending on the guilder/krona exchange rate on April 1. This extreme assumption suppresses the difficult technical problem of continual inventory liquidation within the discrete time period.

Suppose on January 1, he wishes *ex ante* to minimize variance in his anticipated cash flow on April 1. Let us derive the correct hedging strategy, assuming all covering is done in the forward market for foreign exchange.[31]

Let R_s (guilders/kronor) be the spot exchange rate at the beginning of the contract period (January 1).

Let R_f (guilders/kronor) be the rate on January 1 for buying kronor forward to be delivered in 90 days.

---

30. These technical derivations were greatly helped by James Hodder's work in his Ph.D. dissertation, "Hedging of Exposure to Exchange-Rate Movements." Stanford University, 1978.
31. In the next chapter, alternative methods of forward covering will be discussed.

Let R_s^{90} be the actual spot rate on April 1.

Let P_g^{90} be the guilder price of Volvos in 90 days, whereas R_s is their guilder price on January 1 if each Volvo is worth one krona.

The basic idea is that, on January 1, R_s^{90} and P_g^{90} are jointly distributed random variables about which our dealer must make a judgment in deciding how much of his deferred payment of 100 kronor to cover forward. While their variance may be high, let us assume that both random variables have stationary means:[32]

$$E(R_s^{90}) = R_s = R_f \tag{4.1}$$

and

$$E[P_g^{90}] = E[R_s^{90}] = R_s. \tag{4.2}$$

We can first specify the Volvo dealer's income or cash flow Y, as of April 1, on the assumption that he does *not* cover forward:

$$Y = -100\,R_s^{90} + 100\,P_g^{90} = 100\,[(R_s - R_s^{90}) + (P_g^{90} - R_s)] \tag{4.3}$$

$\quad\ $ (cost) $\quad\ $ (revenue) $\qquad$ (profit on $\qquad\ $ (profit on
$\qquad\qquad\qquad\qquad\qquad\qquad$ deferred $\qquad\qquad$ change in
$\qquad\qquad\qquad\qquad\qquad\qquad$ payment) $\qquad\quad$ inventory
$\qquad\qquad\qquad\qquad\qquad\qquad\qquad\qquad\qquad$ value)

Because $E(R_s^{90}) = E(P_g^{90})$, we have $E(Y) = 0$. Moreover, we can partition the net profit in (4.3) into that due to deferring payment to a rate different from R_s, and that due to selling off the inventory at a price different from the cost. Because R_s^{90} need not equal P_g^{90}, there can be substantial *ex ante* variance in Y (in guilder cash flow).

Consider now the introduction of forward covering, where $0 < \alpha < 1$ is that proportion of the 100 krona debt that is covered by a forward purchase of kronor at rate R_f. Remembering that $R_s = R_f$, the random variable Y can now be written:

$$Y = 100\,[(R_f - R_s^{90})(1 - \alpha) + (P_g^{90} - R_s)]. \tag{4.4}$$

The first term represents the net profit on the deferred payment plus forward contract, and goes to zero as $\alpha \to 1$. The second term represents the inventory valuation adjustment as the price of Volvos in 90 days varies with R_s^{90}. While $E(Y)$ is still zero, the two terms jointly determine the *variance* in Y, and to some extent offset each other. This can be seen by writing a general expression for the variance of Y:

---

32. E is the expected value operator.

$$\text{Var } Y = E\,[100(R_f - R_s^{90})(1-\alpha) + 100(P_g^{90} - R_s)]^2. \tag{4.5}$$

The degree of offset, however, depends very much on how one specifies the joint probability distribution of R_s^{90} and P_g^{90}.

CASE 1: *Price fully determined by the exchange rate.*

While retaining the assumption that R_s is indeed a random variable, suppose that P_g^{90} varies exactly proportionately to how R_s^{90} deviates from R_s :

$$P_g^{90} = R_s + \beta(R_s^{90} - R_s) \quad 0 < \beta < 1. \tag{4.6}$$

The Volvo dealer adjusts automobile prices after 90 days by some fraction, β, of the movement in the exchange rate. Substitute equation (4.6) into (4.5) to get:

$$\text{Var } Y = E\,[100(R_f - R_s^{90})(1-\alpha) + 100(R_s^{90} - R_s)\beta]^2. \tag{4.7}$$

Remembering that $R_s = R_f$, we see that the variance of income is precisely zero when:

$$\beta = 1 - \alpha \tag{4.8}$$

where $1 - \alpha$ is that portion of the deferred forward payment that is *uncovered*. For example, if the final price of Volvos in 90 days is adjusted by 40 percent of any exchange-rate change, then 60 percent of the deferred krona payment should be covered by a forward contract at R_f. Because of the deterministic (full information) character of the offsetting price adjustment, this optimum method of hedging leaves no residual variance in income.

CASE 2: *Stochastic uncertainty*

Suppose now that R_s^{90} and P_g^{90} are jointly distributed variables such that:

$$P_g^{90} = F(R_s^{90}) + u \quad \text{where} \quad F' > 0 \tag{4.9}$$

where u is a random disturbance. In other words, movements in the exchange rate influence the price of Volvos 90 days hence, but the relationship is not deterministic so that perfect offsetting is no longer possible: the dealer does not know exactly the relationship between the actual future exchange rate and the actual price of Volvos. Consider the following statistical parameters that *are* known to (or estimated by) the dealer on January 1:

σ_P^2 is the unconditional variance in P_g^{90}.

σ_R^2 is the variance in R_s^{90}

$$\rho = \frac{\text{Covariance } (P_g^{90}, R_s^{90})}{\sigma_P \cdot \sigma_R} \qquad 0 \leq \rho \leq 1.$$

Then one can write the variance of income by substituting these parameters into equation (4.6) to get:

$$\text{Var } Y/10000 = (1 - \alpha)^2 \sigma_R^2 - 2(1 - \alpha) \text{ cov } (R_s^{90}, P_g^{90}) + \sigma_P^2. \qquad (4.9)$$

The variance of income depends directly on the variances of the exchange rate and the price of automobiles, and inversely on the covariance between the two. (4.9) can now be minimized with respect to the control parameter α —the degree of forward cover. The first order optimization condition yields:

$$\alpha^* = 1 - \rho \frac{\sigma_P}{\sigma_R}. \qquad (4.10)$$

This remarkably simple expression for the optimum degree of forward cover, α^*, can be easily interpreted.[33] Suppose $\rho = 0$ because P_g^{90} and R_s^{90} are independently distributed random variables; within the 90-day time horizon, exchange-rate movements have no effect on auto prices although the latter may vary for other reasons. Then $\alpha^* = 1$ and our dealer covers forward 100 percent of the deferred krona payment.

But as ρ increases for given σ_P and σ_R, α^* decreases. That is, the positive correlation between R_s^{90} and P_g^{90} allows inventory valuation adjustment to compensate—at least in part—for the exchange risk on the deferred payment. Similarly, as σ_P increases relative to σ_R for a given $\rho > 0$, the optimum amount of forward cover again declines because the magnitude of inventory valuation adjustment is now larger relative to the variance in the exchange rate. Note that for tradables I, ρ is closer to zero; and for tradables II, ρ is closer to unity.

Because of the stochastic nature of the problem, however, there remains *residual* variance in income even after one chooses the optimum degree of forward cover as described by equation (4.10). To see this, substitute α^* into the general expression for income variance (4.9) to get the unhedgeable residual risk:

$$\text{Var } Y^* = \sigma_P^2 [1 - \rho^2] > 0. \qquad (4.11)$$

Only when $\rho \to 1$, the empirically unlikely case where one can get a perfect

33. This neat algebraic result was derived by James Hodder, op. cit.

inventory valuation adjustment, does the residual income variance become close to zero.[34] In effect, the stochastic case (2) truncates into the deterministic case (1).

On the other hand, when $\rho \rightarrow 0$, and one covers the pure exchange risk fully by 100 percent, the residual variance in income equals σ_p^2 —the price variability over 90 days of the physical inventory of Volvos.

34. This case is unlikely because variance in prices can occur for reasons other than exchange-rate movements—particularly for tradables II.

5

Forward Covering
and Interest Arbitrage
in Imperfect Capital Markets*

Without specifying the financial mechanics, heretofore I have rather cavalierly assumed that an importer or exporter *could* cover deferred payments or receipts by suitable spot or forward currency transactions—although it is generally not optimal to fully cover such deferred commitments. In practice, financial limitations exist on what covering positions any individual trader may choose because he faces a constraint on the amount and cost of capital to which he has access. Just as hedging against currency risk mitigates the capital constraint, so does the capital constraint limit the extent and means by which forward covering takes place. They are mutually determining.

Suppose that our Dutch importer of Swedish Volvos has financial choices that are representative of those open to most traders resident in convertible-currency countries. Take as given a decision to cover fully a payment of 100 kronor in 90 days. The importer can buy 100 kronor to be delivered in 90 days at a forward rate in guilders quoted by his bank.[1] Alternatively, he can purchase spot an interest-bearing krona bill or certificate of deposit that matures in approximately 90 days—again through his bank or in some open financial market in Sweden (exchange controls permitting). In other words, the importer has the option of using the forward foreign exchange market directly, or in undertaking a spot transaction that effectively covers his deferred krona pay-

*I am indebted to Jacob Frenkel for helpful comments on this chapter.
1. The intermediary role of commercial banks in forward transacting is covered in Chapter 9, where interbank market relationships are explored in some depth.

ment. The route he takes will be the one that minimizes his financial costs that, in part, depend on default risk as perceived by his banker.

Before developing a simple analytical model of the minimization process, remember the *partial-equilibrium* nature of this choice. Our importer faces a given krona price for Volvos sold on open-account trade credit. We have considered a three-stage decision procedure where the firm

1)   selects the total volume of business—the number of Volvos to import in any given consignment;

2)   determines the division of hedging against currency risk by financial covering as opposed to relying on inventory valuation adjustments;

3)   decides whether to cover in the forward market or in offsetting spot transactions.

In practice, all three decisions are made jointly—if only implicitly in the importer's mind. However this joint determination involves too many peculiar production, marketing, and financial variables to warrant analyzing in full generality. Hence, I have simply assumed that the production-sales decision (1) is given in the period under consideration, that the optimal degree of financial forward covering vis-à-vis inventory valuation adjustment (2) has been decided according to criteria explained in Chapter 4, and that which remains is the *suboptimization* problem (3) of choosing the most efficient financial technique for covering a given amount of deferred krona payments.

Even so, the study of forward covering by itself has most interesting ramifications for understanding the interaction between national capital markets and the foreign exchange mechanism—particularly in interpreting the economic importance of short-term capital flows in facilitating commodity trade.

The Trader's Liquidity and Spot Versus Forward Covering

Our Dutch importer of Swedish Volvos has a certain opportunity cost of capital. Whether he borrows from a domestic bank or cashes in guilder financial assets to cover the 100 kronor due in 90 days will depend on his own peculiar liquidity position, and on interest yields on money-market instruments available to him. For analytical simplicity, consider only two financial situations for the importer. Either he is *illiquid* in the sense that he must borrow any capital used in covering, or he is *liquid* and has "owned" funds conveniently available within his enterprise.[2]

Let r_b^g be the cost of borrowing from his bank—an interest cost over 90 days denominated in guilders—for the illiquid trader.

2. The liquidity of any one trader can be expected to fluctuate through time as receipts and payments have a random component throughout the range of his commercial activities, which are not fully specified here.

Let r_d^g be the deposit rate of interest on 90-day guilder assets owned by the liquid importer.

The spread between the two reflects "imperfections" in the Dutch capital market.[3]

Let r_d^k be the maximum Swedish rate of interest (free from default) on a liquid krona deposit maturing in 90 days in which all Dutch importers could conveniently invest. (r_b^k is the cost of borrowing in kronor.)

Let R_f represent the forward (90-day) exchange rate at which our importer may buy kronor forward from his bank.

Let R_s represent the spot rate (guilders per krona) quoted the importer by his bank.

The forward premium of kronor over guilders—again taking 90 days as the horizon—is

$$f = \frac{R_f - R_s}{R_s}$$

For example, suppose the spot rate is 1.68 guilders per krona and that the forward rate is 1.71 guilders per krona, then the forward premium is 1.8 percent. f is dimensionally equivalent to rates of interest quoted over 90 days.

One further bit of information is required to determine the appropriate method of covering. What is the cost to our Dutch importer of using the forward exchange market directly to buy kronor forward? Since the importer may face brokerage fees, margin requirements leading to foregone interest earnings, and a bid-ask spread on forward price quotations, let us represent his total costs by the parameter α. If α is the percentage cost over 90 days of forward contracting, $100 \cdot R_f \cdot \alpha$ is the transactions cost in guilders of buying 100 kronor forward.

Because a widened bid-ask spread leads to a higher α on this definition, R_f is interpreted simply as the midpoint in the bid-ask spread that the bank quotes. Hence R_f is *invariant* to a widening or narrowing of the bid-ask spread—an effect captured by α. In the context of the model, R_f is a pure forward rate net of all costs quoted for the nonfinancial firm (importer) by his bank at the "retail" level.

Consider first the problem when the importer's capital position is *liquid*. Will he cover his 100 krona payment due in 90 days spot or forward?

Guilder costs of covering *spot*: Capital outlay plus net interest

---

3. For a fuller analysis using a spread between borrowing and lending rates as a measure of imperfection in the capital market, see Jack Hirshleifer, *Investment, Interest and Capital* (Englewood Cliffs, N.J.: Prentice Hall, 1970), Chapter 7.

$$C_s = 100\,R_s + 100\,R_s(r_d^g - r_d^k) \tag{5.1}$$
$$= 100\,R_s(1 + r_d^g - r_d^k)$$

Equation (5.1) reflects the spot purchase of a 100 krona deposit yielding r_d^k, for which the importer had to sell guilder deposits yielding r_d^g.

Guilder costs of covering by direct *forward contracting*:

$$C_f = 100\,R_f(1 + \alpha)$$
$$= 100\,R_s(1 + f)(1 + \alpha) \tag{5.2}$$
$$= 100\,R_s(1 + f + \alpha)$$

In equation (5.2), I have followed convention and assumed $\alpha \cdot f$ is of a smaller order of magnitude than the remaining terms in the brackets. This is consistent with equation (5.1) where the cost of forward cover for net interest payments is also ignored.

The point of indifference between covering spot or forward is where $C_s = C_f$:

$$r_d^g - r_d^k = f + \alpha \tag{5.3}$$

If the Swedish capital market provides krona assets that are highly attractive compared to deposit yields in Holland, i.e., r_d^k is large relative to r_d^g, the liquid Dutch importer should exploit this convenient financial opportunity and cover spot unless f is highly negative—the Swedish krona is at a sharp forward discount. In the latter case, the importer should take direct advantage of this forward discount and simply purchase kronor forward to mature in 90 days, even though he is liquid and could easily invest in krona financial assets. Nevertheless, for a given f and α, the fact that the importer is financially liquid tilts his decision making towards covering spot.

In contrast, suppose now that our importer is quite *illiquid* and dependent on finance from Dutch banks. The bank lending rate r_b^g in guilders significantly exceeds deposit rates of interest in the Netherlands—deposits that our illiquid importer does not own. Again, compute the alternative costs of covering either by spot or forward contracting. Then whether he contracts forward depends on the left-hand side of equation (5.4) being greater than the right:

$$r_b^g - r_d^k = f + \alpha \tag{5.4}$$

Because $r_b^g > r_d^g$, illiquidity tilts him towards using the forward market to cover. If α is not high and f is not at a sharp premium, the presence of a forward market could substantially relax the liquidity constraint on his financial position. The small margin requirement (incorporated in α) on his forward contract allows him to circumvent the high direct borrowing costs that he would otherwise face. Then too, the fact that he does cover further reduces the riskiness of his enterprise as perceived by outside lenders. Thus the cost of capital r_b^g—which the algebra displayed in the previous equations simply takes as given—might be further reduced. That is, his borrowing costs to finance other aspects of his operation—say inventory accumulation—are thereby lessened.

Although I have divided all traders into fictitious liquid and illiquid groups, such a rigid dichotomy is not necessary for the analysis to go through. Some traders will be partially liquid; still others will find themselves illiquid at some points in time but with a plentiful supply of financial assets otherwise. Thus, the extent to which each trader uses the forward market will vary.

In summary, the existence of an efficient forward market is convenient; but it is not vital to the covering process as seen through the eyes of the individual trader *if* national capital markets operate with tolerable efficiency. On average, the greater flexibility provided by the forward market reduces the financial costs of covering and so relaxes the capital constraint on other aspects of his operation. If an organized forward market did not exist, a trader could still cover spot at a price—higher average interest costs and reduced liquidity. Hence, the forward market can mitigate the effects of substantial imperfections in national capital markets, which may be protected by exchange controls that prevent short-term capital from moving freely.

The Empirical Magnitude of Forward Transacting

Given this inherent flexibility in the financial system, how important are forward exchange transactions by nonbank commercial enterprises? Because such firms operate through authorized commercial banks who frown on the taking of speculative positions free of any immediate commercial justification, data on forward contracting probably pertain to forward covering rather than speculation. Even so, forward contracting is a small proportion of foreign exchange transactions for current goods and services, as Grassman's data given in Table 5.1 indicate.

In the late 1960s in Sweden, Denmark, Britain, France, and Belgium, forward transactions as a proportion of the flow of total current-account transactions are only about seven percent, and are even a smaller proportion of the stock of commercial credits outstanding that typically amount to one or two months' trade flows. These "small" magnitudes led Grassman to conclude that

> It may appear paradoxical that forward transactions, though of minor importance in the foreign exchange market as a whole,[4] have been subjected to much comprehensive analysis; while the behavior of firms giving rise to transactions on the spot market, which are in practice completely decisive, has to a great extent been disregarded.[5]

4. Grassman's data refer only to the retail level between banks and commercial enterprises, not to the high volume of interbank transactions.
5. Grassman, op. cit. p. 89.

TABLE 5.1   Forward Transactions as a Percentage of Trade in Goods and Services (Millions of dollars)

	A	B	C	D	E	F
	Forward purchases	Goods and services (debit)	A as % of B	Forward sales	Goods and services (credit)	D as % of E
Sweden (1969)	431	7,148	6.0	479	7,096	6.8
Denmark (1970)	313	4,954	6.3	70	4,810	1.4
Britain (1968)	3,171	23,501	13.4	2,306	23,479	9.8
France (1969)	68	21,246	0.3	96	20,505	0.4
Belgium (1970)	677	11,896*	5.6	743	12,782*	5.8

SOURCE: Sven Grassman, *Exchange Reserves and the Financial Structure of Foreign Trade*, op. cit. p. 89.

NOTE: When not originally given in dollars the figures have been converted to dollars at the par rate of exchange. For Sweden and Britain the figures on forward transactions have been converted from stocks to flows on the assumption that the average term for forward contracts is three months.

* Includes Luxembourg.

While the analysis of hedging through selecting a currency of invoice, inventory valuation adjustments, flexibility in granting trade credit, and spot covering has been unduly displaced in the literature in order to concentrate on what Charles Kindleberger has called the "mental gymnastics"[6] of the forward exchange market, the role of forward contracting in facilitating trade in goods and services should be kept in perspective. Our analysis has suggested several reasons why the total volume of forward exchange transactions might not be large.

1) There is a significant flow of current payments—cash against documents— whose timing is uncertain and where deferred payments are unnecessary.[7]

2) Insofar as financial predominance is important, invoicing and trade credit in a center country's currency reduces the need for covering back into any single national currency.

3) Under financial symmetry, we showed in Chapter 4 that deferred payments should only be partially covered because an optimal hedge would rely also on inventory-valuation adjustments.

4) Insofar as covering is warranted, it can be executed spot or forward.

6. Charles P. Kindleberger, "Speculation and Forward Exchange," *Journal of Political Economy* (April 1939), p. 163.
7. Production uncertainty is the major reason why primary commodity producers such as farmers do not hedge much by dealing in commodity futures contracts—unlike merchants with given inventories. See R. McKinnon, "Futures Markets, Buffer Stocks and Income Stability for Primary Producers." *Journal of Political Economy* (December 1967).

5)   Insofar as covering entails expense, traders may be induced to "speculate" by
      simply leaving open positions in foreign currency.[8]

Hence one can understand—*ex post facto*—why forward purchases and sales
of foreign exchange by nonbank firms have been small relative to spot transactions. Nevertheless, hedging more broadly conceived remains very important to
exporters and importers.

Grassman drew his data from the relatively calm period of fixed official
exchange-rate parities of the late 1960s. As we pass to the post-February 1973
turbulence associated with floating rates, the preoccupation of importers and
exporters with optimal hedging has likely increased along with the pro rata
share of their purchases and sales in the forward exchange market. But again,
the forward exchange market is unlikely to bear the main burden of adjustment
to floating.

However, if the advent of floating is accompanied by greater illiquidity and
capital rationing in national money markets, the *demand* for forward contracting will increase. And financial ratings—*Aaa*, *Bbb*, and so on—of important
trading corporations fell in 1973–1975, and only partially recovered subsequently, suggesting that illiquidity has become more acute. In addition, any
decline in the financial predominance of center currencies will—*ceterus paribus*—increase the demand for forward cover by exporters and importers.

But this increased demand by commercial traders to buy or sell forward
exchange need not be realized in a greater volume of forward contracts actually
executed if the supply diminishes sufficiently. Suppose the commercial banks
in their capacity as financial intermediaries in the forward exchanges raise their
fees—as measured by our α coefficient—to their retail clients because of
greater perceived banking risk in forward trading under floating rates. Then
whether or not forward contracting flourishes with the advent of floating exchange rates becomes uncertain *a priori*.

Some preliminary data that Grassman has collected on Swedish trade for
1973, paralleling that given for 1969, indicate that forward contracting as
percentage of spot transactions (related to goods and services flows) more than
doubled.[9] That is, nonfinancial trading firms have significantly increased forward transacting with their banks under floating rates.

8. Speculation by commercial traders is discussed below in connection with variations in the credit
period—leads and lags. See Chapter 7.
9. Sven Grassman, "Currency Distribution and Forward Cover in Foreign Trade: Sweden Revisited 1973," *Journal of International Economics* (May 1976), pp. 215–21. This significantly more
intense use of the forward market with the advent of floating exchange rates is documented in more
detail in Stephen Carse, John Williamson, and Geoffrey Wood, *The Financing Procedures of
British Foreign Trade* (London: Cambridge University Press, forthcoming).

Hedging Pressure and Bias
in the Forward Exchange Rate

We have concentrated on the microeconomic problem of the individual trader—a Dutch importer of Swedish Volvos—covering currency risk according to his individual liquidity position and the fixed parameters r_b^g or r_d^g, r_d^k, f and α. But interest rates and forward premia are mutually determined through forward and spot exchange transactions among many similar traders and other market participants. What are the limits within which these parameters can be expected to move vis-à-vis each other? Will there be a systematic statistical bias in this constellation such that the typical risk-averse commercial trader must pay an "insurance" premium to a group of "speculators" who are less averse to currency risk?

Consider now all hedgers similar to our Volvo dealer—including Swedish importers of Dutch tulip bulbs. Suppose that tulips are tradables I, i.e., are sufficiently specialized products to be invoiced in guilders. Then the Swedish importer will tend to cover some of his deferred payments either by buying guilders forward if he is financially illiquid, or by acquiring spot a Dutch bank deposit or other short-term liquid asset if its yield is not unfavorable. If we aggregate over all two-way commerce between Sweden and the Netherlands, there will be hedging pressure in both directions in the spot and forward exchange markets.

Because of the different structure of exports of each country—currency invoicing practices, credit terms, and the timing of forward transactions—it would be sheer accident if the *ex ante* covering pressures from commercial trading in both directions were equal at all terms on any one trading day. Still less likely would the *ex ante* demand and supply for kronor in terms of guilders exactly balance in the forward market, if only because an unknown amount of spot covering occurs. What then is the underlying financial mechanism, or price adjustment process, that satisfies this disparate demand for forward cover at randomly distributed points in time?

While being able to secure forward cover at any term remains very important, let us continue to telescope the forward analysis into a representative 90-day period. The degree of imperfection in the Dutch capital market is represented by the spread γ between borrowing and deposit rates of interest over 90 days facing our hypothetical Volvo importer:

$$r_b^g - r_d^g = \gamma \geq 0 \qquad (5.5)$$

Similarly, represent the degree of imperfection in the Swedish capital market by the interest spread θ facing a typical importer of Dutch tulips:

$$r_b^k - r_d^k = \theta \geq 0 \tag{5.6}$$

In order to focus on imperfections in the spot capital markets *per se*, temporarily assume that the cost of forward contracting, α, is zero. The parameters γ and θ then establish, for given rates of interest, the range of variation in f—the 90-day forward premium of kronor over guilders. (We continue to assume complete currency convertibility between the Netherlands and Sweden: there is no political or administrative risk of exchange controls on spot or forward transactions.)

In order to understand more precisely the range of variation in f and possible bias arising therefrom, suppose initially that the only participants in forward contracting are exporters or importers actually interested in covering exchange risk. Net hedging pressure may then occur in either direction. If Dutch importers are unusually illiquid and/or receive more trade credit than their Swedish counterparts, *ex ante* excess forward demand for kronor in terms of guilders will exist. The forward premium on kronor is pushed towards its upper bound, which is defined by the alternative cost of covering spot $r_b^g - r_d^k$. Hence

$$f \leq r_b^g - r_d^k \tag{5.7}$$

On the other hand, if Swedish importers are particularly illiquid or receive relatively generous trade credits, there will be net *ex ante* forward demand for guilders in terms of kronor[10] bounded by

$$f \geq r_d^g - r_b^k \tag{5.8}$$

A mixture of financially liquid and illiquid importers on both the Dutch and Swedish sides likely exists. Hence, a "corner solution," where either inequality (5.7) or inequality (5.8) is strictly satisfied, is not necessary to clear the market. Yet corner solutions are not out of the question. By combining (5.7) and (5.8) we can establish the relevant range for the forward premium on kronor for given deposit and lending rates of interest accessible to commercial traders in the two countries:

---

10. Because $-f$ is the premium on guilders over kronor, one can view the illiquid Swedish importer's problem as

$$-f \leq r_b^k - r_d^g$$

cost of forward   cost of spot
cover   cover

For forward covering to be attractive, the above inequality must hold in its strong form. Otherwise no forward transactions will occur. Interest rates and forward premia are all defined for a representative 90-day period.

$$r_d^g - r_b^k \leq f \leq r_b^g - r_d^k \qquad (5.9)$$

In the limiting case where the capital-market "imperfections" γ and θ become very small, i.e., $r_d^g \to r_b^g$ and $r_d^k \to r_b^k$, then equation (5.9) becomes

$$f = r^g - r^k \quad \text{where} \quad r_d^g \approx r^g \approx r_b^g \quad \text{and} \quad r_d^k \approx r^k \approx r_b^k \qquad (5.10)$$

The single rates of interest over 90 days prevailing in the Dutch and Swedish capital markets respectively are r^g and r^k. Equation (5.10) describes the famous Interest Rate Parity Theorem (IRPT) in its simplest form.[11] The forward premium on kronor identically reflects a unique short-run interest differential between the two countries when there are no imperfections in capital markets in either country, no costs in forward contracting, and perfect currency convertibility. In this market equilibrium, any individual Swedish or Dutch importer will be indifferent to covering spot or forward—indeed the distinction between financial liquidity and illiquidity loses significance once we impose the assumption of "perfect" national capital markets.

But in the more realistic environment where γ and θ are not zero, f varies within the range established by inequality (5.9); and the existence of a forward market will be a distinct convenience to many market participants—particularly those facing individual capital (liquidity) constraints.

Suppose there is substantial hedging pressure in one direction. If illiquid Dutch importers dominate in purchasing Swedish kronor forward, they will pay a "penalty" forward premium on kronor above the hypothetical interest-rate parity level associated with perfect capital markets. I use the term *hypothetical* because the IRPT is really not well defined once we admit a spread between deposit and lending rates of interest in each national capital market. An algebraic measure of the maximum bias against the Dutch importer can be established by assigning the two *deposit* rates of interest—r_d^g and r_d^k—to be "the" measure of interest-rate levels in each national capital market. Then $d = r_d^g - r_d^k$ is the relevant interest differential; and if $f = d$, there is no bias by this particular statistical index. Substituting d, γ, and θ into inequality (5.9) we obtain

$$-\theta \leq f - d \leq \gamma \qquad (5.11)$$

Hedging pressure from Dutch importers could increase f above d by as much as γ—our measure of "imperfection" in the Dutch capital market. This then is one (but not the only) possible statistical measure of the bias: the excess price the dominant hedger must pay in securing forward cover by forward contract-

11. First formalized by J.M. Keynes in A *Tract On Monetary Reform* (London: Macmillan, 1923), Chapter 3.

ing. This intuitively plausible measure of maximum bias (γ) defines the upper bound by which f can appreciate before all Dutch importers wanting cover are driven out of the forward market.[12]

If such bias exists against illiquid Dutch importers, the unduly large forward discount on guilders will benefit illiquid Swedish importers who cover by purchasing guilders forward. Even those Swedish importers who are financially liquid, and who might not normally cover by means of a forward transaction, will instead sell kronor forward to take advantage of an unusual forward premium on kronor. Indeed, under our limiting assumption that only commercial traders are transacting in the forward exchanges, this would be the mechanism for balancing the aggregate supply and demand for kronor in terms of guilders. Since transactions may take place at any time, such a market would be quite thin if Swedish commercial hedgers were only "incidentally" drawn in as f fluctuated.

What happens to bias and the volume of forward transactions if $\alpha > 0$: we admit significant margin or other costs into taking a forward position? Remember that $f = (R_f - R_s)/R_s$ was defined to be a pure forward premium: R_f and R_s could be quoted to noncommercial firms by banks with no spread between buying and selling rates. Forward contracting costs will narrow the range of f within which forward transacting would still take place—although it wouldn't change our measure of maximum bias against the dominant hedger. That is the limits on the fluctuations in f at which market trading actually occurs would be modified to

$$\alpha - \theta \le f - d \le \gamma - \alpha \qquad (5.12)$$

Clearly, if the cost of forward trading is large relative to imperfections (interest spreads) in international capital markets so that $\gamma - \alpha < 0$ and $\alpha - \theta > 0$, no forward contracting will take place.[13] Financially illiquid traders looking for forward cover simply have to borrow spot and pay the full "cost" of bias due to imperfection in the domestic capital market. International trade becomes distinctly less attractive.

The Importance of Covered Interest Arbitrage

A forward market confined to exporters and importers seeking commercial cover would seem to be very illiquid and, hence, of limited use in hedging.

12. We can see that γ is a maximum in the sense that if one used some weighted average of deposit and lending rates of interest from each national capital market to establish a statistical index of interest-rate parity (instead of just deposit rates of interest), then measured bias against the dominant hedger would be somewhat less.

13. It remains for us to spell out how the cost of forward transacting is mutually determined with interest spreads in national capital markets. The efficiency of banks and other institutions providing spot and forward financial services will be critical in this determination.

against currency risk. Each Dutch importer would have his own particular deferred payment obligation—30 days, 60 days, or whatever—incurred on a particular day that need not correspond to any particular deferred obligation of an identifiable Swedish importer either with respect to term or initial timing.[14] The cost of forward transacting in matching the bids of potential buyers and sellers would be very high in comparison to the spot market with many willing transactors. This market thinness allows random variations in hedging pressure to drive f to one or other of the limits—given by inequality (5.12) above—within which forward contracting is feasible for both participants. *Bias* in the forward premium would be the rule rather than the exception insofar as any forward contracting at all took place.

What then is the principal financial mechanism for introducing more liquidity into the covering process—particularly in forward contracting? Instead of introducing the agile, swashbuckling speculator as the hero of the piece, I break with academic tradition[15] and throw the main burden of adjustment onto the rather conservative and plodding interest arbitrageur. The arbitrageur cautiously remains covered against currency risk while seeking out small gains on interest differentials. The currency speculator, on the other hand, angles for the main chance by taking an open position in a foreign currency—possibly by forward-contracting on a small margin—in the hope of correctly anticipating a change in exchange rates. To what extent can the demand by exporters or importers for forward cover be satisfied without any of the relevant market participants bearing currency risk? To explore this issue narrowly conceived, pure covered interest arbitrageurs are now introduced into the forward market for foreign exchange. Speculators remain absent.

> *Definition:* A covered interest arbitrageur—CIA—is a financial firm that borrows and lends (deposits) freely to exploit interest differentials across assets denominated in different national currencies, while avoiding exchange risk through an offsetting forward transaction.

14. Note that commodity futures trading is organized so that contracts mature on one given day in the month, for only a limited number of months in the year, in order to minimize this matching problem. As we shall see, the liquidity and efficiency of the actual forward market in foreign exchange is much greater in providing a virtual continuum of contracts for a year or two into the future.
15. The usual academic approach is to stress that speculators provide a market-clearing service to covered interest arbitragers—a highly aggregated category that includes commercial traders. The emphasis is on market relationships between "arbitrageurs" and "speculators" somewhat artificially defined. See, for example, the seminal article by S.C. Tsiang, "The Theory of Forward Exchange and Effects of Government Intervention on the Forward Market," IMF Staff Papers (April 1959), pp. 75–106; H.G. Grubel, *Forward Exchange, Speculation and the International Flow of Capital* (Palo Alto, Calif.: Stanford University Press, 1966). The role of speculators remains important and is considered in Chapter 7. However, preoccupation with the speculator-arbitrageur dichotomy seems to have obscured due consideration of the very important service that covered interest arbitrageurs provide to exporters and importers.

Unlike our commercial hedger, the CIA is not tied to a particular set of predetermined commercial commitments arising out of international commodity trade. Rather he is a flexible financier—likely a bank—that can borrow or lend on any term at any particular point in time. Despite his avoidance of currency risk, the individual CIA still faces an effective capital constraint, as does all business enterprise, that ultimately limits the scope of his operations. He cannot borrow an infinite volume of funds in the Netherlands to invest in Sweden. The basic analytical problem, therefore, is to portray this constraint on the operations of CIAs collectively viewed.

The greater flexibility of the CIA in continuous time can be encapsulated into our 90-day discrete time analysis by positing a narrower spread between lending and borrowing rates of interest for the CIA in comparison to the commercial hedger. Not only may a CIA be more flexible in taking advantage of short-run movements in interest-rates vis-à-vis prevailing forward premia, but the fact that he can remain exactly covered according to the terms of his financial commitment means that his borrowing costs may be less than that of a commercial hedger.[16] Both these considerations allow the CIA to have (slightly) higher average deposit yields and lower borrowing costs. Although an individual CIA may face an upper bound on how much he can borrow at a given rate of interest in any national money market, I assume that collectively CIAs have completely elastic access to capital at going rates of interest that are denoted below by i; whereas interest rates facing commercial traders were denoted by r. In the technical note to this chapter, the financial position of CIAs is developed more precisely and fully. Here, however, the important financial service that CIAs provide to the dominant and possibly illiquid commercial hedger is discussed more intuitively.

Assume CIAs are fully liquid financial institutions (commercial banks) with owned capital that can be moved quickly from investments in one currency to those in another.[17] Carrying forward our two-country example, the investment yield open to a Dutch CIA, for example, is either

$$\frac{R_f}{R_s}(1 + i_d^k) \quad \text{or} \quad 1 + i_d^g \tag{5.13}$$

The deposit rate of interest i_d^g is earned by CIAs by keeping one guilder on deposit (invested) in Holland; whereas i_d^k is the yield to CIAs in kronor associated with moving funds to Sweden at a spot rate of $1/R_s$ (kronor/guilders).

16. As we demonstrated in Chapter 4, the optimal hedge requires the trader not to cover all his deferred payments and to rely partly on inventory valuation adjustments to offset exchange-rate changes. But even this optimum hedge will still leave him with some residual currency risk.
17. In the technical appendix, the role of illiquidity among CIAs is more carefully developed. It suffices to say here that the amount of liquid capital owned by CIAs is not indefinitely large.

However, it is inappropriate simply to compare i_d^k to i_d^g because of exchange risk. The Dutch CIA investing in Sweden must buy guilders forward at rate R_f to stay "covered" (maintain his monetary habitat in guilders). Because R_f can differ from R_s, only if the left hand side of equation (5.13) exceeds the right hand side would the CIA choose to invest in Sweden. The difference between the left and right hand sides is the *covered* interest differential—approximated by $f - d_a$, where $f = (R_f = R_s)/R_s$ and $d_a = i_d^g - i_d^k$.

The differential, d_a, in deposit rates of interest facing CIAs can be different from the differential, d, facing commercial traders because CIAs have direct access to the interbank market in deposits. (See Chapter 9.) And $f - d_a$ need only be slightly greater than zero to attract substantial funds to Sweden because, by definition, CIAs are not bearing any exchange risk.

Now consider how the CIA behaves within our hedging pressure model. Suppose that a large consignment of Volvos is contracted by a Dutch importer with payment due in 90 days. Either directly or through his bank as an agent, the Dutch importer *buys* kroner forward and, as the dominant hedger, puts upward pressure on R_f. Then $f - d_a$ becomes positive, thus inducing CIAs to move funds spot to Sweden and *sell* kroner forward to stay covered. Hence CIAs service the commercial traders by selling the kroner the latter are trying to buy with neither party bearing exchange risk!

The CIA need not consciously follow the ebb and flow of commercial trade, but simply stands ready to exploit covered interest differentials as they arise. In so doing, he effectively pools his capital with that of the dominant commercial hedger who is likely to be less liquid. Indeed, one can think of the CIA's acquisition of a Swedish bank deposit as accomplishing indirectly what the hedger would have done to cover his Volvo payments if he were more liquid. The CIA thus acts as a *financial intermediary* in providing less expensive forward cover to the hedger.[18]

The CIA could be the Dutch importer's own bank, which simply buys kronor spot (a deposit to mature in 90 days) as it sells kronor forward to the trader. Or, if the trader's bank found itself somewhat illiquid, it could cover by buying kronor forward in the interbank market. In this latter case, another bank could perform as a CIA by selling kronor forward and buying spot an interest-bearing krona deposit. However the transaction is layered institutionally, covered interest arbitrage remains important in limiting the increase in $f - d_a$, and thus in limiting the bias against the dominant hedger. (See Figure 5.2.)

---

18. Notice that the CIA immediately transmits the merchant's demand for forward kronor into a spot demand (more on this in Chapter 7).

Forward Market Equilibrium
and Interest-Rate Parity

I have argued that the CIA has a comparative advantage in providing forward cover to commerical traders at low cost because the CIA can avoid taking open positions in foreign exchange and thus avoid exchange risk. An incidental general equilibrium effect of providing this forward cover is to align money market rates of interest with the forward premium (or discount): the famous Interest-Rate Parity Theorem or IRPT. Indeed, suppose the international capital market is highly developed such that either potential CIAs have much owned capital on deposit—at rates i_d^g and i_d^k—or they can borrow freely at rates that are not much higher (see technical appendix). Then one would expect that the IRPT would hold:

$$\frac{\bar{R}_f}{R_s}(1 + i_d^k) = 1 + i_d^g \qquad (5.14)$$

where $\bar{R}_f$ is the forward rate that, for a given spot rate R_s, causes (5.14) to be an equality. That is, the actual forward rate $R_f \simeq \bar{R}_f$ such that the covered interest differential is zero. Otherwise, overwhelming flows of capital between the two countries would align R_f/R_s with i_d^k/i_d^g according to equation (5.14). Bias in the forward market, against the dominant illiquid hedger, would be eliminated.

How likely is it that CIAs will have sufficient access to capital, and be able to circumvent exchange controls, so that the IRPT holds? In Chapter 9, I show that the offshore Eurocurrency market provides a way around exchange controls and around imperfections in national capital markets. Equation (5.14) is approximately satisfied when i_d^g and i_d^k are interpreted as interest rates on deposits of Euroguilders and Eurokronor. Eurocurrency trading is now an integral part of the foreign exchange market—both spot and forward—in convertible national monies.

With the fortuitous advent of Eurocurrency trading, one can portray equilibrium in the forward market *as if* the supply of covered arbitrage was virtually perfectly elastic. This is done in Figure 5.1, which is drawn for a given spot rate R_s and given interest rates i_d^g and i_d^k. The resulting R_f is plotted against long (and short) forward positions in foreign exchange. The stable AA schedule represents the net demand for forward exchange by CIAs; whereas the highly variable net demands for forward exchange by commercial traders are represented by the shifting T_1 and T_2 schedules. Equilibrium in the forward market is where the net long (short) position of arbitrageurs equals the net short (long) positions of hedgers.

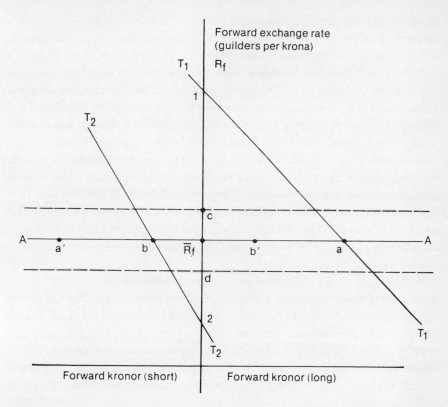

FIGURE 5.1   The forward market under interest-rate parity: Covered interest arbitrageurs and hedgers

NOTE: The forward exchange rate, R_f, is drawn assuming the spot rate, R_s, is given. $\overline{R}_f$ is the parity forward rate defined by equation (5.14) for 90 days hence.

T_1T_1 in Figure 5.1 represents net hedging pressure when illiquid Dutch importers dominate with a strong demand for forward kronor. If arbitrageurs were not in the forward market, the Dutch hedgers would drive R_f upwards towards 1 thereby turning the cost of forward cover against themselves. At point 1 on the vertical axis, enough Dutch hedgers would be driven to the spot market, and Swedish importers would switch to covering in the forward market, that the *net* demand for forward kronor would be zero.

Similarly, T_2T_2 represents a situation where the dominant hedgers are illiquid Swedish importers trying to go short in forward kronor (long in forward guilders). In the absence of CIAs, they would drive R_f against themselves to point 2 on the vertical axis.

However, in the presence of perfectly elastic covered interest arbitrage denoted by the horizontal AA line, R_f is pegged at its parity level $\bar{R}_f$ *despite* variations in hedging pressure (continual shifts in the TT curve). Along T_1T_1 for example, when hedging pressure from Dutch importers predominates, they go long in kronor by the horizontal distance a. However, arbitrageurs would go short by an equal amount, equal to a'. When net hedging pressure comes from Swedish importers (T_2T_2), they would go short in forward kronor by the distance b; whereas CIAs would go long an equal amount, equal to b'. In this way the CIAs reduce the financial costs of the most illiquid of the commercial traders.

It should be stressed that Figure 5.1 only portrays the determination of the *relative* value of R_f for a given R_s. And, in the limiting case where covered interest arbitrage is perfectly elastic along the AA line, R_f is rigidly tied to R_s by the interest differential. But nothing has yet been said to establish the *absolute levels* of R_s and R_f. This remains to be taken up by considering the theory of Purchasing Power Parity in Chapter 6 and the important role of uncovered speculators in Chapter 7.

However, a useful distinction can be drawn between commercial banks in their roles of being sometime speculators and sometime covered interest arbitrageurs. In the short run, the former determines the absolute level of the constellation of spot and forward exchange rates, whereas the latter determines the relative values of spot and forward exchange rates (premiums or discounts) at all terms to maturity.[19] This pooling of capital—by risk-averse and not-so-risk-averse financial enterprises—is crucial for the successful organization of international trade.

Imperfections in the Supply of Arbitrage Funds

Suppose the supply of capital for covered interest arbitrage is neither costless nor perfectly elastic. In Figure 5.1, simple transactions costs, α_a, associated with CIAs taking a forward position are portrayed by the dashed lines on either side of the perfectly elastic supply schedule AA. Roughly speaking, these reflect the spread between bid and ask prices on the forward exchange market. If hedging pressure is T_1T_1, then the illiquid Dutch importer has to pay $\bar{R}_f$ (the unbiased parity rate) plus $\alpha_a\bar{R}_f$. This added cost is represented by the point c on the vertical axis. Normally α_a is between .05 and 0.1 percent of the forward

19. The above algebraic and geometric analysis was encapsulated into a single 90-day interval. Michael Porter has considered the relationship of forward rates to spot for the continuum of forward markets that exist at any point in time. See "A Theoretical and Empirical Framework for Analyzing the Term Structure of Exchange-Rate Expectations," IMF *Staff Papers* (November 1971), pp. 613–42. CIAs can provide liquidity to all forward markets within about two years of time zero. For periods longer than two years, forward markets become thin and the supply of arbitrage capital tends to dry up.

rate (Chapter 1—Technical Note). In times of severe turmoil where forward trading in the interbank market is perceived as being unusually risky—as it was so perceived in 1974 when one or two large banks failed and exchange rates fluctuated sharply—then α_a rose to as much as 0.4 percent. However, usually these costs are close to being negligible for CIAs whose "names" are taken freely in the interbank market for forward foreign exchange.

If there are additional liquidity constraints on CIAs taking positions—borrowing and lending domestic or foreign currencies—then the effective boundaries around the AA line in Figure 5.1 within which R_f fluctuates could be much greater. The algebraic representation of these capital market imperfections is developed more fully in the technical appendix. The percentage spread between borrowing and lending rates in guilders is represented by γ_a; whereas θ_a represents a similar spread in kronor. One would expect γ_a and θ_a to be significantly large if arbitrageurs are confined to taking foreign currency positions in the tightly regulated national money market of the country issuing the currency. That is, all interest-bearing guilder assets (liabilities) must be held in Holland, krona assets in Sweden, and so on across all currencies—as if the Eurocurrency market did not exist.

Figure 5.2 shows a hypothetical profile of the 90-day covered interest differential through time assuming that the imperfections α_a, γ_a, and θ_a are significant. aa' shows the restricted fluctuations in $f - d_a$ when CIAs are in the market; whereas hh' shows the potentially much wider fluctuations from hedging pressure when CIAs are absent. The spread aa' represents twice the total costs of taking a forward position by CIAs before overwhelming arbitrage is induced to limit f—the forward premium. With CIAs in the market, the maximum bias

FIGURE 5.2 The covered interest differential through time: Maximum bias against hedgers

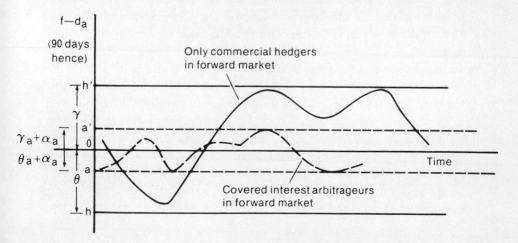

against illiquid Dutch importers is $\alpha_a + \gamma_a$; whereas the maximum bias against illiquid Swedish importers is $\alpha_a + \theta_a$. Exporters and importers can better plan ahead on the knowledge that the cost of forward cover, $f - d_a$, will be confined within predictable limits.

Short-Term Capital Flows
and the Public Interest

From this extensive analysis of hedging against currency risk, what might we conclude about public policy?

Under a system of fixed exchange rates such as that initiated in 1945 under the auspices of the International Monetary Fund, governments were inclined to view free flows of short-term capital as an unmitigated nuisance that, at any time, might cause speculative attacks on a currency and so undermine official parity obligations and exchange-reserve positions. Indeed, the definition of convertibility that member governments were obligated to accept under Article VIII (Chapter 1) specifically left governments free to restrict all capital-account transactions not directly associated with the granting of normal trade credit. Even now many governments with otherwise convertible currencies effectively ban or make short-term capital movements—covered or uncovered—expensive. For example, France and Belgium have, from time to time, split their exchange market; short-term capital outflows are put in a different exchange-rate category from commercial transactions.

Provided changes in official exchange parities were very infrequent, the old Bretton Woods system had a logical rationale because governments did effectively provide forward cover to traders by having the spot rate convincingly fixed through time. Given the shattered state of international capital markets after World War II, covered interest arbitrage may not have worked well anyway, and the speculative threat of unrestrained short-term capital movements was a real one. Prior to the return to full convertibility in 1959, each national central bank was the primary vehicle for making the foreign exchange market: actually matching the needs of exporters and importers at a fixed exchange rate. Private capital movements were *not then* an integral part of this matching process.

However, once central banks withdraw from a strict parity obligation—even to allow exchange-rate fluctuations within a narrow band—the demand for forward cover by commercial traders increases, particularly if spot exchange rates are seen to be unstable. In a period of generally floating exchange rates, unrestricted short-run capital movements become a *vital element* in the matching process. Fortunately, the "accidentally" unregulated Eurocurrency market—described in detail in Chapter 9—allows commercial banks from a variety of countries to borrow or lend foreign exchange from each other at different terms to maturity.

Clearly, the free international movement of short-term capital assumes a more virtuous aspect in a floating exchange-rate regime, and improved efficiency of short-term money markets in each national currency is equally important. While the United States government moved rather vigorously in January of 1974 to remove remaining restrictions on lending abroad by American banks, and to eliminate taxes on the holding of foreign securities by Americans, it remains to be seen whether other governments will take similar measures. Unfortunately, after floating began in 1973, Japan and certain European countries may have intensified their restrictions on residents moving short-term capital out of or into the national currency—even as Eurocurrency transacting among nonresidents remains relatively free (Chapter 9). Perhaps the International Monetary Fund might reconsider its tolerant, even approving, attitude towards such restrictions as it adjusts to a world without official exchange parities.

A TECHNICAL NOTE TO CHAPTER 5:
Covered Interest Arbitrage

This algebraic note formally demonstrates how covered interest arbitrageurs—CIAs—serve to limit fluctuations in the forward premium on foreign exchange, and so limit bias against commercial hedgers using the forward exchange market as portrayed in Figures 5.1 and 5.2.

Representative interest yields and costs facing the CIA over a 90-day interval are denoted by i where

i_d^k is the average krona deposit rate of interest

i_d^g is the average guilder deposit rate of interest

i_b^k is the marginal borrowing cost in Sweden

i_b^g is the marginal borrowing cost in the Netherlands.

These interest variables for the CIA are all comparable in terms and dimension to their r counterparts defined above for the commercial hedger. The i and r interest rates are related by the following inequalities:

$$i_d^k > r_d^k \qquad i_b^k < r_b^k \qquad (5.15)$$
$$i_d^g > r_d^g \qquad i_b^g < r_b^g$$

Inequalities (5.15) imply that the interest spread facing the representative CIA in each national money market is less than that facing commercial hedgers.

$$i_b^g - i_d^g = \gamma_a < \gamma$$
$$i_b^k - i_d^k = \theta_a < \theta \qquad (5.16)$$

where γ_a and θ_a represents the deposit-borrowing spreads available to the CIA in Holland and Sweden respectively.

Hence, the process of covered interest arbitrage will keep the forward premium, f, on kronor within a narrower range than would have been the case in a market where only commercial hedgers are present. Again, temporarily suppose that the cost of forward contracting, α_a, is zero. An *illiquid* Dutch CIA—one who has to borrow funds rather than using owned deposits in guilders—will then be induced to invest in Swedish bank deposits and to cover by purchasing guilders 90 days forward when f rises to the point where

$$(5.17)$$

However, a *liquid* Dutch CIA would move funds to Sweden with less inducement—either a lower deposit rate of interest in Sweden or a smaller forward discount on kronor—because his opportunity cost of capital is lower, i.e., $i_d^g < i_b^g$. Intramarginal pressure to sell kronor forward for guilders develops before f increases as much, as indicated by equation (5.17) where the illiquid Dutch CIAs or Swedish borrowers in Holland are drawn in. Hence equation (5.17) is simply a boundary point where overwhelming covered interest arbitrage develops to sell kronor forward, but not all covered movement of capital from Holland to Sweden need take place at this boundary. It defines a ceiling on the forward premium on kronor such that

$$f \leq i_b^g - i_d^k \qquad (5.17)'$$

Similarly, we define the *maximum* incentive necessary for CIAs to move overwhelming arbitrage funds from Sweden to the Netherlands by:

$$f = i_d^g - i_b^k \qquad (5.18)$$

f cannot fall below $i_d^g - i_b^k$ without inducing a huge movement of funds into the Netherlands with an accompanying demand for forward cover by purchasing kronor forward—these CIAs could be either Swedes placing funds in Holland, or Dutchmen borrowing in Sweden at interest rate i_b^k to deposit in their home country. Either way, the process of forward covering itself puts a floor on the forward premium of kronor over guilders such that

$$f \geq i_d^g - i_b^k. \qquad (5.18)'$$

Combining equations (5.17)' and (5.18)', we can then establish the limits on movement f—the forward premium on kronor—in the presence of unrestricted covered interest arbitrage for a given structure of interest rates:

$$i_d^g - i_b^k \leq f \leq i_b^g - i_d^k \qquad (5.19)$$

Equation (5.19) places somewhat more stringent limits on the range of f than did equation (5.9)—where only commercial hedgers were in the forward market. The economic rationale for the narrowed limits on f is that CIAs can borrow or lend on more attractive terms than can commercial hedgers. With CIAs now in the forward market, let us reconstruct our statistical index of interest-rate parity using deposit rates of interest of the CIAs as the standard of reference. Define the interest differential by $d_a = i_d^g - i_d^k$. Then $f - d_a$ is the covered interest differential "favoring" Sweden over Holland. Substituting from equation (5.16), we establish the range of variation of the covered interest differential

$$- \theta_a \leq f - d_a \leq \gamma_a \qquad (5.20)$$

where θ_a and γ_a represent the lower interest spreads faced by CIAs in comparison to exporters or importers.

Equation (5.20) was derived on the assumption that the brokerage and other charges for forward contracting facing CIAs were zero. If CIAs are largely commercial banks who have direct access to the forward foreign exchange market, then the effective brokerage costs and margin requirements (depending in some measure on name and reputation) may also be less. Denote the cost of forward contracting to CIAs by α_a where $\alpha_a < \alpha$. Then the effective limits on f *seen by commercial hedgers* will be:

$$- (\theta_a + \alpha_a) \leq f - d_a \leq \gamma_a + \alpha_a \qquad (5.21)$$

The range of the covered interest differential $f - d_a$ is enlarged in either direction by α_a before overwhelming movements of covered short-term capital are induced. Remembering that we are encapsulating trading in continuous time into a single representative 90-day interval, commercial hedgers can now take advantage of a system with less bias in the sense that f stays within a narrower range in response to random changes in hedging pressure.[20]

20. A somewhat more general approach to establishing a band within which $f - d_a$ is trapped is to allow the borrowing rates of interest in each national money, i_b^g and i_b^k, to rise with the amount borrowed. See M.F.S. Prachowny, "A Note on Interest Parity and the Supply of Arbitrage Funds," *Journal of Political Economy* (May/June 1970). However, if the number of new arbitrageurs easily attracted is highly elastic, the aggregate result is not significantly different from just assuming a fixed margin between deposit and lending rates of interest for a representative CIA.

6

Purchasing Power Parity

The ways individual banks and merchants use national monies in international pursuits have been sketched. But how does the system fit together to establish equilibrium rates of exchange between commodities and currencies? The insight that national monies tend toward similar purchasing powers over real goods and services provides a valuable general perspective.

The theory of Purchasing Power Parity (PPP) is implicit in the writings of most of the classical authors—David Hume, and particularly David Ricardo on the bullionist controversy. PPP is, however, associated now with the Swedish economist, Gustav Cassel, who used it to explain how the great differential price-level movements in World War I and its aftermath influenced relative exchange rates in the 1920s. Writings in this area have two strands:[1]

1) The extent to which increases in the domestic quantity of money influence the domestic price level—with some possible tradeoff between increases in real output and increases in commodity prices.

2) How the domestic price level is related to foreign commodity prices through the exchange rate.

Because (1) necessitates a complicated exercise in macroeconomic theorizing about national income and its determinants that is beyond the scope of this

1. A useful survey of this literature may be found in Lawrence H. Officer, "The Purchasing-Power-Parity Theory of Exchange Rates: A Review Article," IMF *Staff Papers*, Vol. 23, No. 1 (March 1976), pp. 1–60.

book, I shall truncate the analysis at this stage and concentrate on (2)—as did Cassel who is his own best advocate.

> Our willingness to pay a certain price for foreign money must ultimately and essentially be due to the fact that this money possesses purchasing power as against commodities and services in that foreign country. On the other hand, when we offer so and so much of our own money, we are actually offering a purchasing power as against commodities and services in our own country. Our valuation of a foreign currency in terms of our own, therefore, mainly depends on the relative purchasing power of the two currencies in their respective countries. . . . When two currencies have undergone inflation, the normal rate of exchange will be equal to the old rate multiplied by the quotient of the degree of inflation in the one country and in the other. There will naturally always be found deviations from this new normal rate, and during the transition period these deviations may be expected to be fairly wide. But the rate that has been calculated by the above method must be regarded as the new parity between the currencies, the point of balance towards which, in spite of all temporary fluctuations, the exchange rates will always tend. This parity I call *purchasing power parity*.[2]

In terms of modern price indices—wholesale, consumer, export, and so forth—that were not available in Cassel's time, can we make more precise the circumstances and the time horizons under which a Purchasing Power Parity theory can be expected to hold? What then are the implications of *deviations* from PPP for hedging against currency risk by individual traders in the short run, the need for stabilizing speculation, and comparisons of per capita incomes across rich and poor countries?

The Law of One Price and the Absolute Version of Purchasing Power Parity[3]

Put aside the taking of speculative financial positions in foreign exchange outside of one's home currency habitat until Chapter 7. Are there circumstances where pure commodity arbitrage between two countries is sufficient to establish an equilibrium exchange rate?

Define the purchasing power of money P_t^m to be the reciprocal of some commodity price index. If there are n commodities in the world, this commodity price of money at time t is

2. Gustav Cassel, *Money and Foreign Exchange After 1914* (London: Constable and Co., 1922). This quote was reconstructed from Johan Myhrman's paper, "Experiences of Flexible Exchange Rates in Earlier Periods: Theories, Evidence and a New View," *Scandanavian Journal of Economics* (July 1976), p. 177.

3. I am indebted to Masahiro Kawai for allowing me to adapt this section and the one following from his doctoral dissertation, "International Investment in a World of Flexible Exchange Rates: A Microeconomic Perspective," (Stanford University, 1978).

$$P_t^m = \frac{1}{\displaystyle\sum_{i=1}^{n} a_i P_t^i} \tag{6.1}$$

where P_t^i is the domestic currency price of a unit of good i, and a_i is the importance assigned to commodity i in constructing the domestic price index. Notice that the purchasing power of money declines with general inflation in the prices of commodities.

Similarly, let $^*P_t^i$ be the foreign-currency price of commodity i, with b_i being the set of foreign weights—perhaps reflecting the pattern of final consumption abroad. Then the commodity price of foreign money at time t is

$$^*P_t^m = \frac{1}{\displaystyle\sum_{i=1}^{n} b_i \, ^*P_t^i} \tag{6.2}$$

From Cassel's theory of purchasing power parity in its *absolute* form, we define the PPP exchange rate R_s^{PPP} to be

$$R_s^{PPP} = \frac{^*P_t^m}{P_t^m} = \frac{\displaystyle\sum_{i=1}^{n} a_i P_t^i}{\displaystyle\sum_{i=1}^{n} b_i \, ^*P_t^i} \tag{6.3}$$

The "parity" ratio (R_s^{PPP}) of the purchasing powers of the two monies is expressed in domestic currency (Deutsche marks) per unit of foreign currency (dollars). If R_s is again the spot rate of exchange *actually quoted* in DM per dollar, under what circumstances would R_s^{PPP} exactly equal R_s? The following conditions together are sufficient to guarantee equivalence:

i)   all goods are perfectly tradable with zero transport costs;

ii) there exist no tariffs or other artificial barriers to foreign trade, such as exchange controls;

iii) foreign and domestic goods are perfectly homogeneous within each commodity category in the equations above.

Then assumptions (i), (ii), and (iii) together are sufficient to ensure that the law of one price holds.

$$P_t^i = R_s \, ^*P_t^i \quad \text{for all} \quad i = 1, \dots, n \text{ at any time } t \tag{6.4}$$

That is, perfect commodity arbitrage takes place through the prevailing exchange rate R_s so that prices in dollars are equal to their DM equivalents. But even the law of one price will not ensure that $R_s^{PPP} = R_s$ unless:

iv)   the price indices used in computing the purchasing powers of foreign and domestic monies are the same. That is

$$a_i = b_i \quad \text{for all} \quad i = 1, 2, \ldots, n. \tag{6.5}$$

Under these four very strong conditions, one can then substitute equations (6.4) and (6.5) into equation (6.3) to obtain the absolute version of purchasing power parity where

$$R_s^{PPP} = R_s. \tag{6.6}$$

Indeed, the law of one price is such a strong condition that one can appeal to the relative currency prices of any *single* commodity j, say soybeans, to establish the prevailing R_s that is also equal to the parity rate:

$$R_s = \frac{P_t^j}{{}^*P_t^j} = R_s^{PPP}. \tag{6.7}$$

The law of one price in international commodity arbitrage forces the relative prices of goods in Germany to be the same as they are in America. Hence, it is a matter of indifference as to which commodity one chooses in order to calculate the parity rate of exchange.

The conditions for establishing absolute purchasing power parity are obviously very extreme, and the requisite commodity arbitrage among tradables is likely to be effective only in the long-run sense used analytically in Chapter 1 and discussed below empirically. Thus, in practice, PPP provides only a rough target around which long-run expectations might be able to coalesce.

Counterfactually, suppose for a moment that commodity arbitrage is perfect in the very short run so that equation (6.7) does hold for every commodity. Then there is *no independent role for speculators in exchange-rate determination!* For a given DM price level in Germany, or dollar price level in the U.S., commodity arbitrage in every category will align relative commodity prices *and* exactly determine the spot exchange rate, R_s. Any pressure for, say, price inflation in the United States will result in immediate American efforts to buy goods in Germany. The resulting offer of dollars for DM will drive R_s down exactly proportionately to the price increase in America. This instantaneous commodity arbitrage across the two currencies makes it unnecessary for speculators to carry risky open foreign currency positions in order to stabilize the market for foreign exchange.[4] (Of course, covered interest arbitrageurs would still have a role in establishing the term structure of forward rates of exchange for a given spot rate.)

In practice, however, speculators do have an important role to play precisely because commodity arbitrage across international boundaries is much less than perfect.

Relative Purchasing Power Parity and the "Real" Exchange Rate

Suppose the law of one price, with instantaneous arbitrage in every commodity category, is relaxed. What is an empirically tractable measure of the commodity purchasing power of money in each country that would enable us to predict a long run R_s^{PPP} toward which the actual exchange rate, R_s, might gravitate?

First, one requires national price indices of tradable goods—excluding nontradables such as labor services or very heavy construction materials that cannot enter foreign trade. While the prices of tradable goods are directly linked by international commodity trade, nontradables by definition cannot be so arbitraged.[5] Unfortunately, a simple comprehensive price index for tradable goods is neither currently published by individual countries nor by the International Monetary Fund. Each country publishes a domestic consumer price index (CPI), a GNP deflator, a wholesale price index (WPI), and occasionally an export price index (XPI). Which most closely corresponds to a comprehensive price index of tradable goods?

The CPI includes personal services and housing costs that are clearly nontradable, and the GNP deflator is a comprehensive price index of all goods and services including nontradables. Export price indices are often quite narrowly based because of the way in which countries specialize in international trade. By the process of elimination, I rely mainly on wholesale price indices for cross-country comparisons. Every national WPI is a more or less comprehensive index of agricultural commodities, industrial materials, and manufactured

---

4. The above analysis assumes that the domestic price levels in our two countries are solidly anchored by their respective monetary policies: both the supply and demand for money in each country are determinant as described in Chapter 1. If this were not true for, say, Germany then R_s would be indeterminant—as would the international purchasing power of Deutsche marks—even with perfect commodity arbitrage. Then international currency speculators could be important in determining both R_s and the German price level.

5. Nevertheless, the money prices of nontradables are indirectly determined by international trade—and are an important aspect of overall equilibrium in the foreign exchanges, as we analyze later in this chapter.

goods sold in the domestic economy. Because services are excluded, the great majority of these are at least potentially tradable.

Besides the problem of different commodity weights $(a_i \neq b_i)$ across countries, wholesale and other price indices are always calculated *relative* to some base year. Hence one cannot use them directly to get the absolute purchasing powers of national currencies as per equations (6.1) and (6.2). Rather, the user of national price indices is confronted with

$$PI_1 = \frac{\sum_{i=1}^{n} a_i P_1^i}{\sum_{i=1}^{n} a_i P_0^i} \qquad \text{the domestic (German) price index at} \qquad (6.8)$$
the domestic (German) price index at time one, relative to time zero;

$$PI_1^* = \frac{\sum_{i=1}^{n} b_i {}^* P_1^i}{\sum_{i=1}^{n} b_i {}^* P_0^i} \qquad \text{the foreign (American) price index at} \qquad (6.9)$$
the foreign (American) price index at time one, relative to time zero.

Simply taking the ratio PI_1/PI_1^* would not yield the absolute PPP exchange rate defined by equation (6.3), even if the $a_i = b_i$. Because PI_1 and PI_1^* are price relatives, an additional assumption is required: absolute purchasing power parity must hold in the base period (time zero) such that

$$R_s^0 = \frac{\Sigma a_i P_0^i}{\Sigma b_i {}^* P_0^i} = R_s^{PPP 0} \qquad (6.10)$$

If the actual exchange rate, R_s^0 , prevailing at time zero equals $R_s^{PPP_0}$, one can use that exchange rate and knowledge of subsequent movements in the two countries' price indices to compute R_s^{PPP} at time one:

$$R_s^{PPP} = (PI_1/PI_1^*) \cdot R_s^0 \qquad (6.11)$$

Equation (6.11) yields the *relative version* of purchasing power parity for calculating what the current exchange rate should be vis-à-vis one other country. And, with few exceptions, this relative approximation is how most PPP calculations are made—including those which follow. But the reader should note that the assumptions involved in this approximation are very strong—particularly the need to assume exchange-rate equilibrium (according to PPP) in the base period. However, if we can find a stable base year, or a period of time over which the ratio PI/PI^* moves a great deal, this relative PPP calculation can prove insightful.

This idea of deflating for changes in relative price levels also underlies the increasingly common use of the concept of changes in the real exchange rate. Observing the actual exchange rate R_s at any point in time, and then dividing it by R_s^{PPP}, yields the *real exchange rate*:

$$\bar{R}_s = \frac{R_s}{R_s^{PPP}} = \frac{R_s}{R_s^0} \frac{PI_i^*}{PI_i} . \tag{6.12}$$

By this measure, deviations of $\bar{R}_s$ from unity indicate how the actual exchange rate deviates from purchasing power parity relative to whatever base year (or month) was initially established. Moreover, if $\bar{R}_s$ is plotted through time even without altering the base year of R_s^{PPP}, a good idea of how exchange rates are moving in comparison to domestic price levels can still be obtained. $\bar{R}_s$ then indicates serial changes in the degree of undervaluation or overvaluation of currencies according to the PPP criterion. An observation of $\bar{R}_s > 1$ indicates "undervaluation" of the domestic currency: the domestic price level has fallen relative to the foreign, or that the domestic currency price of foreign exchange R_s has risen with no offsetting movement in relative price levels.

Some Bilateral Statistical Comparisons

Table 6.1 makes a series of relative PPP comparisons on a bilateral basis between each of nine industrial countries—all important trading nations with convertible currencies—and the United States. The base year is 1953 because of the fair tranquility of international price levels following the Korean War, and because no disalignments in exchange rates were obvious after the major European devaluations of 1949—except possibly for France. Annual averages of exchange rates and price levels, all relative to the U.S. dollar, are plotted from 1955 to 1977. Although the consumer price index (CPI) and the export price index (XPI) are presented in Table 6.1, only the wholesale price index (WPI) is utilized in the calculation of the real exchange rate for each country vis-à-vis the United States.

While each country's experience is somewhat unique, what broad trends in the real exchange rate can we discuss from the underlying data? For the period of fixed exchange rates from 1953 to 1970, countries with convertible currencies roughly maintained purchasing power parity with each other. The real rate of exchange with the United States dollar remains in the neighborhood of 1.0 in 1970 for the nine countries in Table 6.1. Commodity arbitrage between each country and the United States seems to be effective in aligning the prices of tradable goods when exchange rates are stable for long periods. The occasional discrete adjustment in exchange rates by Germany, Britain, and the Netherlands offset divergences in internal WPIs vis-à-vis the United States and

TABLE 6.1 Bilateral Comparison of Exchange Rates and Relative Price Indices with the United States (1953 = 100)

	Yearly averages										
	1955	1960	1965	1970	1971	1972	1973	1974	1975	1976	1977
Belgium											
R_s/R_s^o	100.5	99.8	99.4	99.4	97.3	88.1	78.0	78.0	73.6	77.3	71.7
XPI/XPI(USA)	97.0	90.6	86.1	82.3	77.2	76.7	71.6	71.0	65.4	66.0	64.2
WPI/WPI(USA)	100.6	94.4	101.2	98.9	95.1	94.8	94.2	92.5	85.7	87.8	84.7
CPI/CPI(USA)	100.6	99.3	105.7	101.9	101.9	104.1	104.9	106.4	109.9	113.5	114.0
$\bar{R}_s$	1.00	1.06	0.98	1.01	1.02	0.93	0.83	0.84	0.86	0.88	0.85
Canada											
R_s/R_s^o	100.3	98.6	109.7	106.2	102.7	100.8	101.8	99.5	103.5	100.3	108.2
XPI/XPI(USA)	99.7	97.4	99.7	98.1	94.7	95.0	92.9	97.1	96.2	94.8	96.0
WPI/WPI(USA)	98.7	96.3	102.7	102.7	100.6	103.1	110.8	113.8	111.2	110.9	115.6
CPI/CPI(USA)	100.7	100.1	101.8	100.0	98.6	100.0	101.3	101.1	102.7	104.4	105.8
$\bar{R}_s$	1.02	1.02	1.07	1.03	1.04	0.98	0.92	0.87	0.93	0.90	0.94
France											
R_s/R_s^o	100.0	140.1	140.0	158.0	157.4	144.1	127.3	137.4	122.5	136.6	140.4
XPI/XPI(USA)	95.2	123.5	125.3	129.2	132.2	130.0	122.5	121.5	114.0	119.5	125.9
WPI/WPI(USA)	97.7	114.7	125.3	130.7	129.2	129.4	131.2	142.6	123.1	126.4	125.8
CPI/CPI(USA)	101.2	120.3	135.6	136.4	138.0	141.9	143.4	146.9	150.4	155.3	159.6
$\bar{R}_s$	1.02	1.22	1.12	1.21	1.22	1.11	0.97	0.96	0.99	1.08	1.12
Germany											
R_s/R_s^o	100.3	99.4	95.2	86.9	83.0	76.0	63.7	61.8	58.7	60.0	55.3
XPI/XPI(USA)	100.4	100.5	100.8	92.3	91.6	89.7	79.4	71.9	69.0	67.6	65.7
WPI/WPI(USA)	99.7	95.2	99.8	93.4	94.3	92.7	87.3	83.4	79.9	79.3	76.7
CPI/CPI(USA)	101.7	100.7	108.4	99.3	100.2	102.4	103.1	99.4	96.5	95.4	93.0
$\bar{R}_s$	1.01	1.04	0.95	0.93	0.88	0.82	0.73	0.74	0.73	0.76	0.72
Italy											
R_s/R_s^o	100.0	99.3	100.0	100.3	98.9	93.3	93.3	104.1	104.5	133.2	141.2
XPI/XPI(USA)	94.4	82.8	77.4	71.7	73.2	73.3	73.3	81.9	83.0	96.1	110.3
WPI/WPI(USA)	99.6	91.0	102.0	101.3	101.4	101.0	104.5	123.8	123.0	144.5	159.9
CPI/CPI(USA)	105.1	104.3	124.5	117.2	117.7	120.6	125.8	135.0	144.7	159.7	175.3
$\bar{R}_s$								0.84	0.85		0.88

R_s/R_s^o	100.0	99.8	100.2	99.3	96.7	85.4	75.4	80.8	82.3	82.2	74.4
XPI/XPI(USA)	91.0	87.9	70.7	68.9	67.0	64.0	59.4	64.5	58.7	55.4	54.5
WPI/WPI(USA)	97.1	92.2	92.5	90.1	86.5	83.5	85.6	94.6	89.2	89.9	86.0
CPI/CPI(USA)	103.9	103.4	131.5	139.2	141.9	144.1	151.5	167.4	171.9	178.2	180.2
$\bar{R}_s$	*1.03*	*1.08*	*1.08*	*1.10*	*1.12*	*1.02*	*0.88*	*0.85*	*0.92*	*0.91*	*0.87*
Netherlands											
R_s/R_s^o	100.4	99.3	94.8	95.3	92.0	84.5	73.6	70.8	66.6	69.6	64.6
XPI/XPI(USA)	100.3	93.6	91.8	82.3	81.2	79.8	72.9	73.6	68.6	70.5	68.0
WPI/WPI(USA)	103.5	96.9	107.0	102.9	104.6	104.9	99.5	91.5	89.6	91.2	90.1
CPI/CPI(USA)	105.8	109.3	121.1	124.1	128.0	133.6	135.9	134.2	135.5	139.4	139.2
$\bar{R}_s$	*0.97*	*1.02*	*0.89*	*0.93*	*0.88*	*0.81*	*0.74*	*0.77*	*0.74*	*0.76*	*0.72*
Switzerland											
R_s/R_s^o	99.9	100.7	100.9	100.5	96.0	89.1	73.8	69.5	60.2	58.3	56.0
XPI/XPI(USA)	97.7	92.4	101.7	99.4	100.0	102.0	89.7	80.1	73.3	70.5	69.1
WPI/WPI(USA)	100.6	92.8	100.0	95.9	94.9	94.1	92.1	90.1	80.6	76.5	72.3
CPI/CPI(USA)	101.7	97.5	107.5	103.3	105.6	109.1	111.6	110.4	107.9	103.8	98.6
$\bar{R}_s$	*0.99*	*1.08*	*1.01*	*1.05*	*1.01*	*0.95*	*0.80*	*0.77*	*0.75*	*0.76*	*0.77*
United Kingdom											
R_s/R_s^o	100.8	100.2	100.6	117.4	115.1	112.4	114.7	120.3	126.6	155.7	161.1
XPI/XPI(USA)	101.0	101.8	105.3	113.2	115.7	118.4	114.7	115.9	127.4	148.2	166.5
WPI/WPI(USA)	102.5	104.4	115.8	121.7	128.4	129.4	122.9	127.5	144.9	161.2	183.2
CPI/CPI(USA)	105.1	107.0	118.3	120.2	126.1	130.9	134.4	140.5	160.0	176.3	191.6
$\bar{R}_s$	*0.98*	*0.96*	*0.87*	*0.96*	*0.90*	*0.87*	*0.93*	*0.94*	*0.87*	*0.96*	*0.88*

SOURCE: IMF, *International Financial Statistics* (May/June 1977, Apr. 1978) as compiled by M. Kawai, "International Investment in a World of Flexible Exchange Rates: A Microeconomic Perspective" (Stanford University Ph.D. dissertation, 1978).

SYMBOLS: R_s^o = domestic currency/U.S. dollars (1953).
XPI = export price index (1953 = 100).
CPI = consumer price index (1953 = 100).
R_s = domestic currency/U.S. dollars (current).
WPI = wholesale price index (1953 = 100).

$$\bar{R}_s = \frac{R_s}{R_s^0} \cdot \frac{WPI(USA)}{WPI}$$

equals the real bilateral exchange rate (as defined by equation 6.12 in the text) with the United States.
$\bar{R}_s < 1.00$ implies real appreciation of the domestic currency in comparison to 1953.

served to bring their real dollar exchange rates closer to unity. The only seriously disaligned rate in 1970 (by this criterion) was $\overline{R}_s = 1.21$ for France: this reflects in part the surprise discrete devaluation of the franc in 1969 that left it somewhat undervalued. Earlier French devaluations in the late 1950s also suggest that the franc may not have been in equilibrium in 1953, as required by our relative PPP computational technique.

More serious and more general disalignments in real exchange rates become apparent with the advent of quasifixed and then freely floating nominal exchange rates after 1970. In particular, a group of European currencies—of which Germany, the Netherlands, and Switzerland are the strongest representatives in Table 6.1—all appreciated dramatically vis-à-vis the American dollar. Their $\overline{R}_s$ fell to between 0.72 and 0.77 in 1977, and then fell even further in 1978.

These results imply that nominal exchange rate changes (movements in R_s) in large measure need not offset internal price movements so as to maintain purchasing power parity when the direction of exchange-rate fluctuations cannot be easily predicted. Effective commodity arbitrage to align international prices has become more difficult after the fixed-exchange aspect of the Bretton Woods Agreements broke down.

The relative version of PPP performs most impressively, however, when inflation in a single country is extraordinarily high vis-à-vis the outside world. Then statistical worries about obsolete base-year weights, or even the difference between a tradable goods price index (WPI) versus a more comprehensive consumer price index become trivial. For the great German inflation from 1920 to 1923, Jacob Frenkel has plotted the DM/$ exchange rate against (1) a wholesale price index, and (2) a more comprehensive consumer cost-of-living index for Germany. The results are presented on a logarithmic scale in Figure 6.1 on which each variable increased more than several hundred thousand fold!

One can see that the statistical correlation between Germany's exchange rate and internal price level was close to unity—without presuming cause and effect to flow in one direction or another.[6] Even so the WPI is slightly better correlated with the exchange rate than the CPI because the latter contains nontradable services.

In summary, purchasing power parity applied to tradable goods seems to work best in extreme cases where

    i)   we have a long period of exchange stability with currency convertibility that allows uninhibited commodity arbitrage to align prices; or

6. The usual presumption is that the uncontrolled printing of marks in Germany led to domestic price inflation and exchange depreciation.

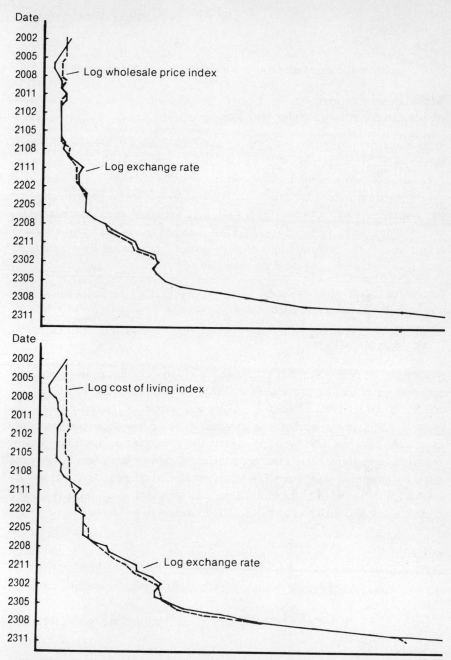

FIGURE 6.1 German price indices and exchange rates under hyperinflation: 1920–1923

NOTE: Vertical axes represent time span from February 1920 to November 1923. The horizontal axes are logarithmic scales where prices (marks) and the cost of foreign exchange (marks per dollar) increase several hundred thousand times.

SOURCE: Figures reproduced without alteration from Jacob A. Frenkel, "A Monetary Approach to the Exchange Rate: Doctrinal Aspects and Empirical Evidence," *Scandanavian Journal of Economics* (July 1976), p. 215.

ii)   price (monetary) inflation is proportionately so high that it must dominate
exchange-rate movements despite imperfections in commodity arbitrage.

Multilateral Comparisons
of Effective Exchange Rates and Prices

The analysis just given, and data presented in Table 6.1, relied on bilateral
measures of exchange rates that are commonly quoted in the financial press
between any two countries. Movements in real exchange rates, measuring
deviations from purchasing power parity, were also bilateral because only the
two countries' internal prices (WPI) were used to deflate movements in nominal exchange rates. However, *multilateral* comparisons of exchange rates and
prices among the principal industrial countries[7] with convertible currencies
may give somewhat more accurate measures of

i)   the persistency of commodity arbitrage in maintaining purchasing power parity
in the tradables sector; and

ii)   the degree of undervaluation or overvaluation of currencies as measured by
deviations from PPP.

First, let us define the *effective* nominal exchange rate for country j against a
specified set of trading partners. In constructing such an index, one could use
weights based on bilateral flows of exports and imports of country j with every
partner. Each country's set of weights would then be unique, depending on its
own trade patterns. The problem is that this procedure does not take export
competition in third markets into account: third markets being largely countries
with inconvertible currencies—socialist or less developed—that cannot be
meaningfully included in the multilateral comparison. Instead, let us develop a
methodology also used by Pentti Kouri[8] and define

$$\alpha_i(t) = \frac{\text{country } i\text{'s total exports (US\$) in year } t}{10 \text{ countries' total exports (US\$) in year } t}$$

$_jR_s$ =   the current spot rate: country j's currency/U.S. dollars

$_jR_s^m$ =   the current multilateral exchange rate of country j with the other nine
countries

With the α_i, a weighted product of ten nominal exchange rates (all measured
with respect to the U.S. dollar) is constructed in equation (6.13) below. For the

7. The ten listed in Table 6.2.
8. Pentti J.K. Kouri and Jorge Braga de Macedo, "Exchange Rates and the International Adjustment Process," *Brookings Papers on Economic Activity*, No. 1 (1978), p. 119.

United States, $_iR_s^{\alpha i}$ is always unity in this index, reflecting the fact that there are only nine independent exchange rates in a ten-country world.[9] Our multilateral nominal exchange for country j is then

$$_jR_s^m = {}_jR_s \Big/ \prod_{i=1}^{10} {}_iR_s^{\alpha i}. \tag{6.13}$$

By itself, the multilateral exchange rate $_jR_s^m$ has no easy intuitive interpretation: it corresponds to no exchange rate quoted on an open market and is a hodge-podge of different currency units. Only when $_jR_s^m$ is judged with respect to some benchmark date is it a useful concept. Let $_jR_0^m$ be a benchmark multilateral exchange rate, as defined by equation (6.13), for some past date, say 1953. Then the *effective* nominal exchange rate can be defined as:[10]

$$_jR_s^{eff} = {}_jR_s^m / {}_jR_0^m. \tag{6.14}$$

Insofar as this effective rate differs from 100 with the passage of time, it measures how country j's nominal exchange rate has changed against the other nine trading partners relative to some base year (1953). For example, if the Deutsche mark has appreciated in nominal terms against the other nine currencies since 1953, R_s^{eff} for Germany will be less than 100. In Table 6.2 the reader can refer to the first row for each country to get measures of its effective nominal exchange rate. The United States is now entered symmetrically with the other nine countries—unlike the purely bilateral comparisons of Table 6.1. And effective exchange rates have moved very substantially. From 1953 to 1976, depreciations occurred of the order of 70 percent for Britain and 50 percent for France; whereas the Swiss franc and Deutsche mark appreciated of the order of 35 percent, with other countries scattered in between.

But these large changes in effective rates are strictly nominal. By the criterion of purchasing power parity, how should "real" depreciations or appreciations be calculated?

Again following Kouri's procedure, define the *international price level*, P_{ALL}, to be:

$$P_{ALL} = \prod_{i=1}^{10} P_i^{\alpha i} \tag{6.15}$$

where P_i is now to be interpreted as an aggregative index of prices in the national currency of country i, and each index is based on 1953 = 100. Thus P_{ALL} is a geometric mean index of prices (either export, or wholesale, or consumer) for all ten countries across ten currencies.

9. The "Nth" currency problem discussed at length in Chapter 2.
10. A more thorough discussion of this concept can be found in R. Rhomberg, "Indices of Effective Exchange Rates," IMF *Staff Papers*, Vol. 23 (March 1976), pp. 88–112.

TABLE 6.2 A Multilateral Comparison of Effective Exchange Rates and Price Indices Among Ten Countries (1953 = 100)

						Yearly averages					
	1955	1960	1965	1970	1971	1972	1973	1974	1975	1976	1977
Belgium											
R_s^{eff}	100.3	96.8	97.3	96.4	96.1	92.4	88.8	87.6	84.0	84.1	80.2
XPI/XPI(All)	98.2	91.6	89.5	89.2	84.7	85.8	85.0	86.9	81.9	82.5	78.5
WPI/WPI(All)	100.4	95.5	98.3	98.7	95.1	95.7	97.3	95.4	90.5	91.6	88.0
CPI/CPI(All)	98.6	96.6	95.5	94.9	93.5	93.7	93.4	93.7	95.0	96.5	94.9
$\bar{R}_s^{eff}$	1.00	1.01	0.99	0.98	1.01	0.97	0.91	0.92	0.93	0.92	0.91
Canada											
R_s^{eff}	100.1	95.7	107.4	103.0	101.5	105.7	115.9	111.8	118.1	109.2	120.9
XPI/XPI(All)	100.8	98.1	103.3	106.5	105.0	106.7	111.3	119.7	121.2	119.2	119.4
WPI/WPI(All)	98.7	97.5	99.7	102.6	100.7	104.3	114.5	117.5	117.5	115.8	119.9
CPI/CPI(All)	98.8	97.3	92.1	93.0	90.3	90.0	90.2	89.1	88.7	88.7	88.0
$\bar{R}_s^{eff}$	1.01	0.98	1.08	1.00	1.01	1.01	1.01	0.95	1.01	0.94	1.01
France											
R_s^{eff}	99.8	135.9	137.1	153.2	155.6	151.2	144.9	154.4	139.8	148.7	156.9
XPI/XPI(All)	96.4	125.1	130.5	140.5	145.3	144.5	145.2	148.5	143.3	150.1	155.4
WPI/WPI(All)	97.4	116.0	121.4	130.4	129.1	130.7	135.6	147.0	129.9	131.9	130.6
CPI/CPI(All)	99.4	117.1	122.7	127.1	126.6	127.8	127.9	129.5	130.2	132.2	133.0
$\bar{R}_s^{eff}$	1.02	1.17	1.13	1.17	1.20	1.16	1.07	1.05	1.08	1.13	1.20
Germany											
R_s^{eff}	100.1	96.4	93.2	84.3	82.0	79.7	72.6	69.4	66.9	65.4	61.9
XPI/XPI(All)	101.4	101.5	104.7	100.0	100.2	99.4	94.0	87.6	85.9	84.1	80.5
WPI/WPI(All)	99.6	96.2	96.7	93.1	94.2	93.5	90.2	85.9	84.3	82.7	79.6
CPI/CPI(All)	99.8	98.1	98.2	92.4	91.9	92.2	91.9	87.6	83.4	81.1	77.4
$\bar{R}_s^{eff}$	1.01	1.00	0.96	0.91	0.87	0.85	0.80	0.81	0.79	0.79	0.78
Italy											
R_s^{eff}	99.8	96.4	97.9	97.3	97.8	97.9	106.2	116.9	119.2	145.0	157.8
XPI/XPI(All)	95.3	83.6	80.3	77.6	79.9	81.1	86.7	99.7	103.3	119.4	134.8
WPI/WPI(All)	99.4	92.0	98.7	100.9	101.1	101.8	107.9	127.6	129.6	150.5	165.7
CPI/CPI(All)	103.1	101.4	112.4	108.9	107.8	108.4	111.9	118.7	124.9	135.6	145.7
$\bar{R}_s^{eff}$										0.96	0.95

Japan

R_s^{eff}	99.8	96.8	98.1	96.3	95.3	88.1	85.6	90.8	93.9	89.5	83.2
XPI/XPI(All)	91.9	88.7	73.3	74.7	73.2	70.8	70.2	78.6	73.1	68.9	67.3
WPI/WPI(All)	96.9	93.1	89.6	89.8	86.4	84.3	88.3	97.5	94.0	93.4	89.2
CPI/CPI(All)	103.3	99.9	116.9	127.4	127.7	126.7	132.1	146.2	147.1	149.5	148.4
$\bar{R}_s^{eff}$	1.03	1.04	1.09	1.07	1.10	1.05	0.97	0.93	1.00	0.96	0.93

Netherlands

R_s^{eff}	100.2	96.4	92.9	92.4	91.0	88.7	83.9	79.6	76.0	75.8	72.3
XPI/XPI(All)	101.3	94.5	95.3	89.5	88.7	88.6	85.6	89.2	85.8	87.3	84.6
WPI/WPI(All)	103.0	98.1	103.4	101.6	104.0	105.9	102.9	93.5	94.2	95.3	93.5
CPI/CPI(All)	103.8	106.3	109.3	115.5	117.1	120.2	121.0	118.0	117.0	118.7	116.0
$\bar{R}_s^{eff}$	0.97	0.98	0.90	0.91	0.88	0.84	0.82	0.85	0.81	0.80	0.77

Switzerland

R_s^{eff}	99.7	97.7	98.8	97.5	94.8	93.4	84.1	78.0	68.7	63.5	62.6
XPI/XPI(All)	99.5	92.9	104.8	108.2	109.8	113.5	106.2	98.2	91.6	87.9	84.5
WPI/WPI(All)	100.4	93.9	96.9	95.7	94.7	95.0	95.1	92.9	84.9	79.7	75.0
WPI/CPI(All)	99.6	94.9	97.0	96.2	96.7	98.0	99.4	97.1	93.2	88.1	82.0
$\bar{R}_s^{eff}$	0.99	1.04	1.02	1.02	1.00	0.98	0.88	0.84	0.81	0.80	0.83

United Kingdom

R_s^{eff}	100.6	97.2	98.5	113.9	113.8	118.1	130.8	135.2	145.1	170.4	180.3
XPI/XPI(All)	101.9	102.8	109.1	127.6	131.6	137.3	138.5	141.3	158.5	183.9	205.1
WPI/WPI(All)	102.3	105.6	112.5	121.7	128.7	131.0	127.2	132.0	153.3	168.7	190.1
CPI/CPI(All)	103.0	103.9	106.8	111.8	115.5	117.7	119.7	123.6	138.1	149.8	159.3
$\bar{R}_s^{eff}$	0.98	0.92	0.88	0.94	0.88	0.90	1.03	1.02	0.95	1.01	0.95

U.S.A.

R_s^{eff}	99.8	97.0	97.9	97.0	98.8	104.9	113.9	112.3	114.1	108.9	111.8
XPI/XPI(All)	101.0	100.8	103.8	108.3	109.4	110.8	118.2	121.8	124.5	123.8	122.3
WPI/WPI(All)	99.8	101.1	96.9	99.7	99.9	100.9	103.2	103.1	105.5	104.3	103.8
CPI/CPI(All)	98.1	97.2	90.4	93.1	91.6	89.9	89.1	88.0	86.4	85.0	83.2
$\bar{R}_s^{eff}$	1.00	0.99	1.01	0.97	0.99	1.04	1.10	1.09	1.08	1.04	1.08

SOURCE: IMF, *International Financial Statistics* (May/June 1977) as compiled by M. Kawai, "International Investment in a World of Flexible Exchange Rates," op. cit.

SYMBOLS: R_s^m = multilateral exchange rate vis-à-vis 10 countries (1953).

R_s^m = multilateral current exchange rate vis-à-vis 10 countries (current).

R_s^{eff} = $.R_s^m/R_s^m$ = effective exchange rate.
XPI = export price index (1953 = 100).

WPI = wholesale price index (1953 = 100).
CPI = consumer price index (1953 = 100).
ALL = weighted average of 10 countries.

$$\bar{R}_s^{eff} = R_s^{eff} \cdot \frac{WPI_{ALL}}{WPI_j}.$$

equals the real effective exchange rate with 9 countries. $\bar{R}_s^{eff} < 1.0$ implies real appreciation since 1953.

In Table 6.2 each country's export, wholesale, or consumer price index is deflated by P_{ALL} . The resulting P_j/P_{ALL} is now a multilateral measure of country j's relative price level within the group of ten convertible currencies. The United States is now treated symmetrically with the other nine countries and had a rate of inflation about equal to the geometric mean for the group. If one focuses on the WPIs, Britain, France, and Italy had the highest rates of inflation in comparison to the rest of the group; whereas the relative price levels of Germany and Switzerland have fallen the most since 1953.

The final step is to calculate the *real effective exchange rate*, $_j\overline{R}_s^{eff}$, for each country j.[11] Again using wholesale price indices as our most basic measure of the prices of "tradable" goods, let us deflate the nominal effective exchange rate with WPI_j/WPI_{ALL} to get

$$_j\overline{R}_s^{eff} = {_j}R_s^{eff} \cdot \frac{WPI_{ALL}}{WPI_j}. \tag{6.16}$$

Again, $_jR_s^{eff}$ is the effective nominal exchange rate for country j, using 1953 for a base year as required by the relative PPP criterion. Similarly, WPI_{ALL} and WPI are price relatives with a 1953 base. Hence, deviations of $_j\overline{R}_s^{eff}$ from unity measure the effective disalignment of national price levels by a PPP standard put on a multilateral (trade weighted) basis. These deviations from relative PPP, as presented in Table 6.2, are somewhat less than the purely bilateral deviations calculated in Table 6.1. In particular, the real appreciation of a cluster of European currencies is less pronounced (but still substantial) in the multilateral as compared to the bilateral case. It is appropriate to give the relatively easy commodity arbitrage within Europe a higher weight than permitted in a purely bilateral comparison with the United States.

Equally striking, however, Table 6.2 shows that large movements in nominal exchange rates—deviations of R_s^{eff} from 100—for Britain and Italy have been eventually offset by relative price movements so as to leave their real effective exchange rates close to unity. In the long run, it seems reasonable to expect that purchasing power parity (modified for statistical errors of measurement) will eventually prevail. And the strength of the underlying commodity arbitrage is best seen on a multilateral rather than a bilateral basis.[12]

Would-be foreign exchange speculators watch out, however! The PPP criterion, where effective real exchange rates are eventually driven back towards unity, can be satisfied by *either* a change in nominal exchange rates *or* a movement in aggregate domestic prices within a country. Whereas Table 6.2

---

11. Pentti Kouri, op. cit. p. 119.
12. Of course, there can be exceptions. Canada's real effective exchange rate might be better calculated on a bilateral basis because the United States so dominates Canadian foreign trade.

seems to suggest that the Swiss franc unduly appreciated in 1976 and 1977, this discrepancy can be eliminated by a gradual fall in the Swiss price level (vis-à-vis the other nine trading countries) without any movement in the effective nominal exchange rate of Switzerland.

Deviations from the Law of One Price Under Fluctuating Exchange Rates

Because the data in Tables 6.1 and 6.2 are based on annual averages of exchange rates and price levels, they conceal the magnitude of quarterly and monthly fluctuations in real exchange rates. Among the major industrial countries with convertible currencies, substantial short-run movements in nominal exchange rates of the order 10 to 20 percent over the course of a few months have not been uncommon since floating began in February 1973.[13] When such short-run movements are neither sustained nor predictable in one direction or another, commodity arbitrage seems quite uncapable of maintaining constancy in real exchange rates. Substantial and continually changing deviations from PPP are commonplace. For individual tradable commodities, violations in the "law of one price" can be striking.

In Chapter 4, a distinction was made between tradables I and tradables II in the invoicing of international trade. The former were manufactured goods likely to be invoiced in the home currency if convertible, while the latter were homogeneous primary commodities more likely to be invoiced in U.S. dollars. Transportation costs aside, if the domestic currency depreciates in international markets, immediate pressure develops to increase the domestic currency price of both importables and exportables belonging to tradables II. Their dollar prices are often registered on an international commodity exchange such as the Chicago Board of Trade. Stocks of domestic tradables would soon leave the country if their prices did not rise to reflect a depreciation. Their owners are price takers and can sell as much as they want at the given international price, but they cannot control that price.

On the other hand, exports (and possible import substitutes) of tradables I are invoiced in domestic currency and are consciously maintained at fairly rigid prices—given the capacity of many manufacturing enterprises to be price setters rather than price takers. A depreciation is less likely to force an immediate increase in the domestic currency prices of these goods, particularly if the firm thinks the exchange-rate change may be transitory.

13. The reader is referred back to Figure 1.1 (Chapter 1) for a more general picture of cyclical short-run movements in nominal exchange rates.

In the tradable goods sector, therefore, we might distinguish three time horizons of response to an unanticipated exchange-rate depreciation:

1) *Momentary equilibrium* where existing stocks and domestic selling prices of tradables cannot be revalued.

2) A *short run* of a few days where domestic selling prices of tradables II rise by the full amount of the depreciation.

3) An *intermediate run* of a few months (years) over which the domestic-currency prices of heterogeneous tradables I rise by the full amount of depreciation— depending on the competitive advantage perceived by domestic manufactures of maintaining an unchanged price to domestic and overseas customers.

For an idea of *differential* price movements among various commodities on a monthly or quarterly basis, it is necessary to distinguish tradables I from tradables II. Unfortunately, completely comparable commodity categories for cross-country comparisons are virtually impossible to find. Nations differ too much in the way they collect statistics. Nevertheless, Peter Isard has compared relative movements of the dollar prices of German goods to their American equivalents—disaggregated down to the 2 and 3 digit levels of the SITC classification.[14] The results for Paper Products and Apparel are presented in Figure 6.2. In response to short-run exchange fluctuations, the quoted prices in DM for Apparel made in Germany seem quite rigid, as if they were tradables I. Hence their relative dollar prices track the dollar/DM exchange rate rather closely. No tendency for the law of one price to hold over months, or even years, is discernable.

Although the category Paper Products is heterogeneous, its profile of dollar prices is more akin to tradables II. While insensitive to very short-run exchange

TABLE 6.3   Exchange Rates and Relative Export Price Indices for Selected Machinery Categories (1970 = 100)

	German dollar price/U.S. dollar price						
	Exchange rate	Internal combustion engines	Agricultural tilling machinery	Office calculating machines	Metalworking machinery	Pumps	Forklift trucks
June 1970	100	100	100	100	100	100	100
June 1971	103.4	104.1	108.9	110.3	110.4	106.2	111.1
June 1972	114.6	119.8	116.6	114.4	125.2	121.2	125.6
June 1973	140.9	155.5	136.2	139.3	153.8	144.7	159.7
June 1974	143.9	147.7	138.1	146.0	144.3	151.7	145.1
June 1975	155.2	148.1	122.5	147.7	141.8	139.3	139.1

SOURCE: Peter Isard, *American Economic Review* (Dec. 1977), p. 946.

14. Peter Isard, "How Far Can We Push the Law of One Price?" *American Economic Review* (December 1977), pp. 942–48.

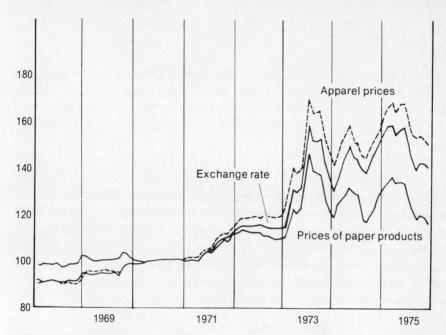

FIGURE 6.2 Dollar price indices and exchange rates: Germany versus the United States (1970 = 100).

SOURCE: Peter Isard, *American Economic Review* (Dec. 1977), p. 944.

fluctuations, their DM price tends to fall with the passage of time given the net appreciation of the German currency. Hence, their dollar price seems to be regressing back towards 100, the American level. The pressure from commodity arbitrage is more visible.

For goods that are clearly brand-specific tradables I, one can disaggregate to the much finer 4 and 5 digit SITC level and still find that the law of one price does not hold. In Table 6.3, Isard's data on the relative dollar prices of various specific classes of German machinery are reproduced. The net appreciation of the DM has simply carried German machinery prices in dollars with it. Hence Isard's conclusion regarding tradables I:

> Students exposed to the pure theory of international trade have been seduced by visions of an imaginary world with few goods, each typically produced by several countries but nevertheless homogeneous. . . . In reality the law of one price is flagrantly and systematically violated by empirical data. . . . Moreover, these relative price effects seem to persist for at least several years and cannot be shrugged off as transitory . . . the products of different countries exhibit relative price behavior which marks them as differentiated products, rather than near-perfect substitutes.[15]

15. Peter Isard, op. cit. p. 942.

In the long run, however, where differential price movements are large, unidirectional and hence easily predicted, internal price-level and exchange-rate movements do compensate each other—as Frenkel's data on German inflation in the 1920s, and many studies of high-inflation in less developed countries, would suggest. Until a more robust theory replaces it, I shall assume that purchasing power parity among tradable goods tends to hold in the long run in the absence of overt impediments to trade and among countries with convertible currencies.

But for tradables I especially, deviations from PPP over months or even years can be very substantial under floating exchange rates. Because commodity arbitrage is so imperfect in this short run, it cannot be relied on to contain nominal exchange-rate movements within the predictable and narrow limits suggested by the law of one price. Thus economists have necessarily fallen back on asset-market or money-market theories of exchange-rate formation in the short run. These new theories require careful incorporation of speculative capital flows across different currencies, and are taken up below in Chapters 7 and 8 where the key role of speculators is spelled out.

Implications for Trader Hedging

These empirical data have strong microeconomic implications for hedging by individual firms against exchange-rate fluctuations. Consider a German importer of American farm machinery, who owes 100 dollars on machinery still to be delivered or already in inventory. There is a certain optimal trade-off between relying on inventory valuation adjustment or covering forward (by a forward or spot exchange transaction) against the date on which the 100 dollars is to be paid. We showed in Chapter 4 that the more perfectly correlated the DM exchange rate and the DM price of machinery, the more the importer could rely on inventory adjustments and the less on forward covering.

With the advent of generally floating exchange rates at the beginning of 1973, the compensating correlations between goods prices and exchange-rate movements declined—with the decline being more severe in European-American trade. This lack of correlation arises out of the unexpected nature of exchange-rate fluctuations that business firms deem to be sufficiently impermanent to make inventory valuation adjustments not worthwhile. Hence, the hedging balance is shifted towards more forward covering. For example, instead of buying only 45 dollars forward, the German importer of farm machinery might purchase 70 dollars against his 100 dollar obligation. And actual forward covering has increased since January 1973 as Grassman's Swedish data (Chapter 5) seem to indicate.

However, it should be stressed that it is not exchange-rate flexibility *per se* that increases the demand for forward cover; *rather it is departures from purchasing power parity* in the markets for individual traded commodities. Because short-run exchange-rate fluctuations since 1973 have been largely unpredictable, forward exchange rates have been poor predictors of future spot rates. (See the technical note to Chapter 1.) Hence, forward covering becomes all the more necessary.[16]

On the other hand, there are circumstances where exchange-rate changes are quite predictable: departures from PPP are minor and forward rates of exchange are good estimators of future spot rates. Suppose a currency is depreciating fairly steadily relative to the outside world because of a higher domestic inflation. But this depreciation is expected and the forward price of foreign currency goes to a sharp premium, domestic nominal rates of interest rise equivalently above foreign rates, *and* commodity prices are continuously adjusted upwards. Given the domestic price inflation, the exchange depreciation has the effect of maintaining PPP and allowing importers to more easily hedge by inventory valuation adjustment. Moreover, the premium on forward foreign exchange (accurately reflecting inflation) also reduces the demand for forward cover. A smooth series of planned mini-devaluations in inflation-prone countries such as Brazil, Chile, and Colombia in certain intervals in the postwar period have allowed importers to hedge primarily through adjustments in the value of their inventories rather than relying mainly on forward cover.

Per Capita Income Comparisons and Exchange-Rate Conversions

The theory of purchasing power parity was initially used by such writers as Gustav Cassel[17] and J.M. Keynes[18] to predict equilibrium exchange rates from data on commodity prices in the days before national income accounting data on consumption, investment, GNP, and so on. Now, more often than not, market exchange rates are used to compare national incomes—particularly per capita incomes—across countries. Any journalist can now open the IMF's *International Financial Statistics*, pick out Switzerland's GNP measured in current Swiss francs, or Indonesia's GNP measured in current rupiahs, or American GNP measured in current dollars. For any given day (or average over a year), our same journalist from the same reference book can find a dollar/rupiah exchange quotation, a dollar/Swiss franc exchange rate, and then a rupiah/Swiss franc exchange rate by simply cross multiplying. To make cross-

16. One difficult question not addressed in this book is whether deviations from purchasing power parity lead to a significant decline in the microeconomic efficiency of foreign trade.
17. Gustav Cassel, op. cit.
18. J.M. Keynes, *A Tract on Monetary Reform* (New York: Macmillan, 1923), Chapter 3.

country comparisons, he then converts the Indonesian and Swiss GNPs to a common currency—say American dollars. Not too much further effort is required to get gross population estimates for each of the three countries to convert his dollar GNP estimates into per capita terms.

Is our reporter now well prepared statistically to write his article on the international distribution of income and wealth? Articles abound in the popular press and in the more technical journals that use current exchange rates to compare per capita incomes. Going beyond this simple technique may be both expensive and difficult. The limitations of using a straight exchange-rate conversion can be conveniently discussed using a shorter and a longer time horizon:

1)   What are the implications of sharp exchange-rate fluctuations for comparing national incomes of industrial countries whose wealths per capita are not greatly dissimilar?

2)   What kind of corrections must be applied to cross-section comparisons of rich and poor countries at any one point in time?

Let us first consider the issues posed by annual exchange-rate fluctuations among countries with convertible currencies of the five to twenty-five percent magnitudes experienced in the 1973 to 1978 period. We established in Tables 6.1 and 6.2 that such exchange fluctuations did not seem to fully offset movements in internal prices. To some considerable extent, exchange-rate changes were associated with movements that led to further deviations from purchasing power parity in the tradable goods sector. Apparently, the unexpected character of these short-run fluctuations led to continual violations of the law of one price among tradable goods—although the "correct" exchange rate could not be determined by our crude statistical methods based on the relative version of PPP. For nontradables, there is even less reason to believe that these sharp and reversible fluctuations were bringing national price levels into closer alignment.

Hence, when the Swiss franc appreciated from US$0.30 in January of 1974 to US$0.41 in January of 1975—over a twenty-five percent increase, and when end-of-the-year exchange rates were used to compare Swiss national income with American for 1974, it suddenly appeared as if the Swiss leapt far ahead of the United States in the per capita national income derby. Commentators noted a similar dramatic improvement in Sweden's position for 1974 (the krona having appreciated similarly vis-à-vis the dollar) over 1973. But since purchasing power parity was being violated, it was quite unreasonable to make a twenty-five percent upward adjustment in European real incomes relative to the United States for 1974. What the correct comparison should be remains very difficult to calculate—requiring a rather thorough and expensive comparison of the same basket of commodities in America as compared to Europe.[19] Swiss or Swedish national incomes per capita might even be higher than American in this more fundamental statistical sense for 1973 or 1974. However, Swiss real national income per capita did not rise suddenly by twenty-five percent relative to American in 1974. In general, short-run movements in the exchange rate have to be discounted in cross-country comparisons.

Putting aside short-run fluctuations in the foreign exchanges, a much higher order-of-magnitude correction is required when comparing national incomes of rich and poor countries—point (2) mentioned earlier. The relative price of nontradables—mainly services—is much lower in poor countries than in wealthy ones. This striking empirical regularity reflects the fact that technical progress in the wealthy economies is concentrated on goods and services that are internationally tradable—see Table 10.1 (Chapter 10) for some evidence on this point. Because expenditures on nontradables amount to about forty percent of GNP in most countries,[20] a straight conversion based on market exchange rates (that tend to align the prices of tradable goods) will greatly understate the "real" per capita incomes of the poorest countries vis-à-vis the wealthier ones.[21]

But how does one correctly price national outputs in diverse countries to obtain comparable income figures that are independent of market exchange rates? For ten representative countries where the relevant statistical information was available, Kravis et al. constructed an average set of international prices over tradable and nontradable goods:

> The world price structure comprises a set of average international prices based on the price and quantity structures of the ten countries included. Each of these ten countries plays a role in determining the structure of international prices, with allowances made for the extent to which each may be considered to represent excluded countries. The international prices have been used to value the quantities of each of the ten countries. The international prices and the product values they are used to obtain are expressed in "international dollars" (I$). An international dollar has the same overall purchasing power as a U.S. dollar for GDP as a whole, but the relative prices correspond to average "world" relative prices rather than to U.S. relative prices. Thus, the purchasing power of an international dollar over footwear or transport equipment, for example, is not the same as that of a U.S. dollar.[22]

19. Such data do now exist, but only for the year 1970 and for a small number of countries. See Table 6.4.
20. I. Kravis, Z. Kennessey, A. Heston, and R. Summers, A System of International Comparisons of Gross Product and Purchasing Power (Baltimore, Md.: Johns Hopkins University Press, 1975).
21. Bela Balassa, "The Purchasing-Power Parity Doctrine: A Reappraisal." Journal of Political Economy, Vol. 72 (1964), pp. 584–96, reprinted in R. Cooper (ed.) International Finance (New York: Penguin, 1969).
22. Kravis et al., op. cit., p. 8.

The results of the huge research project necessary to make such calculations are presented without alteration in Table 6.4 for 1970. Line 12 presents real Gross Domestic Product estimates using a common set of international prices as described above. Line 13 presents much simpler alternative GDP estimates based on a straight exchange-rate conversion. Line 14 then shows the degree to which market exchange rates would have to be corrected in order to give the same results as the real income calculations. For example, India's per capita income using an exchange-rate conversion would have to be increased by a factor of 3.49 to make it comparable with the comparison in terms of international prices. In 1970 the appropriate exchange rate for India, to yield general purchasing power parity with the United States, should be 3.49 dollars/rupees times the market rate—a really sharp hypothetical appreciation of the rupee. On the other hand, a country such as West Germany, which was already close to the American level in 1970, need have appreciated its exchange rate only sixteen percent in order to correctly calculate national income by a straight exchange-rate conversion.

The moral seems to be that, while countries such as Kenya, India, and Colombia are indeed very poor relative to Europe and the United States, simply converting national accounting statistics of GDP by prevailing exchange rates greatly overstates the extent of their relative poverty. Of course, the problem of comparing real welfare across countries throws up complex index number problems that are not completely finessed by simply using a common set of international tradable and nontradable goods prices, because each country consumes goods in different proportions. However, the qualitative direction of these major corrections in exchange-rate conversions would remain unchanged even if refined further. For the most part, wealthier countries do have much higher internal price levels than do poorer ones, and this effect will be more pronounced in higher consumer price indices that include nontradable services than in wholesale price indices that do not.[23]

23. In Chapter 10, a more thorough analysis of the cross-country relationship between WPIs and CPIs under PPP is provided. However, these deviations in the price ratio of tradable to nontradable goods across diverse countries indicate the great difficulty of establishing a "parity" ratio empirically for any one of them. Hence, I have confined the formal discussion of purchasing power parity in this chapter to the tradables sector and have not tried to analyze the parity price of nontradables (including wages) associated with exchange-market equilibrium.

TABLE 6.4 Per Capita Gross Domestic Product in 1970: A Cross-Country Comparison

	Kenya	India	Colombia	Hungary	Italy	U.K.	Japan	Germany (West)	France	U.S.
Valuation at international prices (I$)										
1. Consumption	193	250	555	1,263	1,516	2,050	1,591	2,015	2,238	3,295
2. Capital formation	43	49	166	525	558	627	1,139	1,243	1,138	922
3. Government	39	43	42	148	124	218	222	327	223	584
4. GDP	275	342	763	1,935	2,198	2,895	2,952	3,585	3,599	4,801
Percentage distribution of GDP valued at international prices										
5. Consumption	70	73	73	65	69	71	54	56	62	69
6. Capital formation	16	14	22	27	25	22	39	35	32	19
7. Government	14	13	5	8	6	7	7	9	6	12
8. GDP	100	100	100	100	100	100	100	100	100	100
Per capita quantity indexes based on international prices (U.S. = 100)										
9. Consumption	5.84	7.58	16.8	38.3	46.0	62.2	48.3	61.2	67.9	100.0
10. Capital formation	4.65	5.34	18.0	56.9	60.5	68.1	123.6	134.8	123.4	100.0
11. Government	6.66	7.31	7.2	25.4	21.3	37.4	38.1	55.9	38.2	100.0
12. GDP	5.72	7.12	15.9	40.3	45.8	60.3	61.5	74.7	75.0	100.0
Conversion to US$ at exchange rates for 1970										
13. GDP (U.S. = 100)	3.00	2.04	6.85	21.6	35.4	44.6	41.7	64.2	60.4	100.0
Exchange-rate deviation index (12/13)	1.91	3.49	2.32	1.87	1.29	1.35	1.47	1.16	1.24	1.00

SOURCE: Kravis et al., *A System of International Comparisons of Gross Product and Purchasing Power* (Baltimore, Md.: Johns Hopkins University Press, 1975), Table 1.3, p. 8.

7

Speculation

> A popular stereotype, applied particularly to the case of speculation of all sorts, (is) that the speculator is typically a man who derives a private profit by creating a social woe . . .
>
> Harry Johnson (1976)[1]

Hedging or safety first strategies by banks, firms, and individuals preoccupied us in Chapters 4 and 5. Indeed, the ease with which covered interest arbitrageurs (CIAs) could make an effective forward market, to provide cover for less liquid commercial traders, rested on the principle that CIAs themselves neatly avoid exchange risk. Even if they may have mastered the theory of Purchasing Power Parity, the overwhelming majority of commercial and financial participants in the foreign exchange markets prefer not to risk capital on their abilities to predict future exchange-rate movements in a system from which central banks have withdrawn as the principal market makers.

But Chapter 6 established that commodity arbitrage by itself is quite insufficient to ensure a determinant exchange rate over periods extending for days, months, or even years. A highly developed international market for short-term capital can minimize the social need for market participants to bear exchange risk. Nevertheless, at bottom at least some informed speculation on the direction of future exchange-rate movements is crucial for the successfully monet-

1. "Destabilizing Speculation: A General Equilibrium Approach," *Journal of Political Economy* (February 1976), p. 102.

ized exchange of international goods and services. Indeed, a foreign exchange market composed exclusively of nonspeculative commodity merchants and CIAs is necessarily unstable, as the following discussion illustrates.

In Part I of this chapter, I depict the essential market-making role of *dealer speculators:* mainly, but not exclusively, the foreign exchange departments of large commercial banks from the nonsocialist industrial countries. The battle-field is the system of floating exchange rates among currencies that are freely convertible—with no substantial official restraints on the extension of trade credit, forward transacting, and so on. Exchange rates can move continuously in any direction, and central banks are never caught trying to defend an obviously indefensible parity.

By contrast, in Part II the scene shifts abruptly to the world of pegged exchange rates and detailed financial controls over foreign trade where the central bank views itself as making the exchange market. Most of the other 100+ countries in the world now operate such a regime (Chapter 2), and central banks are frequently faced with the likelihood of having to make dis-crete exchange-rate changes (against some major convertible currency) whose direction but not timing is easily predicted. Unlike the scene in Part I where the professional financial speculator was dominant, nonbank merchants, farmers, and manufacturers now consciously try to anticipate discrete ex-change-rate changes—often for defensive reasons. These *merchant speculators* play a game with the monetary authorities and try to subvert exchange controls in order to prevent capital losses arising out of devaluation. *Leads and lags* associated with giving or receiving trade credit become highly variable, and possibly the most important degree of freedom open to merchant speculators—although other speculative manipulations are brought into play on occasion.

These two common kinds of speculation rest on such different assumptions that the chapter is split into two distinct parts. Nevertheless, a fairly complete picture of the economically important forms of speculation is provided overall. The reader is forewarned that a potentially colorful element is missing from our exposition of speculation. There is no analytical room for popular stereotypes: a sheik of immense wealth, an aggressive multinational corporation unfettered by capital constraints, or a gnome from Zurich.

Part I

FLOATING EXCHANGE RATES
AMONG CONVERTIBLE CURRENCIES

Consider one country, Germany, whose exchange rate R_s (DM/dollars) floats with respect to the United States, which is assumed for simplicity to be the rest of the world. Suppose the monetary policies in each of our two countries are "stable" in the very special sense that the term structure of nominal interest rates is always given exogenously to the market for foreign exchange. That is, deposit (coupon) rates of interest on Deutsche mark assets, as denoted by i_{30}^{DM}, i_{60}^{DM}, i_{90}^{DM} for 30, 60, 90 days, etc., are fixed but perhaps different from those in the United States. Similarly, rates of interest on dollar assets, as denoted by $i_{30}^{\$}$, $i_{60}^{\$}$, $i_{90}^{\$}$ and so on over 180-day and longer-term assets, are also invariant to events in the foreign exchange market. (Worried readers should note that this strong assumption is relaxed in Chapter 8 where varying monetary policies are considered.)

Like ubiquitous bees pollinating an apple orchard in the spring, covered interest arbitrageurs, CIAs, move capital freely in either direction. They exploit minute differences within the interbank market until forward rates of exchange—R_f^{30}, R_f^{60}, R_f^{90}, and so on—are perfectly aligned with the given rates of interest *at every term* to maturity. (For some evidence that this assumption is quite robust empirically, see Chapter 9.) As per our analysis in equation (5.13), the Interest Rate Parity Theorem (IRPT) holds such that:

$$R_f^{30} = R_s \frac{(1 + i_{30}^{DM})}{(1 + i_{30}^{\$})}$$

$$R_f^{60} = R_s \frac{(1 + i_{60}^{DM})}{(1 + i_{60}^{\$})}$$

. . . .

and so on for 90, 180, 360 days, etc. Thus CIAs determine the *ratio* of each forward rate to the prevailing spot rate of exchange across the two currencies.

But, covered interest arbitrage—however useful—cannot determine the *absolute levels* of R_s and R_f^v, where R_f^v denotes a forward rate of any arbitrary maturity "v." Instead, the interaction between merchants and speculators establishes the absolute level of exchange rates overall as we will demonstrate. But either group can hold foreign exchange spot or forward. And forward positions in foreign exchange can be in bills, on-account credits, bonds, or pure forward contracts of varying future maturities. What a bewildering array of financial instruments to portray analytically!

On Aggregating Open Positions Over All Maturities

The usual simplification is to concentrate on one forward contract—say, 90 days—as is done in Figure 5.1 to analyze the way CIAs make the forward market for commercial traders. But this traditional approach is deceptive. First, CIAs are portrayed as if they held open positions in foreign exchange, which they do not if one combines their spot and forward positions. Secondly, speculators are depicted as if they were guessing what the exchange rate would be only at some *specific* time in the future (90 days).

In fact, expectations of the appropriate exchange rate at any particular time are immediately felt in contracts maturing at all terms. If an impulse is transmitted to the market that anticipates a devaluation in 10 days, that devaluation will take place today. The presence of covered interest arbitrage ensures that all exchange rates move up and down in unison. Therefore, the particular term—spot or forward—any one merchant or speculator uses is not important overall. Hence, our analysis is facilitated by aggregating net foreign exchange positions of merchants over all terms to maturity, and then by doing the same for speculators. Consequently, both highly aggregated groups can be portrayed *as if they were interacting only in the spot market,*[2] as in Figure 7.1. Moreover, the

---

2. Or indeed, any particular forward market could also be a basis for the aggregation procedure.

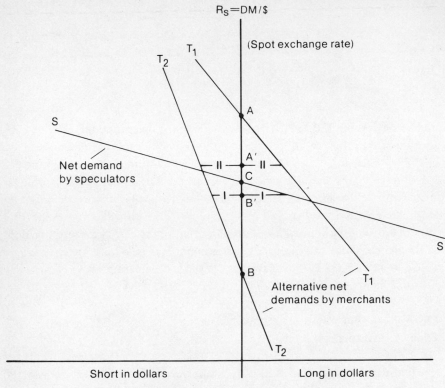

FIGURE 7.1   Merchants and speculators in the foreign exchanges

net foreign exchange positions of CIAs is necessarily zero over all terms to maturity. Thus they are completely excluded from Figure 7.1!

If i_v^{DM} and i_v are given, R_s accurately represents the whole structure of exchange rates. On the vertical axis of Figure 7.1, the spot exchange rate R_s is plotted, and from interest parity we know that all forward rates are proportional to it. For example, R_f^v, an expression for a forward exchange rate of any arbitrary term to maturity, is

$$R_f^v = R_s \frac{(1 + i_v^{DM})}{(1 + i_v^{\$})} \quad \text{where} \quad v = 0, 1, 2, \ldots, \infty, \tag{7.1}$$

On the horizontal axis, the net dollar position in terms of DM of either merchants (the TT schedules) or speculators (the SS schedule) is represented.[3] Long dollar positions are to the right of the vertical axis, and short dollar (long

3. CIAs are not explicitly portrayed because, by definition, they hold no net position in foreign exchange.

DM) positions to the left. What is the aggregation procedure that allows us to add up the dollar positions spot and forward of each group?

Because CIAs fix relative prices, we can use the famous Hicksian composite good theorem.[4] Let X denote the spot equivalent of the net dollar position of agents (speculators or traders). X can then be derived as the sum of all spot and forward positions according to

$$
\begin{aligned}
X &= \sum_{v=0}^{\infty} X_v \frac{(1 + i_v^{DM})}{(1 + i_v^{\$})} \\
&= X_0 + \sum_{v=1}^{\infty} X_v \frac{(1 + i_v^{DM})}{(1 + i_v^{\$})}.
\end{aligned}
\tag{7.2}
$$

X_v can be positive or negative and is the net position of agents at the v-th term to maturity. X_0 is simply the net spot holdings of dollars. Each forward dollar position at time v is weighted by $(1 + i_v^{DM})/(1 + i_v^{\$})$. The *current* opportunity cost of holding dollars instead of Deutsche marks depends directly on how high DM rates a e in comparison to dollar rates of interest. The fact that these interest rates are assumed fixed is crucial in allowing us to portray how the highly aggregated demands of merchants and speculators each respond homogeneously to fluctuations in R_s. It also allows the important analytical simplification of excluding CIAs altogether from having any influence on the single representative exchange rate.

In Figure 7.1 the TT schedules represent alternative net demands for dollars by merchants, who are defined to be nonspeculators: they simply take the current exchange rate R_s as given and do not reorder their affairs in anticipation of any changes. However, merchants can fully cover any *forward* obligations to deliver foreign exchange by simply buying it forward, an impulse that CIAs would immediately transmit to the spot market as an increased demand for spot foreign exchange. Thus, if merchants have a net demand for dollars in Figure 7.1, this does *not* imply that they are uncovered with respect to their forward payments. Rather, a temporary and quite usual imbalance exists in the two-way flow of commercial payments over all terms to maturity.

This normal ebb and flow of commodity trade between Germany and the United States is reflected in the shifting TT curve. Along T_1T_1, German importers (nonspeculative) dominate their counterparts in the other direction so that the net demand for dollars is unusually high. Along T_2T_2, the demand for DM in terms of dollars is unusually high. In the absence of speculation, this normal fluctuation in commercial payments would drive R_s first to A and then to B, in order to clear the market in each case. I call these *real* disturbances in the exchange market—in part reflecting varying tastes for German and Ameri-

4. J.R. Hicks, *Value and Capital*, 2nd edition (Oxford, Eng.: Oxford University Press, 1946), pp. 34–36, 312–13.

can goods—because they are not systematically related to either national money market.

However, suppose intrepid speculators believe that the equilibrium is at C, possibly because of some calculation based on purchasing power parity. Any deviation of R_s from this normal position will (they believe) soon be righted. Because their views are not held with certainty, the SS schedule is less than fully elastic—although more elastic than the demand schedules of merchants. If these dealer-speculators then act on their beliefs, they take a net position equal and opposite to that of the merchants. The range of exchange fluctuation arising out of variations in commercial payments is then sharply reduced to $A'B'$. Badly needed market smoothing is thereby obtained.

As with merchants, speculators are free to enter the foreign exchange market spot or forward with the same effect—as long as CIAs are performing in an uninhibited fashion. If CIAs were not in the market, not only would our analytical aggregation procedure break down, but speculators would have to make a market for merchants at every individual term to maturity. Much natural offsetting of commercial payments between German and American importers would be lost. The total amount of risk (foreign exchange exposure) would increase sharply for all market participants. Merchants would find more bias in the sense of turning individual forward rates of exchange against themselves when they tried to transact.

In summary, both CIAs and speculators are necessary for a system of freely floating exchange rates to work smoothly. Undue day-to-day fluctuations from random variations in international commercial payments, which are aggregated over all spot and forward maturities, can then be avoided.

The Demand for Stabilizing Speculation and the 'J' Curve

Tautologically, "stabilizing" speculation in Figure 7.1 narrows the range of exchange-rate fluctuations arising from the ebb and flow of commercial payments by merchants. Even more cavalierly, Figure 7.1 assumes that merchants have determinant, albeit shifting, net aggregate demands for foreign exchange on any one trading day. As we shall see, the negative slopes of T_1T_1 and T_2T_2 imply sustainable equilibrium at either point A or point B if speculators were absent.

If this basically stable behavior of merchants (albeit with fluctuations) is empirically valid, why risk having speculators in the market at all? Speculation could be destabilizing. To the popular financial press, the unexpectedly wide variations, as much as ten to twenty-five percent per year, in floating exchange rates since February 1973 appear to be *per se* evidence of destabilizing speculation. Moreover, a long and seemingly unending academic dispute over whether destabilizing speculators necessarily lose money, and thus would ultimately be eventually driven out of the market, has proved difficult to resolve.[5] Perhaps risk averse governments should impose more restrictions on international capital flows and forward trading, which are the very embodiment of (destabilizing) speculative activity.

I shall demonstrate that such arguments are dangerously misleading as guides to policy under floating rates. A market consisting only of "legitimate" merchants (and CIAs) is likely to be explosively unstable over short and intermediate time horizons—unlike their portrayal in Figure 7.1. Hence, the old debate over whether destabilizing speculators make or lose money is somewhat beside the main point. Informed speculation is essential to the very existence of a functioning market in foreign exchange.[6]

Proving this fundamental hypothesis required that we circumscribe "pure" merchants rather carefully in their principal role of organizing international trade in goods and services. To avoid introducing a speculative element into their behavior, merchants are narrowly defined such that they take the existing structure of exchange rates as their best guess of the future. Thus, they do *not* try to anticipate movements in exchange rates by deferring or accelerating foreign payments.

In addition, merchants are risk averse and hedge as best they can, as described in Chapter 4. They use partial forward covering in conjunction with inventory valuation adjustments to offset unexpected (*ex post facto*) fluctuations in exchange rates after contracts are signed.

When confronted with known changes in R_s prior to entering into a contract, merchants reorder their affairs by adjusting price quotations and quantities purchased but don't speculate on further changes. Because they have these stationary expectations regarding whatever exchange rates are current, mer-

5. For a recent review of some of this literature, see Susan Schadler, "Sources of Exchange-rate Variability: Theory and Empirical Evidence," IMF *Staff Papers* (July 1977), pp. 253–96. In "The Case for Flexible Exchange Rates," in *Essays in Positive Economics* (Chicago, Ill.: University of Chicago Press, 1953), p. 175, Milton Friedman made the initial seminal suggestion that destabilizing speculators would necessarily lose money.

6. This argument does not preclude central banks themselves from being stabilizing speculators within a no-par system, although my main concern is with private speculation. In the presence of active CIAs, central banks' positions at virtually any term to maturity have approximately the same effect. To leave the domestic monetary base unchanged as per our assumption of stable national monetary policies, however, official transactions in the spot market are best avoided in the face of "real" (nonmonetary) disturbances in foreign payments.

chants respond to such *ex ante* changes in R_s by phasing out some activities that now seem unprofitable, whilst others are favored for expansion.[7]

The stability of a foreign exchange market consisting exclusively of merchants (and CIAs) depends on their collective reaction to arbitrary small fluctuations in R_s. Would any small perturbation of R_s away from its long-run equilibrium value—say, that defined by Purchasing Power Parity—set up forces tending to restore this equilibrium? Or, even when the underlying monetary policies in each of our two countries are stable, would forces be set in motion that move R_s (the whole structure of exchange rates) further and further away from its PPP value? This basic question can only be answered by specifying various time periods over which merchants adjust to some arbitrary change in R_s. For analytical convenience, four consecutive stages will be introduced, without pretending that they do not overlap somewhat in practice.

These stages stand out in sharper relief by assuming that all commodities exported and imported are fixed price tradables I (Chapter 4). The heterogeneous industrial exports of Germany are invoiced only in DM, those of the United States are invoiced only in dollars, and both are invariant to short-run fluctuations in R_s.

Suppose the market for foreign exchange is in full long-run PPP equilibrium, where the law of one price holds and the two-way flow of commercial payments among merchants is exactly balanced. Now a small unanticipated change in the exchange rate occurs. Taken by surprise, merchants respond in four stages:[8]

   (i) During very "short" periods of *currency contract*, neither commodity prices nor amounts traded can be adjusted.

   (ii) After *pass through*, importers in both countries see *ex ante* the altered domestic-currency equivalents of commodity price quotations fixed in foreign currency; but they do not yet have time to alter the traditional flow of goods purchased.

   (iii) In the period of *quantity adjustment*, foreign buyers now alter quantities purchased in response to the changed pass through prices seen in domestic currency.

   (iv) Only in the very long run of *invoice price adjustment* are the domestic invoice

7. Behavior that is not only plausible in of itself, but which is quite consistent with sophisticated "efficient markets" hypotheses that treat the current exchange rate as if it already contained all relevant market information. For example, see Bradford Cornell, "Spot Rates, Forward Rates and Exchange Market Efficiency," *Journal of Financial Economics*, 5 (1977), pp. 55–65.

Remember that the predetermined structure of forward rates related to R_s could already include systematic market indications of movements of the spot rate into the future to which our merchants are free to react.

8. In the context of measuring the impact of devaluation on the U.S. trade balance, the first three of these stages were outlined by Stephen P. MaGee in "Currency Contracts, Pass Through, and Devaluation," *Brookings Papers in Economic Activity* I (Washington, D.C.: Brookings Institution, 1973), pp. 303–25.

prices in DM of tradables I produced in Germany realigned to equal the dollar prices of similar goods produced in the United States at the new exchange rate R_s. The law of one price is reestablished.

Let us now demonstrate that the responses of merchants to small changes in R_s in the short run—adjustment periods (i) and (ii)—is destabilizing, even when covered interest arbitrage is virtually perfect so that the demand and supply of foreign exchange by merchants can be aggregated over all terms to maturity.

Choose units for each tradable German industrial product so that its price is exactly one DM, and for each American industrial product so that its invoice price is exactly one dollar. In the initial full long-run equilibrium at purchasing power parity, suppose R_s = 2 Deutsche marks per dollar; trade and payments are balanced every day with 100 DM worth of German exports being exchanged for 50 dollars worth of American exports. In this steady state equilibrium, no capital is being transferred and the foreign exchange market is balanced at R_s = 2 with no net intervention by speculators.

Suppose now a small surprise perturbation occurs to reduce R_s (appreciate the German currency) by about five percent to 1.9 DM per dollar.[9] Within the immediate *currency contract* period, goods ordered or in transit keep coming. American importers must meet their now more expensive (in dollars) payments obligation in DM, and vice versa for German importers, as old contracts mature. If all merchants were completely uncovered, German importers still pay the full 50 dollars per day for American goods—a windfall gain in DM; whereas American importers now find they must pay $52.50 per day for German goods due for payment and take a windfall loss.[10] Hence, within this currency contract period, an excess supply of dollars develops that tends to drive R_s (depreciate the dollar) further below 1.9. Similar and symmetrical disequilibrating forces are present if R_s is perturbed above 2 DM per dollar. Hence the immediate effect of merchants honoring old contracts in the face of an unexpected fluctuation in R_s is to destabilize the foreign exchange market—aggregated over all maturities.

It is not easy to capture this destabilizing effect in one simple diagram. The downward pressure on the market cumulates through time if the disequilibrium rate of R_s = 1.9 is maintained as more old contracts mature. In Figure 7.2, therefore, the disequilibrating effect over only one trading day is portrayed. Unlike Figure 7.1, stabilizing speculators are not explicitly represented in Figure 7.2—but their (shadow) behavior is important in interpreting the market

9. One could think of a transitory small disruption in German payments for American goods causing such a small depreciation of the dollar.

10. This kind of numerical illustration was given by MaGee, op. cit. pp. 309–10.

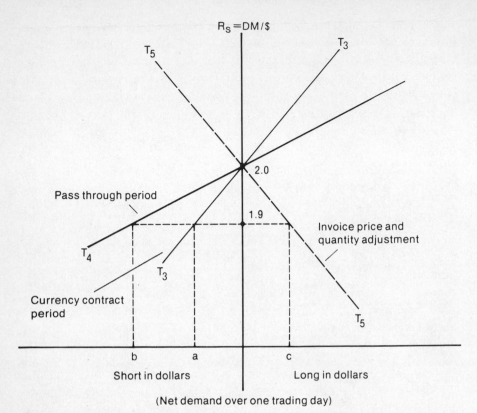

FIGURE 7.2   Exchange instability with only merchants in the market

responses of merchants over three time horizons: currency contract (T_3T_3), pass through (T_4T_4), and the combined invoice price with quantity adjustment (T_5T_5).

The positively sloped currency contract curve represents the immediate response of merchants to fluctuations in R_s away from the point of full long-run equilibrium at $R_s = 2$. If R_s falls to 1.9, and is maintained for one trading day, the net excess supply of dollars (demand for DM) is the horizontal distance a. Within this trading day in the currency contract period, $R_s = 1.9$ could only be prevented from falling further (the dollar depreciating more) if speculators take an opposite position by holding a dollars long. A yet more vigorous net demand *ex ante* for dollars by speculators would be required to drive the exchange rate back to its long-run equilibrium at $R_s = 2$.

How important is our assumption of no forward covering in demonstrating instability in a market consisting only of merchants? Suppose both American and German importers cover 100 percent of their deferred payment obligations. Each group has forward contracts maturing exactly equal to spot payment obligations at the old exchange rate of $R_2 = 2$; thus no windfall gains or losses occur when R_s falls to 1.9 within the currency contract period. Profits on forward contracts offset losses on spot payments so that no further excess supply of dollars develops. No longer destabilizing, the behavior of merchants is now *neutral* with respect to fluctuations in R_s as if T_3T_3 coincided with the vertical axis in Figure 7.2.

In general, however, importers of tradables I do *not* cover fully within the currency contract period because they utilize some (future) inventory valuation adjustments to hedge against unexpected exchange-rate changes (Chapter 4). Suppose each group of merchants had covered forward only one-half their deferred payments so that T_3T_3 in Figure 7.2 is still positively sloped but is now steeper. Then a fall in R_s to 1.9 would still generate an excess supply of dollars: now only $1.25 net over any one trading day, but still sufficient to drive R_s down unless speculators stabilize the market.

Suppose the behavior of speculators is weakly stabilizing: they hold R_s at 1.9 without further decline by cumulating long positions in dollars as more contracts mature.[11] Do matters improve when the higher German export prices in dollars—rising from \$.50 to \$.525—are passed through to American buyers *ex ante* in new contracts, and vice versa?

American importers can no longer cover forward effectively against this higher *ex ante* dollar price for German goods because all forward rates of exchange, R_f^y, will also have fallen five percent. (Forward covering can only offset unanticipated changes in exchange rates.) Therefore, in new contracts American importers must pay higher dollar prices for German goods, whereas German importers face lower DM prices for American goods at $R_s = 1.9$. But the pass through period was defined as one sufficiently short that buyers would be inconvenienced to make significant quantity adjustments in the normal flow of foreign goods purchased. Demand or quantity response for physical goods is inelastic. If so, the excess supply of dollars is further accentuated in the pass through period during any one trading day. Indeed, after pass through, the excess supply of dollars rises to $2.50—comparable to the currency contract period in the extreme case where no importers covered forward.

This accentuated instability in pass through is portrayed by the positive slope of T_4T_4 in Figure 7.2 being flatter than that of T_3T_3. Now, in any one trading day, the excess supply of dollars from merchants—which must be offset by speculators increasing their long positions in dollars to prevent R_s from falling further—has risen from a to b. Obviously, the static portrayal of merchant behavior in Figure 7.2 cannot do full justice to the cumulative increased demands on speculators to buy dollars as we move through the currency contract and pass through periods. But destabilizing pressure from merchants ap-

11. By implication, strongly stabilizing speculation would return R_s to 2.

pears likely to get worse before it gets better if R_s is not returned immediately to its position of full long-run equilibrium.

Eventually, in the *quantity adjustment* stage—say, some months later—the behavior of merchants *may* become stabilizing. American exporters react to the higher dollar prices of German industrial goods and cut back purchases. Similarly, German importers react to the lower prices of American goods by increasing purchases and dollar payments. Whether this quantity response is sufficiently elastic to offset the adverse price effects, and so reduce the excess supply of dollars, remains difficult to resolve statistically.[12]

However, this intermediate run of quantity adjustment still violates the law of one price, even if speculators succeed in preventing R_s from falling below 1.9. That is, each German industrial export still has an invoice price of one DM; whereas each American fixed price export has an invoice price of one dollar. The change from $R_s = 2$ to $R_s = 1.9$ opens up a five percent violation in the law. But with a sufficient lapse in time, even tradables I can have their domestic-currency invoice prices adjusted. The quantity responses eventually set arbitrage forces in motion to reduce the DM prices of German tradables I and raise the *dollar* prices of similar American goods. These price adjustments then further reduce the excess supply of dollars in terms of DM.

Indeed, if monetary policies in our two countries remain stable, strong macroeconomic adjustment forces are now operative. As described and analyzed in Chapter 1, the eventually higher American price level (from the fall in R_s) will reduce American real cash balances, and thus reduce American expenditures for commodities in general including imports. Similarly, the enhanced commodity purchasing power of DM will increase German expenditures and imports. Hence, the ultimate response in commodity markets to an exchange-rate change is strongly stabilizing.

In Figure 7.2, T_5T_5 combines the quantity-adjustment and invoice-price-adjustment phases. The net demand for dollars by merchants is now negatively sloped, so that a perturbation from $R_s = 2$ to $R_s = 1.9$ creates excess *demand* for dollars at point C. Eventually, upward pressure on R_s from the commodity markets acts to restore the exchange rate to its long-run equilibrium level.

This phased behavior of the trade balance following a depreciation of the dollar (a fall in R_s) is often referred to as the "J" curve effect. One reads from left to right along the J indicating that the United States' trade balance first

---

12. See *The Effect of Exchange-Rate Adjustments*, edited by Peter Clark, Dennis Logue, and R.J. Sweeney, The Department of the Treasury (Washington, D.C., 1977). In the same vein of estimating how trade responds to exchange-rate adjustments under different pass through assumptions, see M.E. Kreinin, "The Effect of Exchange-rate Changes on the Prices and Volume of Foreign Trade," IMF *Staff Papers* (July 1977), pp. 297–329.

deteriorates in the currency contract period, declines further in pass through, and then improves with adjustment in quantities and domestic invoice prices. More precisely, in terms of our fictitious foreign exchange market in which only merchants participate, the *J* curve traces their hypothetical excess demand for dollars (in terms of DM) from an accidental but sustained depreciation of the dollar below its long-run equilibrium level. Starting from zero at the left of the *J*, excess demand for dollars becomes increasingly negative in the short run; only in the long run is it restored to zero and then becomes positive.

The *J* curve analysis makes clear that a market for foreign exchange with only merchants—narrowly but reasonably defined to have stationary expectations—is unstable. Even with uninhibited covered interest arbitrage that smoothes demands and supplies of foreign exchange over all terms to maturity, the short-run responses of merchants to random exchange-rate fluctuations is perverse for the market as a whole. Moreover, a bandwagon effect could start once R_s moves below or above its equilibrium values. As old contracts mature and commodity prices are passed through, further pressure develops to keep R_s moving in the same direction.

The Supply of Stabilizing Speculation

On the face of it, the supply of stabilizing speculation during the 1973–1978 experience with floating exchange rates has been disappointing. Writers in the 1950s and 1960s who espoused freely floating exchange rates did not foresee certain peculiar characteristics of the present system:[13]

1) Current movements in spot exchange rates of twenty percent year to year, five percent month to month, or even one percent daily are not now unusual (Figure 1.1 and Table 1.2).

2) Forward rates have been poor (inefficient) although unbiased predictors of future spot rates. That is, rate changes among convertible currencies have been largely unanticipated by the market.[14]

3) Official intervention in the no parity system has continued at about as high a level as in the fixed-rate system.[15]

13. Without attempting to cover the extensive literature on the subject, representative authors are: M. Friedman, op. cit.; H. Johnson, "The Case for Flexible Exchange Rates, 1969," in *Further Essays in Monetary Economics* (London: Allen and Unwin, 1972), pp.198–228; Egon Sohmen, *Flexible Exchange Rates*, (Chicago, Ill.: University of Chicago Press, 1961); Fritz Machlup, *The Alignment of Foreign Exchange Rates* (New York: Praeger, 1972).
14. For a summary of many statistical studies on this subject, see Richard Levich, "On the Efficiency of Markets for Foreign Exchange," in J. Frenkel and R. Dornbusch (eds.), *International Economic Policy: An Assessment of Theory and Evidence* (Baltimore, Md.: Johns Hopkins University Press, forthcoming).
15. John Williamson, "Exchange-Rate Flexibility and Reserve Use," *The Scandanavian Journal of Economics*, Vol. 78, No. 2 (1976), pp. 327–39.

One might contrast this volatility and the high cost of foreign exchange transactions in 1973–1978 with a statement made by Machlup that is indicative of his feeling about the smoothness of adjustment in a flexible rate system:[16]

> Under a system of greater flexibility such serious disalignments of exchange rates would never, or hardly ever, arise, and expectations of change would be confined to minuscule adjustments. Profits from small changes can be only small, inviting only moderate speculation, which can be easily discouraged, if this is wanted, by relatively minor differentials in interest rates.

Machlup was not alone. Other notable writers such as Friedman, Johnson, and Sohmen have maintained similar views on the gradualness of adjustment under floating rates, which they contrasted favorably with the sharp discrete changes and one-way speculative frenzies of the old pegged-rate system.

I would submit that an important institutional element was lacking in the earlier defenses of floating rates, the importance of which has only now become apparent. The questions of *who* was to be a stabilizing speculator, and *what* would be the source of private capital for such speculations, were never directly addressed. Rather, this particular issue was superseded by a rough-and-tumble debate over whether private speculation would be stabilizing or destabilizing. An implicit consensus had been reached that there would be no restraints on the availability of private speculative capital on the huge scale needed.

The contrary hypothesis, advanced here, is that the supply of private capital for taking net positions in either the forward or spot markets is currently inadequate. Exchange rates can move sharply in response to random variations in the day-to-day demands by merchants or from monetary disturbances. Once a rate starts to move because of some temporary perturbation, no prospective speculator is willing to hold an open position for a significant time interval in order to bet on a reversal—whence the large daily and monthly movements in the foreign exchanges and sometimes high bid-ask spreads. Bandwagon psychologies result from the general unwillingness of participants to take net positions against near-term market movements that are necessarily accentuated by the behavior of nonspeculative merchants.

Thus, the problem seems not to be one of excessive destabilizing speculation, but rather one of the absence of speculation over time horizons longer than a day or two. Let us examine this hypothesis by looking first at dealer speculators.

Banking Risk Versus Currency Risk

Commercial banks take open positions in the course of making or receiving foreign payments that themselves cannot be expected to balance in continuous

16. Machlup, op. cit. p. 70.

time.[17] Even when a commercial bank covers in the interbank market, these wholesale transactions are on a much larger scale (Chapter 1) and would not exactly match the positions held at retail with nonbank customers. European commercial banks in particular have prided themselves on mastering the art of making a smooth foreign exchange market; they have been less hesitant in carrying a net open position from one trading day to the next, or even from one week to the next, in order to prevent gyrations in retail price quotations or unduly large bid-ask spreads. Otherwise, nonbank firms would find no particular advantage in using commercial banks as intermediaries in the foreign exchange market—a weaker and less costly brokerage function could supplant them.

In carrying either a spot or forward position—say long in Deutsche marks—through time, however, the bank evidently expects the value of the DM tomorrow or next week to be higher than today; or, equivalently, attempting to cover or eliminate the DM position today will be more costly than holding it. At least over short periods of time, therefore, dealers must systematically form expectations of future spot and forward exchange-rate movements. In this important respect such dealers are speculators.

However agile and prescient, the dealer-speculator remains part of a large commercial bank. He is subject to the capital constraint that the bank faces over all its operations and must worry about views of outside creditors. Stockholders, for example, may not wish to be a party to massive positions in foreign currencies to which they cannot feasibly adjust their own portfolios. Depositors, whose own yields are strictly limited, might well avoid banks that are known to be risk takers. In addition, large commercial banks remain anxious that their names be taken without question in interbank trading. Hence, individual dealer-speculators are limited in what positions they can take. Bank managements see fit to maintain tight controls over their net foreign currency positions.

A trader has a *running position sheet* in each currency. This sheet contains the purchases and sales for a series of dates, and the sum of the net purchases over the entire series of dates. The bank's *position* is the sum of its net purchases and sales for the set of dates in its running position sheet. A position may be *long* or *short*, depending upon whether the bank is a net buyer or seller of foreign exchange over the set of dates.

Most traders have lines, which are the maximum long and short positions they can have in various currencies. The lines given to the trader depend upon (1) the capital of the bank; its ability to withstand losses. An intrepid trader can embarrass his bank

17. In contrast, pure brokers operate to bring buyer and seller together—spot or forward—but themselves do not take a net open position and thus do not speculate.

financially. Positions are checked regularly by the senior trader, who usually is a vice-president, and by the executive vice-president, to prevent the trading department from assuming more risk than senior management deems prudent. The lines also depend upon (2) the volume of business in a given (foreign) currency . . .

Positions have to be managed, for the banks' customers and banks are constantly thrusting positions upon them. The trader must decide what position he wants to take, in each currency, and must react accordingly.[18]

After an initial rash of threatened bank failures in 1973–1974, governments and central banks have now pressed commercial banks to balance more strictly their net position in foreign exchange. Hence, commercial banks are restricted—and perhaps correctly so—from taking speculative positions.

Official restraints on net foreign exchange positions of commercial banks parallel similar restraints on their domestic loan portfolios and liquidity reserves that have long been regulated. Most banking textbooks emphasize the uneasy trade-off between the unique role of the commercial banks in providing a secure *means of payment* against their more general role as financial intermediaries between savers and investors—a role that ordinarily demands aggressive investment and money-market behavior. The commercial banks can attract capital easily by issuing money, legal tender often guaranteed by the state. In return, the government sees fit to limit their aggressiveness in the capital market—possibly reducing immediate real yields in the economy—by safety-first regulations designed to secure money as a means of payment. In addition, reserve requirements permit control over the nominal money base and, ultimately, official control over the nominal price level.

In the international sphere, excessive speculative risk in the foreign exchanges might also impair the security of deposits in purely domestic currency. Hence central banks may well limit the net foreign exchange exposure of their commercial banks to, say, twenty percent of their owners' equity. This and similar constraining regulations are designed to reduce banking risk—the possibility of insolvency on the part of the custodians of the domestic money supply.

However, banking risk pervades international as well as domestic trade. Central banks have largely withdrawn from trading one currency for another at a known parity. But responsibility to clear foreign payments remains with the commercial banks—who buy foreign currencies for customers or honor forward commitments requiring the trade of domestic for foreign money. Large shifts in relative currency values, or the imposition of unexpected foreign exchange controls, militate toward a risk-avoidance view of securing interbank payments in international monies against default. It is one thing for a nonbank individual

18. Jerome L. Stein, "The Nature and Efficiency of the Foreign Exchange Market," Princeton *Essays in International Finance* (October 1962), pp. 16 and 17.

or firm to risk holding a foreign currency unhedged against exchange-rate changes: this currency risk was indeed envisaged by proponents of flexible exchange rates as a real social cost of doing international business. It is quite another matter, however, for the nonbank firm to be continually worried about the insolvency of the bank on which it has a foreign-currency claim. The currency risk was foreseen by the old literature but the banking risk was not. Hence a fairly strong case can be made for banks that specialize in foreign-currency transactions to limit their speculative activities and so reduce the banking risk to other firms and individuals.

Note that our basic aggregation theorem still holds because those same commercial banks that are constrained speculators can function quite freely as covered interest arbitrageurs. The Eurocurrency and forward exchange markets are largely interbank (Chapter 9), and any discrepancies between forward premium and interest differentials on Eurocurrency deposits are quickly eliminated. Therefore, insofar as banks take speculative open positions as dealers for the convenience of their nonbank customers, the particular term to maturity is not of critical concern for the stability of the market as a whole.[19] Their aggregative "running position sheet" can then be encapsulated in Figure 7.1 by the SS curve. The problem remains that, with their rather unique ease of access to the principal foreign exchange markets, the major commercial banks are necessarily conservative in their willingness to bear currency risk. When R_s become "disaligned," and pressure from merchants cumulates to move the rate even further out of line, prudent concern for banking risk inhibits commercial banks from taking large offsetting open positions.

Multinational Corporations and Other Nonspeculators

What ever happened to the multinational corporations, those ogres of speculative runs under the old fixed-rate regime? Surely these giants of unlimited international wealth and power need not hesitate to take a net position in this or that currency if it appears to be seriously disaligned (Machlup's terminology). However, the division of labor seems important to them: they prefer to be merchants

19. The major exception is where covered interest arbitrage is imperfect so that forward markets (perhaps due to exchange controls or imperfect domestic capital markets) become thin. With risk-free CIAs no longer dominating the now fragmented forward market, risk-taking dealer speculators are now called on to "make" the forward market by taking open positions—not easily covered—at several different terms to maturity. In return, they exact substantial fees, perhaps manifested in a wider bid-ask spread for forward exchange, that dissuade merchants from forward covering. This in turn increases the instability of the foreign exchange market during the currency contract period.

and manufacturers rather than foreign exchange speculators. Many companies have clearly defined policies against speculation in the foreign exchanges. Given the current state of the stock market and the financing needs of ordinary business, the freeing of capital for speculative purposes in the foreign exchanges can hardly be given a high priority by big companies whose existence in the long run depends on their expertise in manufacturing or commerce.

With both commercial banks and multinationals minimizing their net foreign exchange exposure, it is not evident that private individuals have sufficient capital, knowledge, or ease of access to the market to take up the slack. Commercial banks have never made it easy for individuals who were not major depositors to take speculative positions. The International Monetary Market of the Chicago Mercantile Exchange does cater to individuals, but the volume of transacting is still tiny in comparison to the interbank market. The contractual obligations for actual delivery of foreign exchange are complex, and trading in foreign currencies is not a game that nonspecialists can easily play.

Speculating Without International Money

Beyond these institutional restraints on banks, multinational corporations, and individuals, there may be a somewhat deeper explanation of the inadequate availability of private speculative capital in the current environment. I refer to the problem of the "riskless asset," alias the "Nth currency," alias "international money."

Let us illustrate with two commonly cited historical examples of smoothly floating exchange rates: the Austro-Hungarian gulden from 1879 to 1892, and the Canadian dollar from 1950 to 1962. In the first case,[20] British sterling served as international money, allowing free access to the London capital markets; in the latter case, the U.S. dollar served as the Nth currency, and the New York capital market was a source of finance to the Canadian economy.

If an individual speculator wanted to be short in gulden, he could do so conveniently by going long in sterling with funds raised or normally held in London. Of course, the speculator would have to follow weather reports on Austrian crops, chart the Austrian money supply, understand Austrian tariff policy, and follow Austria's numerous military imbroglios with diplomatic and strategic insight. Having mastered that, he could safely take his profits in sterling and not worry about being long in sterling half the time. He did not

20. Described in interesting detail by Leland Yeager. "Fluctuating Exchange Rates in the 19th Century: The Experiences of Austria and Russia," in R. Mundell and A. Swoboda (eds.), *Monetary Problems of the International Economy* (Chicago, Ill.: University of Chicago Press, 1969), pp. 61–90.

need to be directly concerned with the N-2 exchange rates between gulden and currencies other than sterling. The presence of secure international money, therefore, allowed the speculator to specialize in knowing Austria—a reasonably big job in itself. The consequent reduction in informational uncertainty increased the availability of capital for taking open positions in 1879–1892 in gulden. Similarly, in 1950–1962, speculators could conveniently use the "stable" U.S. dollar with confidence to take open positions against the Canadian dollar.

Hence, the correct analytical interpretation of the satisfactory Austrian and Canadian experiences with speculation is not quite the obvious one that they were alone in floating while the rest of the world was mainly on fixed rates. Even if most countries had been floating their exchange rates in the 1879–1892 or 1950–1962 periods, the presence of secure international money—sterling or U.S. dollars—would economize on information (provide a riskless asset) and allow speculators to specialize in one currency by always taking their positions in that currency against the international money.

Put differently, in a regime of several floating currencies—say, lire, marks, and dollars—would a speculator always go short in that currency that was judged to be the weakest while simultaneously going long in that judged to be strongest? No, because of the fundamental problem of *timing* based on rapidly changing market information. Having studied the Italian situation with decentralized care, he may find a particular point in time opportune to take a short forward position in lire against U.S. dollars—which is the one currency in which complete forward markets exist against all others. A while later (perhaps never), the German situation may develop favorably enough (according to our speculator's research) to warrant taking a long forward position in marks against U.S. dollars. His net dollar position is now zero. However, he did hold an open long position in dollars for a significant time period whose exact duration was uncertain after his lira transaction. Put more extremely, in the day-to-day or even the hour-to-hour smoothing of random exchange fluctuations, a speculator with highly specialized information on particular countries would prefer to deal only with the intermediary currency if he knew it to be safe.

From the above reasoning, the potential supply of speculative capital for the smoothing of foreign exchange markets in 1973–1978 is much reduced by the decline in the United States dollar as stable international money. For example, to go short in French francs for a year hence, in which currency should one be long at the end of that period? American monetary policy could go awry in the interim and greatly depreciate the U.S. dollar vis-à-vis some average basket of currencies or some representative bundle of tradable goods. Our potential foreign-currency speculator now needs expertise in several currencies in order to find a proper offset for his potential short position in francs. The increased uncertainty reduces his willingness to commit his own equity, and limits his capacity to borrow for speculative purposes.

In short, the markets for foreign exchange can better tolerate diversity in N-1 national monetary policies if the Nth currency is known to be stable. Of course, the more erratic and uncertain the monetary policy in any of the N-1 countries, the more binding becomes the capital constraint on speculators in that particular currency. Monetary disturbances *per se* are analyzed in Chapter 8. On the other hand, if no consensus is reached on what is stable international money, there may be endless surges from one currency to another to find a home. Hot money flows—whether by multinationals or Arabs—are essentially defensive rather than speculative; they may widen rather than dampen fluctuations in relative currency values.

Part II

PEGGED EXCHANGE RATES AND SPECULATION AGAINST CENTRAL BANKS

Under floating exchange rates—Part I—merchants were presumed to hedge against currency risk because of their individual capital constraints, and to take the existing structure of spot and forward exchange rates as their best informed guess of the future. An entrepreneur or management team could then focus on making and selling electronic slide rules or chemical fertilizers rather than on the vagaries of future exchange-rate movements, whose direction is not obvious. And hedging remains normal commercial practice. Yet, speculation by merchants becomes important when (1) expectations of future exchange-rate movements are quite definite and undirectional, or (2) when hedging is costly and inconvenient relative to the ease of carrying open positions.

Let us, therefore, concentrate on the opposite extreme: a central bank intervenes to defend an exchange-rate parity in order to prevent depreciation in face of a persistent deficit in international payments. For example, the Bank of England intervened extensively in the spot market from 1946 to 1948 before finally devaluing sterling from about $4.20 to $2.80 in September 1949 (the forward market was officially closed); and then it intervened extensively in both spot and forward markets from 1964 to 1967 prior to eventually devaluing to $2.40 in 1967. Each time, market participants—banks and firms—were aware of heavy losses in official reserves prior to actual devaluation. Hence full information was telegraphed that the spot price of sterling could only fall or, at most, remain the same.

Similar situations occur continually in less developed countries with inconvertible currencies. For example, Argentinian wholesale prices increased 37 percent in 1974, and at an even faster rate in early 1975, leading to heavy reserve losses. Given Argentina's postwar history of continual devaluations, the market came to expect a devaluation in 1975—which happened in March when the official peso price of U.S. dollars rose from 5 to 10. Similar price inflation in Israel proceeded as fast or faster from 1973 to 1974, culminating in a discrete formal devaluation of the Israeli pound from US$.238 to US$.167 in November of 1974. While not being able to anticipate the date of devaluation exactly, the market knew that the foreign exchange values of the Argentinian peso or the Israeli pound must fall in the near future (despite exchange controls) prior to their actual devaluations. Since virtually all countries with inconvertible currencies maintain a more or less official peg with a convertible currency of a major trading partner (Chapter 2), and many have strong proclivities toward internal inflation, such discrete devaluations occur frequently (see Table 7.3)—without being quite as newsworthy as the saga of major embattled convertible currencies such as sterling.

How then do trading firms and merchants react to strong anticipations of a coming discrete devaluation?

First, consider the two-country example of Holland and Sweden with *convertible currencies*. Convertibility permits commercial enterprises to import and export freely on current account, and grant or receive trade credit (Chapter 1). For the problem at hand, let us broaden this definition to allow merchants to cover future payments easily by forward transactions with duly authorized commercial banks—which the banks could in turn cover in the interbank market. Alternatively, merchants can deal freely in short-term money-market instruments in kronor or guilders—with greater or lesser imperfections in such markets as described in Chapter 5.[22] In this relatively open environment, suppose nonbank firms dealing in Volvos or tulip bulbs have a newly found conviction that the guilder will be discretely devalued (against kronor) in the near future. More or less in sequence commercial traders will:

  i)   alter forward covering on payments due in foreign exchange;

  ii) change the leads and lags in the solicitation and repayment of ordinary trade credit;

---

22. However, I am assuming that movements of short-term capital not associated with, or not justified by, current commodity transactions cannot be undertaken by nonbank firms—and that authorized commercial banks are also quite restricted in this respect. This state of affairs more or less mirrors Japanese and British exchange-rate practices, as well as those of several other European countries, in the postwar period.

iii) perhaps change the currency of invoice;

iv) in the slightly longer run, alter the pattern and composition of trade flows.

While limited by their individual capital constraints and perhaps only reacting defensively, sober merchants and manufacturers thereby transform themselves into speculators in this chronological perspective.

Under (i), consider a prototype Dutch importer who intends to pay 100 kronor for a newly received shipment of Volvos (tradables I) in 90 days; he normally covers forward only a portion of this, say 45 kronor, and relies on inventory hedging for the remainder (Chapter 4). However, a discrete devaluation of guilders now seems likely before 90 days elapse, so he covers forward the whole 100-krona payment. Otherwise, instead of having to pay approximately 60 guilders in total to meet his 100-krona payment (1 krona ≃ .6 guilders), he might find himself having to pay 70 or 80 guilders if a discrete devaluation occurs within 90 days.

Notice that the Dutch importer can immediately adjust his forward cover by a *unilateral decision* that does not require consultation with his trading partner in Sweden. Hence it is likely to be the first speculative deviation from his normal commercial practices. Will he buy 55 additional kronor in the forward market for foreign exchange, or will he buy spot an equivalent interest-bearing krona asset? The answer depends heavily on the means by which the Dutch central bank—Netherlands Bank—is maintaining the pegged guilder/krona exchange rate under pressure.

If the Netherlands Bank is simply buying guilders spot without intervening in the forward market, the krona will go to a sharp forward premium in terms of guilders. Hence forward purchases of kronor will seem expensive, and the Dutch importer will opt instead to buy krona interest-bearing assets spot, and present his 100-krona invoice for Volvos to a duly authorized commercial bank to establish his eligibility to make such a purchase for hedging purposes. The authorities will have no convenient means of distinguishing this application for forward cover from hundreds of other similar requests. Indeed, it seems that the Volvo importer is just covering his 100-krona payment and stands neither to gain nor lose if the guilder is discretely devalued. Yet the importer profits on those Volvos still in inventory at the time of devaluation—a subtle enough adjustment problem for the importer himself let alone the authorities (Chapter 4).

If the authorities are also pegging the forward rate—keeping the krona from going to a forward premium, then the importer may buy the additional 55 kronor in the forward market instead—again with an eye to a speculative profit on inventory valuation adjustment. Either way, such speculation will bring pressure on the Netherlands Bank. Exchange reserves will fall immediately in the first case, whereas the central bank's commitments to deliver kronor forward will increase in the second.

For goods invoiced in guilders, however, the analysis is not quite symmetrical. A Swedish importer of Dutch tulip bulbs invoiced in *guilders*—tradables I again—still need not consult with his Dutch trading partner regarding forward cover. If he has to pay guilders in 90 days, and normally covers 100 out of the 200 guilders that are due, he can speculate by neither covering in the forward market nor buying guilder assets spot. The absence of covering by foreigners is certainly beyond the regulatory reach of the Dutch authorities. Yet just as surely this puts pressure on the official reserves of the Netherlands Bank because the absence of normal covering by foreigners reduces the demand for guilders (supply of kronor) in both the forward and spot exchange markets. Moreover, foreign importers of tradables I can take their profits directly by delivering less of their home currency (kronor) once the guilder is devalued. Disguised speculation, confined to inventory profits, is unnecessary for foreigners.[23]

Leads and Lags

The next stage (ii) of speculative pressure from merchants comes from *exporters leading* in extending ordinary trade credit, and *importers lagging* in obtaining it. This pressure may take a little longer to develop—from the time that ideas become fixed on devaluation—because some cooperation is required between trading partners. Nevertheless such cooperation can be rapidly forthcoming if the authorities tried to prevent importers or exporters from juggling their forward cover, or if restrictions already existed on movements of short-term financial capital as per the IMF's (Article VIII) narrow definition of convertibility.

If Dutch importers of tradables I normally issue krona trade bills payable in 90 days to their Swedish suppliers, such extant trade instruments would have to be renegotiated if the importer wishes to pay immediately, or within the few days prior to when a devaluation seems likely. Even in the absence of such formal renegotiation of old bills, however, new krona bills drawn on Dutch importers in the normal course of trade between Holland and Sweden could be devised so as to have as much shorter maturity—perhaps down to cash on delivery or even krona prepayment. Such a drastic shortening in the term structure of import finance would be equivalent to a sharp net capital outflow from Holland: new imports are paid for immediately while old bills are still falling due.

23. Insofar as the krona price of tulips—still in inventory in Sweden—falls when the guilder depreciates—this will reduce the net speculative profit arising from actually having to deliver fewer kronor in 90 days for depreciated guilders.

Normal commercial practice has shifted away from import bills of a fixed term towards informal on-account credit, as was noted in Chapter 4. If about 70 percent of Dutch imports now carry open-account credits (Table 4.1), the term structure of even "old" import credits is easily shortened without difficult renegotiations. Since credits outstanding can be paid off any time, they can be paid off immediately. Because flexible open-account credits for goods invoiced in the exporter's currency are a quid pro quo for the importer bearing exchange risk, the Netherlands Bank would be hard pressed to prevent Dutch importers from speculating.

On the export side, Dutch growers of tulips could extend abnormally long credits to Swedish customers—or Swedish importers could simply lag in paying their open-account credits. The longer payment for tulips in guilders is deferred, the more likely the importer can reduce his krona costs proportionately to the expected devaluation. Again, the immediate effect is a sharp capital outflow from Holland. While pleased to keep his customers happy, the Dutch exporter might well bargain with his trading partner for a share of the speculative proceeds—particularly if the anticipated devaluation of the guilder arose from continuing wage and cost inflation in Holland. The exporter could charge a very high nominal rate of interest on the extended guilder credits granted to the importer, or raise the guilder invoice price of tulips to reflect expected depreciation. Neither course of action may be entirely satisfactory to both parties: devaluation may not actually occur for all that, and each party has his own peculiar problem of inventory valuation adjustment should it occur. Yet they would have strong incentive to reach some implicit or explicit agreement.

The potential empirical importance of merchant speculators altering leads and lags in commercial credits, or of juggling the normal amount of forward cover on outstanding credits, can be gauged within limits from Sven Grassman's representative Swedish data. In Tables 7.1 and 7.2 foreign assets and liabilities of business firms—dominated by trade credit to (from) suppliers and

TABLE 7.1 Sweden's Portfolio of Foreign Holdings, By Sector, December 31, 1970 (Million kronor)

	Business firms	State and municipalities	Foreign exchange of commercial banks	Riksbank	Total
Assets	13,783	314	4,235	?	(18,332)
Liabilities	13,496	159	3,153	?	(16,808)
Net foreign claims	287	155	1,082	3,624	5,148

SOURCE: Sven Grassman, *Exchange Reserves and the Financial Structure of Foreign Trade* (Westmead, Eng.: Saxon House, 1973), p. 46.

TABLE 7.2   Breakdown of Foreign Portfolio of Business Sector, December 31, 1970
(Million kronor)

	1970	%
Claims	13,782.9	100.0
Cash and equivalent	157.8	1.1
Claims, trade bills, and advances		
to suppliers	8,883.5	64.5
Credits to affiliates	4,168.6	30.2
Other loans	573.0	4.2
Debts		
Debts to suppliers, trade bills and		
advances from customers	5,748.3	42.6
Debts to affiliates	4,232.2	31.4
Other loans	3,515.8	26.0

SOURCE: Sven Grassman, *Exchange Reserves and the Financial Structure of Foreign Trade* (West-mead, Eng.: Saxon House, 1973), p. 47.

affiliates—are fairly evenly balanced at about 13.5 billion kronor each. The average credit period for Swedish imports is about two months, and that for exports about two and a half months. If all Swedish importers suddenly began paying within 30 days instead of an average of 60 days, this moderate shortening of term structure on the import side alone would amount to a capital outflow of 5 or 6 billion kronor—and a reserve loss by the Swedish central bank (Riksbank) of a similar amount.

This loss of 5 or 6 billion kronor seems large when compared either to the foreign assets held by the commercial banks—4.235 billion kronor (Table 7.1)—or to the foreign exchange assets (gross of liabilities) of the Riksbank—about 3.94 billion kronor as of December 31, 1970.[24] Without even considering the export side, such a loss would put the Riksbank into severe difficulty.

While the curtailment of import credits is inherently limited by the volume outstanding[25]—13.5 billion kronor approximately, the extension of new export credits is not so constrained if convertibility is maintained. The full year's flow of Swedish exports in 1970 was about 45 billion kronor.

Clearly merchant speculation through leads and lags, covering or uncovering, can be overwhelming against a convertible currency even when the capital account is otherwise tightly controlled. It was the final trigger (but not the long-run cause) of British devaluations in 1949 and 1967, and discrete French devaluations in the late 1950s. Yet such speculation does require a one-way bet

24. Not shown by Grassman because the data are very rough, but estimated to be about 3.94 billion kronor by the IMF's *International Financial Statistics* (June 1975), p. 358.
25. Not, I suppose, if all potential imports can be prepaid.

that overcomes the strong reluctance of merchants to disrupt normal patterns of commercial payments.

Changing the Currency of Invoice

We have shown how bargaining between exporters and importers to share speculative profits is not easy if the currency of invoice is under pressure. Risk and uncertainty increase for both parties. One way out is simply to change the currency of invoice—strategy (iii) listed earlier.

Suppose again, expectations arise of a discrete devaluation of the guilder, but authorities prevent Dutch exporters from significantly lengthening the term of trade credits to their foreign customers. Exporters may begin to quote prices for tulips in U.S. dollars instead of guilders, and extend only normal trade credit to their Swedish customers at going nominal rates of interest on U.S. dollars. In effect, tulips are reclassified from tradables I to tradables II, where the dollar is taken to be a more stable standard of value. Swedish importers of tulips now have a firm obligation to pay dollars in the future, which they can easily hedge because no discrete one-way change in the krona/dollar exchange rate is expected. Complex negotiations to adjust the contract price of tulips, should devaluation occur in the middle of the credit period, are no longer necessary. The uncertainty and difficulty of dividing speculative profits (or losses) between exporter and importer is avoided because the task of speculating on devaluation of the guilder is now thrown completely onto the shoulders of the Dutch exporter. Additionally, the Dutch exporter may be able to judge his own government's intentions more accurately.

A more general object lesson is that the selection of a currency of invoice is not immutable, even among convertible-currency countries. Arguments were advanced in Chapter 4 linking nonhomogeneous or brand-differentiated products—tradables I—to invoicing in the seller's currency. Yet repeated experiences with discrete devaluations—or other sharp exchange-rate fluctuations—will reduce the convenience yield from invoicing in that particular currency. British sterling has suffered several speculative episodes in the late 1940s, mid-1960s, early 1970, and in 1975–1976. Although in the latter periods Britain was formally on a no-par system, traders could never be sure when the system of official intervention would or would not break down rather suddenly. Hence it is hardly surprising that sterling has lost preeminence as "the" international currency of invoice in trade between third countries. Most international trade was invoiced in sterling prior to 1914, and these practices extended well into the 1920s and 1930s. In contrast, Sven Grassman's most recent data indicate that 17.4 percent of Swedish imports and 11.2 percent of Swedish exports were invoiced in sterling in 1968, whereas only 10.3 percent and 4.6 percent respectively were so invoiced in 1973.[26]

But inconvertible currencies are even less usable for invoicing. Not only is forward covering difficult or impossible by financial means, inconvertible currencies suffer more frequently from major discrete devaluations as we shall establish. In addition to those advanced in Chapter 2, this is another reason why less developed countries and centrally planned economies have a negligible proportion of their exports (and none of their imports) invoiced in their own currency—even for exports of manufactures that might normally be classified as tradables I. It is just too difficult and risky for potential overseas customers to undertake contractual obligations in such currencies. Rather, the use of relatively stable convertible currencies allows overseas suppliers or customers to conveniently hedge their currency risks; but forces profit-minded exporters and importers in LDCs to speculate continually in terms of their own currency—to avoid bankruptcy if nothing more.

Official Speculation and Exchange Controls

While actual international flows of goods and services are more difficult and expensive to alter than their modes of finance, speculation can come to this when currency convertibility is abrogated. Indeed, rather acute disruption in the normal pattern of physical trade—stage (iv) mentioned earlier—depends on how intensively central banks themselves speculate, and then try to support such speculations through the use of exchange controls.

I shall define official intervention in the foreign exchanges to be *nonspeculative* when the exchange-rate target is fully realizable without having to impose exchange controls,[27] or without risking "giving up" so as to allow a discrete devaluation or appreciation to occur. A full exposition of nonspeculative foreign exchange policy would take us too far afield in macroeconomic theory and policy but the central idea can be quickly sketched. An excess demand for foreign currency must reflect an excess supply of domestic currency from residents and foreigners at the official rate of exchange. If, in the course of selling foreign exchange, the central bank retires domestic money from circulation so as to eliminate the excess supply, the rate can be preserved. Retirement of domestic currency is at least a sufficient condition for official intervention to be nonspeculative. Indeed, it is a capability that makes central banks essentially different from private speculators (Chapter 2).

26. "Currency Distribution and Forward Cover in Foreign Trade: Sweden Revisited 1973," *Journal of International Economics*, Vol. 6, No. 2 (May 1976), p. 217.
27. . . . or imposing additional or more stringent trade restrictions than normal.

In practice, however, some other agency of the government may continue to issue excess supplies of domestic currency, or the central bank itself may sterilize (prevent) the retirement of domestic currency as exchange reserves are drawn down. Then the excess supply of domestic money in the foreign exchange market need not be eliminated. The central bank's ability to maintain the exchange-rate target becomes uncertain, and the official intervention itself may be deemed "speculative."

The consequences of speculative official intervention in an *open* convertible-currency system have already been investigated in our guilder-krona example. Counter speculation is generated by merchants and banks with considerable disruption in the financial structure of foreign trade, and sometimes a rather rapid depletion of official exchange reserves. What are the further consequences of supporting speculative intervention by the imposition of exchange controls that escalate in severity as the crisis proceeds? Let the Argentine peso be the analytical prototype of such an inconvertible currency that is officially pegged to the more stable U.S. dollar, which is also the currency of invoice for both exports and imports.

Suppose initially that devaluation pressure is normal. Excess demand for imports is modest and fairly easily rationed by official licensing: say a long free list of essential commodities are imported without restraint, while restrictions remain on "nonessentials." Exporters are content to remit dollars as earned to the central bank at the prevailing peso exchange rate because no devaluation seems imminent. However, exporters do not demand forward cover—i.e., to sell dollars forward—reflecting the past unidirectional nature of exchange-rate changes in Argentina. To prevent capital flight, the government strictly limits the volume of export credits. On the other hand, importers of officially approved goods are anxious to buy dollars forward to cover future payments. Indeed, if allowed, they would cover 100 percent of future payments rather than striking a balance between inventory hedging and forward covering as described in Chapter 4—again because of the unidirectional nature of possible future movements in the peso exchange rate. Although the central bank wants dollar trade credits from abroad (capital inflow), importers are not anxious to defer dollar payments unless forward cover is obtainable.

The Argentinian government sometimes allows importers to buy dollars in advance through an authorized commercial bank to cover at least a portion of the future dollar payments. However, importers can likely cover only at a penalty rate—receiving noninterest-bearing dollar claims on a domestic commercial bank or the central bank itself. Alternatively, advance deposit requirements may actually force importers to put in escrow, say, 150 pesos for payment due in six months, when only 100 are needed at the existing official

exchange rate. If devaluation occurs in the interim, the government appropri-
ates the extra pesos. With these or similar penalties, importers may well decide
to cover only a portion or none of their future dollar payments, and rely on
inventory hedging as far as possible.

Suppose now the system is shocked so that devaluation now seems much
more likely: excess internal money creation in Argentina leads to new demands
for foreign exchange, or exports decline leading to a diminution in its supply.
In neither case is the fall in official reserves allowed to contract the domestic
stock of money. Indeed, the economy may well be caught up in higher domestic price and wage inflation. Merchants now begin to speculate—perhaps only
to avoid exchange losses—against the tightly controlled banking system.

Discouraged from seeking forward cover, importers may try to advance the
dates for making dollar payments—although this may be difficult if old import
licenses have been written on the assumption that longer-term foreign trade
credits would be fully utilized. New import licenses might require increased
trade credits, which many foreign government agencies—such as the U.S.
Export-Import Bank—stand ready to provide. Nevertheless, speculative attempts will be made to drastically shorten the term structure of import finance.
When permission is denied by the authorities, many importers will quit rather
than being left with uncovered dollar obligations.

However, any discouragement to import applications through financial restrictions will be short-lived. As exchange reserves fall and importing becomes
more difficult and expensive, the peso prices of importable goods in Argentina
begin to rise above world levels—as measured by the official exchange rate and
international dollar prices. Where the holding of commodity inventories is
relatively costless, merchants build up domestic stocks in anticipation of higher
peso prices after devaluation. This commodity speculation bids up peso prices
further. Eventually, the gap between Argentinian and world prices in many
categories will be sufficient to overcome any reluctance to import on an uncovered basis so that the exchange-control authority is deluged with new applications. Arbitrary rationing or prohibitions in this or that commodity become
necessary. Each applicant tries to convince the authorities that his particular
import product—fuel, food, ball bearings, medicines, and so on—is in severe
shortage. Gross and costly mistakes in product allocations begin to develop—
and shortages of industrial raw materials, spare parts, or fuels may bring on a
cyclical downturn in the economy.[28]

As reserves fall the overall volume of imports will come to depend on

28. For a more complete description of the cyclical and internal financial complications of such a
foreign exchange crisis, see R. I. McKinnon, *Money and Capital in Economic Development*
(Washington, D.C.: Brookings Institution, 1973), Chapter 11.

continuing foreign exchange earnings. And speculation by exporters is ultimately more difficult to curb. Because exporters do not normally carry forward cover, they will first try to defer the time of future dollar payments by their overseas customers. Elaborate new directives may force exporters to surrender their dollar receipts at the official exchange rate within, say, 30 days of export shipments actually clearing Argentinian ports—irrespective of when goods are sold or what the credit arrangements turn out to be. Since the dollar prices of many primary commodities fluctuate rather sharply on world markets, the authorities may set an official price for wheat or whatever as a basis for calculating what foreign exchange receipts are owed in order to prevent under-invoicing.[29] Insofar as this official price becomes disaligned with actual world prices, additional uncertainty will confront the potential exporter of raw materials.

A determined and well-organized exchange-control authority can block virtually all purely financial avenues by which exporters can speculate against impending devaluation. In so doing, however, the authority may well provoke independent merchants, farmers, and manufacturers into stopping the international shipment of goods and services altogether. Potential exporters either cut production, or build up commodity inventories in Argentina, in the hope of receiving a higher peso price after devaluation. And well they might if caught in an inflationary price-cost squeeze of their own. As export earnings dry up— perhaps aggravating the cyclical downturn—the squeeze on and physical disruption in the import sector becomes more pronounced.

This counter speculation by private traders will only end when the exchange rate is realigned and/or convincing measures are taken to reduce the excess money demand for goods and services in the domestic economy. The longer the exchange-control authority manages to support speculative official intervention without devaluing, the more pronounced become outright shortages and relative price distortions among tradable goods. Often government-to-government aid and official foreign credits may be solicited from abroad in order to let the authorities hang on a bit longer—but this is hardly an efficient way to utilize foreign capital.[30]

Chronic inflationary pressure in many LDCs ensures that their currency pegs are continually changed—with all the speculative disruption attending

29. In the case of coffee, Colombian authorities often fix a standard dollar price per bushel of coffee leaving Colombian ports which is a little bit less than the best guess of average world prices. Irrespective of what the exporter actually receives on world markets, he may be required to surrender 90 percent of this official price within 30 days.
30. A more complete exposition of the utilization of foreign and domestic capital in ending a foreign exchange crisis, together with the appropriate circumstance under which exchange controls and other impediments to trade can be eliminated, is provided in R.I. McKinnon, op. cit., Chapter 11.

TABLE 7.3   Selected Discrete Devaluations in Nonindustrial Countries, 1960–1970

Country	Date of devaluation	Nominal devaluation[a]	Change in domestic currency per dollar
		(Percent)	
Afghanistan[b]	March 22, 1963	55.6	125.0
Burundi[b]	January 26,1965	42.9	75.0
Costa Rica[b]	September 3, 1961	15.3	18.0
Ecuador	July 14, 1961	16.7	20.0
Ecuador	August 17, 1970	28.0	38.9
Egypt	May 7, 1962	19.3	23.9
Finland	October 12, 1967	23.8	31.3
Ghana	July 8, 1967	30.0	42.9
Iceland[c]	August 4, 1961	62.1	164.0
Iceland[d]	November 12, 1968	51.1	104.7
India	June 6, 1966	36.5	57.5
Israel	February 9, 1962	40.0	66.7
Korea[e]	February 2, 1961	61.5	160.0
Mali	May 6, 1967	50.0	100.0
Peru[f]	October 5, 1967	30.7	44.3
Philippines	January 22, 1962	48.5	94.1
Philippines	February 21, 1970	38.7	63.2
Rwanda	April 7, 1966	50.0	100.0
Sri Lanka	November 21, 1967	20.0	25.0
Tunisia	September 28, 1964	19.2	23.8
Turkey	August 9, 1970	40.0	66.7
Zaire[g]	June 23, 1967	67.0	203.0

SOURCE: International Monetary Fund, *International Financial Statistics Annual Supplements*; and data provided by the national authorities. From A. Bhagwat and Y. Onitsuka, "Export Responses to Devaluation: Experience of the Nonindustrial Countries in the 1960s," IMF *Staff Papers* (July 1974), pp. 414–62.

[a]Changes in par value, except as otherwise stated. It should be noted that in many instances the effective devaluation in the economic sense was substantially less than the nominal devaluation shown here.

[b]Establishment of initial par value.

[c]Combined effect of 1960 and 1961 devaluations.

[d]Combined effect of 1967 and 1968 devaluations.

[e]Change in the official rate from Feb. 23, 1960 to Feb. 2, 1961.

[f]Change in the principal rate.

[g]Compared with the average of predevaluation buying and selling rates.

discrete devaluations as described above. Table 7.3 is a nonexhaustive list of 22 representative discrete devaluations that occurred beyond (between) 1960 and 1970. Many were very substantial being of the order of 50 percent or more. Moreover, in the early 1970s similar changes proceeded apace. Stanley Black has tabulated ten additional discrete changes occurring between January 1970 and April 1, 1974 in these and other LDCs.[31]

We know from Chapter 2 that the advent in 1973 of floating exchange rates among Western industrial countries did not much influence the marked propensity of most LDCs to peg to the convertible currency of an industrial economy. Thus the syndrome of periodic discrete devaluations, coupled with speculative crises, is still with us in most parts of the world.

31. Stanley Black, "Exchange Policies for Less Developed Countries in a World of Floating Rates," in *The International Monetary System and the Developing Nations* (Washington, D.C.: U.S. Agency for International Development, 1976), pp. 13–67.

8

Fluctuating Exchange Rates, 1973-1978: A Qualified Monetary Interpretation

Official monetary actions and other money-market disturbances have their own peculiar effects in a regime of floating exchange rates among convertible currencies. Indeed, the equilibrium exchange rate is dominated by market perceptions of monetary policies in the future. Taking output and employment in any one country as given in the short run, I shall examine how exchange rates and interest rates are mutually determined in the national money market: the asset or portfolio approach to the determination of exchange rates.[1]

In Part I of Chapter 7, we assumed that monetary policies were unchanging with a fixed term structure of interest rates in order to focus on the behavior of nonspeculative merchants. That simplifying assumption was quite appropriate when considering random *real* disturbances in trade flows: the shifting tastes of consumers between German and American goods. In this chapter, by contrast, the term structure of forward rates of exchange and interest rates is permitted to vary systematically in response to *monetary* disturbances, along with variations in the spot rate itself. Only then can we get a complete understanding of why exchange-rate fluctuations from 1973 onwards have been so surprisingly large.

1. The more general macroeconomic problem of modelling the determination of income, price levels, and employment is well beyond the scope of this book.

Apart from official exchange parities, should one expect some floating exchange rates across particular pairs of countries to be naturally more stable than others? Combining the old literature on optimum currency areas[2] with the modern asset-adjustment approach to the determination of exchange rates,[3] I develop a theoretical explanation of the *natural degree of exchange-rate variation*. The theory explains the differential movements in relative currency values across differently situated groups of countries. In addition, it explains why some exchange movements have been unexpectedly large with private stabilizing speculation in the foreign exchanges being weak or absent.

A monetary rather than monetarist approach to the short-run determination of exchange rates is employed. Indeed, the Keynesian liquidity preference model of the rate of interest is generalized to the case of an open economy. A novel theoretical twist is to incorporate the demand for domestic money by foreign exchange dealers (speculators) *explicitly*. Then I show how the supply of private speculative capital for stabilizing particular exchange rates in part depends on the degree of economic integration with particular trading partners, along the lines of the older arguments defining optimum currency areas.

Keynesian Liquidity Preference and the Rate of Interest in an Open Economy

Because my main concern is the foreign exchanges, I shall drastically simplify orthodox Keynesian monetary theory for closed economies. Although there are many variants of the Keynesian orthodoxy, all hold that changes in the nominal stock of money affect the final demand for goods and services primarily through the prices of securities in capital markets rather than through any direct wealth effect. Insofar as monetary policy has any influence at all, it operates through the rate of interest as the intermediate policy variable. The negative relationship between the quantity of real money and real interest rates is defined by the liquidity-preference function; and, in a closed economy there is the presumption that monetary authorities can in fact control the real rate of interest and the real stock of money by varying the nominal stock of money. Hence, the real rate of interest and the real stock of money are not endogenous to the economy but can be, to some significant degree, manipulated by the monetary authorities.

2. Ronald I. McKinnon, "Optimum Currency Areas," *American Economic Review* (September 1963), pp. 717–25. Robert A. Mundell, "A Theory of Optimum Currency Areas," *American Economic Review* (September 1961), pp. 657–74.
3. Pentti Kouri, "The Exchange Rate and the Balance of Payments in the Short Run and in the Long Run," *The Scandinavian Journal of Economics*, Vol. 78, No. 2 (1976), pp. 280–304. Rudiger Dornbusch, "The Theory of Flexible Exchange-Rate Regimes and Macroeconomic Policy," *The Scandinavian Journal of Economics*, Vol. 78, No. 1 (1976), pp. 255–75.

Unsurprisingly, since the authorities can increase the real stock of money by increasing nominal cash balances, the Keynesian closed-economy world is one where the price level is stable and expected to remain so over the relevant time horizon. More precisely, any given proportional change in the nominal stock of money leads to a substantially smaller proportional change in the price level. The same would be true for shifts in liquidity preference itself: changes in the private demand for money (for a fixed supply) would lead to much smaller proportional changes in commodity prices. Over prolonged periods, this assumption of stable prices and price expectations seems most plausible when there is substantial unemployment and slack in the economy (prices being fairly sticky in not moving downward), or when individuals have had historical experience with a stable price level at close to full employment and believe that the authorities are committed to, and will be successful in, maintaining that stability. Otherwise, this assumption of sticky prices and price expectations is best confined to the very short run, where firms or individuals are either taken by surprise by shifts in monetary policies or are unable to make price adjustments.

Can domestic prices remain rigid in an open economy subject to exchange-rate fluctuations of the kind observed in 1973–1978? In a world producing and consuming only tradables II—primary commodities—the Keynesian assumption of short-term price rigidity would be untenable. Fluctuations in exchange rates would be quickly transmitted to the domestic price level: a five percent devaluation of a small country's currency leads quickly to a five percent increase in the domestic prices of tradables II. However, if the world is composed largely of nontradables and tradables I—manufactured goods whose price quotations are relatively fixed in terms of the domestic money (for convertible-currency countries)—unanticipated exchange fluctuations lead to much smaller proportional changes in domestic price indices. Indeed, we showed in Chapter 6 that short-run deviations of national price levels from their purchasing power parities, due to fluctuations in exchange rates, were quite pronounced.[4] In this chapter, therefore, *I simply assume that the domestic price level is, in the first instance, relatively invariant to exchange-rate fluctuations.*

This assumption then permits us to interpret Keynesian liquidity-preference theory as if the economy were closed to foreign trade in the goods market, while nevertheless open to capital inflows or outflows from abroad. In Figure 8.1, *LP* represents the domestic liquidity-preference schedule relating the rate of interest to the stock of money in such an economy; and *M* represents the given supply of nominal money under the exogenous control of a government

4. See Chapter 6.

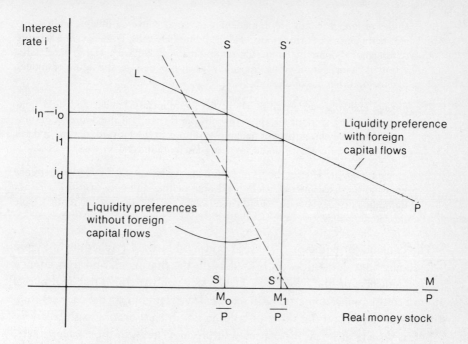

FIGURE 8.1 Liquidity preference in an open economy with a flexible exchange rate

authority who is *not* committed to maintaining a fixed exchange rate.[5] The discrete move from M_0 to M_1 at time zero portrays an unanticipated expansion in nominal money where the real stock increases equiproportionately from M_0/P to M_1/P. The sticky domestic price level within the short time frame under consideration ensures the Keynesian equivalence between real and nominal monetary changes. Given the usual downward slope to the liquidity-preference function, the rate of interest i on 90 day bonds falls at time zero in order to maintain portfolio balance between bonds and the increased supply of real cash balances: the ordinary short-run liquidity effect of easy money.

But how does the money market in an open economy differ from that in a closed one? For analytical convenience, let us distinguish among three classes of financial firms or individuals:

1) *Domestic wealth holders* (DWH) strongly prefer the national currency as their habitat. They hold no working balances of spot foreign exchange and all pur-

5. A pegged exchange rate would, of course, force the monetary authority to endogenize the money supply by buying and selling the domestic currency on demand. One could not then perform the conceptual experiment of arbitrarily varying the stock of money in order to derive the liquidity-preference schedule.

chases of foreign bonds are immediately covered. (Covered interest arbitrageurs are, perforce, part of this group.) Hence domestic wealth holders own a mixture of foreign and domestic bonds. Correspondingly, they have a well-defined transaction demand for domestic currency as a function of the level of money income and the rate of interest.

2) *Foreign-exchange dealers* have no particular monetary habitat and hold non-interest-bearing working balances in both the foreign and the domestic currencies. They freely take open (or hedging) positions in the forward market, and sell cover to domestic wealth holders owning foreign bonds.

3) *Foreign rentiers* sell (or buy) an infinitely elastic supply of foreign-currency bonds at the fixed interest rate i_n, and hold neither domestic cash balances nor domestic-currency bonds.[6] Foreign currency is, therefore, the rentiers' sole monetary habitat.

The demand for domestic money, as portrayed by the *LP* schedule in Figure 8.1, comes from domestic wealth holders on the one hand, and from foreign exchange dealers on the other. The DWH focus on the single nominal rate of interest on bonds—domestic and covered foreign bonds are perfect substitutes—as the opportunity cost of holding noninterest-bearing cash balances, Whereas dealers focus on the expected future movement in the exchange rate, R_s, as the opportunity cost of holding domestic as opposed to foreign cash balances.

Specifically, let us partition domestic currency into M_a held by domestic wealth holders and M_b held by foreign exchange dealers. In order to abstract from the complexities of fractional reserve banking that are not essential to the present analysis, I follow the usual simplification of assuming M to be currency plus demand deposits; reserve requirements of 100 percent are held against the latter. Then holdings of domestic money are completely allocated to DWH or to dealers:

$$M = M^a + M^b \tag{8.1}$$

For our beginning-of-period analysis, the demand for money by DWH is inversely related to the domestic rate of interest i, assuming that both money income Y and financial wealth W^a are given:

6. Somewhat asymmetrically, I am assuming that foreigners do not hold domestic-currency bonds either covered or uncovered, whereas domestic wealth holders can freely take net positions in covered foreign-currency bonds. This asymmetry has the analytical advantage of *not* incorporating the portfolio decisions of foreign rentiers formally into the analysis—other than to say they maintain i_n at a fixed level. At the same time, however, covered interest arbitrage between domestic and foreign currency bonds flourishes through the interaction of foreign exchange dealers and domestic wealth holders.

$$M^a = M^a(i; Y, W^a) \atop \quad - \; + \; +$$

(8.2)

Domestic wealth holders have the conventional function used for closed economies to describe the demand for money as it arises from the transactions and precautionary motives. However, DWH own only a portion—although perhaps the major portion—of the total stock of domestic money.

Notice also that the balance-sheet position of the DWH consists of their holdings of domestic money M^a plus some net holding of bonds. G represents net bonded claims on the domestic government (outside bond holdings) and B represents net covered claims on foreigners such that

$$W^a = M^a + B + G.$$

(8.3)

A government open-market operation can, therefore, be represented as an exchange of M^a for G, i.e., money for bonds in the portfolios of DWH.

Foreign Exchange Dealers and the Domestic Money Market

During the 1950s and 1960s, a mass of literature bourgeoned on whether or not private speculation in the foreign exchanges is stabilizing or destabilizing. Surprisingly, the portfolio position of foreign exchange speculators was never spelled out with any analytical precision. Indeed, events in the foreign exchange market were divorced from direct association with the domestic money and bond markets.[7]

In our monetary approach to exchange-rate determination, on the other hand, dealers (speculators) are important but constrained actors in the domestic money market. Our pure foreign exchange dealers hold no bonds—neither as borrowers nor lenders. Unlike domestic wealth holders, dealers have no preferred monetary habitat and perform the important economic function of clearing international payments. Speculation is incidental to their main business of

---

7. In reviewing this literature, Robert Stern in *The Balance of Payments* (Chicago, Ill.: Aldine, 1973), simply assumed (pp. 77–89) that forward and spot exchange rates are always equal so that domestic and foreign rates of interest are also equalized—even in the short run when the exchange rate is moving. In the absence of speculative activity, contributors to the debate simply posited that the exchange rate moved in certain arbitrary patterns—such as a simple sine wave. Then the question was asked whether speculators without liquidity constraints could make profits by taking long or short positions that aggravate the underlying exchange fluctuations. Counter examples flew thick and fast because of the arbitrary nature of the initial conditions: the predetermined nonspeculative wave motion in the exchange rate. Because the joint determination of interest rates, exchange rates, and the money supply was disregarded in this peculiar literature, rationally based private expectations simply could not be introduced.

TABLE 8.1 The Portfolio Position of Foreign Exchange Dealers

		Spot Position*		
Cash in guilders	M^b	Net wealth	$W^b = M^b + R_s^k M^b$	
Cash in kronor	$^k M^b$			
		Forward Position†		
Long in kronor	B^k	Short in guilders	$R_f B^k = B$	

*R_s is the spot exchange rate (guilders per krona); R_f is the corresponding forward rate.
†Cover for the foreign bonds of domestic wealth holders.

money changing. If the only spot holdings of dealers are working cash balances of domestic and foreign currencies, what determines their liquidity preference between the two?

Focus first on the dealers' spot position. Financing requires capital equal to 100 percent of both their krona and guilder cash balances, which yield no direct interest. On the other hand, forward positions can be held with a much lesser allocation of capital that is assumed here to be negligible—effectively a zero margin requirement. Hence the net wealth position of our foreign exchange dealers W^b is simply the sum of their spot currency holdings as shown in Table 8.1. If more domestic currency is to be acquired, therefore, foreign currency must be given up in exchange. This tight wealth constraint, which forecloses access to the bond market, is not unrealistic in modelling the immediate (beginning-of-period) response of foreign exchange dealers to a discrete increase in the domestic supply of money.[8]

A further consideration in the portfolio selection of guilders and kronor is their effective productivity in allowing dealers to make and clear international payments on behalf of their nonbank customers.[9] On average, dealers collectively viewed will want to hold a balanced portfolio of the two currencies for this purpose of money changing.

However if R_s is expected to increase steadily (guilders depreciate relative to kronor), guilder balances will be reduced in order to raise their marginal product in clearing international payments. This marginal balancing yields a determinant demand for domestic (and foreign) money by dealers that can be written:

8. In effect, all arbitrage between the money and bond markets in response to interest-rate changes is being assigned to firms in their capacity as domestic wealth holders, rather than as foreign exchange dealers.
9. Who remain in the shadows in this chapter. The potentially destabilizing behavior of merchants was analyzed in Chapter 7.

$$M^b = M^b (\dot{R}_s^e; W^b) \qquad (8.4)$$
$$\quad\;\; - \quad +$$

where $\dot{R}_s^e$ is the expected percentage rate of change in the exchange rate (depreciation in guilders); and W^b is the wealth constraint on foreign exchange dealers.[10]

In equation (8.4.), W^b is fixed over the dealer's short decision horizon. However, foreign exchange dealers can freely reshuffle their asset portfolios between guilders and kronor. Indeed, the corresponding asset demand for foreign exchange (kronor) is simply:

$$^kM^b = [W^b - M^b(\dot{R}_s^e; W_b)] \cdot \frac{1}{R_s}. \qquad (8.5)$$

In reducing his guilder balances in response, say, to an increase in $\dot{R}_s^e$, equation (8.5) implies that our dealer acquires an equivalent amount of kronor at the beginning of our 90-day time horizon.

How then can the demand for money by dealers be portrayed as a function of the rate of interest as per Figure 8.1? Before introducing uncertainty, one can comfortably assume that the interest rate parity theorem (IRPT) holds exactly, *and* that the forward rate R_f is an unbiased estimate of the expected future spot rate.[11] If the rate of interest on foreign currency bonds is always inelastically fixed at i_n, these two assumptions imply that:

$$i - i_n = f = \frac{R_f - R_s}{R_f} = \dot{R}_s^e \qquad (8.6)$$

where f is the forward premium on the foreign currency (kronor) in terms of the domestic currency (guilders); and $\dot{R}_s^e$ is the expected percentage movement (gradual) in the exchange rate (depreciation of the guilder) over the next 90 days.

With this asset-adjustment machinery in place, consider the reaction of dealers to a discrete but unanticipated increase in the domestic money supply, assuming that market participants have *full information* about the future course of monetary policy over the next 90 days. If the money supply increases from M_0 to M_1, some of the newly created guilder balances normally flow into the portfolios of foreign exchange dealers. But dealers can only be induced to acquire additional working balances of guilders (in return for working balances of kroner) if R_s is expected to fall smoothly over the next 90 days. Hence, the guilder will depreciate discretely at time zero by an amount sufficient to set up

10. Over longer periods of time, the amount of capital committed to dealing in foreign exchange would depend on the flow of foreign trade.
11. Although much variance in the future spot rate will not be explained by the present forward rate, the evidence indicates that R_f is an unbiased if statistically inefficient estimator.

the expectation of gradual appreciation back to a normal level. That expected appreciation will be exactly equal to the immediate fall in the rate of interest from i_o to i_1, as plotted on the vertical axis of Figure 8.1.

The Interest Elasticity
of the Liquidity-Preference Function

In Figure 8.1, the LP schedule for an open economy is shown to be more interest elastic than the dashed line, which portrays liquidity preference in an economy closed to foreign capital flows. But what allows the domestic rate of interest in an open economy to differ at all from the foreign rate? A rather large literature in macroeconomic international finance now identifies perfect capital mobility with a situation where the domestic rate of interest is firmly pegged to the foreign rate:[12] the LP schedule is perfectly horizontal at i_n over some relevant time horizon. In a regime of floating exchange rates, this literature is in apparent conflict with Keynesian liquidity-preference analysis which presumes that the domestic rate of interest and the real stock of money can be influenced by the monetary authority.

This conflict can be resolved, in part, if we identify Keynesian liquidity-preference analysis with instantaneous beginning-of-period stock *adjustment*. An open-market operation at time zero forces an immediate discrete reshuffling of asset portfolios by domestic wealth holders, foreign exchange dealers, and foreign rentiers. Then a new expectation is established of exchange-rate movement over a finite interval of time—say 90 days or even two years—at the end of which a new equilibrium is established, where new flow additions to wealth could be absorbed. The older macroeconomic literature ignored the continuous transitional movement in the exchange rate that allows temporary interest differentials to develop (my main concern here), and is *implicitly* confined to describing the new equilibrium at the end of the period[13]—where i is again equal to i_n.

Continuing to focus on beginning-of-period adjustment in interest rates, how does the market for domestic and foreign bonds respond to a discrete central bank open-market operation that simultaneously removes bonds and

12. The seminal contribution utilizing this definition of perfect capital mobility is Robert Mundell, "Capital Mobility and Stabilization Policy Under Fixed and Flexible Exchange Rates," *Canadian Journal of Economics and Political Science* (November 1963), pp. 475–85. See also R. McKinnon and W. Oates, "The Implications of International Economic Integration for Monetary, Fiscal and Exchange-Rate Policy," *Princeton Studies in International Finance* No. 16 (1966).
13. For the distinction between beginning-of-period stock-adjustment models and end-of-period adjustment inclusive of flows over the period, see Duncan Foley, "On Two Specifications of Asset Equilibrium in Macroeconomic Models," *Journal of Political Economy*, Vol. 83, No. 2 (1975).

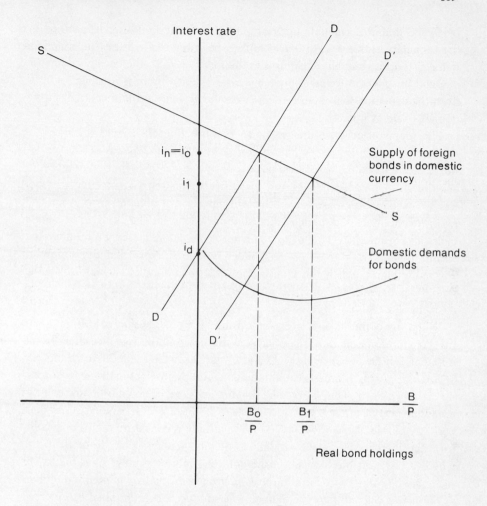

FIGURE 8.2   The domestic market for bonds

injects domestic money? The demand for bonds by domestic wealth holders—
the obverse of their demand for money—depends on the current flow of money
income (GNP) and on their total stock of liquid assets, both of which can be
taken as given at time zero. But the domestic rate of interest, i, measured on
the vertical axis of Figure 8.2, is immediately adjustable to balance the demand
for bonds by DWH with the total supply inclusive of covered foreign bonds.
Graphically, the domestic demand for bonds is most conveniently portrayed as
desired net claims on foreigners, which are measured on the horizontal axis of
Figure 8.2. The line *DD* then represents the net domestic demand for covered
foreign bonds and is simply the difference between the gross demand for bonds

by DWH *and* the available stock of purely domestic bonds as determined by the monetary authority. An open-market operation that reduces the supply of domestic bonds shifts the DD curve to the right to $D'D'$: the effective domestic demand for covered foreign bonds increases. Hence there is a capital outflow from the economy that tends to depreciate the guilder and induce a fall in the domestic rate of interest.

The supply of covered foreign bonds, as a function of the rate of interest, is represented in Figure 8.2 by the SS curve. Its elasticity depends on the portfolio behavior of foreign exchange dealers in two respects: 1) their willingness to acquire guilder cash balances and to reduce their krona balances in the spot foreign exchange market; and 2) the willingness of dealers to provide forward cover for the increased foreign bond holdings of the DWH. Both actions are a necessary counterpart of the purchase of covered foreign bonds by domestic wealth holders with their excess guilder balances. Note that the supply of covered foreign bonds is less than perfectly elastic around i_n—which is why the liquidity-preference schedule LP in Figure 8.1 is also less than perfectly elastic over our short 90-day time horizon.

When the domestic supply expands from M_0 to M_1 as shown in Figure 8.1, the stock of domestic bonds contracts by the same amount as measured by the horizontal distance between the D and D' curves in Figure 8.2. At the old rate of interest, $i_0 = i_n$, domestic wealth holders find themselves with excess domestic cash—guilders. They immediately purchase covered foreign bonds, and the domestic rate of interest is driven down to i_1, because the supply is less than perfectly elastic. Hence the DWH only partially reconstitute their bond holdings: the increase in net bond claims on foreigners increases from B_0 to B_1, which is less than the increase in the domestic money supply. *Thus the fall in the domestic rate of interest induces domestic wealth holders to absorb a portion of the newly created domestic money, whereas the remainder must be absorbed by the foreign exchange dealers.*

Algebraically, one can see that in the new beginning-of-period equilibrium:

$$\Delta M^b = B_1 - B_0 < M_1 - M_0 = G_0 - G_1, \tag{8.7}$$

where $B_1 - B_0$ is the induced bond purchases by DWH from foreign rentiers *and* is also the increment in the money supply flowing into the hands of foreign exchange dealers—ΔM^b. The reduction in domestic bonds is $G_0 - G_1$, which corresponds to the government's open-market purchase. Hence ΔM^a, the increment in the domestic money supply going to domestic wealth holders, is simply:

$$\Delta M^a = (M_1 - M_0) - (B_1 - B_0). \tag{8.8}$$

In an open economy, the interest elasticity of the Keynesian liquidity preference schedule depends, in part, on the willingness of foreign exchange dealers to absorb newly created domestic (guilder) cash balances. But dealers (speculators) face a capital or wealth constraint on what assets they can acquire. Moreover, their business of transacting in the foreign exchanges requires that they keep a balanced portfolio of foreign and domestic monies. Thus dealers do not have an infinitely elastic demand for domestic money, which the DWH wish to sell in order to acquire foreign bonds at the given foreign rate of interest. In the very short run, therefore, an open-market increase in stock of domestic money will force down short-term interest rates *and* raise the domestic currency price of foreign money: a Keynesian liquidity effect. And it remains to be spelled out how much exchange rates will actually fluctuate in response to such monetary disturbances. In the longer run, however, domestic short-term rates of interest will tend to gravitate back to the levels of their foreign counterparts as we shall see.[14]

In summary, Keynesian liquidity-preference analysis, focusing on a variable rate of interest to maintain portfolio balance between bonds and money, holds up well in the very short run when applied to an open economy experiencing discrete monetary shocks. While I have traced out the consequences of one such shock—an autonomous open-market operation by the central bank—the same framework could be used equally well to examine exogenous shifts or instability in the domestic demand for money. As long as the exchange rate can move, in neither case will the domestic rate of interest be rigidly pegged to the foreign rate even when financial capital is perfectly mobile internationally.

Exchange-Rate Fluctuations
Under Full Information

What are the consequences of these monetary disturbances for the foreign exchanges? Modest movements in the domestic rate of interest in our modified model of liquidity preference imply correspondingly modest movements in the premium or discount of the forward exchange rate over the spot, if the IRPT holds. However, I shall show that the spot and forward exchange rates *together* may well vary more widely than either the domestic rate of interest or the domestic money supply. Hence, the surprisingly violent *short-run* fluctuations in foreign exchange rates in the 1973–1978 period could easily be induced by relatively moderate shifts in supplies or demands in each national money market.

---

14. In the absence of any Fisher-like expectations of an exchange rate continuing to move in only one direction—an effect that would show up in permanently higher nominal interest rates on bonds denominated in the depreciating currency.

Given the short-run rigidity in national commodity price levels, the key element that remains to be spelled out is the formation of private expectations regarding short-term movements in the spot exchange rate. Take, for example, the discrete increase in the domestic money supply portrayed in Figures 8.1 and 8.2. If the domestic rate of interest falls by one percentage point on 90-day bonds, the IRPT tells us that the forward premium on foreign currency also falls (or the forward discount widens) by one percentage point. If prior to the monetary disturbance $R_f = R_s$ in long-run equilibrium, then immediately afterwards $R_f < R_s$ because the domestic currency is discretely devalued at time zero.

$$f = \frac{R_s - R_f}{R_s} = .01 = i_n - i_1 \tag{8.9}$$

After this sharp rise in R_s that was unanticipated, equation (8.9) implies that private wealth holders then come to expect that R_s will fall gradually by one percent over the next 90 days. The forward discount on foreign currency to be delivered in 90 days reflects the expected appreciation of the domestic currency.

While all of this is well and good, nothing has yet been said about how much R_s will have to rise initially in order to set up the presumptive expectation that it will fall gradually for 90 days thereafter. The domestic currency can initially depreciate a lot or a little in response to the modest unanticipated domestic monetary expansion because purchasing power parity need not hold in the very short run. The nature and strength of private expectations regarding the equilibrium spot rate in the future will be critical. Is the experienced monetary expansion transitory? Or is it a permanent increase in the money supply? Or is it a harbinger of further monetary expansion? Not only the rise in R_s, but the interest elasticity of the liquidity preference function, depend on how these private expectations are formed.

Even if individual market participants such as commercial banks and merchant traders cannot directly observe what money supply changes occurred or will occur, they can see derivative movements in interest rates and exchange rates. It does not seem farfetched, therefore, to model their behavior *as if* they focused their expectations with greater or lesser confidence on what the future money supply will be, with known consequences for the interest and exchange rate. In other words, private expectations are being rational in focusing on the supply (or demand) of domestic money that really does drive nominal interest and exchange rates in the short run.

In classifying possible expectations effects, let us consider first a hypothetical *full information system*. On the one hand, the quantitative amount of the discrete increase in the money supply is actually published; and then a strong consensus view develops among private speculators regarding future monetary action by the government. This latter effect is equivalent to the government actually publishing credible guidelines on what its future monetary policy will be. (The full information approach has the formal analytical advantage of suppressing the vexing question of uncertainty that must ultimately be considered.) To be concrete, suppose the initial discrete expansion in the money supply at time zero is known to be two percent of the outstanding stock. Within our short 90-day time horizon, consider three possible full information views of the future course of monetary policy:

1) The increase of two percent in the money supply is purely transitory and is reduced gradually back to its normal level within 90 days.

2) The discrete two-percent increase becomes a permanent but nonrecurrent addition to the money stock.

3) The increase signals a policy of further monetary expansion where the money supply increases another two percent in the period following and then ceases to expand.[15]

Each of the three assumptions implies a different initial shock to the exchange rate, and perhaps (but not necessarily) a differently sloped liquidity-preference function over a short time horizon. In order to focus first on discrete exchange-rate movements *per se*, I simply assume that the slope of the liquidity–preference relationship is the same in all three cases: the domestic rate of interest falls by one percentage point. The initial and consequential exchange-rate effects of the discrete monetary expansion are portrayed in Figure 8.3.

In interpreting Figure 8.3 under each of our three full-information patterns of exchange-rate movement, an additional assumption has been imposed that arises naturally out of the monetary approach. Confining our analysis to stationary states, I assume that the domestic price level (tradables and nontradables) and the PPP exchange rate, R_s^{PPP}, are both eventually determined by *the level* of the domestic money supply according to the Quantity Theory of Money:

$$R_s^{PPP} = \alpha M, P_T = \theta M \quad \text{and} \quad P_N = \gamma M. \tag{8.10}$$

where P_T is the price of tradables, and P_N is the price of nontradables.

In the long run the velocity of money is constant and the relative price of tradable and nontradable goods is also fixed. The *sustained* level of the domestic money supply eventually determines the internal commodity price level and the average exchange rate, which is at parity with the purchasing power of foreign currencies as described by equation (8.10). Of course, unanticipated

15. To maintain a stationary economy in which the Fisher effects on interest rates are absent, I rule out for now consideration of a permanently higher rate of monetary growth.

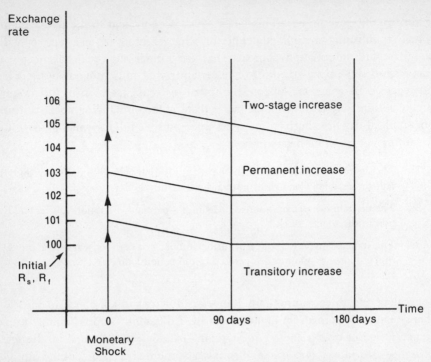

FIGURE 8.3   Alternative exchange-rate effects of a discrete two percent increase in the money supply under full information

short-run variations in the money supply will cause departures from these relationships in the foreign exchange and commodity markets. However, our full information approach does assume that private traders use the relationships in equation (8.10) to establish where they think R_s will ultimately move. And the expected final resting place for the exchange rate is important in understanding short-term exchange-rate movements.

In Figure 8.3, therefore, 100 is the equilibrium PPP exchange rate prior to the exogenous monetary shock. If that two-percent discrete increase is known to be transitory such that the money supply is eventually reduced (falls smoothly) by two percent over 90 days, then R_s will return to 100. The initial one-percent discrete spot depreciation in the foreign value of the domestic currency is the foreign exchange counterpart of the fall by one percentage point in the domestic rate of interest on 90 day bonds.[16] It sets up on the expectation that the domestic currency will appreciate by one percent over 90 days (R_s will fall by

16. Note that for simplicity of exposition all interest rates are being calculated on a 90-day basis corresponding to the time to maturity of short-term bonds. Measured on an annual basis, short-term interest rates would fall by four percentage points to correspond to the fall of one percentage point described above.

one percent) as shown by the downward slope of each graph in Figure 8.3. Reflecting this expectation, R_f would remain unchanged at 100 at time zero in the face of the exogenous shock. Throughout, the sticky commodity price level remains largely unchanged because of the transitory nature of the exchange-rate movement.

Consider the second case of a permanent nonrecurrent increase of two percent in the money stock shown in the middle graph of Figure 8.3. R_s must now increase three times as much—to 103—in order to set up an expectation of a subsequent fall one percentage point on the one hand, and a new long-run equilibrium that is two percent higher (at 102) on the other. That is, the initial fall of one percent in the short-run rate of interest is the same for a permanent change in money stock as with the transitory one analyzed above. But now R_f jumps immediately to 102, so that the IRPT described in equation (8.9) still holds at time zero.

While the interest-rate implications of the permanent increase in the money stock are the same as for the transitory one, the implications for the goods market (as well as for the foreign exchanges) are somewhat different. The new price level in long-run equilibrium is higher: the ultimate PPP value of R_s is 102. The middle graph in Figure 8.3 is drawn as if the commodity price level rises gradually by two percent throughout 90 days. This increase reduces the real value of the money stock by two percent and hence allows restoration of the initial money-market equilibrium. While the domestic commodity price level is invariant to the initial monetary shock and jump in R_s, nevertheless it does gradually rise through time with its stopping place defined by the Quantity Theory of Money.

For comparative analytical simplicity, I have assumed full commodity price adjustment within 90 days to the permanent increase in the money supply. As an empirical matter, the price level could take longer to adjust, in which case, the interest rate would not fall quite as much initially but would be depressed for a somewhat longer period of time. Nothing really essential in this analysis would be altered by this stretching out process. We would still get an initial jump in R_s that was substantially greater in comparison to the transitory case of the lower graph.

By now the analytics of the last two-stage case must be well nigh self-evident to the reader. Because the initial two-percent shock is a precursor of a further monetary expansion of two percent, R_s must jump even more sharply to reflect the total percentage monetary expansion now and in the future *plus* a margin to allow R_s to fall subsequently by two percentage points over 180 days (one percentage point over the immediately succeeding 90 days). Hence, R_s jumps to 106 immediately and then declines gradually to 104 in 180 days. Full monetary equilibrium is restored 180 days later because the price level rises gradually by four percent and reduces the real stock of money back to its original level. The immediate exchange-rate effect is accentuated, however, by the anticipated future monetary expansion.

In summary, the main contention of my full-information analysis is that discrete jumps in the spot exchange rate can, plausibly, be greater in percentage terms than immediate changes in the domestic supply of (or demand for) money, or in the domestic rate of interest. Overshooting occurs in the sense that the immediate effect of a monetary expansion on the exchange rate is greater than the ultimate effect.

Uncertain Expectations

Under uncertainty, a temporary monetary expansion could be mistaken for a permanent one and vice versa. Hence it is difficult to say whether or not exchange-rate fluctuations would be more or less pronounced for any given monetary shock in comparison to the full-information model described.

If the monetary authority's behavior is basically stable over the long run, then this should be well advertised so that short-term fluctuations in exchange rates are reduced to the same order of magnitude as interest-rate changes—as portrayed in the lower graph of Figure 8.3. One way of so stabilizing private expectations is for the government to announce that it will keep the exchange rate within a well-defined band—say, one percent on either side of parity as per the Bretton Woods system or the gold standard. Some short-run manipulation of interest rates is then feasible in the Keynesian mode without inducing major exchange-rate changes. Everyone knows any monetary expansion or contraction must be transitory in order that this band of exchange variation not be violated. The official band, if credible, is a signal to the market regarding the longer-term stability of the government's monetary policy.

Otherwise, if private uncertainty is very great, a transitory monetary expansion such as portrayed in Figure 8.1 could depreciate the currency sharply because foreign-exchange dealers are loathe to unbalance their portfolios by absorbing newly created domestic money. For the same reason, the liquidity-preference schedule portrayed in Figure 8.1 would be less elastic. The domestic interest rate would fall more sharply until domestic wealth holders are sufficiently rewarded to absorb virtually all the newly created domestic money.

Optimum Currency Areas

Consider now the flow of commodity trade—whether any pair of countries is strongly or loosely linked by the exchange of exports and imports. Suppose that the money markets of these two countries are buffeted by essentially transitory disturbances in either the creation of domestic money or the demand for it. Although some uncertainty exists about the future, private traders and dealers (speculators) do *not* expect monetary expansion in any single country to permanently exceed that of its partner. Ruling out conscious official harmonization of short-run monetary policies across closely linked countries, under what circumstances would the Canadian-American exchange rate fluctuate relatively little, while the American-German or Canadian-German exchange rates fluctuate a great deal?

In the Canadian-American case, the normal inventories of Canadian dollars and American dollars held by foreign exchange dealers should be large relative to the volume of Canadian dollars held by domestic wealth holders in Canada. (For this purpose the U.S. can be considered the large outside world.) The greater the proportion of foreign trade in GNP *ceteris paribus*, the larger will be dealer holdings of foreign and domestic currencies. And Canadian imports from the U.S. amount to about 20 percent of Canadian GNP. Hence the wealth constraint on dealers (equation 8.4) should be less binding in comparison to two countries whose trade links are not so close. Any monetary expansion by the Bank of Canada as per Figure 8.1, therefore, could be largely absorbed by dealers. In response to a relatively modest depreciation of the Canadian dollar, dealers would take substantial amounts of Canadian dollars into their portfolios in exchange for American dollars.

Symmetrically, any transitory increase in the American money supply would induce but a moderate appreciation in the Canadian currency because of the willingness of dealers to *dishoard* Canadian dollars in exchange for American. This dishoarding occurs as Canadians attempt to sell bonds (denominated in American dollars) in the United States in response to easier money conditions there. Because the American economy is very large relative to the Canadian, market conditions in the U.S.—as measured by levels of short-term interest rates—will prevail in both countries. But as long as dealers have, at the margin, a plentiful supply of Canadian dollars to dishoard in response to a transitory policy of easy money in the United States, the Canadian dollar should *not* appreciate sharply.

On the other hand, the direct flow of trade between Germany and the United States is much smaller. German exports to the United States amount only to about three percent of German GNP. Hence dealers holding both DM and dollars would not be major factors in either the German or American money markets. But dealers with capital constraints are the relevant institutional embodiment of potentially stabilizing speculators. Only dealers have *both* the financial capacity as well as the knowledge and inclination to alter their short-term foreign exchange positions quickly in response to transitory exchange-rate movements. Because of the incipient capital outflow to Germany, a transitory increase in the American money supply could sharply increase the dollar value of Deutsche marks (DM) before knowledgeable dealers become willing to sell DM from their limited portfolios in sufficient quantities to stop the upward movement. Whence the sharp dollar/DM movements observed in practice in comparison to the milder fluctuations between the Canadian and American dollars.

There is, however, another related reason why economies that are highly integrated in commodity trade might show lesser variance in money-market conditions and in short-term exchange-rate fluctuations. Our use of Keynesian liquidity-preference analysis assumed that domestic price levels are insulated from each other in the short run, and hence fairly invariant to exchange-rate fluctuations. That is, instantaneous purchasing power parity across currencies does not hold even in the sectors producing and consuming tradable goods. These discontinuities essentially allow exchange rates to be volatile in the short run, and to move much more than commodity price indices measured in individual national currencies.

This assumed absence of purchasing power parity may hold up rather less well between economies that are highly integrated. Commodity arbitrage could be more intense and prevent significant deviations from purchasing power parity. Thus the scope for exchange-rate fluctuations, and for short-run interest differentials in the Keynesian mode, would be more limited. For example, an open-market operation that expanded the domestic money supply would cause some exchange-rate depreciation (depending on dealer behavior) that would immediately tend to increase the domestic price level. This rise in prices would raise the demand for money by domestic wealth holders,[17] and thereby eliminate the excess liquidity with its concomitant downward pressure on interest and exchange rates.

Apart from the degree of integration in commodity trade, economies that produce largely primary products (tradables II) would find that domestic prices respond quickly to exchange-rate movements. This again would limit the applicability of our Keynesian liquidity-preference analysis.

But commodity price instability is a poor substitute for exchange- and interest-rate fluctuations in response to short-run shifts in domestic money-market conditions. Indeed, the theory of optimum currency areas[18] would suggest that economies closely integrated in foreign trade might well opt for fixed exchange

17. Assuming that the rate of increase in prices is not projected to continue indefinitely into the future, i.e., Fisher effects are absent.
18. R. I. McKinnon, op. cit. p. 722.

rates precisely to prevent commodity price instability from occurring in response to transitory monetary disturbances that cause exchange-rate variations. For small countries in particular, a transitory disturbance in the money market of a major trading partner might well appreciate the domestic currency and put downward pressure on domestic prices even before the monetary impact was manifest in the price level of the trading partner itself—and might never be manifest if the monetary disturbance was indeed transitory. Commodity traders might then be induced to change their normal purchasing and selling patterns— not because comparative advantage has changed—but simply because of short-run monetary shocks. Hence the welfare costs of volatile exchange rates would seem much higher among highly integrated trading partners.

Intervention by Central Banks: A Concluding Note

In the very short run, a floating exchange rate is *not* tied by purchasing power parity and fluctuates according to the capital constraints on foreign exchange dealers and their views of future domestic monetary policy. If central banks are known to initiate only transitory changes in the domestic money supply (perhaps measured from a trend rate of growth), and if private foreign exchange dealers are not constrained in which positions they may take, domestic short-run rates of interest can be successfully manipulated (according to the canons of the Keynesian theory of liquidity preference) with relatively modest associated movements in exchange rates. However, if private dealers have doubts regarding the future course of official monetary policies, and they face severe capital constraints, the exercise of autonomy in national monetary policy can lead to large exchange-rate fluctuations—perhaps much larger in the short run than changes in either interest rates or in the domestic money supply itself. And this latter situation better describes the experienced instability in rates of exchange among major convertible currencies in the 1973–1978 period.

Now, our analysis from Chapter 7 of destabilizing behavior by merchants can be reintroduced. If money-market shocks move exchange rates from equilibrium levels—say causing a depreciation of the domestic currency—then the "*J*" curve effect becomes operative. During the periods of currency contract and pass through, a further excess supply of the domestic currency from merchants accumulates. Foreign exchange dealers (speculators) are then called on to take even larger supporting positions in the domestic currency, but with capital constraints on their doing so. Overshooting and bandwagon effects develop: exchange rates move much more than the initiating monetary disturbance would seem to warrant.

Thus it is not surprising that central banks have been drawn back to take large balancing positions in the foreign exchange market, although they no longer have official parity obligations. On the information side, central banks have a potential comparitive advantage as "speculators" through their control of the future course of national monetary policy. Unlike commercial banks, moreover, official agencies can take open positions in the interbank market without being so hampered by capital constraints and default risk.

Only if the secular stability of each national monetary policy vis-à-vis other countries is somehow assured, could central banks gracefully withdraw and let the foreign exchanges stabilize themselves. Some possibilities for achieving greater coordination in national monetary policies are explored in Chapters 10 and 11.

9

The Eurocurrency Market[1]

"The volume and nature of transactions in Eurodollars, their large and active turn-over, and the wide range of their employment, has constituted an institutional change of the utmost importance. It has created a truly international money market, and has developed a structure of international interest rates that is entirely without precedent."

Paul Einzig (1973)[2]

Foreign currency deposits—those denominated in a currency other than that of the host country—have risen spectacularly in recent years. As of December 1976, the Bank for International Settlements estimated the stock of Eurocurrency deposits to be about $310 billion—bigger than the domestic banking systems of major European countries, and more than nine times the size of Eurocurrency deposits outstanding back in 1968 (see Table 9.2). The Eurocurrency system is now the focal point of the international market for short-term capital (deposits and loans of a year or less), and intermediate-term credits of three to seven years are increasingly common. Why then was this incredible growth virtually unforeseen by practical bankers or by academic observers?

In principle, the Eurocurrency market is unnecessary. The clearing of international payments, hedging forward against exchange risk, and short-term cred-

1. Ronald I. McKinnon, *The Eurocurrency Market*, Essays in International Finance No. 125, December 1977. Copyright © 1977. Reprinted by permission of the International Finance Section of Princeton University. I am indebted to Peter Kenen, Helmut Mayer, and Jurg Niehans for helpful comments.
2. *The Euro-Dollar System* (London: Macmillan), 5th edition, p. 4.

its for trade finance can all be provided by a system in which commercial banks in any one country accept deposit liabilities from foreigners and domestic nationals that are denominated exclusively in the currency of that country— one in which only Dutch banks accept guilder deposits and make guilder loans, only American banks accept dollar deposits and make dollar loans, and so on. To finance foreign trade for their customers, these commercial banks can easily obtain spot or forward foreign exchange in the interbank market that operates internationally or draw on balances of foreign currency held with correspondent banks abroad.

Let us define *traditional foreign exchange banking* (TFEB) to be this conceptually simple system of on-shore banking supported by foreign correspondents, as described fairly completely in Chapter 1. Traditional foreign exchange banking arises naturally from the role of domestic commercial banks as custodians of the national money supply and intracountry payments mechanism. Historically, TFEB has dominated international finance, including the twenty years of rapid growth in trade following the Second World War. For understanding the causes of exchange-rate fluctuations at the present time (Chapter 8)—or the invoicing and hedging strategies of nonbank merchants and manufacturers engaged in foreign trade (Chapter 4), the implicit assumption of TFEB is sufficient.

In a *Eurocurrency market*, by contrast, banks resident in country A accept deposits and make loans in the currencies of countries B, C, D, and so on; depositors and borrowers are often nonresidents. Despite the semantic connotations, a Eurocurrency system is not necessarily located in Europe. Major Eurocurrency markets exist in Canada, Singapore, Japan, and the Caribbean as Table 9.2 makes abundantly clear. Because the U.S. dollar is usually the principal currency traded abroad (see Table 9.1), the expression Eurodollar market often connotes trading in many convertible currencies. Here, however, the term *Eurodollar* is used narrowly to refer only to deposits of U.S. dollars held outside the United States. The term *Euroguilders* refers to deposits of guilders in banks not resident in the Netherlands; offshore markets do exist in many convertible currencies other than U.S. dollars as indicated in Table 9.1.

The rapid emergence in the 1960s of a worldwide Eurocurrency market that coexists and competes with TFEB resulted from the peculiarly stringent and detailed official regulations governing residents operating with their own national currencies. These regulations contrast sharply with the relatively great freedom of *nonresidents* to make deposits or borrow *foreign currencies* from these same constrained national banking systems. On an international scale, offshore unregulated financial markets compete with onshore regulated ones. Gurley's and Shaw's standard analysis of unregulated versus regulated financial

TABLE 9.1 External Positions in Dollars and Other Foreign Currencies of Reporting European Banks from Eight European Countries (Billions of U.S. dollars)

	Dollars		Other Foreign Currencies						
End of year	Total	Vis-à-vis nonbanks	Total	Vis-à-vis nonbanks	Deutsche marks	Swiss francs	Pounds sterling	Dutch guilders	French francs
Assets:									
1968	$ 30.4	$ 5.2	$ 7.3	$ 1.2	$ 3.9	$ 1.8	$ 0.6	$ 0.3	$ 0.2
1969	47.6	6.1	10.5	2.2	6.0	3.0	0.6	0.4	0.2
1970	60.4	11.9	17.9	4.7	10.1	5.1	0.6	0.6	0.4
1971	71.5	14.4	28.6	6.8	16.2	8.2	1.6	0.7	0.5
1972	98.0	18.3	33.8	8.0	20.4	7.8	2.2	0.7	0.7
1973	132.1	24.7	55.5	14.0	31.4	15.0	3.1	1.2	1.8
1974	156.2	34.9	58.9	18.1	35.0	14.4	2.1	1.9	1.5
1975	190.2	40.9	68.0	20.5	41.6	15.4	2.0	2.1	2.6
1976	224.0	50.8	81.3	22.7	48.7	17.9	2.2	3.8	2.6
Memorandum-item positions vis-à-vis residents:									
1975	66.5	17.4	22.8	6.6					
1976	74.7	21.3	26.9	7.6					
Liabilities:									
1968	26.9	6.2	6.8	1.5	3.0	2.3	0.8	0.3	0.2
1969	46.2	10.5	10.5	1.3	4.6	4.0	0.8	0.4	0.2
1970	58.7	11.2	16.6	2.5	8.1	5.7	0.9	0.6	0.4
1971	70.8	10.0	27.0	2.7	14.6	7.8	2.1	0.9	0.4
1972	96.7	11.8	35.2	3.6	19.5	8.8	2.2	1.4	1.1
1973	131.4	17.5	60.7	5.6	32.0	17.2	4.6	2.3	2.1
1974	156.4	22.2	64.3	8.1	34.4	18.3	3.6	2.8	2.3
1975	189.5	24.3	69.2	6.7	39.9	15.3	3.1	3.6	3.4
1976	230.0	29.6	80.6	9.0	47.2	15.9	4.0	3.5	3.2
Memorandum-item positions vis-à-vis residents:									
1975	58.2	9.4	19.8	3.2					
1976	64.1	10.7	23.7	4.3					

SOURCE: *47th Annual Report, 1976–77*, BIS, 1977.

NOTE: Countries include Belgium-Luxembourg, France, Germany, Italy, Netherlands, Sweden, Switzerland, United Kingdom.

intermediaries shows why it is not surprising that the former grow rapidly at the expense of the latter.[3]

The quirks in foreign exchange controls and national regulations of commercial banking that have created the huge Eurocurrency market remain to be spelled out. But their financial consequences are striking:

1) There is an important *foreign exchange aspect:* by trading with each other in the Eurocurrency market, commercial banks can more conveniently cover the forward foreign-currency obligations undertaken on behalf of their nonbank customers and engage in covered interest arbitrage—functions that have assumed critical importance (see Chapter 5) with the advent of floating exchange rates.

2) The Eurocurrency market has a purely *domestic intermediation aspect* within the confines of a single national currency: it supplants financial intermediation between savers and investors that might otherwise flow through a purely domestic capital market, as in the case of the United States during the monetary crunch of 1969.

3) The Eurocurrency market is a great *international conduit* for funneling short- and medium-term capital from surplus (net saver) countries to deficit (net borrower) countries, as with the huge flow of funds arising from the formation of the OPEC oil cartel in 1973–1974.

The competitive strength of the Eurocurrency market in all three roles accounts for its astonishing growth and resiliency on the one hand, and the great difficulty academic economists have had in developing a single theoretical model to describe it, on the other. Freedom from restraint has created a paragon of international banking efficiency. Yet, the underlying asymmetry vis-à-vis domestic banks has also created an acute problem of second-best optimization for any single monetary authority, and national central banks have responded differently to this problem of regulating transactions in foreign currencies.

Somewhat surprisingly, however, the unregulated Eurocurrency market does not compete with TFEB in all respects. TFEB continues to provide the actual *means of payment* in international commodity trade and in capital-account transactions.

Regulatory Asymmetry: A Potted History

Why should so much Eurocurrency transacting (about 40 percent, according to Table 9.2) be concentrated in London? One explanation relies on historical

3. J. G. Gurley and E. S. Shaw, *Money in A Theory of Finance* (Washington, D.C.: Brookings Institution, 1960). Gurley and Shaw analyzed purely domestic financial intermediaries such as tightly regulated commercial banks versus loosely regulated savings and loan associations.

experience. Over many decades, financial wisdom and technical skills have accumulated in the great merchant banks, discount and acceptance houses, commodity and stock exchanges, foreign exchange brokerages, and all-purpose insurance companies located in the City.[4] Prior to 1914, not only was Britain a huge net supplier of saving to the rest of the world, but most world trade was invoiced in sterling. The sterling bill (often discounted or accepted by a London financial house) was the prime instrument of trade finance. In contrast, Britain is now a significant international debtor, and the use of sterling by third countries as an invoice currency has sharply declined (Chapter 4). But once firmly in place, it is often hypothesized, the accumulated expertise and associated economies of scale in financial transactions are sufficient to allow Britain to thrive as a financial entrepôt by transacting in foreign currencies and managing the savings of foreigners.

There is an alternative explanation. Among major industrial countries, the British have imposed the least regulation of offshore transactions in *foreign* currencies. At the same time, the decline in the international role of sterling has been hastened by an increasingly complex web of exchange controls on sterling transactions. How did these two dramatic, and related, changes in British financial policy come about?

For many years after the Second World War—the era of the great dollar shortage—European governments tightly controlled private transactions on current and capital account that involved making payments in U.S. dollars. Purely intra-European payments were progressively liberalized, however, and, as a result, the City of London provided sterling finance for many individual European firms engaged in European trade. In addition, London provided trade finance for the old sterling area—a large group of excolonies such as Australia, Kuwait, India, and Nigeria—which also maintained an imperfect web of exchange controls vis-à-vis the dollar area. Then in 1957–1958, two regulatory changes triggered the decline of this TFEB in sterling:

1) Partly because of the Suez crisis, but mainly because of higher inflation in Britain than in other European countries, a speculative run on sterling in 1957 threatened the Bretton Woods sterling parity of US $2.80. The British authorities placed severe new restrictions on sterling credits to nonresidents, and even imposed restraints on sterling credits to countries engaging in third-party transactions *within* the sterling area. Concomitantly, British monetary policy (in sterling) was made very tight, with a sharp increase in bank rate to a "sensa-

---

4. For a detailed description of the unrivaled scope of commercial and financial institutions in London serving the international markets before the emergence of a substantial Eurocurrency market, see William Clarke, *The City in the World Economy* (London: Institute of Economic Affairs, 1965).

tional" seven percent that was very high in view of the limited inflationary expectations of the time. In addition, direct ceilings were imposed on bank lending for domestic and foreign purposes; these were later relaxed and reimposed in a cyclical fashion in subsequent years.[5]

2) In December 1958, Western Europe returned to full current-account convertibility, including short-term credits incurred in the financing of foreign trade (as described in Chapter 1). While some countries retained restrictions on many purely capital-account transactions by nonbanking firms, overt discrimination against dollar transactions was terminated. Authorized commercial banks and major European exporters were given wide latitude to take long or short positions in U.S. dollars, or indeed any other currency in which they had a trading interest.

These changes, taken together, suggest a shift away from financing third-party trade through sterling credits and deposits in London. The natural beneficiaries were New York banks, which financed trade between third parties using dollars, and TFEB in each of the newly convertible European currencies. Indeed, vigorous TFEB has been restored in many European centers as well as in Japan, where full currency convertibility came somewhat later.

Nevertheless, lingering restrictions on international capital movements in Europe—with the major exceptions of Germany and Switzerland—and the sometimes heavy-handed regulation of domestic banking systems in the form of high reserve requirements, interest ceilings, and arbitrary allocations of bank credit for domestic purposes often served to limit the efficiency and flexibility of European and Japanese commercial banks engaged in TFEB.[6] While subject to much ebb and flow, such regulatory curbs remain in Europe to the present time and were even intensified by many governments (e.g., the French) during the breakup of the Bretton Woods system in 1973 and the advent of floating exchange rates.

In contrast, in 1959–1960 the United States imposed no restrictions on capital movements, had modest reserve requirements on commercial banks, and ran a highly developed international market for primary securities of all kinds (including a huge liquid stock of short-term treasury bills in which foreign central banks held much of their exchange reserves). Thus the decline of sterling finance in London and the restoration of dollar convertibility for European currencies left the United States well placed to be the dominant world financial center, based on the techniques of TFEB. But this idyllic develop-

5. See Leland Yeager, International Monetary Relations: Theory, History, and Policy, 2nd edition (New York: Harper & Row, 1976), pp. 441–72.
6. Often with a zero ceiling on nonresident bank accounts in the domestic currency—see the Swedish regulations quoted in Chapter 1.

ment, as seen through the eyes of the New York banking community, was soon to be disrupted by the American government.

First, restraints were imposed on the flow of both long-term and short-term capital from the United States by (a) the Interest Equalization Tax introduced by President Kennedy in 1963, which imposed a substantial levy on the sales of foreign bonds and equities in the United States; (b) guidelines imposed in 1965 on American commercial banks that limited their acquisitions of foreign assets (i.e., curtailed short-term lending to foreigners); (c) the 1968 requirement that American multinational corporations raise funds for new direct investment (reinvestment) outside the United States.[7]

Second, interest ceilings were imposed on time and savings deposits in American banks. These usury restrictions also became more onerous as nominal rates of interest rose in the uncontrolled open market because of heightened inflationary expectations, while the ceilings on nominal deposit rates of interest remained relatively inflexible.

Hence, both on the lending and deposit sides, TFEB in the United States became distinctly less attractive in the early 1960s. While these regulatory distortions were intensified throughout the later 1960s, most were eventually terminated. In 1974, as concern for specific balance of payments targets diminished, the controls and levies on capital outflows were lifted entirely. Although now much less onerous, these American controls undoubtedly did much to shift international finance to the Eurocurrency market during its period of rapid adolescent growth.[8]

While the American financial system was thus tying itself in knots, the British authorities began separating deposit and loan transactions in foreign

7. For a more complete history of these controls, see Leland Yeager, op. cit., Chapter 27. The imposition of exchange controls on capital account by the American authorities, despite surpluses in the current account of the balance of payments, arose partly from a peculiar accounting definition of a deficit in international payments to which the American authorities responded. Almost two decades later, in May 1976, the American authorities wisely discarded any formal definition that involves an implicit assessment of equilibrium or disequilibrium capital-account transactions in U.S. foreign payments, given the complex role of the American capital market as an international financial intermediary. Also, European governments at that time could and did convert their official dollar holdings so as to deplete the American stock of gold. For a more detailed discussion of the failure of the American authorities to understand their proper monetary role in the world economy, see R. McKinnon, "Private and Official International Money: The Case for the Dollar," *Princeton Essays in International Finance*, No. 74 (1969).

8. Because of competition from the Eurodollar market, the Federal Reserve System allowed the development of a new kind of financial instrument, the certificate of deposit, on which interest ceilings were eventually abolished and against which reserve requirements are kept low. Much like Eurocurrency deposits, certificates of deposit are confined to firms making very large financial transactions: the minimum deposit size permitted by law is $100,000. Repressive controls still exist on smaller scale time and savings deposits in the form of interest ceilings and reserve requirements.

currencies from those in sterling. An important class of British merchant banks—many of which are British residents but American owned—could accept deposits and make loans in *dollars* (or any currency but sterling) completely free of regulatory restraint. Neither interest ceilings nor reserve requirements are imposed, and only informal monitoring of these transactions is undertaken by the Bank of England. The big British clearing banks, on the other hand, were initially confined to sterling transactions and to TFEB because of their customary cash and liquidity requirements. Now, even the clearing banks are allowed to undertake Eurocurrency transactions, which are exempt from these requirements.

From the point of view of the British government, an essential element in maintaining this oasis of freedom in foreign-currency transactions is strict control on the conversion of sterling assets owned by British residents into assets denominated in any other currency—particularly into foreign-currency deposits that also happen to be direct claims on London banking establishments! Except for specially authorized direct investments abroad or the granting of trade credit by exporters, nonbank firms and individuals in Britain can acquire foreign-currency assets only by buying special investment dollars at a high premium over the regular commercial exchange rate—say, 30 to 50 percent.[9] And when such foreign exchange assets are eventually liquidated, an additional 25 percent of the proceeds must be surrendered to the exchange authorities so that the pool available for purchases of foreign exchange diminishes continually. The purpose of this investment dollar control mechanism is to prevent capital flight from sterling by restricting portfolio diversification by British residents into foreign financial assets and real estate. Only British companies with a large stake in international trade can hold Eurocurrency deposits. Hence the unregulated part of the British banking establishment serves mainly *nonresidents*— although in recent years local governmental authorities and private firms in Britain have been entering the Eurocurrency market as net *borrowers* and, as such, have incurred substantial obligations in foreign monies.

Is this remarkable freedom from regulation sufficient to establish London as the principal center for Eurocurrency transactions? Eurocurrency markets still exist in Paris, Frankfurt, Amsterdam, and elsewhere. Why should London

9. Needless to say, strict controls also exist on Britons trafficking in foreign exchange at the ordinary commercial exchange rate. The *Economist* (May 1976), pp. 78–79, gives some of the legal constraints: All British residents must surrender immediately any foreign currency they own. That includes exporters who are paid in foreign currency. Foreign-currency payments for exports must be received no more than six months after the goods are shipped. Any businessman wishing to buy foreign currency (to pay for imports, for example) must provide his bank with documentary evidence of the underlying transaction. Further detailed and complex rules exist for forward transacting.

dominate? The answer is that, except for small countries such as Singapore, the Cayman Islands, and Hong Kong, which may be mainly tax havens, other European centers are not so free of regulation. At the other extreme, for example, Germany does not accord special treatment to foreign deposits. In normal times, the same reserve requirements and interest ceilings apply to deposits in Deutsche marks as to deposits in foreign currency. Because the Deutsche mark (DM) is also a relatively stable currency, moreover, most banking transactions with foreigners are denominated in DM according to the canons of TFEB (see Table 9.2). Frankfurt has not become a major Eurocurrency center. (The other major country that does not discriminate in favor of offshore banking is the United States, where Eurocurrency transacting is negligible.) Other European countries and Japan lie somewhere between the extreme British and German approaches to the regulation of Eurocurrency transactions, so that Eurocurrency trading predominates over TFEB except in Germany and the United States.

Countries with convertible currencies and active Eurocurrency markets, such as Belgium, France, Italy, and Japan, often insulate the purely domestic portion of their banking systems by a web of exchange controls on capital-account transactions similar to the British. The logic here is straightforward. If there are no controls on capital-account transfers into foreign monies by domestic residents, the authorities tend to regulate foreign-currency deposits more severely to prevent a decline in the use of the domestic currency as domestic money. Among major countries, Britain seems to grant the greatest regulatory freedom to commercial banks accepting deposits and loans in foreign currencies. Consequently, Britain has the greatest need to protect the domain of sterling with exchange controls. The other countries mentioned, however, are not too far behind.

To summarize by returning to the question posed at the beginning of this section, financial expertise—the debris of history—is only a partial explanation of London's importance. On the supply side of financial services, freedom from reserve requirements or interest-rate restrictions gives London in particular— and Eurocurrency centers generally—a competitive advantage in providing higher deposit rates of interest and lower lending rates to each class of borrower. On the demand side, freedom from exchange controls on capital account for nonbanks is necessary in at least some countries (say, Germany and the United States) to create a pool of funds to be invested in Eurocurrency markets in yet other countries (say, Britain). In addition, most countries permit their *domestic commercial banks*—which are also authorized dealers in foreign exchange—to freely take positions in foreign currency in these offshore centers.

TABLE 9.2 External Assets and Liabilities of Banks in Individual Reporting Countries, the United States, the Caribbean Area, and Singapore, in Domestic and Foreign Currencies (Billions of U.S. dollars)

	Domestic currency			Foreign currency		
	1974	1975	1976	1974	1975	1976
Belgium-Luxembourg						
Assets	$ 1.7	$ 1.7	$ 2.4	$ 32.2	$ 39.1	$ 49.4
Liabilities	2.5	2.7	3.4	31.3	37.9	47.5
France						
Assets	1.1	1.2	1.5	31.8	39.0	48.0
Liabilities	3.7	4.4	3.8	32.5	38.1	48.7
Germany						
Assets	14.2	21.0	25.9	8.4	10.6	14.3
Liabilities	11.3	13.6	17.4	7.7	9.3	13.7
Italy						
Assets	0.6	0.4	0.3	12.5	15.0	12.3
Liabilities	1.3	1.6	1.4	13.6	15.0	15.0
Netherlands						
Assets	2.7	3.5	4.2	13.4	17.4	22.0
Liabilities	2.1	2.2	4.1	12.6	16.4	19.6
Sweden						
Assets	0.4	0.6	0.8	2.1	2.6	2.9
Liabilities	0.5	0.6	0.7	1.0	1.8	2.3
Switzerland						
Assets	9.2	9.1[a]	10.9	12.3	16.3	18.4
Liabilities	8.5	4.6[a]	5.1	10.6	12.0	15.3
United Kingdom						
Assets	1.9	1.7	1.8	102.6	118.2	138.0
Liabilities	9.5	9.2	7.1	111.5	128.2	148.6
Total						
Assets	$31.7	$39.2	$47.7	$215.2	$258.1	$305.3
Liabilities	39.4	38.9	42.9	220.8	258.7	310.7
Canada						
Assets	$ 0.4	$ 0.5	$ 0.5	$ 13.5	$ 13.4	$ 17.1
Liabilities	1.6	2.0	2.0	11.7	12.1	14.6
Japan						
Assets	1.4	1.5	2.1	19.2	18.8	19.6
Liabilities	0.9	1.5	1.9	24.1	25.2	27.2
United States						
Assets	45.0	58.3	78.8	1.3	1.4	1.8
Liabilities[b]	59.6	58.2	69.8	0.8	0.6	0.8
Caribbean area and the Far East[c]						
Assets[d]				33.2	51.1	74.9
Liabilities[d]				33.2	51.0	74.1

SOURCE: BIS, *47th Annual Report, 1976–77*, p. 106.
[a]Break in series due to change in coverage.
[b]Excludes U.S. Treasury bills and certificates held in custody for nonresidents.
[c]Figures for 1974 relate to branches of U.S. banks in the Bahamas, Cayman Islands, and Panama; data for 1975 and 1976 cover branches of U.S. banks in Hong Kong and Singapore as well.
[d]Includes negligible amounts in domestic currencies.

Hence we can begin our analysis by presuming that banks and nonbanking enterprises, which are not subject to effective exchange control and which acquire and want to hold convertible foreign monies, are likely to place much of this money with a Eurocurrency bank.

The Mechanics of Transacting and the Scope of the Market

A Eurodollar claim on a London bank has an exchange rate that is exactly one-to-one with a dollar deposit located in New York or San Francisco. This complete absence of currency (exchange-rate) risk is reflected in the fact that checks drawn on U.S. banks are the means by which payments are made (dollar claims are transferred) within the Eurocurrency system. However, banking risk still exists in the sense that depositors have to be worried about the solvency of London banks, mostly affiliates of U.S., Japanese, and continental European banks.

Almost all Eurocurrency transactions are interbank, and most outstanding deposits are interbank claims, reflecting the highly developed intermediary role of the banks on behalf of their nonbank customers. Much like the spot and forward market for foreign exchange (Chapter 2), these interbank loans "are unsecured credits, hence the importance of names attached by would-be lenders."[10] When a Eurocurrency bank receives a deposit not already committed on the lending side, the immediate placement of such funds (although not necessarily the ultimate destination) may well be with another Eurobank. The lending bank typically uses a broker, who disguises the names of the potential transactors until the deal is near conclusion in order to secure the best offer of an interbank deposit rate of interest. This procedure enables banks to avoid publicizing a firm bid-ask spread at which less than first-rate credit risks may wish to trade—but ultimately allows trade among established names at very close to a standard rate of interest. Indeed, LIBOR is the acronym for this standard London interbank offer rate of interest paid by name banks of the highest credit standing. LIBOR is plotted in Figure 9.1.

Suppose now, for illustrative purposes, that Barclays' merchant Eurobank affiliate in London sets up in business with a deposit of $1,020,000 from a French exporter. Having no nonbank customer to service, Barclays then agrees to lend $1,000,000 to the Bank of Tokyo (also located in London) for a period of three months at 4½ percent per annum (LIBOR). Suppose, for simplicity, that Barclays and the Bank of Tokyo both retain checking deposits with Chase Manhattan in New York. The way in which the transaction influences the

10. Einzig, op. cit. p. 19.

balance sheet of all three banks is shown in Table 9.3. The Barclays' checking account in New York declines by $1,000,000, whereas that of the Bank of Tokyo increases by the same amount.

Neither Barclays nor Chase Manhattan questions or puts restraints on what the Bank of Tokyo then does, as they would with commercial credits to their nonbank customers. This is the meaning of the taking of names and the use of unsecured credits in the interbank market. However, if the Bank of Tokyo used its New York checking account (or at least part of it) to make payments on behalf of a Japanese commercial importer of Australian wheat, the goods themselves or other securities in the form of commodity invoices from the importer might be required. Indeed, while the Bank of Tokyo pays 4½ percent interest on its Euroloan from Barclays, the interest yield normally escalates to, say, 6 percent on the commercial loan to the Japanese wheat importer, because of the administrative cost and increased riskiness of the commercial loan compared with the interbank deposit.

The Bank of Tokyo (London branch) is free to lend anywhere in the world at its discretion. And outside the inner group of name banks that provide the wholesale market for Eurofunds, the credit ratings of potential borrowers of Eurocredits at retail (those requiring credit investigations) are typically classified as so many points above LIBOR: the Polish state trading agency may be two

TABLE 9.3 Interbank Transacting in the Eurodollar Market

Barclays (London)		Step One: Prior to Interbank Loan Chase Manhattan (New York)		Bank of Tokyo (London)	
Assets	Liabilities	Assets	Liabilities	Assets	Liabilities
$1,020,000 (Deposit in Chase Manhattan)	$1,020,000 (Deposit by a French exporter)	$1,020,000 (Domestic loans and reserves)	$1,020,000 (Deposit of Barclays)	0	0

Barclays (London)		Step Two: After the Interbank Loan Chase Manhattan (New York)		Bank of Tokyo (London)	
Assets	Liabilities	Assets	Liabilities	Assets	Liabilities
$20,000 (Deposit in Chase Manhattan)	$1,020,000	$1,020,000 (Loans and reserves)	$20,000 (Deposit of Barclays)	$1,000,000 (Deposit with Chase Manhattan)	$1,000,000 (Deposit from Barclays)
$1,000,000 (Deposit in Bank of Tokyo)			$1,000,000 (Deposit of Bank of Tokyo)		

points above, the central bank of Zaire perhaps four points above, Exxon Corporation possibly one-half of one point above. You and I cannot borrow at all on personal account—the minimum transaction required is simply too large. An increasing number of large loans of intermediate term credit—three to seven years—are lent by banking consortia who pool the risks involved. To finance a large loan to Brazil, the Bank of Tokyo might team up with the Bank of America (London), Morgan Guaranty (London), the Royal Bank of Canada (London), and so on over as many as a dozen consortium partners, one of whom usually leads in doing the credit investigation and managing the consortium.

Alternatively, the Bank of Tokyo could simply make a low-cost quick turn by lending the funds in a lump sum to another name bank at, say, 4¾ percent—if LIBOR had risen by one-fourth of one percent in the interim. Yet another simple transfer of checking deposits within Chase Manhattan in favor of this new Eurobank could follow; or Chase might lose the deposits if, say, First National City was the American correspondent of the new bank.

We see, therefore, that the great volume of dollar transactions among Euro-banks results in a mirror image shuffling of dollar claims (usually demand deposits) among American correspondent banks in New York, Chicago, or San Francisco. The proximate *means of payment* within the Eurocurrency system is M_1 in the form of American demand deposits, while the ultimate means of payment among the American correspondents is federal funds (high-powered deposits with the Federal Reserve System). Eurosterling or Euroguilder transactions work in an analogous fashion. For example, Eurosterling transactions in Paris would have their counterpart in the shuffling of sterling demand deposits among the large London clearing banks.

Thus currency convertibility in the mother country, whose currency is being used for offshore transacting, is essential to provide the means of payment in the system. Even when the United States imposed certain capital-account restrictions in the 1960s, foreigners remained free to place deposits in, or withdraw deposits from, American banks in New York or San Francisco. This freedom is essential to Eurodollar transacting. In contrast, Euroyen transacting has not developed to any substantial extent—even in natural offshore markets like that provided in Singapore. Foreigners may be too much hampered by official restrictions in turning over their yen demand deposits with Tokyo banks, and the Japanese government may prefer to keep it that way.

In summary, the popular image of Eurodollars as U.S. dollars that flee to Europe in brown leather satchels and then circulate *independently* abroad is simply incorrect.

Problems of Statistical Measurement:
Some Conceptual Difficulties

Because the Eurocurrency system is largely a wholesaler that connects national money markets, it is difficult to choose an appropriate level of aggregation for measuring its size and growth. The most widely accepted statistical series on outstanding *gross* foreign-currency deposits and credits is published by the Bank for International Settlements (BIS). It is reproduced in Table 9.1, and in the middle total in Table 9.2, for a group of eight reporting European countries whose collective net positions vis-à-vis outsiders defines the extent of the "market."

More revealing of the scope and nature of the Eurocurrency system is the more net compilation in Table 9.4 of sources and uses of foreign currencies for the same inner group of reporting banks. All commercial and merchant banks accepting foreign currency deposits in eight European countries (Belgium-Luxembourg, France, Germany, Italy, the Netherlands, Sweden, Switzerland, and the United Kingdom) are included in the BIS reporting procedures. All net foreign currency placements (say, a franc deposit in a German bank) within this inner circle of banks, plus payments by outside banks, are then counted as *sources* of finance to the market. Similarly, all net foreign-currency loans to nonbanks, plus deposits made in banks *outside* this inner circle, are counted as *uses* of Eurocurrency resources. Because reporting banks undertake extensive borrowing and lending among themselves, all such interbank deposits of foreign currencies are netted out for the inner eight countries to avoid double or triple counting the same funds passing through several institutions. Thus, much of the purely wholesale interbank transacting—which itself may serve an important economic function—that appears in Table 9.1 is eliminated from the BIS data presented in Table 9.4.

Yet, despite this netting out, neither the sources nor the uses of Eurocurrencies so measured (US$247 billion in 1976) reflect a purely retail relationship with nonbank enterprises—a conceptual state of bliss for which we strive in defining domestic monetary aggregates. First, banks outside the BIS inner group are major borrowers and depositors in the market. Second, as demonstrated below, switching between foreign and domestic currencies by any reporting bank itself can influence the total size of the sources or uses statistical aggregate. Thus the BIS statistical concept stops well short of netting out all interbank transactions. Indeed, interbank deposits still account for 70 percent of the BIS sources, as shown in Table 9.5. Hence, the commonly accepted BIS measure of the size of the Eurocurrency market is not comparable to domestic monetary aggregates, which measure stocks of monetary assets held by individuals and firms that are not themselves banks.

TABLE 9.4 Estimated Sources and Uses of Eurocurrency Funds (Billions of U.S. dollars)

End of year	Reporting European area		United States	Canada and Japan	Other developed countries	Eastern Europe[c]	Offshore banking centers[d]	Oil-exporting countries[e]	Developing countries	Unallocated[f]	Total
	Total[a]	Nonbank[b]									
Uses:											
1973	$49.0	$29.5	$13.5	$12.7	$14.7	$ 7.4	$18.7	$ 3.3	$11.0	$1.7	$132.0
1974	61.5	41.3	18.2	18.2	20.4	10.1	26.7	3.5	15.7	2.7	177.0
1975	63.0	43.6	16.6	20.2	25.8	15.9	35.5	5.3	19.5	3.2	205.0
1976	75.1	51.5	18.3	21.6	33.0	20.8	40.7	9.6	24.7	3.2	247.0
Sources:											
1973	50.8	27.5	9.5	9.8	17.7	3.7	12.5	10.0	14.6	3.4	132.0
1974	67.8	36.2	11.9	8.7	18.5	5.1	17.8	29.1	15.5	2.6	177.0
1975	79.5	38.5	15.4	8.3	19.9	5.4	21.8	34.6	16.2	3.9	205.0
1976	87.6	44.7	18.3	10.5	21.3	6.4	30.1	45.2	21.3	5.8	247.0

SOURCE: BIS, *47th Annual Report, 1976–77*, p. 109.

[a]Includes: (1) under "Uses" the banks' conversions from foreign into domestic currency and foreign-currency funds applied by the reporting banks to the commercial banks of the country of issue of the currency in question (such as DM funds deposited with German banks); (2) under "Sources" deposits by official monetary institutions of the reporting area, the banks' conversions from domestic into foreign currency and foreign-currency funds obtained by the reporting banks from the banks in the country of issue of the currency in question (such as funds received in DM from German banks).

[b]On the "Sources" side includes trustee funds to the extent that they are transmitted by the Swiss banks to the other banks within the reporting area by the Swiss banks themselves.

[c]Excludes positions of banks located in the Federal Republic of Germany vis-à-vis the German Democratic Republic.

[d]Bahamas, Bermuda, Cayman Islands, Hong Kong, Lebanon, Liberia, Netherlands Antilles, New Hebrides, Panama, Singapore, Virgin Islands, West Indies.

[e]Algeria, Bahrain, Brunei, Ecuador, Gabon, Indonesia, Iran, Iraq, Kuwait, Libya, Nigeria, Oman, Qatar, Saudi-Arabia, Trinidad and Tobago, the United Arab Emirates, Venezuela.

[f]Includes positions vis-à-vis international institutions.

TABLE 9.5   Sources of the Eurocurrency Market (Mid 1975)

Banks:	
Commercial banks in the reporting area	16%
Banks outside the reporting area	29%
Central banks and other official monetary agencies	25%
Total Banks	70%
Nonbanks:	
Domestic nonbank depositors	6%
Nonresident nonbank depositors	15%
Trustee funds, including some funds placed in the market by financial holdings and investment trusts	9%
Total Nonbanks	30%

SOURCE: Helmut W. Mayer, "The BIS Concept of the Eurocurrency Market," *Euromoney* (May 1976), p. 63.

A further difficulty with the BIS "net" statistical aggregate is its parochial European nature. For example, it omits growth in the Asian dollar market centered in Singapore. Like its European counterpart, the Singapore market presents a mixture of wholesale transactions among banks and retail transactions with nonbank firms for which a satisfactory statistical aggregate is difficult to define. Total gross foreign-currency assets of Eurobanks in Singapore rose from about nothing in 1968 to over US$12 billion by the end of 1975.[11]

Despite this proliferation of Eurocurrency trading in other parts of the world, the European (London) segments seem to predominate in providing a central market for interest-rate determination. "The opening quotations in the Singapore market are the previous day's closing rates for Eurodollars in London and Europe. During the day there are only minor fluctuations in the rates until late in the afternoon when trading between Singapore and London/Europe commences. Then any difference in the rates between the two markets quickly disappears and the rates equalize at whatever level the Eurodollar market dictates."[12] There would thus be some reason for the BIS to stick to its European reporting procedures even if there were sufficiently detailed statistics on other offshore centers. Nevertheless, the scope of the Eurocurrency market is indeed worldwide, with open access to banks or commercial enterprises that are not limited by exchange controls and who feel comfortable in dealing with deposits of the order of US$250,000 or more. It is not a game in which individuals— the little man—can easily participate.

11. BIS, *Annual Report, 1975–76* (Washington, D.C.: Bank for International Settlements, 1976).
12. Robert F. Emery, "The Asian Dollar Market," Federal Reserve Board *International Finance Discussion Papers* (November 1975), p. 15 (processed).

The Foreign Exchange Aspect:
Covering and Interest Arbitrage

Table 9.5 reveals the huge share that interbank trading comprises in the Eurocurrency market even when all interbank foreign-currency transactions among the eight reporting countries are netted out. This dominance is superficially puzzling. A certain amount of churning of transactions at wholesale is perhaps necessary to match lenders with ultimate borrowers, but the vast amount of interbank transacting within the Eurocurrency system seems disproportionate if treated merely as a substitute for domestic financial intermediation within the confines of a single currency. And most formal academic models have treated the Eurocurrency market as if it were merely an extension of domestic financial processes. (See the commonly used model of the *money multiplier* discussed in the next section.)

The statistical paradox can be resolved, however, if we consider two important economic functions of interbank transacting in Eurocurrencies other than the traditional intermediation between primary savers and final borrowers. First, in countries where national capital markets are imperfect, domestic banks may find they can best adjust their reserve positions in the national currency by Eurocurrency transacting, much as the virtually perfect United States federal funds market allows American banks to swap reserves. (This function is discussed in the following section.) Second, interbank transacting in the Eurocurrency market has a key *foreign exchange* aspect. It allows banks to exchange one national currency for another (a) in covering forward foreign exchange commitments they make to their nonbank customers, whose need to hedge against currency risk has become more acute under floating exchange rates (Chapter 4); and (b) in undertaking covered interest arbitrage that aligns interest differentials with forward premia or discounts in the forward exchange markets, which in turn reduces the cost of hedging for nonbanks (Chapter 5).

To get a feeling for the importance of foreign exchange transactions, note that BIS reporting banks are counted as original suppliers (sources) if they use funds obtained in domestic currency for switching into foreign currencies and are counted as users when they switch foreign currency into domestic currency. Helmut Mayer gives an example. "For instance, a bank in Germany may use Deutsche marks to buy dollars and place the dollars with a bank in London; the London bank may relend the funds to a bank in France which may convert them into French francs. In such a case, the German bank would be shown as a supplier, and the French banks as an end-user of Eurocurrency funds."[13]

Item (1) in Table 9.5 captures this switching between a domestic and foreign

13. Helmut Mayer, "The BIS Concept of the Eurocurrency Market," *Euromoney* (May 1976), p. 60.

currency by reporting banks. Of course, switching confined between different foreign currencies by the reporting banks would be netted out and not shown.

It is also likely that banks outside the reporting area—item (2)—are, in significant measure, simply covering in the Eurocurrency market the forward transactions undertaken on behalf of their nonbank customers. For example, an Austrian bank may sell DM three months forward to a commercial firm, and then cover by switching schillings into DM spot and placing the proceeds in a Euromark deposit in London that matures in about three months. This last transaction would show up as a source of Eurocurrency funds under item (2), whereas the initiating forward exchange transaction with the commercial firm would not appear. Not only do banks have the peculiar advantage that their names are accepted in Eurocurrency transacting, but foreign exchange restrictions on capital account often force nonbank enterprises to work through authorized commercial banks in their home country—a restraint that can preclude direct Eurocurrency transacting by nonbanks.

Because forward covering operations of banks have important economic implications in diminishing the risks associated with flexible exchange rates, perhaps the BIS measure of sources and uses in Table 9.4 nets out too much. At least some of the excluded foreign currency transactions among banks in the BIS inner eight group of countries may reflect hedging or covering operations, as when a German bank switches out of francs and into U.S. dollars held in London. (Note again that switches from DM into foreign currencies would be captured as a source by the BIS.) The conceptual conflict in what the BIS is trying to measure becomes readily apparent. To construct an international monetary aggregate analogous to M_1 or M_2, as applied within any national monetary system, all interbank transactions must be consolidated to get a single net position of the banking system as a whole vis-à-vis nonbanks. However, to measure the importance of *foreign exchange* hedging and covering operations, we do *not* want to consolidate all interbank foreign-currency transactions.

In addition to the prevalence of interbank transacting, further indirect evidence of the importance of transactions *across* national currencies is the very limited amount of *maturity transformation* undertaken in trading among Eurocurrency banks. Table 9.6 reproduces data on the maturity structure of assets and liabilities of London-based Eurobanks as of September 1973[14] and separates data on interbank transacting from claims and liabilities to nonbanks. The latter exhibit substantial transformation: the average term to maturity of loans to nonbanks (claims) exceeds that of deposits (liabilities). Whereas the more prevalent interbank trading is nicely balanced at every term to maturity.

To interpret these data, suppose for a moment that *interbank* transactions arose exclusively from hedging pressure by nonbank enterprises. (Other reasons

14. The Bank of England, *Quarterly Bulletin* (March 26, 1974).

TABLE 9.6 Maturity Transformation: Claims and Liabilities in Nonsterling Currencies of all U.K.-based Eurobanks (September 30, 1973)

Maturity	Total		With banks		With nonbanks	
	Claims	Liab.	Claims	Liab.	Claims	Liab.
	(percent)					
Less than 8 days	14.9	19.1	17.1	17.4	8.9	28.4
8 days to <1 month	18.9	19.4	20.6	19.8	13.5	17.6
1 month to <3 months	24.8	26.2	25.7	26.8	22.3	22.3
3 months to <6 months	20.8	20.9	21.6	22.0	18.8	14.9
6 months to <1 year	8.2	8.8	8.8	8.8	6.6	8.8
1 year to <3 years	4.8	2.5	2.9	2.5	9.8	2.7
3 years and over	7.7	3.1	3.3	2.8	20.0	5.4
All maturities	100.0	100.0	100.0	100.0	100.0	100.0
			(millions of £s)			
All maturities	49,774	49,664	36,354	42,313	13,420	7,351

SOURCE: The Bank of England, *Quarterly Bulletin*, March 26, 1974.

for interbank transacting are provided below.) Importers buy foreign exchange forward and exporters sell it, meeting under the auspices of their banks in the Eurocurrency market. While purchases and sales of foreign exchange might take place at several maturity dates, generally one would expect no *net* hedging pressure in one direction for any given maturity in any one currency, because the flow of foreign trade is in both directions. Therefore, these purely forward foreign exchange operations would not cause the deposit side to become more liquid than the loan side. In addition the tremendous depth of available forward deposit and loan maturities allows Eurocurrency banks to quote forward rates of exchange tailored quite precisely to the diverse needs of their nonbank customers, unlike trading in commodity futures where contracts are written on particular months, and given days in those months (see Chapter 5).

A final, striking piece of evidence that the Eurocurrency market is heavily used for forward covering is provided by the measurement of covered interest differentials. National money-market instruments are still subject to various degrees of regulatory control, interest restrictions, and surveillance. Because of this asymmetrical regulation, foreigners may perceive the political risk incurred by investing in a domestic-currency instrument in a national money market to be higher than that incurred by investing in foreign-currency deposits in the same country. Moreover, national interest rates on bank deposits and loans are often rigidified by cartellike arrangements. Because of either exchange controls or cartels, therefore, the covered interest differential across Eurocurrency deposits should be closer to zero than across national money-market instruments with the same time to maturity. Robert Aliber has confirmed this hypothesis with evidence that is reproduced in Table 9.7.[15]

15. Robert Z. Aliber, "The Interest Rate Parity Theorem: A Reinterpretation," *Journal of Political Economy* (November/December 1973), p. 1455.

TABLE 9.7   Comparative Deviations of Predicted Forward Rates from Actual Forward Rates (Percent per annum)

Interest agio (1)	Mean deviation (2)	Median deviation (3)	Minimum deviation (4)	Maximum deviation (5)	Range of deviation (6) = (5) − (4)	Standard deviation of mean (7)
U.S.–U.K. treasury bills	1.94	1.348	−0.25	8.40	8.65	1.93
London dollars– Paris sterling	0.273	0.168	−0.51	1.72	2.23	0.40

SOURCE: Robert Z. Aliber, "The Interest Rate Parity Theorem: A Reinterpretation," *Journal of Political Economy* (Nov./Dec. 1973), p.1455. The observations pertain to the three-year period January 1968 to June 1970.

Aliber's example compares forward rates and interest rates on sterling with those on U.S. dollars. Suppose that

R_s is the spot exchange rate in dollars/sterling;

R_f is the actual forward exchange rate;

r^s is the interest rate on sterling assets; and

r^d is the interest rate on dollar assets.

Further, define $\bar{R}_f$ as that *hypothetical* forward rate such that—for given R_s, r^s, and r^d—the interest-rate parity theorem (Chapter 5) holds exactly:

$$\frac{\bar{R}_f}{R_s} \cdot \frac{(1 + r^s)}{(1 + r^d)} - 1 = 0.$$

Aliber's testing procedure amounts to comparing R_f with $\bar{R}_f$ when the two interest rates are defined first by national money market instruments and then by the LIBOR on dollar and sterling Eurodeposits. In the latter case, R_f more nearly approaches $\bar{R}_f$ because freer capital mobility greatly reduces covered interest differentials across Eurocurrencies.

Perhaps one can go beyond simply relying on the relative ease of taking foreign-currency positions in the Euromarkets. The standard model of covered interest arbitrage presumes that forward rates are separately determined, and that arbitrageurs then match forward premia or discounts against intercurrency interest differentials. The real story may be simpler. It seems to be common knowledge that foreign exchange traders actually use the Euro interest-rate quotations (LIBOR) on different currencies to determine their forward bid-offer quotations.[16] Since these traders know that they must cover in the Eurocurrency market anyway and that this market is deep relative to the forward market itself, it would seem that Eurocurrency interest rates dominate forward-exchange quotations. In general equilibrium, of course, forward exchange rates and Euro interest rates are simultaneously determined variables.[17]

One small puzzle remains. If the Eurocurrency system has evolved into an integral part of the forward market for foreign exchange, why should transactions in Euro*dollars* predominate as seen in Table 9.1? Because most world trade takes place outside the United States, should we not observe relatively more active Eurocurrency transacting in other convertible currencies—such as kronor and guilders—by countries that are substantial exporters?

The puzzle can be dispelled, however, by noting that the U.S. dollar is the principal *vehicle* currency in the spot or forward markets for foreign exchange.[18] Forward contracting by Dutch or Swedish traders would normally use the dollar as an intermediary currency anyway (Chapter 2) because a direct market between kronor and guilders does not exist. For example, a Swedish importer of Dutch tulip bulbs that must be paid for in guilders in three months would contract with his bank to buy guilders for kronor three months hence. To cover itself, the Swedish commercial bank might well buy *dollars* forward for kronor in the interbank market and then sell the dollars forward to obtain guilders: kronor/guilders = kronor/dollars · dollars/guilders.

This chain of transactions can take place through the forward market directly or, alternatively, by swapping Eurocurrency deposits. For example, the Swedish bank might buy (with kronor) a Eurodollar deposit maturing in three months or so, and then sell that deposit forward in the active forward exchange market between dollars and guilders. This intermediary role of the dollar in foreign exchange operations would show up statistically as an increase in *Eurodollar* deposits outstanding, making the latter seem disproportionately large vis-à-vis other Eurocurrency holdings as seems to be the case in Table 9.1. Effective covered interest arbitrage between interest-bearing krona and guilder assets also might well take place triangularly, the vehicle currency being the dollar.

16. I am indebted to two foreign exchange traders, Edward Aronson and Peter Naylor, on this point.
17. On this point, see Richard J. Herring and Richard C. Marston, *National Monetary Policies and International Financial Markets* (Amsterdam: North-Holland, 1976), Chapter 4.
18. Indeed, this central role of the U.S. dollar as a vehicle currency is the main theme of Alexander Swoboda in "The Euro-Dollar Market: An Interpretation," *Princeton Essays in International Finance*, No. 64 (1968). For Swoboda, banking systems in other countries are simply bidding for some of the seigniorage that would otherwise accrue to the United States because of the central role of the U.S. dollar as interbank money.

Liquidity Creation and Domestic Financial Intermediation

Rather than the foreign exchange aspect, most academic observers focus on whether the Eurocurrency system is an uncontrolled vehicle for the creation of "money"—a gigantic international liquidity machine under nobody's control. What are the analytical and empirical roots of this concern?

Because the term "deposit" is used to describe the placement of funds in the Eurocurrency market and also connotes the means of payment within a country, Eurocurrency deposits have often been considered a competing form of money for each national currency. And, in recent years, the absolute growth of Eurodollar claims as measured by the BIS has been of the same order of magnitude as the growth of the domestic stock of money held by firms and individuals in the United States—as measured by M_1 or M_2. Moreover, the emergence of worldwide price inflation in the late 1960s paralleled the remarkable growth of the Eurocurrency system in the world economy.

If Eurocurrency deposits are treated as money and we have fractional reserve banking, then the old idea of multiple deposit creation from some reserve base seems relevant. Indeed, in Table 9.3, Barclays' EuroBank in London holds only a US$20,000 demand deposit in Chase Manhattan New York as a reserve against outstanding deposit liabilities of US$1,020,000. Let us then formalize algebraically the process of increasing Eurocurrency reserves, and multiple deposit creation arising therefrom, within the confines of a single currency.[19] Let r be total demand deposits held by Eurobanks in American correspondents, with r amounting to a small fraction ρ of Eurodeposit liabilities e.

$$r = \rho e. \tag{9.1}$$

Assuming some notion of portfolio balance between American and overseas dollar holdings, suppose that Eurodollar deposits are a linear function of *total* liquid dollar assets M^*, where M^* is defined as the United States money supply M (deposit claims on American banks plus coin and currency) less Euroreserves plus Eurodeposits:

$$e = \epsilon M^* + \alpha \tag{9.2}$$

where

$$M^* = M - r + e. \tag{9.3}$$

19. I am using the notation and analytical procedure suggested by Jürg Niehans and John Hewson, "The Eurodollar Market and Monetary Theory," *Journal of Money, Credit, and Banking* (February 1976), p. 3. Earlier articles on the subject of multiple deposit creation are Milton Friedman, "The Euro Dollar Market: Some First Principles," *Morgan Guaranty Survey* (Oct. 1969), and Fritz Machlup, "Euro Dollar Creation: A Mystery Story," *Banca Nazionale del Lavoro Quarterly Review* (September 1970).

For a given M, equations (9.1), (9.2), and (9.3) together describe the effect of a shift in asset preferences from U.S. dollars to Eurodollars—the shift being conveniently embodied in a change in the parameter α. This sets in train a multiple expansion in M^* when new Eurocredits are granted. The proportion ϵ of the proceeds of these dollar credits are redeposited in Eurobanks. In final equilibrium, the total incremental creation of Eurodollars is thus given by the multiplier:

$$\frac{de}{d\alpha} = \frac{1}{1 - \epsilon(1 - \rho)}. \tag{9.4}$$

Clearly $de/d\alpha$ is positively related to ϵ—the redeposit rate—and negatively related to ρ—the reserve ratio. The fact that ρ is very low—of the order of two to five percent—is offset by ϵ also being low (i.e., the leakage from the Euro-currency system is high). Niehans and Hewson compare the broad definition of the American M_2—say \$641.3 billion at the end of 1973—to the BIS estimate of net sources of Eurodollar deposits of more than \$100 billion for the end of 1973. For illustrative purposes, let $\rho = 0.033$, and $\epsilon = 0.16$. From equation (9.4), the total increase in Eurodeposits from an increase in α can then be calculated: $de/d\alpha = 1.18$—a relatively modest number of the same order of magnitude as the initial transfer of dollar claims from the United States to Europe.

More revealing is the multiplier impact on M^*—the total stock of dollar liabilities—of a shift in dollar deposits from the United States to Europe. Solving equations (9.1), (9.2), and (9.3), but this time eliminating e, we have:

$$M^* = \frac{1}{1 - \epsilon(1 - \rho)} + \frac{(1 - \rho)\alpha}{1 - \epsilon(1 - \rho)} \tag{9.5}$$

From an exogenous shift in α the multiplier is:

$$\frac{dM^*}{d\alpha} = \frac{1 - \rho}{1 - \epsilon(1 - \rho)} = 1.15 \tag{9.6}$$

Given that ρ is small, and accepting Niehans's and Hewson's parameter estimates for ϵ, a shift from the United States to Europe increases the total stock of dollar deposits by slightly more than the amount of the transfer. Hence, multiple deposit creation from any single isolated transfer of funds from the United States is of limited importance, and the model seems quite stable in the context of this kind of shock. However, *continual* movement from the United States to Europe would be capable of increasing the outstanding stock of dollar deposits virtually without limit, even though the multiplier impact of any one such shift is modest.

How likely is the continual shifting of dollar deposits from the United States to Europe? Unlimited multiple deposit creation from an increasing reserve base of the standard textbook kind implicitly assumes that interest rates are fixed and that there is an excess demand for bank credit at those interest rates.[20] Niehans and Hewson suggest that a flow of deposits to Europe (because of changed portfolio preferences) will bid down Eurodeposit rates of interest that are unregulated and are ultrasensitive to demand and supply. This bidding down of interest rates in Europe will dampen the flow of deposits or drive them back to the United States because American banks are actively providing a competing monetary asset in the form of interest-bearing certificates of deposit. Assuming that the commodity price level exhibits stability in the short run, it seems unlikely that a monetary explosion could be generated from a series of exogenous shifts in dollar deposits from the United States to Europe.

Uncontrolled deposit creation in Europe could occur only if misguided regulatory policy rendered American time deposit rates of interest uncompetitive and gave undue incentive to large American business firms to hold dollar deposits overseas so as to earn much higher rates of interest. Such perverse policy did in fact occur in 1969, when nominal rates of interest on Eurodollar deposits rose sharply above the Q ceilings on equivalent assets in the United States and American parent banks in New York could borrow freely from their European affiliates with, effectively, a zero reserve requirement against such borrowing. The consequences are portrayed in Table 9.8. Multinational corporations switched their holdings on a large scale from dollar deposits in New York to dollar deposits in London. The result was a sharp and artificial run-up of Eurodollar deposits that were borrowed back by New York banks. However, the whole process was quickly reversed in the early 1970s when certificates of deposit in large American banks were freed of interest restrictions, and American reserve requirements against certificates of deposit were reduced to about three percent and a ten percent reserve requirement on overseas borrowing by American banks was imposed by the Federal Reserve Board.

There is a more basic reason, however, for not worrying about excess liquidity creation in the Euromarkets. The statistical aggregates compiled by BIS, measuring the size of the Eurocurrency market, are simply not comparable to M_1 or M_2 as currently measured in the United States. Helmut Mayer makes dramatically clear that only thirty percent of the sources to the Eurocurrency market specified by the BIS represents deposit claims by *nonbanks*—Table 9.4, items (4) to (6). Of these nonbank foreign-currency deposits, those owned by domestic residents—item (4)—are already counted in the monetary aggregates

20. See James Tobin, "Commercial Banks as Creators of Money," *Essays in Economics: Vol. 1 Macroeconomics* (Chicago, Ill.: Markham, 1971), Chapter 16.

TABLE 9.8   Borrowings by U.S. Banks in the Eurodollar Market (Billions of U.S. dollars)

Years	Size of Eurodollar market*	Borrowings from branches by U.S. banks
1963	5.0	1.04
1964	9.0	1.18
1965	11.5	1.35
1966	14.5	4.04
1967	17.5	4.24
1968	25.0	6.04
1969	37.5	12.81†
1970	46.0	7.68
April 1971	47.0	5.17

SOURCE: BIS *Annual Reports* and *Federal Reserve Bulletin*, compiled by Patricia Brenner.

*As measured by the BIS for the U.K., Belgium, the Netherlands, France, Germany, Italy, Sweden, and Switzerland.

†Maximum 14.35 in September 1969.

of reporting countries, whereas trustee funds—item (6)—have financial liabilities that may well be less liquid than their Eurocurrency claims. Only the stock of nonresident deposits held by nonbanks—item (5)—is a strong candidate to be classified as an alternative monetary asset that is now *not* counted in national monetary aggregates. As of mid-1975, item (5) represented only 15 percent of the BIS sources aggregate; in any case, it is *quasi* money more akin to certificates of deposit than to demand deposits.

Nevertheless, allowing banks in any one country to adjust their liquidity positions in the Euromarket may be important when national money markets are imperfect. If a domestic bank in country A found itself with a reserve shortage, it could (by raising interest rates) bid for Eurodeposits directly in currency A. If a Euromarket in currency A was not well established or regulations prohibited taking offshore deposits in domestic currency, then the domestic bank could bid for Eurodollars and swap them for domestic reserves. In a floating rate system where A's central bank is *not* obligated to purchase dollars and provide domestic reserves on demand, there would be no net increase in domestic bank reserves nor any loss of monetary control.

Once it is understood that Eurocurrency deposits are primarily of an interbank character and that little maturity transformation takes place between deposits and loans (Table 9.6), it can be seen that relatively little *net* liquidity is created. The liabilities of the Eurobanks are about as liquid as the claims. The Eurocurrency market is therefore, mainly a vehicle for readjusting the liquidity positions of financial institutions (for domestic reasons or due to foreign exchange transactions) rather than being a net creator of liquidity. As such, the direct inflationary consequences of the market's growth need not induce indigestion or heartburn.

As Helmut Mayer points out, however, the *indirect* consequences may well be important if the Eurocurrency system more quickly transmits monetary disturbances from one country to another, as happened in the last years of the old fixed-rate Bretton Woods regime. If the expansionary effects in some countries are only slightly offset by contractionary effects in others, inflationary impulses will show up in the rapid growth of *domestic* monetary aggregates in most participating countries.

International Capital Transfers

Minimizing the importance of the Eurocurrency market as a net creator of liquidity in no way detracts from its role as a great international conduit for transferring capital net from one country to another. The enormous recycling of funds made necessary by the formation of the OPEC oil cartel in 1973 would not have proceeded so smoothly in the absence of the Eurocurrency system. However, one must carefully distinguish *gross* from *net* capital flows. The spectacular growth of the market's size, as measured by the BIS statistical aggregates in Tables 9.1 or 9.4, does *not* reflect a one-to-one correspondence with net international transfers of capital:

1) The forward covering of foreign exchange positions assures us that importers and exporters—as represented by their banking intermediaries—will normally take somewhat offsetting positions in the Eurocurrency market. For example, liquid importers (in the sense used in Chapter 5) from country A may be holders of Eurodollar deposits against forward exchange obligations; so might liquid importers from country B. Exporters from both countries might then be borrowers of Eurodollars—either directly or indirectly. Any number of such gross flows of capital may arise out of granting or receiving trade credits that are then covered against foreign exchange risk.

2) The unregulated Eurocurrency market extends financial intermediation between savers and investors within the same country, and often within the domain of the domestic currency. The sharp run up of Eurodollar deposits in 1969 by American firms, which were simply withdrawing their certificates of deposit from New York, did not reflect any international net transfer of capital. Insofar as regulation of domestic capital markets in convertible-currency countries remains onerous, the Eurocurrency market will continue to grow at the expense of purely domestic financial intermediaries.

However, a substantial but unknown proportion of what remains undoubtedly represents a net transfer of claims on real resources from one country to another. For the oil-exporting countries alone, the excess of exports over imports in 1972 was about US\$13 billion; it then rose to a peak of more than \$86 billion in 1974. Subsequently, in 1975, this trade surplus declined to about \$58 billion and declined further in 1976 through 1978. Of course, trade surpluses are not the same as total surplus to be financed on current account, but the order of magnitude and the ebb and flow are indicative. On the other side of the same coin, we note that the most liquid part of OPEC's claim on foreigners—what are officially called OPEC's International Reserves by the IMF[21]—rose from \$8.5 billion at the end of 1972 to about \$62.1 billion at the end of 1977. Perhaps as much as two-thirds of these were held as Eurocurrency deposits.

The complex layering of financial intermediaries in the Eurocurrency market and the latter's close connection to purely domestic capital markets make it next to impossible conceptually and statistically to ascribe definite amounts of the recycling to the Eurocurrency market, to the American capital market, to official international institutions such as the IMF or World Bank, and so on.[22] Nevertheless, it is clear that the anonymity, the flexibility in swapping among various currencies (the foreign exchange aspect), and the ultrasensitivity of short-term Eurodeposit rates of interest to demand and supply make the market valuable at the margin to those creditworthy borrowers or depositors without access to other well-defined financial channels. And, judging by the very rough BIS estimates of the deployment of OPEC's investible surpluses in 1974–1976, reproduced in Table 9.9, the Eurocurrency system was particularly important in 1974 when the magnitude of the oil surplus seemed to take all participating countries by surprise.

The flexibility of the Eurocurrency system is important in avoiding two kinds of mismatching in the recyling process:

1) Mismatching across currencies, where the mix of convertible-currency assets desired by OPEC investors differs from the mix of currencies in which oil-importing countries wish to borrow. As a practical matter, countries with inconvertible currencies cannot issue acceptable debt in domestic money to foreigners; even most debtor countries with convertible currencies find the credit market limited unless they borrow in well-known currencies such as DM,

21. See *International Financial Statistics* (Washington, D.C.: International Monetary Fund, 1978).

22. This layering of financial intermediaries also makes the assets of any one country more difficult to expropriate, and thus reduces the political risk within the Eurosystem. For example, if relationships between Russia and the U.S. were to deteriorate, Russia might default on those loans that come directly from the United States but could not identify the sources of American funds channeled through London. On the other hand, the U.S. might freeze direct Soviet dollar deposits in New York but would have little control over indirect dollar claims channeled through the Bahamas.

TABLE 9.9   Oil-Exporting Countries: Estimated Deployment of Investible Surpluses (Billions of U.S. dollars)

Item	1974	1975	1976
Bank deposits and money-market placements:			
Dollar deposits in the U.S.	$ 4.0	$ 0.6	$ 1.6
Sterling deposits in the U.K.	1.7	0.2	−1.4
Deposits in foreign-currency markets	22.8	9.1	12.6
Treasury bills in the U.S. and U.K.	8.0	−0.4	−2.2
Total	36.5	9.5	10.6
Long-term investments:			
Special bilateral arrangements	11.9	12.4	10.3
Loans to international agencies	3.5	4.0	2.0
Government securities in the U.S. and U.K.	1.1	2.4	4.4
Other[a]	4.0	7.4	8.0
Total	20.5	26.2	24.7
Total new investments	57.0	35.7	35.3

SOURCE: BIS *Annual Report, 1976–77*, p. 92.

[a]Includes equity and property investment in the United States and the United Kingdom, and foreign-currency lending.

United States dollars, Swiss francs or—in an earlier era—British sterling. Among these internationally acceptable currencies, however, loans must still be matched to deposits. Fortunately, the interest sensitivity of the Euromarket can fairly easily balance net supply and demand in each currency for given expectations of future exchange-rate movements on the part of both depositors and lenders. Even if primary depositors and ultimate borrowers are rather interest insensitive, a highly developed forward market for foreign exchange permits banks to engage in covered interest arbitrage across currencies. Hence, the menu of currency obligations of final borrowers can differ from the menu of currency assets held by primary savers—with banks acting as financial intermediaries in making this currency transformation.

2)   Mismatching across countries where OPEC depositors hold claims on some convertible-currency countries in excess of their oil deficits—say, Switzerland, Germany, and the United States—while other creditworthy countries with large oil deficits do not receive such a direct capital inflow from abroad—say, Sweden, Korea, or Brazil. But capital is fungible. Eurobanks in London can use the proceeds from dollar deposits to lend to Brazil. Either London banks can offer a higher rate of interest than American or German banks, or they can borrow dollars from their American affiliates (in the absence of U.S. exchange controls) if OPEC depositors are determined to hold their funds in the United States. Of course, American banks—even if regulated—can compete in provid-

ing the same intermediary service in the absence of exchange controls, which fortunately were finally phased out in 1974. And from Table 9.2, dollar claims of American banks on foreigners also increased substantially from 1974 to 1976.

Thus, the world capital market facilitates both currency transformation and country transformation in the international recycling of oil revenues and other monies—always in the context of the convertible currency system. What might have been major bottlenecks in a world of rigidly controlled national monetary systems in 1973–1978 are nonproblems in free Euromarkets—supplemented by greatly improved regulatory conditions in the United States. (Of course, countries with little or no debt service capacity cannot borrow in a free market and must rely on government-to-government grants or loans from official international agencies.)

Flexible as it was, why then did the international capital market appear temporarily to seize up in mid-1974? Stories appeared in the financial press in 1974 that some Eurobanks refused to accept large OPEC deposits, some creditworthy borrowers were being turned away, and there was insufficient equity capital in the Eurobanking system to service the oil transfers. The situation was exacerbated at the time by the failure of two large banks, Herstatt and Franklin National, because of unsuccessful speculation in foreign exchange. This temporarily dampened interbank trading on the basis of names—the very heart of Eurocurrency transacting. The disappearance of this seeming financial incapacity by the end of 1974 was due, I believe, to a realignment of short- and long-term rates of interest in the Eurocurrency market (and in the United States) and to the restoration of general confidence in the major name banks.

What caused the initial disalignment in the term structure of interest rates? Business activity in the United States and in much of Europe culminated in a cyclical peak in 1973 and 1974, at a time when the monetary authorities were determined to slow inflation. As a result, a situation of tight money drove short-run deposit rates of interest extraordinarily high relative to longer term bond rates—see Figure 9.1. Call interbank lending (deposit) rates of interest— those based on first-class credit names—rose to 12 or 13 percent in the Eurocurrency market in 1974, while comparable long-term rates remained at 9 to 10 percent. This unusual conjunction of interest rates was the same in the United States and other major national money markets. Thus short-term rates exceeded long-term ones when the full force of the oil shock—the need to transfer huge funds from OPEC to oil-importing countries—struck in mid-1974. (The acute financial shock somewhat lagged the actual rise in oil prices because payments by the oil companies to OPEC lagged, as per normal commercial practice.) I hypothesize that *this inverted maturity structure of interest rates*, arising out of a particular stage in the business cycle, *was precisely wrong*

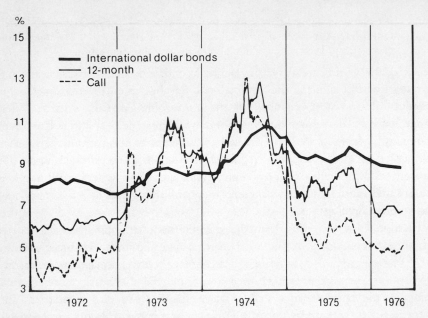

FIGURE 9.1   Eurodollar deposit rates and Eurodollar bond yields (end-of-month rates and weekly averages)
SOURCE: BIS *Annual Report*, 1975–76, p. 91.

for matching the portfolio preferences of OPEC depositors (lenders) to final borrowers—firms and governments in the rest of the world that were net importers of oil. It also accentuated the crisis in bank confidence because many commercial banks ran at a bookkeeping loss in paying more on their short-term deposit liabilities than they were earning on their older, but longer term, loans to nonbanks.

Unaccustomed to such a deluge of revenue and nervous about possible retaliation through expropriation of their convertible-currency assets and significant fluctuations in exchange rates, the OPEC investors tried to invest mainly at very short term. Indeed, time deposits for seven or eight days—or simply overnight money—in relatively large discrete lumps were commonplace. In contrast, governments and enterprises in the oil-importing countries wanted to borrow at much longer term, because several years might elapse before their exports expanded sufficiently to cover the amortization costs of current borrowings. These inconsistent preferences were greatly accentuated by the unusual inversion of the interest-rate structure. It prevented banks from engaging in their normal limited amount of maturity transformation: borrowing at short term and lending at long term to nonbanks. Banks became unwilling to transact at the inverted interest rates, and both potential depositors and borrowers were turned away.

Fortunately, however, interest rates were not pegged. The pressure from depositors drove down short-term rates of interest rather sharply by early 1975 to less than half their former levels (Figure 9.1), whereas the demand for the longer-term Euro and other credits maintained long rates of interest. (This unravelling of the interest-rate inversion was accentuated by the cyclical downturn in business activity in late 1974.) When short-term rates of interest fell, the portfolio preferences of depositors for longer-term assets were enhanced, as was the willingness of the private banking system to engage in maturity transformation. The apparent impasse in the deposit-lending process was resolved, and talk in the financial press of the inadequate capacity of the international banking system simply disappeared. The flexibility of the Eurocurrency system undoubtedly contributed to this successful resolution of the financial aspect of the transfer problem, as did the fall in yields on American certificates of deposit.

But this brief interest-rate impasse did not cause even a temporary breakdown in the recycling process! OPEC countries receive oil revenues in convertible foreign currencies—largely U.S. dollars. This means of payment ensures that financial recycling will occur automatically irrespective of whether such funds are successfully "invested" in Eurocurrency deposits—or in national money markets in Germany, the United States, or other countries. The interest-rate impasse mentioned above did complicate the problem of distributing OPEC resources to needy borrowers, but not the aggregate transfer itself. In making payment to Saudi Arabia, one can imagine Exxon's checking account in Chase Manhattan Bank (New York) falling by $1,000,000 and Saudi Arabia's checking account in the same American bank rising by $1,000,000. The funds have been automatically recycled the instant that payment is made! Of course, Saudi Arabia may not be happy holding a noninterest-bearing checking account in New York; and Chase Manhattan may not be able to lend immediately to some oil importer outside of its normal commercial ambit. The portfolios of all participants are hardly in equilibrium. But recycling has occurred nevertheless. Talk in 1974–1975 that private channels in the international financial system were incapable of effecting such an enormous financial transfer was based on a misconception of how the system works. (Again one should mention that the treatment of countries that are worthy, but not creditworthy, potential borrowers is necessarily more the concern of government and official agencies.)

An important consequence of eliminating the inverted structure of interest rates of 1973–1974, and of dampening inflationary expectations over 1975–

TABLE 9.10 International Bond Issues (Millions of U.S. dollars)

Borrowing countries or areas	Eurobond issues				Foreign issues			
	Total	U.S. dollars	Deutsche marks	Private placements	Total	In U.S.	In Switzerland	Private placements
Western Europe								
1974	$ 1,430	$ 430	$ 370	$ 800	$ 1,400	$ 360	$ 650	$1,130
1975	4,570	1,350	1,770	1,450	2,840	840	1,760	1,360
1976	5,440	3,750	1,200	850	4,860	1,180	3,210	2,730
Canada								
1974	440	380	—	350	1,960	1,930	30	800
1975	1,150	610	—		310	3,380	3,100	280
1976	3,010	1,570	40	150	5,870	5,530	340	3,850
U.S.								
1974	110	100	—	10	80	—	80	30
1975	310	220	—	80	140	—	40	120
1976	410	400	—	120	30	—	—	30
Other developed countries[a]								
1974	330	220	110	10	150	30	120	130
1975	2,220	1,340	700	610	1,010	380	600	650
1976	2,070	1,510	510	310	1,480	690	790	660
Rest of the world[b]								
1974	140	120	—	10	790	650	20	520
1975	470	230	80	150	480	460	20	240

International
institutions

1974	2,070	1,830	160	1,780	3,410	620	90	2,650
1975	1,480	1,060	340	840	3,980	1,980	670	1,340
1976	2,960	2,050	730	1,710	4,960	2,270	770	1,650

Total issues
placed

1974	4,520	3,080	640	2,960	7,790	3,590	990	5,260
1975	10,200	4,810	2,890	3,440	11,830	6,760	3,370	4,540
1976	14,930	9,730	2,780	3,300	18,010	10,270	5,220	9,120

SOURCE: BIS *Annual Report, 1976–77*, p. 118. Based on IBRD and OECD sources.

[a] Australia, Japan, New Zealand, and South Africa.

[b] Includes Eastern European countries.

1977, was to lengthen the term structure over which international borrowing and lending take place. Confidence is still somewhat fragile and can easily be upset by renewed inflationary expectations. Yet the lengthening term structure of the international capital market is rather well reflected in the increased importance of new international bond issues. Although still small in comparison to bank deposits and loans, total bond placements increased from about $12 billion in 1974 to about $33 billion in 1976, as indicated in Table 9.10. Besides the large increase in Eurobond issues from $4.5 billion to $14.9 billion, foreign bond issues in domestic capital markets—almost wholly confined to the United States and Switzerland—also increased remarkably from 1974 to 1976 (see Table 9.10).

A Concluding Note on Regulation

My analysis suggests:

—that the uncontrolled Eurocurrency system is not now directly an engine of inflation, of excess liquidity creation, as is often posited.

—that the foreign exchange aspect of the market is particularly valuable in a regime of floating exchange rates.

—that the growth of the market would slow naturally if onerous regulation of domestic money markets were relaxed.

—that the flexibility of the Eurocurrency system has at times served the world economy extraordinarily well in transferring capital, and no *prima facie* case for joint international regulation or supervision exists under current institutional arrangements.

—that countries and islands continue to set policy individually regarding the use of exchange controls to shield differential regulation of domestic- and foreign-currency deposits or bond issues if and only if at least some major international currencies remain freely convertible on both current and capital accounts.

Besides the more general third-party benefits they confer to socialist and less developed countries, freely convertible national currencies remain the life blood of the Eurocurrency system. Valuable though it is, the Eurocurrency market itself provides no substitute for using a few widely accepted national monies to organize international trade.

10

Monetary Unions
and Fixed Exchange Rates

The international payments system, inclusive of Eurocurrency transacting, depends on the exchange of convertible national currencies.[1] Relatively modest disturbances in domestic money markets, however, can move floating exchange rates a great deal (Chapter 8). What then constitutes a mutually consistent set of monetary policies among countries desirous of maintaining fixed parities or virtually stable exchange rates?

A group of countries that are highly integrated in commodity trade, allow free factor movement, and have effective currency convertibility may be classified as an optimum currency area[2]—an area where the establishment of a common monetary policy and virtually fixed exchange rates has potentially high social benefits. Within such an area, discrete and unanticipated exchange-rate changes are highly disruptive—even though the natural degree of exchange-rate variation may be less. Not only are attempts to establish common official prices for agricultural products thwarted, but the law of one price for industrial goods in private trade may also be undermined by exchange-rate fluctuations (Chapter 6).[3]

1. This chapter builds on my article, "Beyond Fixed Parities: The Analytics of International Monetary Agreements," R. Z. Aliber ed., *The Political Economy of Monetary Reform* (Chicago, Ill.: University of Chicago Press, 1977), pp. 42–46.
2. Robert A. Mundell, "A Theory of Optimum Currency Areas," *American Economic Review* (September 1961), pp. 657–65; and Ronald I. McKinnon, "Optimum Currency Areas," *American Economic Review* (September 1963), pp. 717–65.
3. The Common Agricultural Policy in Europe is being continuously upset by exchange-rate fluctuations because the appropriate support price in each national currency for a given farm product becomes ambiguous. See T. Josling and S. Harris, "Europe's Green Money," in *The Three Banks Review*, No. 109 (March 1976).

Despite the periodic fall from grace of several members, industrial Western Europe, as represented by the European Economic Community, is a potential optimum currency area; whereas the Latin American Free Trade Association is not a candidate because most Latin currencies are not convertible into foreign exchange and most of their economies are not highly integrated with each other in foreign trade. Even less is Comecon in Eastern Europe a candidate to be an effective currency area because of both foreign exchange and commodity inconvertibility practiced by member countries (Chapter 3).

In this chapter, I sketch a set of rules of *minimum stringency* for harmonizing monetary policies in a potential currency area, such as the European Monetary Union, under the assumption that monetary nationalism can be curbed although not completely eliminated.

A maximum sufficient condition for success is, of course, to establish a single central bank issuing a single currency over a domain consisting of all the countries in the optimum currency area. Yet this condition is terribly strong in its implications for political and economic sovereignty, and is likely only feasible in imperial regimes.

At the other extreme, one has what W. M. Corden has called a "pseudo exchange-rate union" in which "member countries agree—no doubt solemnly—to maintain fixed exchange-rate relationships within the union but there is no explicit integration of economic policy, no common pool of foreign-exchange reserves, and no single central bank."[4] More specifically for our purposes, a pseudo exchange-rate union is one where there is no effective international coordination of open-market operations, discounting, or forward exchange operations by national central banks. Only pseudo exchange-rate unions have been legally concluded in the postwar period, although *de facto* harmonization of national monetary policies has been achieved in certain subperiods under Bretton Woods (see Chapter 11).

Yet the minimum conditions for success are not so difficult to spell out as is commonly supposed, and are much less stringent than the requirements of a single international currency. Nevertheless, monetary guidelines for a successful agreement are stronger than those prevailing in the pseudo unions to which we have become accustomed. The two key elements are:

1) To agree on a mutually consistent price-level target to which national monetary policies can be adjusted.

2) To agree on the appropriate division of the supply of money from domestic sources among the members of the fledgling union.

4. W. M. Corden, "Monetary Integration," *Princeton Essays in International Finance* (April 1972), p. 3.

Secular Growth in the Money Supply and the Prices of Tradable Goods

Monetary authorities seldom distinguish secular growth in the monetary base from transactions designed to influence the money supply on a day-to-day basis. However, a long-run or secular monetary policy can be defined for each member of a proposed monetary union.

Suppose initially that the partners wish to stabilize relative exchange rates *without* direct official intervention in the markets for foreign exchange. (Later we shall examine the circumstances under which direct intervention may be warranted.) They want relative rates of national monetary growth to be consistent with no net upward or downward movements in exchange rates, which are not directly pegged. A second equally important objective is to control the growth in the aggregate money supply of the union as a whole in order to avoid general price inflation, as defined more precisely below.

To simplify further, assume that the problem of long-run control is one of managing each national monetary base—narrowly defined to be commercial bank reserves held with the central bank plus coin and currency held by the public. That is, secular growth in the monetary base is strongly positively correlated with long-run growth in other monetary aggregates, such as demand or time deposits. (This assumption may be violated if there are regulatory changes in reserve requirements or effective interest ceilings, or significant growth in unregulated financial intermediaries.) With no direct official intervention in the foreign exchange markets, each national monetary base expands *pari passu* with expansion in domestic credit from its central bank. How fast then should central bank credit expand in each participating country? What should be the target for the price level?

For closed economies, the merits and demerits of alternative monetary standards have been widely discussed.[5] A wage standard fixes average nominal wages in money terms while commodity prices fall smoothly in the face of general technical progress. A more common approach, and one more consistent with international harmonization, if growth in labor productivity differs across countries, is to choose some general price index of goods and services as the target to be stabilized—while allowing money wages to rise secularly. But how does one choose among the consumer price index (CPI), wholesale price index (WPI), or possible GNP deflators as the targets of monetary policy? Over long periods of time in any one country, these indices can diverge substantially.

5. J. M. Keynes, *A Treatise On Money*, Vol. 1, Chapter 4 (New York: Macmillan, 1930), pp. 47–57; Milton Friedman, *The Optimum Quantity of Money and Other Essays* (Chicago, Ill.: Aldine, 1969), pp. 46–47.

For open economies striving for exchange stability, one price index naturally suggests itself. The maintenance of fixed exchange rates implies that the prices of goods that enter foreign trade (exportables or importables) are tied together across countries. Although some short-term variation is possible, no one member of a union of fairly diversified industrial countries can continually inflate its domestic prices of tradable goods at a rate faster or slower than the mean for the union. And our empirical analysis in Chapter 6 suggests that, over long periods of time, national wholesale price indices yield an adequate approximation to the prices of tradable goods.

Although the prices of tradable goods (WPIs) would be bound together across countries within the union, national indices of consumer prices or GNP deflators need *not* move in unison. Indeed, countries experiencing the most rapid productivity growth, in which some tradable goods industries are almost invariably the leading sectors, will find real wages and the prices of nontradable services rising more rapidly. Hence consumer price indices, including nontradable services, may rise substantially faster than wholesale price indices from which nontradable services are excluded. Using data from the relatively stable 1953–1970 period before large shifts in national price indices began, the differences in the secular movement among indices becomes readily apparent in Table 10.1. In Japan, a very high growth economy, the WPI rose 14 percent from 1953 to 1970 while the CPI almost *doubled*. Slower growing countries such as the United States, maintaining fixed exchange rates with Japan, experienced substantially less upward movement in their consumer price indices over the seventeen-year period. Thus the choice of a suitable price index to be stabilized can make a big difference to the conduct of secular monetary policy in each participating country. Growth in the nominal money supply in Japan in the postwar period would have been much slower if Japanese authorities had concentrated on stabilizing the CPI.

Members of a potential monetary agreement have, therefore, a vested interest in stabilizing *tradable goods prices*—while allowing residual movements in the prices of nontradable services to reflect differential productivity growth. Only then would each national price-level target be consistent with exchange-rate stability within the currency area. After agreeing to a common price level for tradable goods, a zero rate of change in that index is the easiest target around which private expectations and diverse national monetary policies can coalesce. Any specified rate of growth in P_T different from zero, say eight percent per year, would be essentially arbitrary and therefore less credible.

Once zero long-run growth in an index of tradable goods' prices P_T is established as a mutual target of long-run monetary policy, the appropriate secular rate of domestic credit expansion by each national central bank can be

TABLE 10.1 Movements of Prices in Domestic Currency and Rates of Growth in Real Output, 1953–1970

	First Quarter of 1970 (1953 = 100)					
	(1) Output per man-hour*	(2) Consumer price index (CPI)	(3) Wholesale price index (WPI)	(4) Export price index (EPI)	(5) CPI / WPI (2)/(3)	(6) CPI / EPI (2)/(4)
Rapidly growing economies						
Germany	251.0	145.2	116.6	107.1	125.2	135.4
Italy	260.9	166.3	126.3	91.6	131.7	181.6
Japan	406.8	197.3	114.1	94.8	173.0	208.2
				Mean	143.0	175.1
Slowly growing economies						
Canada	185.2	142.5	129.8	129.7	109.8	109.9
United Kingdom	173.8	175.6	147.6	143.6	119.0	122.3
United States	154.9	141.4	125.3	129.6	112.8	109.1
				Mean	113.9	113.8

SOURCE: R. I. McKinnon, "Monetary Theory and Controlled Flexibility in the Foreign Exchanges," *Princeton Essays in International Finance*, No. 84 (April 1971), p. 22.

* 1953–69 only. Taken from unpublished estimates supplied by the U.S. Department of Labor.

calculated. One procedure would be for each member country to project (based on historical experience) average real GNP growth for a year or more into the future. For a mature economy not experiencing major changes in financial regulation or inflationary pressure, a fairly constant ratio of money to GNP may also be projected. That is, suppose the demand for money can be specified as

$$\frac{M}{P_g} = YL(i), \quad \text{where} \quad i = r + \frac{d \log P_T}{dt} \quad (10.1)$$

P_g is the GNP deflator, M is the nominal stock of domestic money under some consistent definition, and hence M/P_g represents real cash balances. Then equation (10.1) says that the demand for real cash balances by the nonbank public is a function of real GNP (Y) and the nominal rate of interest (i) on nonmonetary assets where L is the liquidity-preference function. The income elasticity of the demand for money is close to unity by assumption.

Further suppose that i shows no secular trend because the price of tradable goods P_T—whose rate of change defines the Fisher price expectations effect on interest rates—shows no secular trend under the terms of the agreement itself.[6] Indeed, if P_T is stable and expected to remain so, then i equals r, where r is the real rate of interest that is presumed constant.

Thus equation (10.1) tells us that the demand for nominal cash balances will increase proportionately with real income *and* with increases in the GNP price deflator.

Each national monetary authority would then have a fairly simple rule governing the secular increase in the domestic nominal stock of money as derived by differentiating equation (10.1) logarithmically to get the percentage rates or change over time:

$$\frac{1}{M} \cdot \frac{dM}{dt} = \frac{dY}{dt} \cdot \frac{1}{Y} + \frac{dP_g}{dt} \cdot \frac{1}{P_g}. \tag{10.2}$$

The projected increase in the domestic money supply would be equal to $dY/dt \cdot 1/Y$, the projected increase in real GNP, plus $dP_g/dt \cdot 1/P_g$. The latter can be interpreted as the projected percentage change in the GNP price deflator assuming that tradables goods prices P_T—and hence the wholesale price index—is approximately constant. One would expect the GNP price deflator to rise slightly in the course of the year because of the increase in price of nontradable services—which may be substantial in rapidly growing economies and could differ across members of the monetary union.

Central bank credit is usually closely linked to the money supply as defined in equations (10.1) and (10.2). A key to successful international monetary agreement is, therefore, for each member country to expand central bank credit smoothly as described by equation (10.2) to ensure that relative exchange rates do not move persistently in one direction or another. Speculators (foreign exchange traders) would then have full information on how central banks were obligated to behave. Once the biggest single uncertainty in the system, i.e., the behavior of central banks, is reduced, private intervention in the foreign exchange markets would become of a more stabilizing character (Chapter 8).

In addition, the price level of tradable goods for the union as a whole would be anchored. Indeed, one can imagine a monetary agreement with strong transnational implications, but with no mutually supporting official intervention in the foreign exchange markets! I emphasize this possibility because most monetary agreements focus on official intervention to fix exchange rates, rather than stress the importance of precisely targeting domestic rates of monetary

6. In R. I. McKinnon, *Money and Capital in Economic Development* (Washington, D.C.: Brookings Institution, 1973), pp. 96–97, I make the argument that long-run movements in the prices of commodities rather than services dominate the Fisher effect. And P_T is mainly a commodity price index whereas the CPI and GNP deflator have large service components.

expansion. A successful agreement may be able to do without the former, but it must have the latter.

What instrument of domestic monetary policy is best suited to maintain smooth secular growth in the national monetary base as calculated in equation (10.2)?

Again, provisionally assume that national central banks do not intervene directly in the foreign exchanges. Then, each central bank changes the domestic monetary base either through open-market operations—say, purchases of government securities in some market that broadly influences all domestic financial institutions—or through the discounting of private bills and government bonds. (Changes in reserve requirements cannot be an instrument of long-run expansion in the effective monetary base.) For those countries with broadly based markets in government securities, open-market operations are the preferred instrument for achieving steady secular growth in the money supply because they occur at the discretion of the central bank, can be executed smoothly, and need not particularly influence one sector of the economy or another. This last characteristic is important if the monetary union is also a common market, where governments are supposed to behave neutrally with respect to individual industries or sources of finance.

On the other hand, with a completely open discount window, where the discount rate of interest is equal to prevailing market rates, monetary expansion depends on the volition (discretion) of individual eligible borrowers. Smooth secular growth overall is then difficult to achieve by continually manipulating the discount rate. Moreover, open-market operations may be confounded by an open discount window because the purchase of government securities is offset by a reduction in the outstanding volume of rediscounts. The trade-off between the two modes of creating money may generate substantial uncertainty.

A controlled discount window is one where at least some discount rates are kept below market levels so that there is excess demand for loans. For secular growth, the central bank must continually allocate new loan tranches to particular borrowers while preserving penalty rates or arbitrary rationing for others. Again, this has nonneutral financial implications which are best avoided. Yet, in the absence of convenient open markets in government securities, the discount window may have to be so used. For example, most secular growth in the Japanese monetary base from 1950–1967 was achieved through increased rediscount tranches to favored institutions, unlike the U.S. and Britain who could rely more on open-market operations.[7]

7. Hugh Patrick, "France, Capital Markets and Economic Growth in Japan" A. Sametz ed., *Financial Development and Economic Growth* (New York: New York University Press, 1972), pp. 109–39.

Because open-market operations are best assigned to smoothing long-run growth in the monetary base, they should not be used for other undermining objectives—such as pegging interest rates on government securities. Indeed, price support operations are best outlawed by the international monetary agreement itself in order that member countries can have confidence in each other's policies. From time to time, both the U.K. and the U.S. have engaged in operations designed to fix interest rates on certain classes of government securities, with unfortunate losses of control over their respective monetary bases.

Official Intervention and Nonsterilization

When private suspicions of official monetary actions are acute and unsettling, formal foreign exchange parities may stabilize the expectations of traders regarding the consistency of national monetary policies. They can provide concrete indications of official intentions for the future.

Dropping the provisional ban on official foreign exchange transactions, assume now that, wisely or unwisely, member countries commit themselves to a regime of fixed parities. To keep matters simple, suppose the initial constellation of rates is an equilibrium set in that a common bundle of tradable goods costs more or less the same in each country at the parity rates of exchange.[8] What rules then are needed to ensure the credibility of the official parities?

A parity commitment—even in the form of a modest band within which exchange rates can move—may entail official intervention on a day-to-day basis. Any resulting official-settlements deficit in the balance of payments will contract the domestic monetary base because the central bank must sell foreign exchange and hence withdraw domestic high-powered money from circulation to maintain the official parity. These foreign exchange transactions can be expected to dominate short-run monetary policy (changes in the supply of money) if open-market operations are assigned to smooth secular purchases of domestic securities. Indeed, consistent behavior requires that this secular growth in *domestic* central bank credit not be disrupted by swings in the balance of international payments. In other words, a short-run monetary contraction due to a deficit should not be sterilized, and such a *nonsterilization rule* needs to be built into the monetary agreement.[9]

8. Whether or not a single intervention currency is designated to maintain the parity system, or whether there is multiple currency intervention with multiple reserve holdings, is an important issue not addressed here because it depends on the special character and purposes of the proposed monetary union. There is no universally best system. Whereas the restraints on expansion of domestic central bank credit outlined in this chapter are generally necessary whatever specific system of foreign exchange intervention is used.
9. By "sterilization" we mean allowing the central bank's domestic credit, items (a) or (c) in Table 10.2, to expand and fully offset the monetary contraction coming through the foreign exchanges—item (b).

TABLE 10.2   The Balance Sheet of a National Central Bank

Assets	Liabilities
(a) Government securities from open-market operations	(d) Coin and currency held by public
(b) Net foreign exchange reserves	(e) Reserves of commercial banks
(c) Discounts (loans) to commercial banks	Monetary base = (d) + (e) = (a) + (b) + (c)

What is the basic rationale for the nonsterilization of short-run deficits or surpluses in the balance of payments? Suppose the long-run demand for the monetary base in the economy is correctly approximated by equation (10.1), and is met by the expansion of domestic credit by each national central bank. One might still expect substantial short-run variation in the demand for money (or supply of deposits) in any one country. Under a fixed exchange-rate regime, excess domestic demand for money would show up as a surplus in the balance of payments, whereas excess supply would show up as a deficit. Correct monetary policy would then allow the surplus in the balance of payments to clear the excess domestic demand for money by expanding the monetary base—and vice versa in the case of a deficit. And it doesn't matter whether the balance of payments surplus is on the current or on the capital account. Domestic firms and households can sell goods *or* securities to foreigners to satisfy their excess demand for money, although the sale of securities may be the primary mode of adjustment in the short run if there is an open international capital market.

This nonsterilization policy is related to the balance sheet of the central bank in Table 10.2.

Let us temporarily defer considering the proper role of discounting by commercial banks with their central bank as depicted in line (c) of Table 10.2, and instead focus on the other two assets held by the central bank. From our rule governing domestic credit expansion, suppose the increase in central bank holdings of government securities, line (a), represents the whole of secular domestic credit expansion—which rises smoothly through time according to the rule given in equation (10.2). Then, item (b), the net foreign reserve position of the country, will fluctuate according to short-run changes in the domestic demand for high-powered money as manifested in balance of payments surpluses or deficits. The national money supply in our fixed exchange-rate regime is thus *endogenously determined in the short run*, although not in the long run, as shown in Figure 10.1.

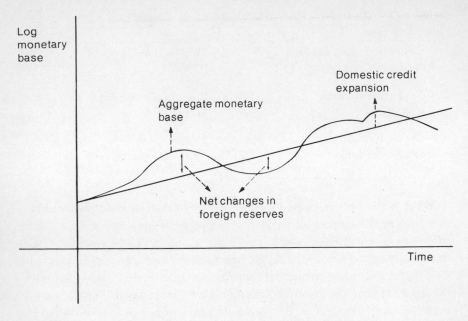

FIGURE 10.1   The domestic monetary base under fixed exchange rates

On the other side of the coin, a nonsterilization rule assures foreign exchange traders that the fixed parity is invulnerable. If a deficit itself clears a temporary excess supply of domestic money as official reserves are drawn down, everyone knows that the excess money supply and the deficit will soon be eliminated. Deficits will be self-liquidating if secular monetary expansion from domestic sources is restrained. Hence, the foreign exchange authority would never be in the role of the unsuccessful official speculator described in Chapter 7, Part 2. Instead, the domestic monetary base would always change in the short run to support the official intervention.

The Symmetry Rule and the Aggregate Monetary Base

So far, only domestic monetary management in a single member country has been related to official foreign exchange transactions. Yet, short-run monetary policy must be coherent for the proposed union as a whole. Whatever the system of official intervention, a rough symmetry should prevail by having deficit countries contract their monetary base by quantitatively the same amount as surplus countries expand—at least from the inital impact of the international payments imbalance. In this way the overall monetary base of the union is stabilized, and assurance is given that partner countries share the adjustment burden fairly.[10]

Although not considered carefully in Europe and elsewhere, currency pyramiding within the union is not difficult to prevent and should be an important part of any agreement allowing substantial official intervention in the foreign exchanges. For example, suppose the monetary authority in the surplus country intervenes by selling its own currency (high-powered money) and acquiring commercial bank deposits in the deficit country. An unfortunate asymmetry then exists: the supply of high-powered money in the surplus country expands whereas only low-powered money is withdrawn from domestic nationals in the deficit country. The currency area's money supply would then expand in the aggregate as a result of ongoing payments imbalances among member countries. This pyramiding can be avoided, however, if the surplus country's foreign claims are impounded in a special account in the central bank of the deficit country, so as to reduce symmetrically that country's monetary base.[11]

The obvious implication of foreclosing short-run variation in the aggregate supply of money (remembering that secular monetary growth has been predetermined) is that the union as a whole would not engage in discretionary short-run monetary policy. This limitation is consistent with the absence of a single international central bank whose liabilities are accepted as money within the currency area. Fortunately, this loss of discretionary monetary authority may be as much an advantage as a disadvantage. National central banks will be more tightly constrained from using the monetary system to support the prices of government securities, or covertly provide cheap credits to particular pressure groups within the economy.

On Flexing the System:
Discounting and Short-Term Capital Flows

Many readers will balk at what seems to be excessive rigidity in, and the overly simplistic nature of, the model of monetary union outlined above. Long-term secular growth in the domestic credit portion of each country's monetary base is projected on a once-and-for-all basis at the beginning of each year; whereas only foreign exchange transactions can move each national monetary base significantly above or below this secular trend—and only then

10. While commonly used, the phrase "burden of adjustment" has an unfortunate semantic connotation. In the present context, adjusting to the balance of payments need not be a burden at all when deficits or surpluses clear domestic excess demands or supplies of money and so enhance monetary stability.

11. As described by R. I. McKinnon in "On Securing a Common Monetary Policy in Europe," *Banca Nazionale del Lavoro Quarterly Review* (March 1973), pp. 3–30.

for short periods of time. Yet the potential flexibility of such a monetary union is greater than it may first seem.

First, symmetrical international adjustment is consonant with a wide variety of regulatory systems whereby each national central bank controls its commercial banks. Reserve requirements do not have to be identical, and differing national classifications of commercial banks, savings banks, merchant banks, and so on need not be altered. National interest-rate restrictions or usury laws that force money-market yields below international levels will lead to unwarranted capital flight, but this would be true whether or not a formal monetary union exists. In short, as long as each central bank does have control over the domestic credit portion of its national monetary base, and the monetary base overall is firmly related to money holdings of individuals, a successful union would not require the same regulatory modes in each participating country.[12]

Secondly, the apparent harshness of short-run adjustment to imbalances in international payments can be ameliorated through two channels: (1) the free international flow of portfolio capital that responds quickly to small interest-rate differentials; and (2) short-term and automatic rediscounting by commercial banks, who are losing reserves, with their national central banks.

Consider a shock, a deficit in the balance of trade or in foreign capital flows, whose direct impact is to reduce the domestic monetary base on a dollar-for-dollar basis as per our nonsterilization rule. This loss of reserves causes short-term interest rates to rise in the domestic money market generally, and on the liabilities of commercial banks in particular. Hence, domestic financial institutions facing a short-term liquidity squeeze borrow on the international money market, thereby replenishing their reserves, and dampening the international deficit of the country in question. Since the maintenance of official parities is guaranteed, small interest differentials should attract stabilizing flows of short-term capital from abroad in the classical manner—as described by James Ingram for the case of Puerto Rico and the United States.[13] The pressure on the deficit country is eased further by our symmetry rule that requires mirror-image adjustment in surplus countries, from which portfolio capital is expelled.

If international markets in financial instruments are not well developed within the union, a carefully designed form of automatic discounting by commercial banks with their respective national central banks can, in part, replace short-term foreign borrowing. Suppose, again, that a deficit in international

---

12. The Bank of England somehow contrived in the British monetary reforms of 1971 to lose control over the monetary base by allowing treasury bills and some short-term commercial paper to be included in the reserves of the commercial banks.
13. James Ingram, *Regional Payments Mechanisms: The Case of Puerto Rico* (Raleigh, N.C.: University of North Carolina Press, 1962).

payments causes commercial banks in one country to lose reserves. With limitations on borrowing abroad, they are driven to the discount window of their own central bank. The central bank then discounts freely but at a penalty rate—a rate of interest that is kept slightly above the market and perhaps automatically raised when an unusual demand for loans appears. A serious liquidity squeeze on the commercial banks is thus avoided, but their reserve positions are not completely restored because the penalty rate of interest (or an upward sloping supply curve for central bank finance) will make it unprofitable to do so. A lesser, but perhaps smoother, domestic monetary contraction remains to ensure the elimination of the deficit in international payments. And because of the partial sterilization due to discounting, offsetting capital inflows are not quite sufficient to prevent a temporary loss of national exchange reserves: a fall in item (b) in Table 10.2 associated with a lesser rise in item (c).[14]

The shock causing a deficit in the balance of payments and compensating increases in domestic rates of interest was—implicitly—nonmonetary in nature: domestic nationals did not care to reduce their demand for the domestic money. For example, domestic consumers could unexpectedly increase their demand for internationally tradable goods at the expense of domestic nontradable goods and services: a purely goods market disturbance. In the short run, however, a tendency for a counterpart trade balance deficit would develop whose unwanted domestic monetary consequences (a contraction in the supply of money) are largely offset by a combination of international capital inflows and increased advances (discounts) to the commercial banks. And the capital inflow covers the temporary trade balance deficit until domestic producers adjust.

Indeed, the great advantage of the automaticity of the discounting process— combined with short-term capital flows—is that the authorities need not know *ex ante* what the source of the disturbance in the foreign exchange market might be in order for the system to adjust in the correct direction. Suppose in contrast to the shift between domestic and foreign goods described above, there was an exogenous shock in the money market where domestic nationals reduced (temporarily) their demand for domestic money in favor of bonds. Then an incipient fall in the domestic rate of interest and a capital outflow (purchase of foreign bonds) would follow, perhaps accompanied by a reduction in volume of outstanding discounts of the commercial banks with their central bank. The fall in both items (b) and (c) in Table 10.2 would then reduce the monetary base to reflect the reduced demand for domestic money. (The domestic price level is maintained at the community level by the fixed exchange rate.)

14. Under fixed exchange rates in the 1950s and early 1960s, monetary adjustments of this kind apparently did take place in Europe and Japan. See Michael Michaely, *The Responsiveness of Demand Policies to Balance of Payments* (N.B.E.R., Columbia University Press, 1971), Chapter 2.

In each of the above situations, we have a surprise deficit in the balance of payments accompanied by quite different but correctly accommodating adjustment at the discount window. But a further fine distinction in the passive use of discounting combined with free international capital flows can be made. The fall in the demand for domestic money described above did not distinguish low-powered money M_1 from high-powered money in the form of commercial bank reserves.

Suppose the commercial banks in Country A must maintain a 10 percent required reserve against deposits, but they find themselves with excess reserves of 10 as shown in Step One of Table 10.3. At the prevailing interest structure, however, the demand for domestic loans is insufficient to warrant extending domestic credit to absorb these excess reserves. However, reserves are truly in excess because lending opportunities elsewhere in the monetary union are attractive, and 10 units of foreign loans are undertaken as shown in Step Two of Table 10.3. The result is that commercial banks succeed in reducing their reserves to the required minimum, and the central bank experiences a counterpart loss of 10 units of foreign assets. Hence, the excess supply of domestic high-powered money—commercial bank reserves—is drained off directly by the balance of payments deficit and no commercial bank need feel pressed to appear at the discount window. (Of course, reducing the volume of discounts outstanding with the central bank would be an alternative adjustment mechanism if foreign lending seems unattractive.)

Suppose instead the fall in demand for domestic money were to take the form of a decline of 10 units in the demand for commercial bank deposits

TABLE 10.3   The Elimination of Excess Commercial Bank Reserves

Step one				Step two			
Commercial banks				Commercial banks			
Reserves	20	Deposits	100	Reserves	10	Deposits	100
Domestic loans	80			Foreign loans	10		
				Domestic loans	80		
Central bank				Central bank			
Domestic assets	5	Reserves of commercial banks	20	Domestic assets	5	Reserves of commercial banks	10
Foreign assets	15			Foreign assets	5		

TABLE 10.4　A Reduction in the Demand for Domestic Deposits

Ex ante (without discounting)			Ex post facto (with discounting)		
Commercial banks			Commercial banks		
Reserves	0	Deposits 90	Reserves	9	Deposits 90
Loans	90		Loans	90	Advance from central bank 9
Central bank			Central bank		
Domestic assets	5	Reserves 0	Domestic assets	14	Reserves 9
Foreign assets	−5		Foreign assets	−5	

(low-powered money) by the nonbank public, who buy foreign securities net—a financial shift that puts maximum pressure on the domestic banking system. We start from a position shown in Step Two of Table 10.3 where commercial banks are fully loaned up; then Table 10.4 shows the reduction in deposits from 100 to 90. If the commercial banks were helpless in immediately adjusting their portfolios either by discounting from the central bank or borrowing in the international capital market, their reserves would fall to zero as deposits were reduced by 10 units. They would be in violation of their reserve requirements as shown in the *ex ante* panel of Table 10.4, and a rather violent, and needless, multiple contraction in the commercial banking system would be set in motion.

However, to accommodate the reduction in demand for low-powered money without engendering on equivalent reduction in high-powered reserves, the commercial banks could immediately appear at the discount window and get 9 units of advances from the central bank. This is shown in the *ex post facto* panel of Table 10.4. Then deposits only fall by the correct amount of 10 currency units, bank reserves are reduced only by one unit, and no false multiple contraction is set in motion.

Notice from Table 10.4 that if the central bank discounts to provide all the needed 9 units of commercial bank reserves, it will lose 10 units of foreign exchange assets. As domestic nationals sell off the domestic currency to buy foreign bonds, the central bank must draw down its exchange reserves (or borrow from other members of the union) to preserve the fixed exchange rate. This is the counterpart of letting the supply of domestic money fall exactly by the reduced demand for it in the short run. To better protect its reserve position, the central bank could raise the discount rate to a penalty level and force the commercial banks to offset some of their reserve losses by borrowing in the international capital markets, thus engendering a countervailing capital inflow. Indeed, this could be a normal part of the rules of the game for short-run adjustment that I have patterned after the old pre-1914 world gold standard. The more highly developed the international capital market, the less the consequent fluctuations in national exchange reserves and the less the need for the discount mechanism to ameliorate monetary shocks.[15]

However, our currency union remains unlike the gold standard in the mechanism for ensuring secular expansion in the monetary base. But how rigid and accurate need be the rule that governs the long-run expansion in domestic central bank credit? If the domestic demand for money in one country rises faster secularly than money GNP, the demand for high-powered money will likely exceed domestic open-market purchases as prescribed by equation (10.2). This secular excess demand will be cleared through the foreign exchange markets by a persistent tendency towards surplus in the balance of payments. Correspondingly, all other members of the union will experience a persistent deficit on current or capital account. If the tradable goods prices—P_T—are stable overall, we know that the monetary base of the union as a whole is tracking accurately. Hence mutual accommodation requires that domestic credit expansion by the central bank in the surplus country be annually increased a percentage point or two, while other members of the union adjust downwards their credit expansion by a commensurate amount. If tradable goods prices had been falling slightly, perhaps only the former adjustment would be necessary.

Such rough tailoring can occur annually under international auspices without significant upheaval in the foreign exchange markets or in domestic monetary policies. The parameter estimates of the long-run demand functions for money would simply be updated every year or so. Indeed meetings and tailorings should be infrequent to avoid the ever-present temptation to direct the secular instruments of monetary policy towards short-term national goals, thus undermining the full-information character of the union.

An example of a national policy that is clearly inconsistent with the secular growth rule outlined above is that of postwar Germany. In part because the German monetary reform of 1948–1949 eliminated (froze) all government open-market securities leaving the Bundesbank without a convenient vehicle for conducting open-market operations, and in further measure because Germany aimed for a lower rate of inflation than that prevailing elsewhere, most of

15. Discounting would be less useful in a regime of floating exchange rates and an independent national monetary policy. Here the primary reliance is on open-market operations and one does not have to worry (as much) about changes in the monetary base arising from foreign exchange transactions.

the postwar growth in the German monetary base can be explained by official intervention to acquire foreign exchange which was then either kept as reserves or disposed of through official channels. Clearly, this secular strategy puts continual upward speculative pressure on any official parity for the German exchange rate. To become a well-behaved member of a negotiated monetary union, Germany would have to expand domestic open-market operations until no further net accumulation of foreign exchange occurred. This would only be satisfactory to Germany if partner countries limited their domestic credit expansion so as to stabilize international prices at an agreed-upon level.

Concluding Note

Perhaps the foregoing analysis of a monetary union with fixed exchange rates can be summarized thus:

1) The long-run target for price stability should be precisely defined by an index of tradable goods prices for the union as a whole, rather than by a consumer price index or GNP deflator for each individual country.

2) A Friedmanlike rule specifying the rate of secular growth in domestic central bank credit by open-market operations can be applied to each country in a manner consistent with the overall price-level target.

3) No country should allow official foreign exchange transactions either to expand or to contract its monetary base on a secular basis, but all members would allow deficits or surpluses to dominate short-run changes in their domestic money supplies.

4) Passive discounting with the central bank—along with free movements of short-term capital—can prevent disturbances in foreign payments from destabilizing any participating country's monetary system.

11

America's Role in Stabilizing the World's Monetary System[1]

Since 1945, the United States dollar—and American financial policies toward foreigners—have been the central elements in the international monetary system. Despite events that would seem to point to the contrary, the evolving key-currency role of the dollar has shown surprising robustness. The articles of the International Monetary Fund (IMF) and other international agreements, however, treat all nations as equals and somewhat disguise this underlying reality. And American authorities themselves often fail to appreciate the singular economic position of the United States in keeping the world's money machine going.

Signed at Bretton Woods, New Hampshire, in July 1944, the IMF articles remain the principal legal basis of the world's monetary system, even though they have been substantially amended since then.[2] They have been ratified by almost all noncommunist countries. Nations were anxious to avoid returning to the chaotic exchange-rate practices of the 1930s that severely attenuated international commerce. Thus each participating country committed itself to maintain free currency convertibility (under Article VIII) as well as a stable par value for its currency (Article IV). A parity once fixed was to be changed only when threatened by a fundamental disequilibrium in the exchange market, and only

1. Reprinted by permission of DAEDALUS, Journal of the American Academy of Arts and Sciences, Boston, Massachusetts. Winter 1978, A New America?
2. The articles were the product of purely British-American negotiations. Canada acted as an umpire between the British delegation headed by John Maynard Keynes and the American delegation headed by Harry Dexter White. The White Plan eventually became the principal basis of the IMF charter.

then with the mutual agreement to the IMF. In a formal sense, these rules applied symmetrically to all countries—including the United States.

Fixed exchange rates among convertible currencies of the major industrial countries were, on balance, well maintained into the late 1960s.[3] Together with the General Agreement on Tariffs and Trade (GATT), this international economic order was associated with unprecedented growth in world commerce that was essential to the postwar prosperity enjoyed by Europe and Japan, and enjoyed by a few developing countries—such as Taiwan, Korea, and Israel—which did not unduly restrict their own participation in international trade.

How worried then should we be about the disintegration of the fixed exchange-rate system in the late 1960s? Strenuous efforts to enforce a new legal basis for fixed exchange rates, which was agreed to at the Smithsonian Institution in December 1971, collapsed completely in February 1973. The present regime of free floating is subject to only the loosest kind of supervision by the IMF.[4] The recent marked divergences of exchange rates (against the U.S. dollar) of major industrial economies are portrayed in Figure 1.1. Important monetary values such as the Deutsche mark/dollar exchange rate now seem to fluctuate about 15 to 20 percent in the course of a year, whereas under the old system the rate fluctuated within a 2 percent margin.

Fortunately, a regime of common law in international monetary affairs continues to operate vigorously even if some of the important statutes of the 1944 Bretton Woods agreement have been suspended. Much of this book has been devoted to outlining these conventions of international exchange. But the present (apparently disordered) system is viable only if the rules of the game are understood by all the players, particularly the American government. The markedly asymmetrical but central role of the United States can best be understood by tracing its evolution through four distinct phases: the Marshall Plan and European Recovery (1948–1959), realization of the Bretton Woods agreement and fixed exchange rates under the dollar-gold standard (1959–1968), uncertainly pegged exchange rates (1969–1973), and finally the present regime of uninhibited floating of the freely convertible currencies of major industrial economies.[5]

3. From the outset of the Bretton Woods agreements, many countries in Latin America, Asia, and Africa continually adjusted (devalued) their largely inconvertible currencies mainly to compensate for high and unstable internal rates of inflation.
4. "The significance of the (IMF) agreements reached in Jamaica in January 1976 is that they make provision for legalizing the existing nonsystem governing international monetary relations. . . . " John Williamson, "The Benefits and Cost of an International Monetary System," in E. M. Bernstein et al., *Reflections on Jamaica, Princeton Essays in International Finance*, No. 115 (April 1976), p. 54.
5. It is interesting to note that only 11 currencies are independently floating, seven are floating jointly (the European Snake), and the 105 remaining members of the IMF (mainly less developed countries) peg to a convertible currency of a major industrial economy. IMF *Annual Report* (Washington, D.C., 1975). Due to waivers for less developed countries in the IMF's charter, most of the 105 currencies are inconvertible for international commerce.

Because somewhat differing American obligations and policies have been appropriate (and not always followed) in each of the four phases of the evolving world dollar standard, let us distinguish among them by discussing each in turn.

The Marshall Plan and the Remonetization of Western European Trade (1948–1959)

In the recovery of Western European trade from the paralysis with which it was afflicted in 1946–1947, the International Monetary Fund was not operational. None of the previously belligerent countries had multilaterally convertible currencies in the sense of Article VIII, and none would make payments in terms of gold or dollars (which they did not have) to support an officially fixed parity in the sense of Article IV. All made use of various escape clauses in the Fund's charter. Moreover, the Fund's bylaws would not permit lending gold or dollars in substantial amounts to build up European reserve positions when prospects for repayment were dubious. Instead, in its early years, the Fund specialized in helping a few less developed countries that had better repayment prospects and less massive borrowing needs.

But the European trade and payments mechanism was sunk in a mire. The absence of owned reserves of gold or internationally convertible foreign exchange, coupled with their voracious appetite to absorb industrial goods and primary products, meant that European countries quickly spent dollar earnings from their limited exports. They then rationed in great detail—through exchange controls and quota restrictions—the potentially huge excess demand for further imports available only from hard currency countries such as the United States and Canada. This was indeed the era of the world dollar shortage that many people projected to be chronic.

Discriminatory trade restrictions against the importation of American goods were only part of the problem, however. Europeans had potentially strong reciprocal demands for each other's goods, but each of their currencies was inconvertible. Nonresidents, unlucky enough to acquire balances of inconvertible European currencies, could freely buy neither commodities nor convertible currencies without going through a complex licensing process. Therefore, any one European country would try to avoid acquiring inconvertible monetary claims on any European trading partner. This froze multilateral trade within Europe: country A could not effectively use credits from a trade surplus garnered from country B to offset a trade deficit with country C.[6]

6. The same problem afflicts multilateral trade among Eastern European countries—none of which has convertible currencies—to the present day. (See Chapter 3.)

By 1947 . . . the system was in deadlock. Debtors were not prepared to make payments in gold or dollars, and creditors were not prepared to extend credit beyond existing limits. Thus there was an incentive to discriminate in trade, debtors discriminating against imports from their creditors in favour of imports from those countries with whom they had a bilateral surplus, hoping that this would prevent a drain on reserves and encourage a repayment of previously extended credit. The consequence of such trade restrictions and discrimination was a stagnation in the growth of intra-European trade in 1947. Europe . . . was being choked by the self-imposed collar of bilateralism.[7]

The resulting bilaterally balanced trade diverted production and consumption from the most efficient sources and uses by country. Moreover, decision making was largely taken out of the hands of individual firms and households in Europe and placed with the foreign exchange licensing authorities in national central banks, who then negotiated the bilateral exchange of exports for imports with their counterparts in other national central banks.

The United States European Recovery Program in its most general form, commonly known as the Marshall Plan, was not enacted by the American Congress until April 1948. Previously, some piecemeal bilateral aid had been extended in 1946 and 1947 for famine relief to particular countries, and to support an abortive effort to restore nonresident convertibility for the pound sterling in 1947. But whatever its initial institutional shortcomings, the 1948 Marshall Plan funneled aid in the form of generally usable dollar credits to Europe as a *whole*. Indeed, the Organization of European Economic Cooperation (OEEC), consisting of 17 European countries, was formed in 1948 to help the Economic Cooperation Administration of the United States administer American aid on a multilateral basis.[8]

In retrospect, why was the Marshall Plan so successful? The quantitative magnitude of American balance of payments support for Europe (mainly official credits supplemented by some private investment) was very large in absolute terms by the standards of the time: $4 to $5 billion annually from 1948 to 1951. Yet conceived of as simply making possible additional consumption plus investment in Europe, the magnitudes were not large relative to the total size of Europe's own gross income:

The total supply of goods and services available to Western Europe is estimated at $145 billion in the year 1948–49, of which Western Europe's gross national product accounts for $140 billion and net imports of goods and services from the outside

7. See Peter Coffey and John R. Presley, *European Monetary Integration* (London: The Macmillan Press, Ltd., 1971), p. 5.
8. With, of course, substantial effort being made to ensure that each European country got a fair share.

world for the remainder. Thus, the external deficit has recently been providing only four percent of the goods and services available to Western Europe, the remaining 96 percent coming from Europe's own production.[9]

Although they were only about 4 percent of Europe's collective GNP, American capital transfers did amount to about 40 percent of Europe's total receipts of "hard" foreign exchange—that which could be spent freely anywhere in the world. Yet, subsequently, similar amounts of aid directed towards less developed countries such as India had nothing like the enormous payoff in augmented growth that seemed to characterize the Marshall transfer to Europe.

To explain the apparently high leverage from Marshall Plan aid, one has to look for a lever. The first temptation is to consider specific shortages or materials bottlenecks in Europe. Basic food grains (wage goods) for consumption might come to mind. But the dominant image is the restocking of war-torn European factories with American machines, spare parts, and perhaps even industrial raw materials from third countries financed by dollar credits. To take a hoary example, the want of specialized ball bearings, whose European output sources were flattened during the war, might keep a complete European factory closed save for a trickle of ball-bearing imports from America that, in monetary value, need only be a trivial proportion of the factory's gross output. And Marshall financed industrial procurement by Europeans in American was undoubtedly one important reason for the remarkable European recovery.

However, to base the leverage argument solely on the transfer of key physical commodities—those in accidentally short supply in Europe—implies that the system would have worked equally well even if American aid had been bilaterally given, with separate arrangements for each European country. In an economic sense, the multilateral character of OEEC would have been largely redundant, and the financial deadlock in intra-European trade described above would not have been important in real terms. Moreover, Europe's limited exports to hard currency countries still amounted to about six percent of European GNP from from 1948 to 1952—more than enough by themselves to overcome many highly specific shortages such as that of ball bearings.

To supplement this standard argument, I would emphasize the *financial* leverage achieved by Marshall Plan aid, with the flow of finance from America (inclusive of unutilized precautionary credit lines) being ultimately successful in eliminating the money muddle that was repressing intra-European trade. Hence, the relatively slender American financial resources directed toward this

9. See *International Economic Reform—Collected Papers of Emile Despres*, ed. G. M. Meier (New York: Oxford University Press, 1973), pp. 30–31.

particular end sharply increased real output—once multilateral trade revived and resources in Europe came to be more efficiently allocated.

But how was this financial lever applied? Only after partial success in 1948 and 1949, the European Payments Union (EPU) was formed in 1950 under the auspices of the OEEC.[10] The United States provided the initial capital fund of $350 million. The American dollar was formally set up as a unit of account in which intra-European receipts and payments would be denominated as *claims against the clearing union (EPU) itself*; each European currency was pegged at a fixed dollar parity.[11]

At monthly settlement dates, national central banks would submit a record of receipts from—and payments to—all other members of the union. For country A, the EPU secretariat would then offset the sum of bilateral deficits with countries B, C, D with the sum of bilateral surpluses with E, F, and G. Thus, every month, the multilateral net debtor-creditor position of each national central bank vis-à-vis the union was established, and settlements were made. The means of settlement was initially 40 percent gold or dollar payments by debtors, and 60 percent net credit extension to the EPU by creditor countries. With the American financial backing, the EPU itself would make gold-dollar settlements if any debtor country should default. Similarly, guidelines for maximum credits from the EPU were imposed on debtor countries. Thus, creditor countries within Europe could be assured of eventual payment in truly hard money, and they no longer had to strive for bilateral balance with each trading partner in order to avoid acquiring unusable soft currency claims. Moreover, the clearing mechanism within the union—and the credit lines provided—greatly economized on the scarce gold and dollar exchange reserves held by each European country.

Multilateral trade within Europe was no longer inhibited for monetary reasons; after 1950, the European countries moved vigorously to remove tariffs and quantitative restrictions on particular commodites imported from European trading partners. The surge in trade was dramatic. With 1949 as 100, the

10. The first intra-European payments scheme in 1948 was still mainly bilateral in character: Certain bilateral deficits between any pair of European countries were financed by Marshall dollar credits, thus avoiding the need for strict bilateral balance in trading transactions. The second intra-European payments scheme in 1949 took some small steps towards multilateralism, but intra-European trade was still negotiated through formal bilateral agreements. For a more detailed account of these early schemes, see Peter Coffey and John Presley, op. cit., and Robert Triffin, *Europe and the Money Muddle* (New Haven: Yale University Press, 1957).

11. Without even a small margin or band of exchange-rate variation of the kind that was permitted under the Bretton Woods agreements, and was to later characterize the fixed exchange-rate system of the 1960s (Chapter 2). This avoided ambiguity in ascertaining the exact dollar value of monetary claims within the union at the end of each month.

volume of intra-European imports rose to 141 in 1950; by 1956 it had climbed to 226.[12]

Throughout this period of European recovery, the United States tolerated discriminatory tariff and quota restrictions on many potential American exports to Europe—thus allowing the individual European countries to build up their dollar and gold reserves more rapidly and so set the stage for the return to full currency convertibility in 1959, when such restrictions were removed. Afterwards, it became appropriate for the United States to lobby hard to have payments restrictions removed whenever possible, as with the achievement of full convertibility by Japan in 1964. Unlike the industrial economies, however, less developed countries have not been similarly pressured by either the United States or the International Monetary Fund to eliminate financial or other restraints on their foreign trade.

Realization of the Bretton Woods Agreement and the Dollar-Gold Exchange Standard (1959–1968)

With all its great advantages in reestablishing a monetary basis for intra-European trade, the EPU in its initial form had certain economic limitations:

1) Intra-European payments were placed on a substantially different basis from trade with non-European countries. The latter had to be financed by open-market purchases and sales of foreign exchange. The clearing machinery of the EPU permitted discrimination against purchases or sales of commodities outside of the union.

2) The EPU relied heavily on national central banks for recording all settlements, and indeed this funneling of transactions through central banks facilitated the maintenance of exchange controls and payments restrictions.

Hence, on December 24, 1958, the European Payments Union was officially disbanded and exchange restrictions against dollar area imports were removed. Fourteen Western European countries—including all the industrial ones—made their currencies fully externally convertible for current transactions, and finally made fully operational the par-value obligation under Article IV of the 1944 Bretton Woods agreements:

12. Randall Hinshaw, "Toward European Convertibility," *Princeton Essays in International Finance,* No. 31 (November 1958), p. 16. Hinshaw also demonstrates how a more normal open market in foreign exchange transacting developed after 1953. Within Europe, traders began to exchange one currency for another through the medium of commercial banks. The proportion of transactions channeled through, and approved by, central banks—to be cleared through the EPU—progressively diminished.

1)   The par value of the currency of each member shall be expressed in terms of gold as a common denominator or in terms of the United States dollar of the weight and fineness in effect on July 1st, 1944.

2)   The maximum and minimum rates . . . shall not differ from parity, in the case of spot transactions by more than one percent. . . . [13]

As a practical matter, it was awkward to buy and sell gold directly for fiat currencies in the open market in order to maintain exchange margins. Gold is costly to store and transport, and the world gold supply was still asymmetrically concentrated in the United States in the late 1950s. Moreover, European countries had already been maintaining exact dollar parities as part of EPU agreement. Thus, in 1959, Article IV was interpreted such that member countries of the IMF all pegged their currencies to the U.S. dollar within a one percent margin on either side of parity. Each national central bank kept reserves to buy or sell dollars for the domestic currency in the open market for foreign exchange in order to maintain the two percent band width for all who wished to trade with the country in question. Thus the dollar became the *official intervention currency* used by European and other central banks the world over.[14]

What were the reciprocal American obligations in the brave new monetary order? The formal obligation under Article IV was to fix the dollar's parity in terms of gold. While all other counties pegged to the dollar, the American authorities agreed to sell (or buy) gold to foreign central banks upon demand in exchange for dollars at a fixed parity of US $35 per ounce with no band of variation. Such government-to-government transfers took place outside the open market for foreign exchange. Thus, the world was put on a full-fledged dollar-gold exchange standard.

The second important American obligation under the dollar-gold exchange standard was implicit. Because all foreign central banks were intervening with their own currencies against the dollar to maintain parities that were occasionally changed, the American government essentially stayed out of the open foreign exchange markets in order to avoid conflict.[15] The Bank of England, for example, would buy or sell dollars for sterling to maintain the exchange rate

13. *The International Monetary Fund 1945–65, Volume III: Documents* (Washington, D.C., 1969), p. 189.
14. An ever-decreasing number of ex-British colonies continued to fix their exchange rates in terms of sterling, and a similar overseas franc area was maintained in Africa among ex-French colonies. Canada floated without an official par value from 1950–1962. Otherwise, virtually all other members of the IMF did define their exchange parities in dollars.
15. Among LDCs these parities were frequently changed. Notice that it is sufficient to establish *all* the cross rates of exchange in the system if each country intervenes against a common intervention currency, e.g., the U.S. dollar.

between US \$2.78 and US \$2.82, but the Federal Reserve Bank would stay out of the dollar-sterling market—and also stay out of a hundred or so other markets in foreign currencies. Indeed, the U.S. didn't hold reserves of other currencies with which to intervene. And this American passivity in allowing other countries to choose their exchange rates against the dollar was, and still is, an essential element in the harmonious working of the global monetary system. (The analytical details of this asymmetrical system are developed in Chapter 2.)

An important consequence, however, was that the American government did not have direct control over the state of its balance of payments in the 1960s—nor should it have. As long as other countries succeeded in setting their exchange parities at desired levels vis-à-vis the dollar so as to have a payments surplus that allowed them to accumulate reserves (U.S. dollars) as they wanted, the state of the American balance of payments was residually determined. But American authorities responded with alarm to the resulting accounting deficits in American foreign payments, even when America was running large trade surpluses in the early 1960s. Instead of welcoming the voluntary build-up of dollar reserves by foreigners in a period of worldwide price stability (Table 2.1), in the 1960s the American authorities made the mistake of restricting some kinds of capital outflows from the United States (as discussed below and in Chapter 9).

As a partial *quid pro quo*, however, the U.S. could use its own dollars to cover payments deficits as they developed, whereas other countries had to use scarce foreign exchange. This asymmetry in the dollar standard was called by Charles de Gaulle an "exorbitant privilege of the United States"—indicating that official misinterpretations of international monetary phenomena were not confined to the American side of the Atlantic.

Before discussing the reasons for the inevitable collapse of the pure dollar-gold exchange standard, let us describe its rather remarkable accomplishments. For the industrial economies, it allowed free multilateral exchange of their convertible currencies among private commercial banks and trading firms without having to channel foreign payments through central banks. Within the one percent margins on either side of parity, exchange rates were very stable and payments restrictions absent so that domestic monies in the industrial economies were virtually as good as international money. Meanwhile, under GATT, tariff and quota restrictions on commodity trade with industrial countries were progressively reduced. Foreign trade grew even more rapidly than national incomes in the 1960s, so that all the industrial economies became more open to foreign trade, as output per capita rose impressively by any historical standard.

(It should be noted that most LDCs maintained inconvertible currencies in the late 1950s and 1960s, and also intensified payments restrictions as well as tariff and quota barriers to their own external trade. This import-substitution strategy of economic development meant, effectively, that most did not participate in the world trade boom and their economies became more closed. Indeed, we have a paradox. U.S. aid in the late 1950s and 1960s to less developed countries was often associated with more centralized planning (India, Latin America) and the imposition of restraints on foreign trade, whereas the earlier more successful Marshall Plan aid to Europe was associated with the removal of trade restrictions! Quite possibly, AID administrators in the 1950s and 1960s failed to recognize the monetary reasons for the Marshall plan's success.)

Stability in a macroeconomic sense was also achieved. Those countries that effectively fixed their exchange parities to the U.S. dollar, and kept convertible currencies as well, had their price levels (in terms of tradable goods) pegged to that in the United States—the latter being quite stable from 1951 to the mid-1960s, as indicated in Table 11.1.[16] Their domestic monetary policies had to be passively adjusted to maintain this fixed exchange rate, while accommodating quite high rates of growth in real output. (The details of this adjustment mechanism were described in Chapter 10.) Indeed, a convincing peg to the U.S. dollar allowed Germany and Japan, which had experienced traumatic monetary upheavals in the late 1940s, to restore confidence in the Deutsche mark and yen faster than would otherwise be the case. Inflationary expectations were also dampened elsewhere in Europe if citizens came to believe their government was committed to a fixed dollar parity. (This earlier favorable experience induced many countries to continue their dollar parities into the early 1970s, well past the point that it was desirable to do so.)

A truly international capital market was an outgrowth of the dollar-gold exchange standard, and essential to its smooth functioning. Countries and individuals who were net savers (surplus units in a financial sense) could deposit in New York banks or buy bonds in New York, whereas countries that had a need for investment resources (deficit units in a financial sense) could borrow in New York, with both creditors and debtors using the dollar as a vehicle currency to finance this *net* international transfer of capital. And in the late 1950s and early 1960s, New York was the dominant entrepôt center for international capital, although not on the grand scale that London had been prior to 1914 under the old gold standard.

---

16. Of course, countries suffering from often massive internal inflations—such as Argentina, Brazil, Chile—could maintain neither fixed parities nor convertible currencies.

TABLE 11.1   The World's Dollar Price Level (U.S. Wholesale Price Indices)

Year	Price level	
1951	82.5	
1952	80.3	
1953	79.2	
1954	79.3	
1955	79.5	
1956	82.2	
1957	84.5	
1958	85.7	
1959	85.9	Dollar price stability and internationally
1960	86.0	fixed exchange rates
1961	85.7	
1962	85.9	
1963	85.6	
1964	85.8	
1965	87.5	
1966	90.4	
1967	90.6	
1968	92.8	
1969	96.5	
1970	100.0	
		Accelerating world inflation and the break-
1971	103.3	down of fixed exchange rates
1972	107.9	
1973	122.0	
1974	145.0	
1975	158.4	
		High world inflation and freely floating
1976	165.7	rates
1977	175.8	

SOURCE: *International Financial Statistics* (various issues).

Besides bringing net savers and investors together, financial intermediation through New York had another important aspect. Governments abroad had a continuous need to tailor their owned reserves of freely usable dollars for intervention or precautionary purposes; and commercial banks also had a demand for dollar checking accounts and term deposits because of the dollar's role as a vehicle currency. Either group was then free to borrow at long term— say, by issuing bonds—in New York, and use the proceeds to build up their short-term liquidity: freely usable deposits in New York.[17] This freedom to borrow long and lend back (deposit) short in dollars did not result in any *net* international transfer of capital. Yet foreigners could acquire international liquidity when they needed it, and hence more easily preserve currency convertibility with fixed exchange rates.

In discussing the collapse of the dollar-gold standard and fixed exchange rates, I shall first look at the proximate reasons for virtually ending in 1968 American gold sales to foreigners—and then discuss the deeper reasons rooted in the increasing instability of the American economy in the late 1960s. Gold could have been phased out of the system—and indeed some kind of gold crisis was inevitable—without causing the collapse of the fixed exchange-rate regime.

After the European recovery, the world's stock of monetary gold changed little because the official price was fixed at $35 per ounce until 1971, and the net flow of newly mined gold relative to industrial usage was—and remains— small relative to existing stocks (see Table 11.2). In 1951, the total official gold reserves of IMF members amounted to $33.5 billion and were $38.7 billion in 1968. Of this, official American holdings amounted to $22.9 billion in 1951, but fell to $10.9 billion by 1968. As rapidly growing European economies allowed their reserve positions to grow commensurately by purchasing dollars in the open markets for foreign exchange, some chose to convert their dollars into gold that the American Treasury was obligated to supply.

More impressive to American authorities was the rapidly rising stock of dollar claims on the United States held by foreign banks (commercial and central) that had not yet been converted. These rose from about $8.9 billion in 1951 to $38.5 billion in 1968 (Table 11.2). Thus claims potentially convertible into gold in 1968 amounted to more than three and a half times the remaining American gold! Concern with protecting the last American gold reserves and avoiding the inevitable run on the bank prompted the American authorities in

17. This process is described in more analytical depth in C. P. Kindleberger, "Balance of Payments Deficits and the International Market for Liquidity," *Princeton Essays in International Finance*, No. 46 (May 1965).

TABLE 11.2   Official Gold Holdings and External Dollar Liabilities of the United States (Billions of dollars)

Year	Official world gold holdings*	Official U.S. gold stocks*	Outstanding dollar claims on U.S. held by foreign banks
1951	$33.5	$22.9	$ 8.9
1956	35.7	22.1	15.3
1960	37.7	17.8	21.0
1964	40.5	15.4	29.4
1968	38.7	10.9	38.5
Closing of the American gold window			
1972	38.5	10.5	82.9
1974	43.3	11.8	119.1
1976	41.3	11.2	144.7

SOURCE: *International Financial Statistics* (various issues).

* Gold is evaluated at official dollar prices through time. After 1968, the open-market price for gold was two or three times this official price. Nevertheless, no major country could sell all of its official gold in the open market without driving the price down quite drastically. Therefore, choosing a correct price for evaluation is difficult.

the mid 1960s and afterwards to pressure friendly governments not to convert existing dollar holdings, as was their right under Article IV. Finally, on March 15, 1968, official sales of gold by a consortium of central banks (including the United States Federal Reserve System) on the open private gold market in London were terminated, thus segmenting the official price of gold from the free market price. And subsequently the free-market price has fluctuated well above the official price of $35 per ounce, which was raised to $42 in 1971. Although, the American gold window was not closed officially by President Nixon until August 1971, negligible American sales of gold to foreign central banks took place after 1968.

Worse than simply leaning on foreign central banks not to convert dollars into gold, was the spate of balance-of-payments restrictions on capital outflows imposed by presidents Kennedy and Johnson: (1) the interest-equalization tax on foreign securities sold in the United States in 1963, (2) the restrictions on bank lending to foreigners in 1965, and (3) attempts to force multinational corporations in 1968 to finance their foreign operations overseas. These were concrete responses to accounting balance-of-payments "deficits"—the overseas build-up of dollar claims on the United States (see Table 11.2)—that in turn augmented official fears of losing gold. If effective, such restraints would have seriously impeded the key role of the New York capital market in providing dollar liquidity to the rest of the world. Fortunately, these regulatory efforts were undercut by the development of the Eurodollar market centered in London, outside the web of American capital controls.[18] Hence, an international capital market continued to provide dollar liquidity as well as to bring net savers and investors together. And the American balance-of-payments restrictions themselves were eventually terminated in 1974.

From Table 11.2, it is clear that the build-up of dollar claims on the American gold stock as the world economy grew would sooner or later force termination of the American Treasury's unlimited obligation to convert extant dollars into gold, and that balance-of-payments restrictions that contributed to the market's nervousness would be ultimately self-defeating.[19] America's principal international monetary obligation was not the *pro forma* link to gold but rather to maintain stable dollar prices of internationally tradable goods as well as an open capital market. This it did successfully throughout the 1950s and early 1960s (see Table 11.1). However, severe inflationary pressure developed in the United States in the middle and late 1960s that ultimately cracked the system of fixed exchange rates. The harmonization of stable monetary policies across the world's major industrial economies came to an end.

Uncertainly Pegged Exchange Rates and the International Transmission of Inflation (1968–1973)

There has never been a great inflation that has not been preceded or accompanied by large increases in the nominal supply of money. Nevertheless, plenty of observers, including government authorities, are always available to point out special nonmonetary circumstances associated with high or rising prices. In the great German hyperinflation of 1922–1923, where both prices and cash balances increased by several thousandfold, people could blame the unfair burdens imposed on Germany by the Treaty of Versailles and the French occupation of the Ruhr as somehow directly pushing prices up.[20] Similarly, in the great world inflation that began in the late 1960s but broke with full force in 1973–1975 (Table 11.3), "special" circumstances abounded: crop failures in Russia and India, the disappearance of anchovies off the coast of Peru, the formation of the OPEC oil cartel in 1973–1974, and so on. Into 1976, one

18. A more complete description of the fascinating financial phenomena of Eurocurrency trading can be found in Chapter 9.

19. Britain managed the pre-1914 gold standard with even more slender gold reserves behind extant sterling claims. But everyone realized that the Bank of England would undertake a contractionary monetary policy to defend itself against gold losses—unlike the Federal Reserve System in the 1960s.

20. It would, of course, be legitimate to go one step further and ask the additional question of whether these externally imposed burdens made it inevitable that the Weimar authorities would lose monetary control.

TABLE 11.3   Inflation in Consumer Price Indices of Ten Countries: 1960–1975

From prior year (percent change)	U.S.	Canada	Japan	U.K.	Germany	France	Italy	Netherlands	Belgium	Switzerland	10 countries combined
Weights	.4705	.0518	.1257	.0630	.1108	.0830	.0481	.0192	.0150	.0130	
Actual 1960	1.5	1.3	3.7	1.0	1.5	4.1	2.3	2.7	0.3	1.4	2.0
1961	1.1	0.9	5.2	3.5	2.3	2.4	1.2	2.1	1.0	1.9	2.0
1962	1.2	1.2	6.8	4.1	3.0	5.2	4.7	2.4	1.4	4.3	2.8
1963	1.2	1.7	6.3	2.1	3.0	5.0	7.4	3.2	2.1	3.4	2.8
1964	1.3	1.8	3.8	3.2	2.3	3.2	5.9	5.9	4.2	3.1	2.4
1965	1.6	2.4	6.7	4.8	3.3	2.7	4.5	4.8	4.1	3.4	3.0
1966	3.0	3.8	5.0	3.8	3.5	2.6	2.4	5.7	4.2	4.7	3.4
1967	2.8	3.6	4.0	2.6	1.7	2.8	3.2	3.5	2.9	4.0	2.9
1968	4.2	4.1	5.3	4.7	1.7	4.5	1.3	3.7	2.7	2.4	3.9
1969	5.4	4.5	5.3	5.4	3.1	6.0	2.7	7.4	3.7	2.5	5.0
1970	5.9	3.4	7.6	6.4	3.3	5.8	4.9	3.6	4.0	3.6	5.6
1971	4.3	2.8	6.1	9.4	5.3	5.4	5.0	7.5	4.3	6.6	5.1
1972	3.3	4.8	4.5	7.1	5.5	9.2	5.6	7.8	5.5	6.7	4.8
1973	6.2	7.6	11.8	9.2	6.9	7.4	10.8	8.0	6.9	8.7	7.7
1974	11.0	10.9	24.4	16.0	7.0	13.5	19.2	9.6	12.7	9.8	13.2
1975	9.2	10.7	11.9	24.3	5.9	11.8	17.0	10.2	12.8	6.7	10.8

SOURCE: H. Cleveland and B. Brittain, *The Great Inflation: A Monetarist View* (National Planning Association, 1976), p. 54.

could note the freezing of Brazilian coffee trees and the general feeling of the Club of Rome that we are running out of natural resources.

Some of these special circumstances may have had indirect monetary consequences. However, I shall stress the remarkable loss of monetary control among the major industrial economies concurrently in the last years of the fixed exchange-rate regime. Taking ten industrial countries combined, their aggre-

:ent per annum in the 1971–1973 period

ıt per annum in the preceding ten years

ınfortunate orchestration of international

:d States, incipient or actual balance of

ed according to the official settlements

ct of increasing (reducing) the domestic

German Bundesbank actively enters the

rs with Deutsche marks to prevent the

reserves of German commercial banks—

's monetary base—are increased directly.

direct countervailing action (which is

f Deutsche marks available to individual

ll expand. This increased monetary li-

se their demand for both tradable and

ıs bids up their prices measured in DM.

1973, the Bundesbank purchased about

ɔr foreign exchange, with the extraordi-

base indicated in Figure 11.1.[24]

therefore, inflationary pressure originat-

United States, took two complementary

of the world: (1) The direct increase in

ıble 11.1) automatically raised tradable

r, sterling, and so on unless these coun-

dom, Germany, France, Italy, Netherlands, Bel-

of official purchases of foreign exchange (U.S.

in an official exchange-rate peg.

23. See *International Financial Statistics* (May 1976).

24. Although such overt balance-of-payments surpluses in 1969–1973 best explain monetary expansion in countries such as Germany, Japan, and Scandinavia, incipient balance-of-payments surplus still contributed to monetary inflation in countries such as Britain, Italy, and France. Incipient surpluses in these latter countries allowed faster monetary expansion by domestic means without incurring unmanageable foreign payments deficits. For a nice description of these various monetary transmission mechanisms see Harold Van B. Cleveland and W. H. Bruce Brittain, op. cit.

TABLE 11.4 Annual Increases in Money Supplies of Ten Countries: 1960–1975

From prior year (percent change)	U.S.	Canada	Japan	U.K.	Germany	France	Italy	Netherlands	Belgium	Switzerland	10 countries combined
Weights	.4705	.0518	.1257	.0630	.1108	.0830	.0481	.0192	.0150	.0130	
Actual 1960	−0.1	1.3	19.9	3.3	9.3	11.2	13.0	5.2	2.1	7.3	5.5
1961	2.1	5.2	25.1	0.7	9.3	16.4	14.1	7.8	5.2	14.7	8.0
1962	2.2	3.3	16.0	0.0	11.0	16.9	17.8	5.7	7.0	10.4	7.0
1963	2.9	5.9	26.4	6.2	7.3	16.7	17.1	9.7	9.9	8.0	8.8
1964	4.0	5.1	16.8	5.4	8.4	10.1	7.3	8.5	5.6	5.5	7.0
1965	4.3	6.3	16.8	3.1	8.9	9.1	12.7	10.9	7.8	4.5	7.4
1966	4.6	6.9	16.3	3.1	4.3	8.9	15.1	7.2	6.7	2.6	7.0
1967	4.0	9.7	13.4	3.8	3.4	7.1	13.1	7.0	4.3	3.0	6.1
1968	7.1	4.3	14.6	4.6	7.5	5.7	13.3	8.8	6.6	9.5	8.0
1969	6.0	7.5	18.4	5.2	8.2	4.3	15.1	9.5	4.8	5.4	8.2
1970	3.9	2.2	18.3	6.7	6.5	0.2	21.7	10.6	5.6	4.9	6.8
1971	6.7	12.8	25.5	12.9	11.7	13.5	22.8	16.7	9.9	16.5	12.0
1972	7.1	13.9	22.0	14.7	13.8	12.9	17.9	17.8	12.7	17.5	12.0
1973	7.5	14.5	26.2	8.6	5.9	10.8	21.1	7.4	12.7	2.2	11.0
1974	5.5	9.8	13.2	5.5	6.0	10.8	17.1	3.1	8.6	0.1	7.6
1975	4.2	13.7	10.4	16.3	14.1	11.8	7.7	18.6	11.7	4.6	8.5

SOURCE: H. Cleveland and B. Brittain, *The Great Inflation: A Monetarist View* (National Planning Association, 1976), p. 56.

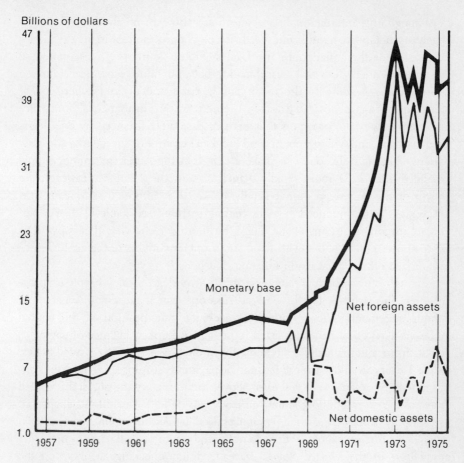

FIGURE 11.1 Sources of the German monetary base

NOTE: Components are converted using current exchange rates for the years shown.

SOURCE: H. Cleveland and B. Brittain, *The Great Inflation: A Monetarist View* (National Planning Association, 1976), p. 36.

tries took discretionary action to appreciate their currencies in terms of dollars. (2) The heavy pressure on aggregate demand in the U.S. also sharply deteriorated the American trade balance. This deterioration helped to precipitate capital flight from the United States as people speculated that the dollar would eventually be devalued. These current and capital-account movements together caused inherently stable countries like Germany to run large balance-of-payments surpluses—the foreign counterpart of the American deficits. This led to unwanted increases in the domestic money supplies in Germany, Japan, Sweden, and so on that added further pressure to increase the world price level—perhaps with a lag of one or two years.

Although this international mechanism for the transmission of inflation is largely monetary in nature, one need not be a pure monetarist in explaining the origins of the inflation in the United States. With the inauguration of President Kennedy in 1961, fiscal policy became more expansionist in the United States, leading to the major policy error under Lyndon Johnson of spending to fight a substantial war in Vietnam while simultaneously introducing costly new social programs that were inadequately financed by duly legislated taxation, and which were beyond the fiscal control of succeeding administrations. Alternatively, one can make a case that the American money supply expanded after 1961 more rapidly than it had in the 1950s.[25] However, the growth of the American money supply 1971–1973, although significant, was not as great as that induced in many trading partners (see Table 11.4). Perhaps lags are important. In any event, I take the more eclectic view that expansionary macroeconomic policy with fiscal and monetary origins in the center country touched off the great world inflation that is with us yet.

Although only a moderate increase in the American money supply is apparent from the statistics for the early 1970s, one can make a somewhat more definite statement. The asymmetrical exchange-rate position of the United States vis-à-vis other countries acted to prevent American balance-of-payments deficits from automatically contracting the monetary base of the United States. While European and Japanese balance-of-payments surpluses induced substantial monetary expansion as described above, the monetary impact in the United States of the corresponding American payments deficits was fully sterilized. To oversimplify somewhat, when foreign central banks buy dollars in the open markets for foreign exchange they do not withdraw those dollars from monetary circulation in the United States. Instead, dollar checking accounts on the Federal Reserve or on American commercial banks are used immediately to buy U.S. Treasury bills or longer-term Treasury bonds. Hence, no monetary contraction within the United States automatically occurs.[26] In summary, in the world economy the expansionary monetary effect of European and Japanese balance-of-payments surpluses in the 1969–1973 period was not offset by any monetary contraction due to the equivalent American deficits.[27]

Automatic sterilization of the center country's payments deficits becomes a

25. As has been done very impressively by Jurg Niehans in "How to Fill an Empty Shell," *American Economic Review* (May 1976), pp. 177–83.
26. Unlike the workings of the classical gold standard prior to 1914 when gold losses would have induced an automatic American monetary contraction.
27. A description of the technical details associated with this automatic sterilization, and what might be done to change it, can be found in R. McKinnon, "A New Tripartite Monetary Agreement or a Limping Dollar Standard?," *Princeton Essays in International Finance*, No. 106 (October 1974).

defect in the world's monetary system only when that country itself is unstable—as the United States has been from the late 1960s. If not abused, however, this unique monetary independence given to the center country in a world of fixed exchange rates can work well. American dollar prices were very stable from 1951 to the mid 1960s (see Table 11.1), making it much easier for other countries to maintain their own macroeconomic stability. Therefore, allowing the accumulation of dollar claims by Europeans in, say, the 1950s, to force a monetary contraction in the United States would have been entirely inappropriate. Thus it need not be desirable to force American monetary policy to respond mechanically to the state of American foreign payments, unless such monetary rules are carefully hedged.

While not playing by the mechanical rules of the classical gold standard, America still had the important international responsibility to maintain price stability in dollar terms. The abrogation of this obligation after 1968 (1966?) was finally enough to drive other industrial countries away from fixed exchange-rate parities by 1973 in a crisis atmosphere.[28] The new regime of floating exchange rates then allowed other industrial economies to establish independent control over their domestic money supplies. The dollar standard in its *strong* form, where the United States determined world monetary policy, came to an end.

Freely Floating Exchange Rates (1973–Present)

After such a debacle in the foreign exchange markets, and with the residue of high world price inflation that is not yet under control, the world dollar standard—which has been with us in one form or another since 1945—would seem to be finished. Yet, I suggest that much of the substance remains and a *weak* form of the dollar standard survives.

Although traumatic at times, the transition to floating exchange rates among the currencies of the major industrial economies allowed the preservation of currency convertibility for both residents and nonresidents of these countries. Thus, the socialist economies of Eastern Europe, the hundred or more less developed countries, and the residents of the industrial economies can continue to use 20 or so Western currencies to invoice their exports and make payments for imports. In contrast, the inconvertible currencies of these socialist economies and LDCs still are unusable as monetary vehicles for international trade (see Chapters 2 and 3). Fortunately, we have been spared the proliferation of exchange controls among industrial countries that characterized the floating

28. Except for some very loose arrangements among a small group of European countries with a nonpermanent membership—the European snake.

exchange-rate system of the 1930s. Private individuals or firms or communist state trading monopolies can freely buy or sell goods in international markets by using one of the convertible currencies as a unit of account and means of payment. Poland may invoice many of its exports in Deutsche marks, whereas Argentina invoices most of its exports in U.S. dollars. The demonetization of international trade and relapse to bilateral barter that characterized the 1930s has been avoided. Indeed, world trade has continued to grow relative to national outputs since 1973.

But among the twenty or so effectively convertible currencies, an asymmetrical two-tier system still exists. Nonbank enterprises may invoice or make payments in any of the twenty convertible currencies as described above. However, banking systems everywhere continue to rely heavily on the U.S. dollar as the prime vehicle currency for commercial banks and intervention currency for central banks. The American dollar is still interbank money internationally, even where nonbank firms and enterprises do not use it directly (Chapters 2 and 9).

Any international monetary "reform" that attempted to terminate the key-currency role of the United States dollar simply to make the system more symmetrical among nations in a *pro forma* sense would be quite dangerous; it could mistakenly encourage the American government to undertake an independent exchange-rate policy.

For example, in the early months of 1977, high American officials expressed unhappiness about the alleged "undervaluation" of the Japanese yen in terms of dollars.[29] Whatever the dubious advantages of publically chastising the Japanese, it would be entirely inappropriate for the Federal Reserve to enter the foreign exchange market directly and purchase yen with dollars. To avoid international conflict, the Japanese government should be discreetly persuaded of the merits of the American case. Then the Bank of Japan could take the appropriate action in the foreign exchange markets. Germany and Japan are probably the only two countries large enough to warrant even this limited pressure from the United States—and then only in unusual circumstances.

Thus benign passivity by the United States in its official exchange-rate targets, and a willingness to let the dollar be used on a worldwide basis as interbank money, remain key elements in maintaining currency convertibility under fluctuating exchange rates. And having an open capital market in dollars (inclusive of Eurocurrency transacting), where foreigners can deposit or borrow freely, is an essential source of international finance for the rest of the world, a source that

29. The large Japanese trade surplus in 1977 need not reflect undervaluation of the yen. American and Japanese price levels do not appear to be disaligned. Rather, the surplus more likely reflects the high propensity to save in Japan relative to the current flow of investment opportunities.

cannot easily be replicated by any other country or institu\
International Monetary Fund. Today what America does\
whether or not international trade will remain monetized and r\

In the breakdown of fixed exchange rates, what has been lost\
worse—is the direct and pervasive influence that the United Sta\
on the *domestic* monetary policies of other industrial countries. \ ⁀ᴀɪble exchange rates better allow other countries to insulate their money supplies not only from American policies, but from each other's policies as well. Instead of having the more or less common international price level for tradable goods of the 1950s and 1960s, in the mid 1970s Germany and Switzerland are selecting lower rates of price inflation than the United States, whereas the United Kingdom, Italy, and France are selecting markedly higher rates (see Table 11.3). Unfortunately, continuing uncertainty about these differing relative rates of inflation is the prime cause of substantial day-to-day and month-to-month fluctuations in foreign exchange rates (see Figure 1.1). Hence, the international values of national monies are not as stable as before, and international commerce—on both the production and consumption sides—is somewhat less efficient.

Of course, a return to monetary stability in the United States could induce other industrial countries to voluntarily fix their exchange rates vis-à-vis the U.S. dollar again, resulting in greater international monetary harmony.

Even under flexible exchange rates, however, the dollar-based convertible currency system can still be undermined. Suppose that monetary instability of the kind generated in the later 1960s in the United States was to escalate, making the dollar unacceptable either as a reserve asset or as a vehicle currency. Attempts to unload existing dollar reserves could cause wild exchange-rate fluctuations and payments restrictions among Western convertible currencies that would send us back to bilateral barter and uninhibited protectionism.

Hence, America's own role in stabilizing the world's monetary system should be, first, to avoid further debasement of the U.S. dollar—i.e., to avoid domestic price inflation—and secondly, to maintain a passively open foreign trade and payments mechanism. President Carter's dollar stabilization program of November 1, 1978 was a hopeful sign. Finally, the United States seems willing to consciously adjust its monetary base to international needs, rather than automatically sterilizing the domestic impact of large balance-of-payments deficits.

Appendix
Proposals for International Monetary Reform:

I have argued that the monetary basis for world trade since 1945 has been an evolving dollar standard—complemented by a firm commitment to currency convertibility on the part of noncommunist industrial economies. The road to "reform" was to examine ways in which these industrial economies might better stabilize their monetary policies vis-à-vis each other. Exchange-rate fluctuations and associated deviations from purchasing power parity could thereby be reduced, making it easier to retain convertibility among important national monies. And this rather pedestrian approach seems the only practical avenue for improving the workings of the international monetary system at the present time.

This appendix, on the other hand, makes no pretence of being "practical"; it analyzes some common—and rather sweeping—suggestions for change. Since the breakdown of the sterling-gold exchange standard in 1931, dozens of schemes for introducing a more purely international money—with no particular national origin—have been proposed. By and large these proposals tend to be variants on two broad themes:

1) an international *commodity-reserve currency*, where the gold standard is but a special case; and

2) an international *fiat money* of which the Special Drawing Rights (SDR) facility of the International Monetary Fund (IMF) is an example.

But widespread inconvertibility of national currencies would undermine any international standard. Hence, increasing the number of national currencies that are internationally convertible is discussed first. Then the merits and demerits of proposals under (1) and (2) are sketched. I conclude with a general discussion of the controversial seigniorage problem. What are the social costs or benefits to an issuer of international money under (1) or (2), or gains to the United States itself under the dollar standard?

On Extending Currency Convertibility to Less Developed and Centrally Planned Economies

Deliberate pressure to encourage currency convertibility in LDCs such as India, and even some centrally planned economies, is a neglected aspect of reform. Trade is a two-way street: free international access to earn Indian rupees that accurately reflect the social costs of producing Indian goods at prevailing exchange rates confers mutual trading advantages on foreigners *and* on Indian nationals. The second and third party benefits of international money are best provided on a quid pro quo basis. Not only do we have a wider ambit for the international division of labor, but the capacity of the international economy to act as a shock absorber for a crop failure or a similar random shift in production or consumption is enhanced the wider the effective area of currency convertibility.[1]

The international economy would be much less stable if all economies behaved like, say, the Russian. Foreigners have no free access to Russian resources in times of crisis given the absolute commodity inconvertibility of the ruble (Chapter 3). Yet Russia can use foreign exchange reserves (or obtain Eurocredits) to cover shortfalls in her own grain production; and she can dump excess goods on world markets—a vent for surplus—when her domestic plans don't mesh. Russia benefits substantially from the existence of effective international money without contributing to it. Fortunately other socialist economies such as Yugoslavia and Hungary show signs of evolving a more internationalist or open foreign trade system with at least limited currency convertibility.[2]

A common counter argument is that the needs of less developed countries—their economic backwardness and often desperate poverty—should allow them to conduct their domestic monetary and fiscal policies free of international restraint or sanction. Specifically, LDCs may become members of the International Monetary Fund, drawing on its low-cost credits and technical advice, without

1. This reduction in social uncertainty is argued by R. A. Mundell in "Uncommon Arguments for Common Currencies," *The Economics of Common Currencies*, ed. H. G. Johnson and A. Swoboda (London: George Allen and Unwin, 1973), Chapter 7.
2. As a consequence of moving away from central planning by materials allocations. The use of market prices in internal trade makes currency convertibility in foreign trade possible to attain (Chapter 3).

making any serious effort to accept Article VIII—the article that defines the obligation to strive for current-account currency convertibility (Chapter 1). In the other great forum for promoting freedom in international commerce—the General Agreement on Tariffs and Trade—member countries are eligible to receive the benefits of "Most Favored Nation" treatment from other members if they do not arbitrarily impose tariff or quota restrictions on their own imports.[3] Under Article XVIII of the GATT, however, a waiver is provided allowing poor countries unilaterally to impose tariffs or quotas on imports for "development" purposes, which means in practice no restraint on tariff and quota manipulation. In effect, LDCs are allowed to practice monetary and fiscal nationalism in foreign trade in a manner that is (fortunately) denied the wealthier industrial economies under the IMF and GATT agreements.

If these exemptions from established international protocol did indeed promote more rational development policies, they would be worthwhile. Yet the available empirical and theoretical evidence points strongly to the contrary: uninhibited national manipulation of the trade and payments mechanism seems to reduce the economic wealth of the country in question. In LDCs, the whole panoply of detailed exchange restrictions, multiple exchange-rate categories, trade quotas on particular products, advance deposit requirements for imports, high tariffs, and so on *ad infinitum* are an order of magnitude higher than the remaining trade barriers in the industrial economies. They were a principal reason for most LDCs missing out on the great boom in world trade after 1948, and for their inadequate export performance at the present time.[4]

Thus, one worthwhile reform within the existing framework of the IMF and the GATT is to treat less developed countries more symmetrically in comparison to the industrial ones: convertibility obligations could be more generally enforced and pressure to reduce barriers to trade applied more evenly.

A Commodity-Reserve Currency?

A full-bodied commodity-reserve currency is one where commodities themselves circulate—such as gold and silver coins; or it consists of warehouse receipts that are a direct claim on a given stock of commodities, measured by their weight and fineness. The volume of such money in circulation cannot exceed the stocks of commodities that are held by a monetary authority—the warehouse custodian.

3. In exporting to any other member, a given country would face the lowest tariff or most generous quota governing that member's import policy.
4. These points are developed in detail—both empirically and analytically—by R. I. McKinnon, *Money and Capital in Economic Development* (Washington, D.C., Brookings Institution, 1973), Chapters 3 and 10.

Under a pure gold standard, coins or receipts (issued by a bank—goldsmith—which actually holds that amount of gold printed on the receipts), can both circulate. The amount of money in circulation, therefore, depends on the vagaries of goldmining technology and on new discoveries.[5]

A more general commodity-reserve currency is backed by a wider variety of goods which have direct value in use as well as being less subject to uncertainties in the production of or demand for any one of them. All such goods, however, must be sufficiently *homogeneous* to be assayed to a given physical standard that is commonly accepted: Number 1 Northern Red Winter Wheat; 24 karat gold; refined copper of a given grade; and so on. This rather stringent criterion eliminates manufactured goods that are (slightly) heterogeneous with respect to function, size and shape, or brand name. And rather few primary commodities—mainly base metals and the most homogeneous agricultural produce that does not incur unacceptable deterioration in storage—can feasibly be included. Albert Hart's listing of possible candidates, including commodities suggested by the United Nations' Conference on Trade and Development (UNCTAD), is reproduced in Table A.1.

Only with such homogeneous commodities can the basic monetary unit be defined unambiguously in physical terms, say

> 1 ounce of gold + 3 ounces of copper + 20 bushels of wheat
> + 18 cwt of frozen pork bellies + 100 cups of coffee + . . .
> = 1 Commodity Reserve Unit (CRU).

The CRU defined above includes these various commodities in *fixed proportions*—sometimes called symmetalism. Because only quantities are in fixed proportions, relative prices of the underlying commodities are free to vary—as are their absolute prices in CRUs.

More recently, Jon Luke has proposed allowing commodities to be combined in variable proportions, but with purchase prices varying according to a rule such that an acceptable price index of what one CRU will buy (in terms of the included commodities) is exactly stabilized.[6] Thus, we retain the big advantage of a commodity-reserve money: having a unit of account precisely defined in real terms even as paper notes or depository claims are allowed to circulate.

5. Any persistent tendency for too much gold to be mined so as to cause general price inflation would eventually be stopped by the relative fall in the price of gold that forces the closure of marginal mines; the reverse would be true in the case of too little gold being mined and general price deflation.
6. Jon C. Luke, "Inflation-Free Pricing Rules for a Generalized Commodity-Reserve Currency," *Journal of Political Economy* (August 1975), Vol. 83, No. 4, pp. 779–90.

Although technically sophisticated, the additional advantage of Luke's approach is that CRUs (warehouse receipts) can be issued when any single homogeneous commodity is tendered to the monetary authority. (Under the old fixed proportions approach, a whole basket had to be tendered—even when some of the commodities in that basket were in short supply.) The pricing rule is such that, in the aggregate, if more wheat is tendered than copper at some initial set of value weights, the authorities would lower the price of wheat in CRUs and raise that of copper so that the initial value weights are maintained.

Even this neatly generalized version of a commodity reserve currency, however, requires precise homogeneity in each underlying commodity. (Natural rubber of flexible quality wouldn't do.) Along with the additional need to avoid significant deterioration in storage, the total value of the flow of new output of

TABLE A.1   Potential Reserve Commodities for Commodity-Reserve Currency from UNCTAD, and Other Lists

Commodities apparently well-standardized and durable in storage				Other suggested commodities
Grains, etc.	Other foods	Fibres, etc.	Minerals	
i. UNCTAD list of 18 commodities				
Wheat	Sugar	Cotton	Copper	Iron ore
Maize	Coffee	Wool	Zinc	Bauxite, alumina
Rice	Tea	Rubber	Tin	
	Cocoa	Jute	Lead	
		Hard fibers[a]		
ii. Additional items with New York Times futures quotations				
Soybeans	Frozen pork bellies	Plywood	Silver	Eggs (shell)
Oats	Frozen orange juice	Lumber		Live beef cattle
iii. Additional items on older lists in literature				
Linseed	Butter	Silk		Tobacco
	Lard	Newsprint		Coal
	Milk, dried	Wood pulp		
iv. Items under UNCTAD consideration				
Groundnuts				Copra
				Palm oil
				Coconut oil

SOURCE: A. G. Hart, "The Case as of 1976 for International Commodity-Reserve Currency," *Weltwirtschaftliches Archiv*, Band 112, Heft 1 (1976), p. 6.
[a]Sisal, henequen, abaca.

included commodities can, at best, amount to a very small proportion of the world's GNP—say, of the order of five percent.[7]

Unlike a pure gold standard that includes the circulation of gold coins, a commodity-reserve money would circulate only as paper notes or as deposit claims. Otherwise, tolerable homogeneity, divisibility, and portability in the medium of exchange would be absent. Who wants to be paid with 10 bushels of soybeans or 100 cans of frozen orange juice? Banknotes worth 10 CRUs would, however, be perfectly acceptable. Presumably, such notes and checking accounts denominated in CRUs would be the only legal tender in international transactions among enterprises, individuals, and governments apart from the money-issuing authority itself. The commodity-reserve bank, of course, would have to stand ready to accept (buy) the designated commodities and issue CRUs in exchange. Indeed, this would be the sole mechanism for increasing the volume of *full-bodied* commodity-reserve currency in monetary circulation.

Should our monetary warehouse—jam packed with a mélange of scarce commodities—provide storage facilities for the ordinary commercial merchandising of these commodities?[8] Suppose the buying price exactly equals the selling price—say CRU.05 per ounce of copper, and that the storage facilities for copper were conveniently located geographically. Then the unwitting monetary authority would be the principal stock holder and source of supply to users, and producers would sell all their newly refined copper to the monetary authority for CRUs. The absence of any spread between buying and selling price amounts to a heavy implicit subsidy to having the monetary authority undertake a dominant merchandising role—and to driving all the commercial traders in (stock holders of) refined copper out of business. Much of the monetary authority's holdings would be working or productive stocks, and hence CRUs issued by the monetary authority—when copper was sold to it—would at least partly reflect this nonmonetary merchandising aspect. It would be analogous to having money issued according to the old *real bills* doctrine based on the extension of short-term bank credits for inventory financing, rather than the modern technique of estimating what the social demand for money might be.[9]

---

7. Milton Friedman makes this necessarily rough estimate in "Commodity-Reserve Currency," in *Essays in Positive Economics* (Chicago, Ill.: University of Chicago Press, 1953), p. 228.
8. Of course, one doesn't have to think of these commodities as all being stored in one physical location.
9. According to the real bills doctrine, the banking system as a whole should be allowed to expand the money supply freely as long as loans are made for productive purposes—largely the purchase of short-term trade bills from sellers of commodity merchandise.

Without rehearsing all the well-known faults of the real bills doctrine, comparative advantage seems to suggest that specialist profit seekers in the copper trade are likely to be more efficient merchants than central bankers. And the commodity-reserve bank should disengage from the multiplicity of problems associated with the marketing of copper, groundnuts, wheat, soybeans, and so on by simply imposing a spread that comfortably exceeds the private merchants' normal profit margin between buying and selling prices.

For example, the authority might now offer to buy copper for CRU.045 and sell it for CRU.055 at any point in time with the parity in the middle varying flexibly through time according to Luke's rules. Now the world's stock of refined copper would be partitioned into (1) the idle hoard of the monetary authority that is the real backing for the issue of CRUs, and (2) the working inventories of copper merchants. If the price of copper did not tend to move much one way or another, the monetary authority would be neither buying nor selling. Decentralized merchants would service the huge flow of day-to-day transactions associated with copper production and consumption—and similarly with all the other commodities in the monetary basket. Only when the CRU price of copper (or other commodities) tended to fall substantially would copper be tendered to the monetary authority who would issue CRUs in exchange: the supply of copper (and the other commodities) being simply the obverse of the monetary demand for CRUs. And this increase in the monetary stock of commodities would be taken out of commercial circulation.

Although not always very clear about it, the older writers[10] seem to advocate this partitioning between the monetary and commercial stocks of the relevant commodities. Unfortunately, this partitioning makes the social cost of any substantial issue of Commodity Reserve Units (CRUs) unacceptability high. In order for the world's money stock in CRUs to expand, valuable physical commodities would be impounded so that they were no longer available either for consumption or as an intermediate input in production. Suppose the stocks of CRUs were substantial—say 30 percent of world trade.[11] Besides the incredible initial social cost of building up the commodity stockpile, as the world economy grows 30 percent of any increase in international trade would be diverted to this monetary hoard!

This heavy social cost would prevent CRUs from being used *voluntarily* as an international means of payment or as a precautionary store of value. The cost to individual nations or firms of acquiring CRU balances net would be too

10. Benjamin Graham, *World Commodities and World Currency* (New York: McGraw Hill, 1944); Frank D. Graham, *Social Goals and Economic Institutions* (Princeton, N.J.: Princeton University Press, 1942); and A. G. Hart, op. cit.

11. Each country held a monetary reserve equal to two or three months' imports.

high, and they would continue to exchange national monies directly unless all were simultaneously ruined by some catastrophe such as hyperinflation.

Suppose, however, a very strong international authority imposed an all-inclusive international clearing union, where each national central bank kept exact tabulations on all its country's international payments and receipts. Then, monthly settlements in CRUs, where bilateral deficits and surpluses were cleared multilaterally, could be forced through the single world clearing bank.[12] And proposals to introduce a commodity reserve money have (unsurprisingly) been accompanied by the suggestion that nations and individuals be prevented from holding monetary reserves in the form of gold or other countries' currencies— particularly U.S. dollars.[13] But this dramatically increased role for national central banks in the clearing process would make the imposition of restrictions on trade or capital flows uncomfortably easy! Even under the old fixed exchange- rate regime of Bretton Woods, the designers were careful to allow a one percent margin of variation on either side of parity in order that commercial banks and private firms could make day-to-day foreign payments and receipts without refer- ence to the national central bank (Chapter 2). To have central banks become the sole intermediaries in the foreign exchanges, in order to ensure the use of commodity-reserve money, would be socially retrogressive.

While retaining its usefulness as a real unit of account, two financial tech- niques have been suggested for reducing the inventory costs of commodity- reserve money:

1) The commodity backing could be *futures contracts* ("long" positions) in the relevant commodities, thus avoiding the physical warehousing of the goods.

2) Instead of having full-bodied commodity-reserve money, one could have *frac- tional reserves* against outstanding CRU liabilities.

If the CRU system ever got going, one could imagine futures trading in homogeneous primary commodities where these contracts are denominated in CRUs. Then the authority could create CRUs by buying commodity futures to provide financial cover for private merchants who did the physical warehousing and covered themselves by selling commodity futures. No longer would there be a sharp separation between idle monetary commodity reserves and active merchandising reserves. The net incremental social cost of the CRU system would be reduced because normal working inventories of the commodities would become part of the monetary reserve.[14] This use of futures markets is

12. Perhaps on the model of the old European Payments Union (EPU) where monthly settlements were made in gold or dollars. See Chapter 11.

13. Hart, op. cit. pp. 9 and 10.

14. Presuming that the normal stocks of commercial inventories of copper exceeded the normal demand by copper users to buy the product forward, and that wanton speculators did not try to exploit the international monetary authority.

clouded, however, by subtle problems of contract enforcement in a world subject to crop failures, famines, embargoes, etc. If the goods are not actually in the official warehouse, can one count on forward delivery commitments across very diverse countries in the family of nations? Moreover, existing futures trading is mainly organized in national monies—principally the U.S. dollar (Chapter 4). How would the CRU authority operate in national money markets in its purchases or sales of commodity futures?

The second financial technique for economizing involves moving away from a full-bodied commodity-reserve currency. The CRU authority would be empowered to create money by lending CRUs at interest—while keeping sufficient physical commodities as a fractional reserve. The interest earned could possibly offset storage costs so that the whole system yields a modest deposit rate of interest to the holders of CRUs. Indeed, if full-bodied CRUs ever began to circulate successfully, private banking entrepreneurs would emerge who issued their own CRU notes at more attractive interest rates, and kept only modest commodity reserves (10 percent of deposits?) to guard against a run on the bank. Fractional reserve money, of course, brings with it this new kind of potential instability. However, the consequent reduction in the stock of idle commodity hoards would be an important social saving.

But any physical commodities that are held as reserves are still costly. And the commodity-reserve currency would continue to depend heavily on political sanctions that force all international payments or receipts through a centrally supervised and controlled clearing union. Market pressure by private traders would always exist to exchange one (convertible) national currency for another without going through this rather expensive supernational clearing device.

Does the CRU system have any particular advantages in promoting freer international trade? If a common commodity-reserve money was to replace national fiat monies in domestic circulation in each participating country, the international means of payment would become the same as that within individual nations. With free trade in the underlying commodity basket, free convertibility and stable exchange rates would automatically ensue just as in the case of the classical gold standard. Unfortunately, there is no reason to believe that introducing a commodity-reserve currency as the basis for world trade would encourage an increase in the number of national currencies that are internationally convertible. Would countries in Latin America, Africa, or Asia be more likely to have an open domestic foreign exchange market in CRUs as compared to U.S. dollars? LDCs retain restrictions on convertibility as an adjunct to practicing covert taxation of their national fiat monetary systems (Chapters 2 and 7). It seems unlikely that they could be persuaded to give up this degree of national monetary autonomy in return for adopting a (socially costly) commodity-reserve currency for domestic circulation that is controlled by an international institution. And for the industrial countries with convertible currencies, the expensive CRU system seems somewhat redundant.

Despite some possible benefit as a world price index or unit of account, I conclude that the on-going social costs and the tremendous wrenching of existing institutions for international exchange hardly warrant a commodity-reserve currency as the principal international means of payment or store of value.

Of course one might well wish to consider international commodity-price stabilization programs *separately*, and consider the holding of some buffer stocks in common. But purchases and sales of individual commodities would use existing national currencies (singly or in combination) as a unit of account and means of payment. It would merely confuse the operation of these buffer stocks to associate them with some notion of creating a new international money.

Artificial Currency Units and Special Drawing Rights

Suppose commodity-reserve currency is deemed infeasible, but one still wants a purely international money that is symmetrical in use with respect to all nations: that is not unduly dependent on any one of them. Is it possible for the International Monetary Fund (or similar agency) to issue a relatively cost-less fiat money that becomes generally acceptable as an international unit of account, means of payment, and store of value? In particular, what are the prospects for the Special Drawing Rights (SDR) facility of the IMF evolving *independently* into the principal form of international money?

Starting with the old European unit of account (EUA) worth exactly one United States dollar associated with the European Payments Union in the 1950s (Chapter 11), there is some history of artificial units of account being used for international purposes. Joseph Ascheim and Y. S. Park have collated a number of these official and private units of account (Table A.2). All are simply composite bundles of individual national currencies.[15] For units of account only, Ascheim and Park develop the concept of "functional currency areas": how different currency baskets are appropriate for various classes of international transactions in a world of fluctuating exchange rates.

From being worth exactly one American dollar in 1950,[16] the official Euro-

15. Joseph Ascheim and Y. S. Park, "Artificial Currency Units: The Formation of Functional Currency Areas," *Princeton Essays in International Finance*, No. 114 (April 1976).
16. Although formally specified in terms of gold content.

pean unit of account changed to a basket of nine currencies of the members of
the European Economic Community in 1975. And this new unit of account
may well be more appropriate for keeping track of budgetary allocations, taxes,
common agricultural prices, and so forth within the community.

1 EUA = DM 0.828 + F 1.15 + £ 0.0885 + Lit 109 + f 0.286
        + BF 3.66 + DKr 0.217 + £Ir 0.00759 + Lux F 0.14.

Similarly, Special Drawing Rights were initially valued at exactly US$1.00
in 1970 (again with the *pro forma* specification in terms of gold content), and
then were changed in 1974 to a basket of 16 of the world's principal convertible
currencies as shown in Table A.2. Given the rather large exchange-rate fluctuations of recent times, this basket may be a more appropriate average for
determining the contributions that individual members pay to the IMF in
terms of their own currencies and for denominating the outstanding value of
IMF loans that must be repaid in convertible currency(ies). The amount of
these repayments depends on the exchange rate between that currency(ies) and
the composite SDR basket at the time the loan is due.

1 SDR = $ 0.40 + DM 0.38 + £ 0.045 + F 0.44 + Y 26 + Can$ 0.071 + Lit 47 + f 0.14
        + BF 1.6 + SKr 0.13 + $A 0.012 +DKr 0.11 + NKr 0.099 +Pta 1.1
        + S 0.22 + R 0.0082.

Using the daily market exchange rates of the component currencies against
the U.S. dollar, the IMF calculates every day the rate for the new SDR in
terms of the U.S. dollar by summing up the dollar value of the currency
fractions. It then derives rates for the SDR in terms of other currencies by
converting the dollar value of the SDR into other currencies at that day's
market exchange rates.[17]

The SDR unit of account may come into some limited uses outside of the
IMF. The International Air Transport Association did fix air fares in a modified
version of the SDR, so that ticket agents recalculated the domestic-currency
equivalents of these fares. This practice has been discontinued, however.

In parallel, some private currency baskets or units of account, such as the
Eurco (Table A.2), have been used by banking houses such as N.M. Roth-
schild and Sons to denominate a few private bond issues—with the loan proceeds and repayments in any convertible currency in accordance with its exchange rate for the basket as a whole. However, these private transactions
involving currency cocktails remain very minor in comparison to international
bond issues denominated in a single currency such as U.S. dollars or Deutsche
marks.

17. Ascheim and Park, op. cit. p. 10.

TABLE A.2   Summary Classification of Artificial Currency Units

Type of ACU	Year of creation	Value tied to	No. of currencies in basket
Official			
EUA			
Old	1950	Gold	—
New	1975	Currency basket	9
SDR			
Old	1970	Gold	—
New	1974	Currency basket	16
AMU	1974	Currency basket	16
Private			
EUA			
Old	1961	Gold	—
New	1972	Gold	—
ECU or EMU	1970	Immutably fixed exchange rates	—
Eurco	1973	Currency basket	9
Arcru	1974	Current exchange rates	8 of 12
B-Unit	1974	Currency basket	5
IFU	1975	Currency basket	10

SOURCE: Joseph Ascheim and Y. S. Park, "Artificial Currency Units: The Formation of Functional Currency Areas," *Princeton Essays in International Finance*, No. 114 (April 1976) pp. 7, 8, 9, 18.
NOTES: EUA = European unit of account.
SDR = Special drawing rights.
AMU = Asian monetary unit.
ECU = European currency unit.
EMU = European monetary unit.
Eurco = European composite unit.
Arcru = Arab currency-related unit.
B-Unit = Barclays unit.
IFU = International financial unit.

1 Eurco = DM 0.90 + F 1.20 + £ 0.075 + Lit 80
+ f 0.35 + BF 4.50 + DKr 0.20 + £ Ir 0.005 + Lux F 0.50.

Note that a national convertible currency has always been used as a *means of payment* in transactions with the IMF or in private capital markets—even in those functional currency areas where the unit of account is a currency basket. Does this continuing dependence on national monies reflect an inadequacy in our international institutions that could be overcome by some technically skillful reform of the IMF articles defining Special Drawing Rights? My tentative answer is that *no* such reform is possible without impinging in an unacceptable way on the freedom of trading enterprises, individuals, and commercial banks to make and receive international payments without restraint. Why should the prior existence of national fiat monies, which are freely convertible, tend to preempt the emergence of any purely international one as a means of payment?

Each national currency is legal tender and has the full force of state sanction requiring people to use it for the circular flow of production and consumption within the nation in question. The domain for which a demand exists for the *stock* of domestic money is thus quite well defined. Even here, however, each national central bank only controls the real value of its currency indirectly by financial techniques—rather than operating directly in the market for commodities. The purchase of domestic bonds through open-market operations—or through discounting—is a way of adjusting the supply of national money to the estimated demand for it. And in a fixed exchange regime, the purchase or sale of foreign exchange is another financial technique for adjusting the stock of domestic money available for people to hold (Chapter 10). Although these financial techniques are imprecise, normally the need for domestic money is sufficiently stable that a reasonably competent monetary authority can tailor the supply of money to approximate the demand[18]—and thus stabilize the purchasing power of the domestic currency in terms of goods and services.

Unfortunately, a purely international fiat money has no natural and uniquely defined monetary domain. The nexus of the international exchange of commodities and services is not the exclusive province of any purely international money because convertible national monies can always be traded directly. There is no equivalent to a legal tender provision for international transactions, and thus a stable—indeed any substantial—private demand for SDR is hard to specify. Even if the supply of international money was not in the hands of a huge bureaucracy representing more than one hundred countries, the world's leading financial wizard could hardly be expected to use open-market operations or discounting successfully to adjust the supply of international money to the elusive (and possibly nonexistent) private demand for it. In short, such an attempt at monetary independence would likely leave indeterminate the real purchasing power of the international money in question.

Governments could collectively establish a demand to hold a stock of international fiat money—as was seen necessary in the case of a commodity-reserve currency. An exclusive international clearing union could be set up among national central banks. Each national authority would monitor all its country's external payments and receipts. At the end of each month, bilateral deficits and surpluses would be cleared through the union, and net debtors would have to pay up in SDR or something like it. Alternatively, to allow more scope for direct private exchange, all exporters or sellers of securities would be required

18. Unless undermined by fiscal inadequacies—such as uncovered government budgeting deficits.

to invoice and receive payment exclusively in the international money. All exchange rates would be established in terms of the official international money. The direct use of national monies as a currency of invoice (unit of account) or a means of payment would be forbidden.

This would indeed be establishing international money by fiat! While politically very difficult to administer, in a technical economic sense a stable demand for the international money might well result. Then through judicious financial procedures for money creation, the international central bank might well have a determinate price level for tradable goods.

However, the coercion involved and the increased surveillance (and possibly exchange controls) by national central banks of private trading enterprises—including commercial banks—would hardly encourage freer trade. What is left, therefore, is what we observe. Because of the difficulties of establishing an independent value for international fiat monies, they see limited use as units of account whose real purchasing power is linked to convertible national currencies.

The Seigniorage Problem and the Link to Less Developed Countries

Without coercion, perhaps the door can be left open for a purely international money that is held *voluntarily* by private traders and governments because of its attractive yield and liquidity properties. In the case of the special drawing rights, this latter possibility is closely related to the seigniorage problem.

The *Oxford English Dictionary* defines seigniorage as "a duty levied on the coining of money for the purpose of covering the expenses of minting, and as a source of revenue to the crown, claimed by the sovereign by virtue of his prerogative."[19]

Let us formulate the revenue or seigniorage flow from the issue of money in a more general form.[20] Consider first the balance sheet of our money-issuing institution: deposits are recognized money for international settlements, reserves are the backing for deposits outstanding in the form of some more fundamental asset such as commodity reserves, and investments refer to interest-bearing assets purchased on an open capital market such that their yield approximates the opportunity cost of capital in the world economy.

19. *The Compact Edition of the Oxford English Dictionary*, Vol. II (1971), p. 2712.
20. My analysis draws heavily on H. Grubel, "The Distribution of Seigniorage from International Money Creation," and H. G. Johnson, "A Note on Seigniorage and the Social Saving from Substituting Credit for Commodity Money," both in *Monetary Problems of the International Economy*, ed. R. A. Mundell and A. K. Swoboda (Chicago Ill.: The University of Chicago Press, 1969).

Money-Issuing Institution

Assets		Liabilities	
Reserves	R	Deposits	D
Investments	I		
	total assets $=$	total liabilities	

Seigniorage can be considered a flow per year associated with net money issue, or as the present value of all the present and expected future gains to the money-issuing authority. While remembering that seigniorage may well be assigned to claimants on a flow-per-year basis, let us define algebraically the more inclusive present value concept, S, over the years $1, 2 \ldots , n$:

$$S = \frac{I_1 r_1 - D_1 i_1 - C}{1 + r_1} + \frac{I_2 r_2 - D_2 i_2 - C_2}{(1 + r_1)(1 + r_2)} \tag{A.1}$$
$$+ \ldots + \frac{I_n r_n - D_n i_n - C_n}{(1 + r_1)(1 + r_2) \ldots (1 + r_n)}$$

where r is the open-market rate of interest on investments, i is the deposit rate of interest accruing to the holders of international money, and C represents the costs of servicing the outstanding stock of money including the management of deposits, investments, and reserves. Clearly seigniorage is only positive when $rI - iD - C > 0$ on an average (appropriately discounted) through time.

It is important to distinguish between the *nominal* value of seigniorage S and the *real* value S/P, where P is a price index of what money will buy. Despite its overwhelming social cost, a commodity reserve currency has one big advantage: the real value of the monetary unit—one CRU—is precisely established in terms of the underlying commodity bundle. P always equals one. True, that commodity bundle may not be broadly representative of all goods—particularly manufactures—that enter international trade. But the value in use of the unit of account is itself independent of the amount of nominal money actually issued—which is endogenously determined and outside the control of the monetary authority.

Quite different is a national or purely international fiat money whose real value depends heavily on the amount of nominal money issued relative to the demand for it. For example, suppose the real demand to hold the fiat money in question in any period is:

$$\frac{D}{P} = L(Y, r - i) \tag{A.2}$$
$$\quad + \quad -$$

where Y is the relevant flow of real income within the monetary domain. In the international sphere, Y would have to be interpreted as the flow of world trade.

From equation (A.1) by itself, and if $rI + iD - C > 0$, seigniorage appears to increase when more nominal money is issued: I and D rise proportionately. However, the price level, P, is now an endogenous variable. Suppose at time zero, one exactly *doubled* all nominal money currently in existence, and also doubled expected cash balances and investments in the future. That is, $D_1, D_2, \ldots D_n, I_1, \ldots I_n$, and $C_1, \ldots C_n$ all are doubled. If this is a once-and-for-all change, then both S and P will also double. The *real* value of seigniorage garnered by the money-issuing institution will remain unchanged. Thus, simply issuing more of a purely international[21] money, with a market demand to hold it given by equation (A.2), will not necessarily increase the flow of real seigniorage. The multitude of proposals for arbitrarily increasing the distribution of international fiat money often lose sight of this uncomfortable fact.

If one entertains the notion of continuous inflation in the international money—D and P rise through time—then the seigniorage flow may or may not increase depending on how much D/P contracts as r rises.[22] Indeed, the position of (demand for) any purely international money is likely to be so precarious, for the reasons just discussed, that any substantial continued depreciation in its real purchasing power would drive it out of existence. People would tend to exchange national currencies directly. Thus, in the analysis to follow, I assume that the money-issuing institution is restricted to a level of D in each period that is consistent with no price inflation: P is constant or at least rises no faster than the average of competing national currencies. This is true for the SDR, which is tied to a basket of national currencies, and has also been approximately true for the U.S. dollar.

Various candidates for international money can now be classified according to their seigniorage flow.

CASE I: A COMMODITY-RESERVE CURRENCY

For a full-bodied community-reserve currency we have:

$$R = D, \quad \text{and} \quad I = 0.$$

Income flow from investment is zero, and even if deposit holders are paid nothing, positive storage costs imply that the seigniorage flow to the money-issuing authority is negative. In a formal sense, there would be no seigniorage

21. One not based on a basket of national currencies.
22. As the Fisher effect, incorporating the expected rate of inflation, is built into the open-market rates of interest.

to dispense—although proponents of a commodity-reserve currency often see it
as a vehicle for raising the relative prices of those particular products included
in the commodity basket. The storage costs of the commodity stockpile would
have to be financed by levying taxes elsewhere.

If only fractional commodity reserves are kept against outstanding deposits,
then

$$R < D, \quad I > 0.$$

For r sufficiently great, and C sufficiently small, S could be positive. Thus, the
commodity reserve scheme could pay for itself. Indeed, the severe pressure for
a full-bodied commodity reserve currency to break down into a fractional one,
with either official institutions or wildcat private banks garnering some of the
resulting seigniorage, was analyzed above.

CASE II: A FULLY COMPETITIVE FIAT MONEY

Suppose there is no more fundamental asset, such as commodity reserves, so
that $R \simeq 0$ and $I \simeq D$. The money-issuing institution uses "virtually" all the
proceeds from deposit growth (maintaining our assumption of a stable price
level) to purchase interest-bearing investments. The cost, C, of servicing these
investments and the cost of settling international payments—say check clearing
on the deposit side—includes both the salaries of bankers and a normal yield
on the capital put up by banking institutions.[23] Under what circumstances
would we expect a competitive solution: the deposit rate of interest is bid up so
that seigniorage is driven to zero?

Under the world dollar standard, the New York banking community and its
unregulated progeny—the Eurodollar market—may approximate this competitive solution at the present time. Suppose $rI - iD - C > 0$ so that seigniorage
exists in the collecting of deposits and making loans. Then either new banks
will be tempted to enter the world's money market or existing banks will try to
expand their business. In order to do so, a small increase in i will be necessary
to attract the new deposits, and this increase in i will continue until $rI - iD -
C \simeq 0$. Seigniorage has been eliminated.

If a regulatory agency, such as the U.S. Federal Reserve Bank, successfully
placed a direct ceiling on i—or did so indirectly by imposing heavy official
reserve requirements (noninterest bearing) against outstanding deposits—then

23. For private banking systems, the owners' equity should appear above on the right-hand side of
the balance sheet of the money-issuing institution. However, this would not influence the seigniorage calculation in equation (T.1).

significant positive seigniorage would potentially exist. This seigniorage could be collected by the U.S. government or be assigned to a private claimant— e.g., a favored group of borrowers. In the 1960s, however, such regulatory efforts were thoroughly undercut by the development of Eurodollar transacting (Chapter 9). The minuscule voluntary reserves held in New York by Eurobanks are the working means of payment—and their effect on i is negligible. Hence, the worldwide use of the dollar as a vehicle currency in private transacting is not associated with a significant flow of seigniorage to the United States, and approximates a fully competitive international fiat money.[24]

Could a monetary claim, such as special drawing rights, on an official international institution become a competitive form of international money in private capital markets? To be voluntarily held as a store of value and means of payment in private portfolios, its deposit yield, liquidity, and stability as a unit of account must approach that of the fully competitive dollar-based system that now exists. Perhaps such properties could be simulated by the International Monetary Fund directly, or could be farmed out to private banks who use the SDR as a reserve asset. Even then, there are economies of scale in having a single international vehicle currency—and the dollar certainly has a big head start in familiarity and organization.

Presently, however, the question of an internationally competitive SDR is moot. The deposit rate of interest, i, has been kept artificially low, necessarily confining the circulation of SDR to official reserves—as is discussed in Case III.

CASE III: POSITIVE SEIGNIORAGE AND SPECIAL DRAWING RIGHTS

At least for official reserve assets that are only circulated among central banks, we can safely assume that the cost of administering these transfers is close to zero, i.e., $C \simeq 0$. Then, the flow of seigniorage depends on keeping i low relative to r—the relevant yield that measures the opportunity cost of capital. When SDR were first introduced as a reserve asset for national central banks in 1970, the effective rate of interest earned was 1½ percent on any accumulation of SDR beyond the initial tranche assigned to each member country (Table 2.1). That is, if country A acquired 100 SDR as a result of a payments surplus with country B, A would earn 1½ percent per year on its new holding; whereas country B would pay 1½ percent per year. And countries could draw down (spend) up to 100 percent of their initial allocations

---

24. More debatable is whether foreign official holders of U.S. Treasury Bills earn a yield, i, that is close to open-market rates of interest. Among the major industrial economies, central banks have agreed not to hold other kinds of dollar assets and their demand for reserves may unduly depress the yield on U.S. Treasury bills and bonds.

providing they reconstituted 70 percent within a few years time. Effectively, users of SDR could borrow at 1½ percent, and since this was well below open market rates of interest, *users* would be collecting the seigniorage S as defined in equation (A.1).

More recently, the IMF has raised the deposit rate of interest to approximately a weighted average of the treasury bill yields of the 16 currencies underlying SDR. From this, however, it subtracts a *liquidity* premium. The result is to leave i in the range of four to five percent. This still seems significantly less than the relevant r—measured, say, by deposit on lending rates of interest in the Eurocurrency market.

In order to prevent all recipients of SDR from selling them in order to acquire foreign exchange assets with a higher interest yield (thereby collecting the seigniorage), the IMF strictly limits the situations where SDR can be spent by any one member and assigned to another. The former can only draw down SDR if they have a genuine deficit in foreign payments, and are not simply adjusting their portfolios and acquiring other foreign exchange assets. Whereas the latter are required to accept SDR if (1) they have a genuine balance-of-payments surplus, and (2) their existing holdings of SDR are not more than 200 percent greater than the cumulative sum of their free tranches. The free tranches to individual countries are assigned according to IMF quotas (the importance of countries in world trade) if they choose voluntarily to participate in the SDR system.

Are the surplus countries receiving SDR actually paying seigniorage *net* to the deficit ones? The answer depends on the initial conditions.

Suppose, at the existing price level (determined by the purchasing power of the basket of national currencies underlying the SDR), there was a liquidity shortage. On balance, reserve holdings were felt to be too low and the international capital market was such that governments could not borrow freely to build up their liquidity positions. Then the general distribution of SDR—even with a zero yield on the initial free tranche—and only four to five percent on incremental earnings—would be attractive to many countries. The imperfection in the international capital market would, by hypothesis, foreclose exchanging the SDR for an equally liquid, but higher yielding, foreign-currency assets.

In Figure A.1, dd' represents the steady-state demand for international reserves as a function of the spread between the opportunity cost of capital r and the deposit rate i. The percentage cost—C—per year of servicing a given level of real reserves (deposits) outstanding could be close to zero. Let i_b be the initial deposit rate such that $r - i_b > C$; and let a be the arbitrarily given initial reserve holdings that are posited to be in short supply. Then, new reserves could be increased from a to b so as to fully satisfy the demand to hold them at

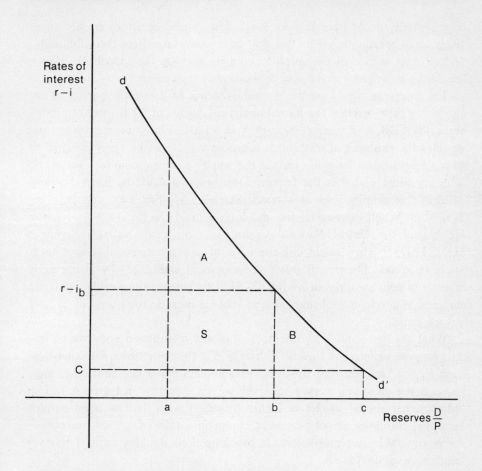

FIGURE A.1   The demand for international reserves

the deposit rate of interest i_b. The reserve shortage would be eliminated. Insofar as the area under the aggregate demand curve (above the cost of servicing reserves) accurately represents incremental welfare from having international money, the social gain from increasing reserves is simply the triangle A plus the rectangle S.[25]

But who gains and who loses by the increase in reserves? Consider the extreme case where all the new reserves are given only to those countries with incipient deficits. They are immediately spent and transferred to surplus countries. Then S neatly represents the seigniorage that the monetary authority assigns to the deficit countries—revenue that, in principle, the sovereign mone-

25. An analytical oversimplification that monetary theorists are fond of using. In this analysis, I assume that users of reserves pay the service charge C.

tary authority could have kept for itself. The surplus countries are not effectively taxed because they want the additional reserves to relieve their illiquidity. Indeed, the welfare of the surplus countries rises by the triangle A. Hence everybody is better off as the reserve shortage is overcome!

The foregoing, based on the posited existence of a reserve shortage at the prevailing price level, is the formal analytical argument for the need to introduce the SDR as a reserve asset (store of value). The same argument then justifies the existence of unrequited seigniorage that can be safely assigned to poor (deficit) countries while leaving the wealthy (suplus) countries better off. The argument underlies the famous Link proposal made by many eminent academic economists such as Maxwell Stamp, Tibor Scitovsky, and Jan Tinbergen on behalf of agencies like the International Development Association (IDA) and the United National Commission on Trade and Development (UNCTAD).[26] They would link the issue of new international reserve assets such as Special Drawing Rights to development assistance—by giving SDR directly to poor countries or having the SDR tranches of the wealthy countries assigned to development banks (such as IDA) to increase their capacity to lend on soft terms.

What are the counter arguments to this well-intentioned endeavor to improve world welfare and income distribution at the same time? The analytical case for the Link rests heavily on the presumption that a reserve shortage now exists at the prevailing world price level: we are at point a in Figure A.1. The international capital market is highly imperfect such that incipient surplus (wealthy) countries cannot borrow at competitive rates of interest—or collectively run trade surpluses—so as to build up their liquidity (official reserve) positions to desired levels.

Suppose instead that an open American capital market, together with unregulated Eurocurrency transacting, constitutes a nearly perfect international capital market. The competitive pressure within this banking system raises deposit rates of interest on highly liquid dollar assets very close to competitive lending rates—save for a small margin that just pays for the bankers' salaries and other costs. That is, $rI - iD - C \approx 0$. Then we have full liquidity *without* any SDR issue, as represented by point c in Figure A.1. At point c, the international supply of liquidity, D/P, is already expanded to its social optimum, given the cost of producing it under competitive conditions. In comparison to the suboptimum at b, potential world welfare is greater by the triangle B.

This alternative uncomfortable presumption implies that neither seigniorage

26. The contributions of many authors in many international forums over a 20-year period are well summarized by Y. S. Park, "The Link Between Special Drawing Rights and Development Finance," *Princeton Essays in International Finance*, No. 100 (September 1973).

nor the welfare of the potential surplus countries increase with new tranches of relatively low yield and illiquid SDR. Unexploited social gains as represented by the areas S and A no longer exist. Being fully liquid already, the surplus countries see the SDR system as a potential claim against their real resources—when they have to accept unwanted SDR in return for running a trade surplus with poor countries.

For philanthropic reasons, the wealthy countries may not object to modest aid giving in this form, but they will want to carefully hedge their liabilities. Hence, the restriction that they need only accept additional SDR up to twice their initial tranche, that any single country can opt out of new tranches, and why the facility itself has not been expanded very far relative to other forms of reserve holding. From Table 2.1, we note that SDR remain less than four percent of total holdings of official reserves.

In summary, a direct conflict exists between achieving full liquidity internationally and using the same monetary vehicle as a clandestine credit line to subsidize worthy borrowers—the link to less developed countries. As long as they are meant to be a subsidy device to users—and in practice less developed countries tend to spend their SDR allocations rather quickly—then potential private "depositors" for holding SDR voluntarily will be even fewer and farther between than official holders are now. The consequent tax on depositors (reduction in interest rates) probably ensures that the SDR facility will never be able to substantially displace national monies as a means of international payment or as a store of value. However, SDR are likely to continue as a useful unit of account for many international purposes.

Index